NO LONGER
SEATTLE PU

Family and Society in American History

Family and Society in American History

EDITED BY JOSEPH M. HAWES

AND ELIZABETH I. NYBAKKEN

UNIVERSITY OF ILLINOIS PRESS

URBANA AND CHICAGO

© 2001 by the Board of Trustees of the University of Illinois
All rights reserved
Manufactured in the United States of America
1 2 3 4 5 C P 5 4 3 2 1

∞ This book is printed on acid-free paper.

Frontispiece: Polish Immigrant Family. Private Collection.
Courtesy of John and Jeanne Marszalek, Starkville, Mississippi.

Library of Congress Cataloging-in-Publication Data
Family and society in American history / edited by
Joseph M. Hawes and Elizabeth I. Nybakken.
p.   cm.
Includes bibliographical references and index.
ISBN 0-252-02567-9 (cloth : acid-free paper)
ISBN 0-252-06873-4 (pbk. : acid-free paper)
1. Family—United States—History.
2. Domestic relations—United States—History.
I. Hawes, Joseph M. II. Nybakken, Elizabeth I.
HQ535.F318   2001
306.85'0973—dc21   00-011382

We dedicate this volume to all of our kin—
those who are with us now and those who came before.

Contents

Preface

Family and Society in American History is both an introduction to the literature on the history of American families and a reflection of the diversity of that literature. We have included essays that vary in their approaches to the topic by chronological period, by region, and by race, class, and gender. All demonstrate how family patterns have responded to changing circumstances from the eighteenth through the twentieth century. The anthology can stand by itself in inducing further exploration or it can be used to complement a general account of the history of American families by offering more depth and specificity to generalizations. It is designed not to increase the literature on the subject but to make it more accessible.

No collection of essays can do full justice to a field so vast and complex as the study of families in America's past. The rich and diverse literature available in journals made our selection process difficult; many fine and timely articles had to be excluded because of the limitations of space. Documentation for all essays has been retained but in a revised format to provide consistency. Our historical sensibilities have led us to choose essays covering a period that ends in the middle period of the twentieth century, when historical perspective fades in deference to contemporary sociological studies. A discussion of the recent status of trends noted in the Introduction concludes the Epilogue.

We have juggled a number of variables in developing this collection. Selections are grouped into broad chronological periods to indicate that scholarly discourse about families varies among these periods. We have also tried to maintain a balance among regions. Likewise, we have sought work that highlights the varieties of families that coexisted with the European-American middle-class "norm" and illustrates the importance of class, region, and ethnicity.

What follows is an eclectic collection of scholarly writings that we hope will provide a window into the rich mosaic of past families and introduce a wide variety of methods and approaches used to study them. We hope that these essays will help to dispel the myth that there is one universal and static American family and, perhaps more important, that they will entice readers to undertake a deeper inquiry into the field of family history.

Historians use a variety of approaches in order to understand families and their histories. Some are primarily concerned with structure, whereas others look at the changing legal climates in which families functioned. Some historians try to understand the reasons for such family-oriented behaviors as the limitation of fertility or even the triggers for domestic violence. Still others have studied the material culture found in portraits, architecture, and household possessions in order to understand changing family dynamics. Another popular approach is to study the effect of various influences on family patterns, for example, ethnicity or the impact of major events such as the depression and World War II. Finally, rather than assuming that individual family members acted according to socially constructed gender roles, historians have sought greater understanding of their actual behavior.

The creative use of sources to tease out vital information about this most fundamental of human institutions has characterized the field of family history since its inception. All the essays attest to the success of that endeavor and point to a future understanding that will be limited only by the imagination of scholars.

In preparing this volume, we have incurred a variety of debts. We are especially grateful to Richard Wentworth of the University of Illinois Press for his continued support and encouragement. We appreciate very much the help of Pattie Dillon, Peggy Bonner, Patsy Humphrey, Lonna Reinecke, and John Hawes for their roles in the preparation of this volume. Special thanks are due to Patricia V. Higgs of the *William and Mary Quarterly* for help in securing photographs. We wish also to acknowledge the support of our respective departments and institutions: the Departments of History at Mississippi State University and the University of Memphis. And, most emphatically, we wish to emphasize the support provided by our spouses, Gail Murray and William H. Graves III.

Family and Society in American History

PART 1

An Overview of the American Family

Before we begin to look at the many variations in American families in chronological periods, it may be useful to consider the broader patterns of American family history. We open with this caveat: There has never been one single family form in America. The nuclear family consisting of father, mother, and children living together within a privatized household has often served as the model of the American family. Many families, however, did not fit into that mold.

Most families in early America were nuclear, but their household often included non-related members, and they were dependent on extended kin networks for conducting business, educating and marrying children, and offering whatever support was necessary for survival. These family connections often crossed ethnic, racial, and class lines. In the South, three very different cultures shaped families: European, African, and Native American. Each influenced the others and had a significant impact on family life. Some Europeans intermarried with Native Americans, and the children who resulted were raised within a blended culture. Slaves in North America lived in families but also with families. The ownership of slaves made a major difference in the way that white southern families regarded and protected property and transmitted it across generations.

The nineteenth century elevated the middle-class nuclear family to the level of a cultural icon even though countless other Americans lived in very different sorts of families. Working-class families were larger, on the whole, than middle-class families, and their households sometimes included a number of unrelated adults. Native American families retained vestiges of a matrilineal structure and communal functions. African American families under slavery exhibited a variety of patterns, including that of marriage partners living apart from each other, either on separate plantations or in different statuses—free and slave. Beginning in the late nineteenth century, millions of small farmers, especially in the South, left the land when they could not

Urban family. (Private collection, courtesy of Connie Schulz, Columbia, S.C.)

Farm family. (LC-USF 34T01-72355, courtesy of the Library of Congress)

African American family of Aberdeen, Mississippi. (John E. Rodabough Papers, courtesy of Special Collections, Mitchell Memorial Library, Mississippi State University)

Family picnic. (LC-USF 3301-13067-M3, courtesy of the Library of Congress)

survive as farmers in a market economy. Sometimes a family moved to a mill town, where it entered as a unit into the paternalistic mill village system. Immigrants crowding into the ghettos of American cities found family formation to be difficult and were forced to pool resources to survive.

Other Americans sought their fortunes by moving west, where they encountered different cultures and family traditions. In the Southwest, Latino families either enjoyed elite status as major landowners or, especially if the family was partly of Native American descent, struggled to survive by employing strategies similar to those adopted by their counterparts in the East. Latino families of northern New Mexico cooperated in order to make the maximum use of limited resources, and their men traveled north to work on the railroads and in the sugar beet fields. In California, family formation for Chinese immigrants was very difficult because very few women immigrated until the men could afford to send for them. A more balanced sex ratio among the Japanese allowed families to be the norm within that immigrant group.

The point is, there have always been a variety of family patterns in America. Their forms and strategies varied with the circumstances they encountered. The middle-class nuclear family might have been the "ideal," but it has never been universal in its pristine form. Yet because all American families, to some degree, have aspired to this ideal, it is important to note that the form has changed.

The most prominent changes in mainstream American families since the early colonial period have concerned alterations in the functions that families have been expected to perform, the individualization of their members, and the concomitant modification in the internal dynamics of the family. Although these changes occurred in a continuum, they can be more readily discerned by focusing on the archetypal family of the colonial period, the nineteenth century, and the twentieth century.

In the seventeenth century, the family was the primary and all-competent social institution. It was expected to be self-sustaining, with all members subsuming their individual desires to the common good of the unit. Households were the primary units of production. Tilling small plots of land, family members grew crops, raised livestock, and manufactured what was essential. Thus, they survived without generating much of a surplus and with little need for cash. They did, however, work to acquire enough property to give their children a start in life. A son received the means to make a living; a daughter, the necessities to start her own household. Servants, too, at their majority could expect a stake with which to begin their adult lives. Children were expected to support their aged parents, who often held onto property as a way of ensuring that this occurred. Widows were not left destitute but were entitled by law to the use of a third of their deceased husbands' estate. Families took in aged or disabled relatives and cared for them.

Society looked to families to maintain order and to support, care for, and police their own members. Patriarchy was designed to ensure that this happened. The husband/father was legally the ruler of the household and as such shouldered responsibility for all activities of the household and actions of its members. Within a family, all deferred to the husband/father, who was its only public representative and controller of its property. Wives could stand in for husbands but only in a temporary capacity. Children and servants ranked below husbands and wives in this hierarchical family and in the larger society, where power and property conferred status.

Families alone were responsible for preparing their young for adulthood. If literacy was desirable, parents taught offspring to read and write. All socialization occurred within the unit. Fathers bore primary responsibility for the moral and religious instruction of the young. Families also provided vocational training, and children were expected to contribute as they learned. Boys learned their trade as apprentices to a master craftsman or from their fathers; girls learned household duties by assisting adult women in these tasks. Newly formed families with small children imported older children from established families, teaching, socializing, and supervising them all.

Over the course of three centuries, families have seen many of these primary functions taken up by other social institutions. Responsibilities that once belonged exclusively to a father became diffused among a variety of people and agencies. Other individuals, beginning with the mother, shared in familial tasks and in the process renegotiated relationships among family members.

As society became more complex in the increasingly commercial world of the nineteenth century, families began to lose their primacy in economic production to more complex entities such as the factory or the market. Increasingly, wages replaced the domestic production on family farms as small farmers lost out to the advancing forces of mass production. A family system of wage working persisted in southern cotton mills into the twentieth century. By the end of the nineteen century, however, most Americans contracted for wage work on an individual basis. Even young women were migrating to the expanding cities, seeking jobs and marriage. At first they regarded their jobs as temporary until they could find husbands; later they began to consider remaining single as a viable option.

Families now had to redefine what was necessary to prepare children for an independent life. The demand for educated workers increased, so families had to find the means to send children to specialized schools and to manage without their labor. Instead of providing young men with land, families now invested in their future through education. The content and duration of education continued to expand, and girls were included in the process as educated men perceived the need for educated wives. Families still bore the primary responsibility for children's moral training and early socialization, but now they were sharing it more with external institutions. Churches expanded their role in instilling morality in the young through the development of Sunday schools, which had begun as literacy schools for poor children.

As families continued to lose functions throughout the nineteenth century, their internal dynamics changed as well. This happened in stages. Because of their extended absences from their homes, the all-encompassing authority of fathers within the family declined and the moral authority of mothers rose. The cult of domesticity developed, which advanced the moral stature of women and designated them as the inculcators of virtue in the young. According to this ascriptive cult, women were to manage the private, domestic sphere as their men filled the role of breadwinners in the public world. These separate spheres were not equal, but their existence granted more autonomy to mothers and respect for their domestic responsibilities. The focus of families shifted from economic production to moral development, and the family became a refuge from the world of work rather than a principal player in it.

The primary function of the family shifted to become one of nurturing the individual development of the children and preparing them to make their own ways in the world. No longer could parents expect that the future lives of their offspring would mirror their own. In this less patriarchal and more democratic family, more assertive mothers sought to develop the individual personalities of, first, their sons and, later, their daughters. Mothers were to instill self-control and moral rectitude in their children, who could then restrain themselves rather than depend on other family members to police their actions. In addition, sons had to learn how to choose virtuous wives and be good providers, and daughters were to preserve their moral characters and reputations. A declining birthrate made it easier to accomplish this mission. The family was becoming a collection of individuals in pursuit of different goals. It was a sharp contrast to the earlier patriarchal family engaged in collective action for the survival of the whole.

The rise of individualism accelerated in the latter part of the nineteenth century and became the dominant theme of the twentieth. In the mid-nineteenth century, urban middle-class families sought to develop the individual abilities and personalities of their sons as a way to foster their success in the public, business-oriented world. By the late-nineteenth century, daughters began to develop an interest in the same sort of personal growth and fulfillment and, later, even in having careers of their own. Consequently, families became even more focused on the individuality of all their members.

In the twentieth century, a wide variety of experts on the family, such as physicians, sociologists, social workers, psychiatrists, and psychologists, appeared and began to develop a body of advice on family life. Their views stressed the importance of individual development and personal satisfaction of children at each stage of maturation. Families were urged to continue to provide the early moral development and socialization of young children but to allow a stronger influence to managers of schools, peer organizations, and religious institutions because of their greater expertise.

Increasingly, daughters as well as sons were expected to pursue post–high school educations, not just for personal growth but also to acquire the ability to be self-supporting. As the century progressed, that expectation grew as more and more married women entered the work force, attaining some economic autonomy and even pursuing careers for personal satisfaction.

This process of individualization and loss of family functions was temporarily reversed during the depression as many families reverted to a self-sufficient unit of kinfolk, with all members contributing what they could in order to survive. World War II removed many fathers from homes and encouraged wives to combine with related families. In the early 1950s a reaction set in against the preceding disruptive years, and Americans sought to recreate the model middle-class family of the nineteenth century. Such strategies only underline the flexibility of families in making temporary adjustments to meet current contingencies. Earlier trends, however, soon reasserted themselves and have continued.

One by-product of increasing individualism has been a rapidly rising divorce rate. More than half of all marriages begun since the middle of the twentieth century now end in divorce. The search for individual self-realization and personal happiness helps to explain that phenomenon as well as the propensity of many divorcees to remarry. Many single-parent households result from social circumstances rather than choice. The rate of out-of-wedlock births among inner-city dwellers, for example, is strongly influenced by the lack of good job opportunities there for fathers. Most single-parent households are headed by women, who, on average, earn less than men, so many female-headed households must struggle to provide for their children. Blended families of previously married spouses and their children are becoming more common. Such families have existed in the past, but they never conformed to the dominant family model that continues to be the norm to which most Americans aspire.

The model middle-class family norm has itself undergone continual changes from the colonial period to the latter part of the twentieth century. In his useful survey of family law (chapter 1), Steven Mintz traces the changing relationship between the model family and the state, which mirrors alterations in the general perceptions of the family, its dynamics, and the societal roles it is expected to fill in any given period. Mintz traces four main themes for the model family: social functions of the law; reflection of social values in the law; relative responsibilities of the public and private sector in enforcing these values; and ways in which the law intervenes in family matters based on class and wealth.

1

Regulating the American Family

STEVEN MINTZ

Until quite recently, American family historians tended to focus their attention on what might be termed the inner dimension of family life: the family's functions and structure, its division of domestic roles and economic strategies, and its developmental cycle and emotional and power dynamics. In the last few years, however, a growing body of scholarship has turned outward to the legal and institutional context of family life: the laws, institutions, and policies that define normative family relations, stigmatize deviance, and regulate domestic behavior. What this large body of research has decisively demonstrated is the consistent belief throughout American history that there is a strong public interest in regulating what occurs within families as a way, at various times, of promoting social order, reducing the costs of caring for the poor and the infirm, discouraging divorce, encouraging population growth, and curbing domestic violence and abuse. This scholarship has also shown that a full understanding of family life in the past must take account of the shaping legal and institutional framework in which the family is embedded.

This essay, a synthesis of recent scholarship on family law and family policy over the past three centuries, examines the legal and institutional context of American family life. It argues that the history of government regulation of the family can best be understood as a discourse involving the shifting balance of four primary and changing constructs: conceptions of the functions of family law; notions of the values family law should promote; views of the relative role of private individuals and government in regulating families; and forms of public intervention within families.

Early colonial New Englanders conceived of family law as moral pedagogy in which law's primary function was to articulate a religious ideal of hierarchy and patriarchy. A mutually reinforcing matrix of civil and religious authorities developed a range of formal instruments of familial oversight, yet enforcement of family norms rested largely on informal mechanisms except in cases involving the poor or flagrant and repeated violators of communal norms.

By the early nineteenth century, public discourse on the family had radically shifted. A republican conception of law promoted a contractual ideal of social relationships stressing individual responsibility within the family as well as in commerce. Although early-nineteenth-century popular culture tended to picture the family as a private haven or retreat, it was, paradoxically, during this period that reformers and local governments, eager to rectify parental failures, acquired new authority to act in loco parentis, creating a variety of surrogate families, including orphanages and houses of refuge for wayward and neglected youths.

In the late nineteenth and early twentieth century, family law increasingly began to be conceived in therapeutic terms—a trend evident in the development of new notions of "parental fitness," "parental duty," and "child welfare." Child-savers, family preservationists, and state and municipal governments invoked therapeutic ideals to justify new programs to reclaim delinquent youths and to keep families intact, including the development of juvenile and family courts and marriage counseling.

In recent years, legal discourse has taken a fresh turn toward an instrumental conception of family law stressing equality, individual rights, diversity, and the terminability of family relationships and obligations. Ironically, at the same time that the courts have upheld broad conceptions of familial privacy, encompassing such matters as birth control and abortion, jurists have also permitted new forms of intervention into areas previously regarded as bastions of family autonomy.

REGULATING THE COLONIAL FAMILY

As Marylynn Salmon has shown, the colonial law of the family varied sharply from one colony to another, reflecting differences in religious ideology, regional economies, and demographic circumstances. Colonies actively involved in trade with England, including Maryland, New York, South Carolina, and Virginia, created chancery courts modeled on those in England and retained English common-law principles more readily than Connecticut, Massachusetts, and Pennsylvania, where religious ideas led authorities to reject English common law and equity.[1]

During the seventeenth century, lawmakers in Massachusetts and Connecticut revised English common law and created a new system of family law that reflected certain broad assumptions about how families were to be ordered and authority distributed, the nature of the marital bond, and the proper roles of married women and children. This body of law embodied and enforced basic religious and ideological beliefs: the hierarchical and patriarchal nature of familial relationships, marriage as a civil contract, an emphasis on family unity and interdependence, wifely submission to her husband's will, and children's dependent and subordinate status.[2]

In Puritan Massachusetts and Connecticut, local governments encouraged all individuals to marry and live in "well-ordered" households by taxing bachelors and single women who failed to marry, fining couples who lived apart from each other, and requiring unmarried persons to enter established households as boarders or servants.[3] Because marriage was regarded as a public act and an alliance among families, town governments in New England compelled brides and grooms to submit to extensive community and family supervision. A father had a legal right to determine which men could court his daughters and a legal responsibility to give or withhold consent from a child's marriage, although he could not "willfully" or "unreasonably" deny his approval. No couple could legally join in marriage without announcing their intention to do so at three successive public meetings or by posting a written notice on the meetinghouse door for fourteen days.[4] In all colonies, however, a shortage of clergy and onerous regulations contributed to large numbers of "informal" marriages lacking legal sanction. In eighteenth-century Virginia, where a marriage license cost the equivalent of 465 pounds of tobacco and the only officials authorized to sanctify marriages were ministers of the Church of England, informal marriages appear to have been particularly common.[5]

Because Puritan lawmakers considered marital unity under the authority of the husband a prerequisite of social stability and because they assumed that husbands (or grown sons) would provide for their wives and widows, they tended to eliminate certain English common-law protections for married women that assumed that husbands and wives had separate interests within the family. Both Massachusetts and Connecticut rejected English ideas of separate estates for women, dower interest, prenuptial contracts, and suits in equity as well as certain common-law protections for women from coercion by their husbands. In sharp contrast, in Maryland, South Carolina, and Virginia, where the death rate was higher and widows were more likely to be left with young children, dower was extended to personal and real property. These colonies also retained English protections against coercion by husbands by requiring wives to acknowledge their consent to the conveyance of property in a private examination apart from their husbands. New York and South Carolina recognized separate estates, extending women limited rights to own and control property apart from their husbands.[6]

Although married women in colonial New England were legally subordinate to their husbands, they did have limited legal rights and protections. Husbands who refused to support or cohabit with their wives were subject to legal penalties. Because Puritans regarded marriage as a civil, not a sacred, contract, they permitted divorce in cases of a husband's impotence, cruelty, abandonment, bigamy, adultery, incest, or failure to provide. Massachusetts granted approximately forty absolute divorces between 1639 and 1692; another twenty-three divorce petitions were brought to the Governor's Council from 1692 to 1799. In contrast, such colonies as Maryland, New York, and Virginia strictly opposed absolute divorce with right to remarry, although allowing divorce *a mensa et thoro* (separation from bed and board) and private separation agreements.[7] In addition to authorizing divorce as protection for women, the Massachusetts Bay and Plymouth colonies also enacted the first laws in the Western world protecting "marryed women . . . from bodilie correction or stripes by her husband . . . unless it be in his own defense."[8]

The law in New England treated children, like married women, as subordinate and dependent beings. In exchange for paternal support, education, and training, children's service and earnings were their father's property. In order to support paternal authority over children, one statute adopted by the Massachusetts General Court in 1646 made it a capital offense for a "stubborn or rebellious son, of sufficient years and understanding (viz.) sixteen years of age" to strike or swear at his parents. In Connecticut and Rhode Island, a rebellious son could be confined in a house of correction. Rebellious daughters and sons under sixteen were subject to whippings. The Massachusetts code did extend children certain minimal protections. Just as the code outlawed wife-beating, it prohibited "any unnatural severitie" toward children.[9]

Because the family was the foundation stone of the Puritan social order and disorderly families defiled God's injunctions, the larger community gave fathers legal authority to maintain "well-ordered" families. If they failed, then the community asserted its responsibility for enforcing morality by punishing misconduct and intervening within households to guide and direct behavior. If a family failed to properly perform its responsibilities for teaching religion, morality, and obedience to law, then town selectmen had orders to "take such children or apprentices" from neglectful masters "and place them with some masters . . . which will more strictly look unto, and force them to submit unto government."[10]

Each year, courts tried a few dozen cases of spouse abuse, cruelty to children and servants, threats against parents, child neglect, adultery, and, above, all, fornication.[11] In 1648 the Massachusetts Bay Colony, fearing that "many parents and masters are too indulgent and negligent," ordered selectmen to keep "a vigilant eye over their brethren and neighbors to see . . . [that] their children and apprentices [acquire] so much learning as may enable them perfectly to read the English tongue and knowledge of the capital laws." Between 1675 and 1679 the selectmen in every town were given authority to appoint tithing men, "each of whom shall take the Charge of Ten or twelve Families of his Neighbourhood, and shall diligently inspect them."[12]

In practice, Puritan law tended to reinforce a hierarchical and paternalistic conception of the family. In order to obtain a divorce, a wife had to prove that she had "acted dutifully" and not given her husband "provocation."[13] In a number of instances, authorities allowed husbands to punish an abusive wife or a disobedient child by whipping.[14] Perhaps as a result of the emphasis attached to order and patriarchal authority, women were more likely than men to be punished for adultery, fornication, and bastardy.[15]

Even in cases of abuse, Puritan magistrates commanded wives to be submissive and obedient. They were told not to resist or strike their husbands but to try to reform their spouses' behavior.[16] Women who refused to obey injunctions about wifely obedience were subject to harsh punishment. Courts prosecuted 278 New England women for heaping abuse on their husbands and meted out punishments by fines or whippings. In general, colonial New England valued family preservation above the physical protection of wives or children and seldom granted divorce on grounds of cruelty, punished only the most severe abuses, and generally meted out mild punishments to men.[17]

To what extent did seventeenth-century New Englanders use courts to encourage and enforce proper domestic behaviors? Not as frequently as popular attitudes about Puritans suggest. Only rarely did courts become involved in cases of domestic violence. Only one rebellious adult son was prosecuted for "reviling and unnatural reproaching for his natural father," and he was punished not by hanging but by whipping. Similarly, only one natural father was prosecuted for excessively beating his daughter.[18] Prosecutions for wife-beating were relatively infrequent. Between 1630 and 1699, 128 men are known to have been tried for physically abusing their wives. The punishments for wife abuse were generally mild, usually amounting only to a fine, a lashing, a public admonition, or supervision by a town-appointed guardian. In two instances, however, colonists lost their lives for murdering their wives.[19]

Although early New Englanders paid close attention to the domestic and sexual behavior of individuals, prosecutions were generally infrequent, except in cases of repeated offenses or especially disruptive behavior or in cases involving the indigent. In those cases, lawmakers separated children from parents and required them to work for strangers, required paupers and their families to wear the letter *P* on the sleeve of their outer garment, warned indigent families out of town, and compelled relatives, including grandparents, to support grown children or grandchildren at risk of fines or imprisonment.[20] Punishment of offenses was designed to strengthen communal norms by bringing deviation into the public realm and eliciting proper attitudes on the part of the convicted—shame and recantation. Couples whom a church court found guilty of fornication had to repent publicly before their child could be baptized. Public humiliation, confession, and repentance affirmed the boundaries of acceptable behavior.[21]

By the mid-eighteenth century, the decline of community regulation of the family was manifest in rising rates of illegitimacy and premarital pregnancy, the abolition of many church courts, and declining legal prosecution of sexual offenses. Courts and town selectmen were less concerned about married couples guilty of premarital pregnancy and more about the economic maintenance of the illegitimate children born to single women.[22]

FAMILY LAW OF THE POOR

Throughout American history, there has been a dual system of family law, treating poor families differently from better-off families. Even in the seventeenth century, a dual system of family law existed, with one set of principles—of patriarchal authority, family unity, domestic privacy, and the primacy and inviolability of the family—applying to most families and a different set of principles applying to the families of the poor. As Maxwell H. Bloomfield has demonstrated, four key principles characterized the colonial family law of the poor: local responsibility for assisting poor families, outdoor relief (that is, assistance for the destitute in their own homes), the legal obligation of family members to support relatives, and apprenticeship of minor children.[23]

Eligibility for public relief was defined by settlement and removal laws. Colonial settlement laws, which grew stiffer with time, authorized local authorities to deny residence to newcomers who might become a burden on the town, required newcomers without means of support to post bond, and barred property owners from selling land to newcomers without prior approval by local authorities. During the nineteenth century, residency requirements for public relief were lengthened and penalties for those who brought the indigent into local communities were toughened; in a number of cases, courts split up indigent families and transported sick or elderly paupers across local boundary lines.[24] Other regulations empowered local officials to remove children from indigent and neglectful parents and apprentice them with a master and required parents, grandparents, children, and, in Massachusetts and New York, grandchildren to provide support for poor relatives.[25]

During the colonial era, most indigent individuals received assistance in their own homes, although some elderly, widowed, sick, or disabled persons who were unable to care for themselves were placed in neighboring households. It was not until the mid-eighteenth century that a small number of towns erected almshouses or workhouses to serve individuals without families, such as vagrants, dependent strangers, deserted children, or orphans. Yet as David J. Rothman has observed, even these institutions were modeled upon families; they were built in the style of ordinary residences and patterned after the organization of the family.[26]

CREATING A NEW CONCEPTION OF FAMILY LAW

During the first decades of the nineteenth century, American jurists, legislators, litigants, and legal commentators reformulated English and colonial legal rules and doctrines dealing with families and created a new system of family law. As Michael Grossberg has shown in his study of nineteenth-century family law, this new set of rules, regulations, and practices rearranged the balance of power within the home and dramatically altered the relationship between family members and government.[27]

Early-nineteenth-century domestic relations law drew upon two major sources. One was republican ideology, with its aversion to unaccountable authority and unchecked government activism and its tendency to define human relations in contractual terms. A second major influence stemmed from emerging "republican" or "democratic" notions of what constituted a proper family: a new conception of women's role (known as the "cult of true womanhood") that defined the ideal wife and mother in terms of piety, virtue, and domesticity; a new sentimental conception of children as vulnerable, malleable creatures with a special innocence; and a romantic conception of marriage based on free choice and romantic love.[28] Further contributing to the impulse to reorder domestic relations law were a rash of upsetting social trends: an erosion of paternal authority, an upsurge in illegitimate births and premarital pregnancies, and a growing number of women who were delaying marriage or not marrying at all.[29]

A belief that choice of a spouse should be based on romantic love rather than parental arrangement led judges and legislatures to make matrimony easier to enter. State legislators lowered marriage fees and authorized an increasing number of churches and public officials to perform marriages, while courts rejected colonial rules that made marriage licenses or banns and parental consent necessary for a valid marriage. Judges voided state statutes setting a minimum age of marriage and reduced restriction on marriages among affines (such as marriages between a widower and his sister-in-law). They also tended to uphold the validity of common-law marriage (in sharp contrast to English courts, which rejected "irregular marriage" as invalid) on the grounds that a prohibition on informal marriages would throw into question the legitimacy of such unions and "bastardize" many children.[30]

A belief that the primary object of marriage was the promotion of personal happiness (as well as a growing judicial commitment to a contractual view of legal relations) encouraged jurists and legislators to increase access to divorce and remarriage in instances of adultery, physical abuse, or failure of a marriage partner to fulfill his or her proper role. Before the nineteenth century, divorce was exceedingly difficult to obtain, and the number of divorces granted was minuscule. In a number of colonies, divorce was unavailable, and in those colonies where divorce was possible, it could only be obtained on the limited grounds of adultery, nonsupport, abandonment, or prolonged absence. Colonial law did not in general permit an injured spouse to remarry, except in instances in which the marriage could be annulled (such as impotence or bigamy). In many colonies, divorce was only available through a special act of the colonial legislature. Given the difficulty of obtaining a divorce, unhappy couples were more likely to separate formally. In eighteenth-century Massachusetts, only 220 couples divorced, but 3,300 notices of separation were printed in colonial newspapers.[31]

In the early nineteenth century, the availability of divorce as a remedy to intolerable marriages expanded as states transferred jurisdiction over divorce petitions to courts. By the 1830s, a number of states, led by Indiana, adopted extremely permissive divorce laws, allowing a divorce to be granted for any misconduct that "permanently destroys the happiness of the petitioner and defeats the purposes of the marriage relation."[32] In conception and practice, nineteenth-century divorce law tended to reinforce contemporary notions of wifely and husbandry behavior. Divorce laws were built around the concept of fault or moral wrongdoing, and in order to obtain a divorce it had to be demonstrated that a husband or wife had violated his or her domestic role in a fundamental way. In his study of divorce in nineteenth-century California, Robert Griswold suggests that husbands were most frequently sued for nonsupport, intemperance, and "indolent," "profligate," and "dissipated" behavior, whereas wives sought to demonstrate their "frugality" in managing the home.[33]

Of greater importance than divorce in altering the position of women in the nineteenth-century American family was the gradual improvement in the legal status of married women, symbolized by the enactment of married women's property acts that gave them limited control over property they brought to marriage or inherited afterward, rudimentary contractual capacity, and the right to sue or be sued. It must be stressed, however, that despite enactment of married women's property rights statutes, married women continued to be treated as a separate and special class in the eyes of the law. Norma Basch's detailed study of married women and the law of property in nineteenth-century New York found that judges severely restricted women's contractual capabilities and strictly construed statutory provisions in order to maintain husbands' common-law right to their wives' earnings and services, for example, by holding that ambiguous or intermingled assets belonged to the husband; that women's customary way of earning money, such as taking in boarders, did not meet the legal requirements of a separate estate; and that wives could not establish a separate estate without their husband's consent. In practice, judges tended to uphold the common-law fiction of marital unit represented by the husband.[34]

The new domestic ideology—as well as the rise of a contractual view of legal relationships—was also recognized in legal changes involving child support, child custody, and illegitimacy. During the middle decades of the century, New York state judges were the first to establish the principle that parents had a legal obligation to support their children, reversing the old common-law doctrine that parents had only a nonenforceable moral duty to support offspring. Many courts went even further and rejected the notion that fathers had an unlimited right to their children's earnings and services, ruling that emancipated minors had full control over their own earnings.[35] A growing number of judges also moved away from the common-law principle that gave fathers almost unlimited rights to the custody of their children. By the 1820s, however, the growing stress on children's welfare, and the special child-rearing abilities of women, led American judges to limit fathers' custody rights. In determining custody, courts began to look at the "happiness and welfare" of the child and the "fitness and competence" of the parents. As early as 1860, a number of states had adopted the "tender years" rule, according to which children who were below the age of puberty were placed in their mother's care unless she proved unworthy of that responsibility.[36] Nineteenth-century American law also broke with English common law by extending many legal rights to illegitimate children and making it easier to legitimate children born out of wedlock by permitting adoption.[37]

THE PARADOX OF THE MODERN FAMILY

The late eighteenth and early nineteenth centuries witnessed a fundamental redefinition of the boundaries of private and public spheres. In the early seventeenth century, the family's functions were broad and diffuse. The family was the fundamental unit of society. It educated children; it cared for the elderly and ill; it transferred property and skills to the next generation; and, most important, it was the economic center of production. By the early nineteenth century, nonfamilial institutions came to perform many of these functions. The middle-class family's primary roles were to provide emotional support and affection and contribute to the socialization of children.[38]

While in one sense the family became more private by appropriating the realms of feeling and emotion, this was essentially a means geared to a public end. In the eyes of a growing number of commentators, America's experiment in republican government depended on the capacity of families to produce good citizens. The family was expected to serve the political order by diffusing self-serving needs and instilling the values of willing obedience, service, and rational impartiality—the values of good citizenship. Failures of the family, in turn, seemed to explain an alarming increase in violence, robbery, prostitution, and drunkenness. In order to rectify parental failures, reformers created such substitute families as public schools, houses of refuge, reform schools, YMCAs for young rural migrants to cities, orphanages, and penitentiaries.

The blurring of boundaries between public and private life encouraged the transference to public agencies of moral prerogatives and of presumed benevolence and goodwill that had grown out of kinship bonds.[39] As early as the 1820s, Americans discovered that the nation's growing cities teemed with young people who had gone through "infancy and childhood without a mother's care or a father's protection."[40] Responsibility for these children lay not simply with their parents but with the state. As legal writer Joel P. Bishop noted, "Children are not born for the benefit of the parents alone, but for the country; and, therefore, . . . the interests of the public in their morals and education should be protected."[41] According to this view, the state had a moral duty to intervene to advance the best interests and welfare of children.

During the mid–1820s, Boston, New York, and Philadelphia established the nation's first publicly funded children's asylums for the moral rehabilitation of delinquent, incorrigible, and neglected youths. To combat delinquency, houses of refuge separated children from "incompetent" parents; removed them from the sources of temptation, pauperism, and crime; and instilled habits of self-control through moral education, work, rigorous discipline, and an orderly environment. Further underscoring the blurring of public and private boundaries, advocates of houses of refuge and prisons proposed that families adopt the system of surveillance and calculated privation that had supposedly proved effective in their institutions.[42]

Early-nineteenth-century houses of refuge set four important precedents. The first was that civil officials had a right to act in loco parentis by removing children deemed unruly, incorrigible, in need of supervision, or abused or neglected and placing them in foster homes or institutions. In a landmark 1839 decision the Pennsylvania supreme court upheld the commitment of an "incorrigible" girl to the Philadelphia House of Refuge, asking rhetorically, "May not the natural parents, when unequal to the task of education, or unworthy of it, be superseded by the *parens pariae,* or common guardian of the community?" Second, the houses of refuge established a formal distinction between children and adults before the law. Drawing upon the emerging sentimental conception of childhood, which drew a sharp distinction between childhood and adulthood, many jurists held that a child could not be considered criminally responsible "by reason of infancy." They also contended that a concerted effort should be made to rehabilitate rather than punish the child, and the child should be placed in a specialized institution for juveniles. Third, juvenile statutes placed noncriminal behavior, including incorrigibility, habitual disobedience, and vicious and immoral behavior, under the jurisdiction of the courts. Fourth and finally, the new system embodied two key characteristics of the modern juvenile justice system: commitment of juveniles to institutions after summary or informal hearings and indeterminate sentencing.[43]

Highly publicized charges of child abuse within houses of refuge, almshouses, and orphanages contributed to growing public revulsion against institutional confinement of indigent, neglected, or abused children. Orphanages in particular tended to be quite large and poorly supervised. In New York state in 1915 the average orphanage held 230 children; twelve institutions housed eight hundred. In a reaction against the impersonality and workshop discipline of houses of refuge, in the 1850s a number of states experimented with the "family reform school" in which between one and three dozen children were cared for in a cottage setting by a parent surrogate.[44] During the second half of the nineteenth century, reformers increasingly called for the placement of dependent or wayward children in foster homes and demanded enactment of adoption laws to give adopted children the same rights as natural children. Massachusetts became the first modern jurisdiction to adopt a comprehensive adoption law in 1851.[45]

CHILD-SAVING AND FAMILY PROTECTION

Few issues haunted the imagination of late-nineteenth- and early-twentieth-century reformers more than the future of the family. A precipitous rise in the divorce rate, delayed marriage, a shrinking birth rate, and a growing tendency among middle-class women to attend college and pursue careers raised fear that the family, "the original germ-cell which lies at the base of all that we call society," was disintegrating.[46]

Growing anxieties over the family encouraged unprecedented arguments for public paternalism and provided new kinds of justification for intervention in the family by secular authorities. During the late nineteenth century, many states imposed physical and mental health requirements for marriage, established a waiting period before marriage, instituted a higher age of consent, and adopted procedures for public registration of all new marriages (by 1907 twenty-seven states required registration). Polygamy was outlawed in Idaho and Utah, and interracial marriages in the border states and lower South. A growing number of states barred first-cousin marriages and other marriages between blood relations, and an increasing number of judges refused to accept the validity of common-law marriages.[47] Convinced that family limitation was an assault on the home, legislators and judges held abortion to be a criminal offense and restricted the dissemination of birth control materials and information.[48]

The publication of an 1886 report estimating that the United States granted more divorces than all other Western countries combined encouraged states to make it more difficult to obtain divorces by raising the age of marriage, restricting remarriages after divorce, lengthening residence requirements for divorce, and reducing the grounds for divorce from more than four hundred to fewer than twenty. In 1900 just three states—Kentucky, Rhode Island, and Washington—permitted courts to grant divorces on any grounds the court deemed proper.[49]

Starting in the 1870s, two reform causes—child-saving and family protection—stimulated public intervention within the family. Children's aid societies and societies for the prevention of cruelty to children (the first was founded in New York in 1875) sought to assist orphaned, destitute, deserted, and illegitimate children and rescue ill-treated children from neglectful and abusive parents. Advocates of child labor laws and compulsory education sought to take children out of the labor force and keep parents from exploiting their children economically. Other child-savers created kindergartens and playgrounds and led campaigns to remove children from poorhouses and other institutions and place them instead in "familylike" arrangements such as apprenticeship and foster homes. Still others tried to reform the juvenile justice system by establishing juvenile courts and to aid children born out of wedlock by increasing paternal support requirements. Public health reformers sought to reduce infant and child mortality, pasteurize milk, and cut the death rate from such diseases as tuberculosis and diphtheria. Family-savers attacked the double standard of sexual morality, worked to reduce rates of venereal disease, advocated closing red-light districts, and supported pensions for indigent mothers.[50]

Child-savers and family protectors were a diverse lot. They included social hygienists eager to reduce prostitution and venereal disease by instilling continence in young men, woman's rights advocates hoping to restrain male licentiousness, purity crusaders seeking to reduce vice, eugenicists trying to improve the hereditary qualities of the population, and charity workers attempting to use "scientific philanthropy" to combat poverty and cruelty.[51] They varied widely in their assumptions about such issues as the propriety of religious or benevolent organizations running child- or family-saving institutions, the appropriate role of the state and private agencies acting as *parens patriae,* and the relative merits of custodial institutions and the family. They were united, however, by a conviction that many of society's most intractable social problems originated in deformed or dysfunctional homes and that it was necessary to expand the state's supervisory and administrative authority over the family.[52]

Perhaps the most dramatic attempt to save the family was the movement to prevent cruelty to wives and children. During the last third of the nineteenth century, concern about family violence and child abuse mounted, and philanthropists founded 494 child protection and anticruelty societies; several states passed laws allowing wives to sue saloonkeepers for injuries caused by a drunken husband; and three states (Maryland in 1882, Delaware in 1901, and Oregon in 1905) passed laws punishing wife-beating with the whipping post.[53] These late-nineteenth-century reformers largely blamed cruelty to children on drink and the flawed character of immigrant men—in sharp contrast to their counterparts of the 1930s and 1940s who downplayed male violence and blamed abuse on mothers who nagged their husbands and children and refused to accept the female role.[54] After the turn of the century, the anticruelty movement declined rapidly for two reasons: Opponents were convinced that the societies were prejudiced against the poor and the working class and that they much too frequently removed children from parents' custody.[55]

The extension of the state's authority over children was also apparent in new policies toward "wayward" children. New legislation, drawing on the old legal doctrine that the state had an obligation to protect children from "imminent harm," gave public agencies power to remove neglected and vagrant children from parents; construct industrial-training and reform schools; and invoke criminal penalties against parents for abandonment, nonsupport, and contributing to the dependency or delinquency of a minor.[56]

Concern over the lack of supervision of children also led to the launching of pioneering efforts to provide day nurseries for the children of working mothers and to enactment of mothers' pensions for poor mothers. By 1910, 450 charitable day nurseries had been opened in working-class neighborhoods, supplemented by a small number of for-profit centers.[57] To help indigent mothers preserve their families, thirty-nine states enacted mothers' pensions during the second decade of the twentieth century. Initially, these laws restricted aid to widows with dependent children but were eventually broadened to provide aid to needy families in which the father was physically or mentally incapacitated or in which the mother had been divorced or deserted or was unmarried.[58]

By the beginning of the century, a new mode of discourse and a new set of standards dominated discussion of government policy toward the family. Jurists, charity workers, settlement house workers, and other professionals dealing with family problems evolved new notions of "parental fitness," "parental duties," "child welfare," and "children's rights and needs" that justified state supervision of the family "for the protection of society, and the welfare of the child himself—to prepare him for honest and intelligent citizenship."[59] Nowhere was that viewpoint more apparent than in the reconstruction of the juvenile justice system. In an effort to give special attention and rehabilitative opportunities to youngsters who broke the law, Illinois established the first juvenile court in 1899. By 1917, all but three states had enacted juvenile justice legislation. Within these separate tribunals for young people, informal hearings were supposed to replace adversarial proceedings, and diagnostic investigations, psychological assessment, and rehabilitation were to replace judgments of guilt and innocence and the imposition of punishment. In these courts, however, young people were deprived of constitutional safeguards that would apply in a criminal trial, including protections over the admission of hearsay and unsworn testimony, criminal standards of proof, privilege against self-incrimination and double jeopardy, and right to bail and counsel.[60]

The new outlook was also exemplified by the establishment of separate family courts charged with resolving a variety of family-related problems, including desertion, parental neglect or maltreatment of children, adoption, and juvenile delinquency as well as divorce. Proponents believed that separate family courts, dedicated to the welfare of families and children, would offer a less formal and less adversarial mechanism than regular courts for settling domestic disputes. Many sponsors of family courts were inspired by the example of divorce proctors, hired by a number of jurisdictions before World War I to investigate petitions for divorce, make recommendations to the court, and try to achieve reconciliation of the parties. Following the advice of social workers and psychologists, family courts emphasized family rehabilitation and tried to urge reconciliation of spouses whenever possible.[61] In practice, however, overcrowded dockets and a lack of funds prevented family courts from conducting careful investigations of petitions for divorce or reconciling differences between spouses. Yet they did assert the state's special interest in family welfare.[62]

After 1920, a growing number of reformers, convinced that the law's adversarial approach to divorce was harmful both to spouses and children, recommended a variety of changes in divorce proceedings, including mandatory counseling of parties seeking divorce, nonadversarial divorce proceedings, and greater availability of divorce on grounds of mental cruelty and incompatibility. Two states—New Mexico and Oklahoma—revised their divorce statutes to allow divorce on grounds of incompatibility, and three other states—Arkansas, Idaho, and Nevada—shortened residency requirements and liberalized divorce codes in order to attract couples seeking divorce.[63]

Convinced that the major problem confronting the twentieth-century family was not divorce but a breakdown of love and companionship within marriage, a number of social workers, physicians, and psychologists joined together during the 1920s to promote court-based, private and public marriage reconciliation and counseling services. These authorities maintained that marriage required special instruction in the art of personal interaction and that, contrary to older ideals of romantic love, conflict and tension were normal parts of married life. They believed that the major source of marital instability included a lack of communication and cooperation, unsatisfactory sexual relationships, and psychological maladjustments that might be prevented by sex education, counseling, and clinical therapy. By the early 1930s, courses in marriage and family living had spread across the country, dealing with such topics as dating, courtship, reproduction, birth control, and divorce. One of the reformers' most visible successes was the establishment in California in 1939 of Children's Courts of Conciliation, empowered to hold informal hearings on divorce, annulment, and separation suits and family conflicts involving minor children.[64]

From the early 1920s onward, family law was increasingly influenced by psychological and clinical studies of the family. Custody law was recast in light of new notions of "psychological parenthood" and the importance of continuity and stability in caretakers (assumptions that led jurists to frown upon joint and divided child custody arrangements).[65] In divorce proceedings, judges tended to dilute stringent legal statutes. In 1931 only seven states specifically permitted divorce on grounds of mental cruelty, but judges in most other jurisdictions reinterpreted laws permitting divorce on grounds of physical cruelty to encompass such conduct as constant nagging, humiliating language, unfounded and false accusations, insults, and excessive sexual demands. In these ways and others, psychological and clinical research was incorporated into family law.[66]

One ironic consequence of the continuing academic and clinical research into the family was the questions it raised about certain assumptions held by family professionals, notably the emphasis attached to preserving the family unit. Studies of divorce, for example, posed the problem of the psychological and emotional implications of divorce for children. In the 1920s, authorities on the family, using the case-study method, had concluded that children experienced the divorce of their parents as a devastating blow that stunted their psychological and emotional growth and caused maladjustments persisting for years. Beginning in the late 1950s, a growing body of research argued that children from conflict-laden, tension-filled homes were more likely to suffer psychosomatic illnesses, suicide attempts, delinquency, and other social maladjustments than were children whose parents divorce; that the adverse effects of divorce were generally of short duration; and that children were better off when their parents divorced than when they had an unstable marriage.[67]

Professional concern about child abuse and family violence also increased, leading a growing number of physicians and psychologists to call for the expansion of child-protection services and separation of abused children from parents. In 1954 the Children's Division of the American Humane Association conducted the first national survey of child neglect, abuse, and exploitation. Three years later, the U.S. Children's Bureau launched the first major federal study of child neglect, abuse, and abandonment. Child cruelty captured the attention of a growing number of radiologists and pediatricians who found bone fractures and physical trauma in children, suggesting deliberate injury. After C. Henry Kempe, a pediatrician at the University of Colorado Medical School, published a now-famous essay on the "battered child syndrome" in the *Journal of the American Medical Association* in 1962, legal, medical, psychological, and educational journals began to focus attention on family violence. Growing professional concern about child abuse led to calls for greater state protection and services for abused and neglected children and their parents.[68]

GOVERNMENTAL REGULATION OF THE FAMILY TODAY

Over the last two decades, a radical transformation has taken place in the field of family law as traditional familial expectations collided with changing conceptions of liberty and autonomy, as familial relationships have grown increasingly fluid and detachable, and as the law has relinquished its earlier policing functions over spousal and parental roles.[69] Older legal definitions of what constitutes a family were overturned. In cases involving zoning and public welfare, the courts have declared that local, state, and federal governments cannot define "family" too restrictively, holding that common-law marriages, cohabitation outside of marriage, and large, extended households occupying the same living quarters are entitled to protection against hostile regulation. In other cases, the Supreme Court has ruled that government cannot discriminate against groups of unrelated individuals living together (as, for example, in communes) in providing food stamps (while upholding zoning ordinances that limit occupancy of homes to members of families related by blood, marriage, and adoption) and that state legislatures cannot designate one form of the family as a preferred form.[70]

Nineteenth-century legal presumptions about the proper roles of husband and wife were called into question. Until recently, the law considered the father to be "head and master" of his family. His surname became his children's surname, his residence was the family's legal residence, he was immune from lawsuits instituted by his wife, and he was entitled to sexual relations with his spouse. Several state supreme courts, however, have ruled that husbands and wives can sue each other, that a husband cannot give his children his surname without his wife's agreement, and that husbands can be prosecuted for raping their wives.[71]

Perhaps the most sweeping legal changes have occurred in divorce law. State legislatures, following California's adoption of the nation's first no-fault divorce law in 1970, responded to the sharp upsurge in divorce rates by radically liberalizing their divorce statutes, making it possible to end a marriage without establishing specific grounds, and in many states, allowing one spouse to terminate a marriage without the consent of the other.[72] Every state except South Dakota has enacted some kind of no-fault statute. Rather than sue the other partner, a husband or wife can obtain a divorce simply by mutual consent or on such grounds as incompatibility, living apart for a specified period, or "irretrievable breakdown" of the marriage. In an effort to reduce the bitterness associated with divorce, many states changed the terminology used in divorce proceedings, substituting the term *dissolution* for the word *divorce* and eliminating any terms denoting fault or guilt.[73]

In recent years, courts have tended to abandon the "tender years" doctrine, which holds that a young child is better off with the mother unless the mother is proved to be unfit. The current trend is for the courts not to presume in favor of mothers in custody disputes over young children. Most judges now only make custody awards after considering psychological reports and the wishes of the children. To spare children the trauma of custody conflict, a number of jurisdictions now allow judges to award divorced parents joint custody in which both parents have equal legal rights and responsibilities in decisions affecting the child's welfare.[74]

Likewise, courts have moved from the concept of alimony and replaced it with a new concept called "espousal support" or "maintenance." In the past, courts regarded marriage as a lifelong commitment and in cases in which the husband was found guilty of marital misconduct have held that the wife was entitled to lifelong support. Now, maintenance can be awarded to either the husband or the wife. As the legal system has moved away from the principle of lifelong alimony, growing attention has been placed on the distribution of the partners' marital assets and property at the time of divorce.[75]

Another dramatic change in the field of family law is the courts' tendency to grant legal rights to minor children. In the past, parents enjoyed wide discretionary authority over the details of their children's upbringing. More recently, the nation's courts have held that minors do have independent rights that can override parental authority. In deciding such cases, the courts have sought to balance two conflicting traditions, the historic right of parents to control their children's upbringing and the right of all individuals, including children, to privacy, due process, and equal rights. The U.S. Supreme Court has struck down state laws that give parents an absolute veto over whether a minor girl can obtain an abortion but upheld a Utah statute requiring doctors to notify parents before performing an abortion and upheld a New York statute prohibiting the sale to minors of publications that would not be obscene to adults. Two states—Iowa and Utah—have enacted laws greatly expanding minors' rights. These states permit children to seek temporary placement in another home if serious conflict exists between the children and their parents, even if the parents are not guilty of abuse or neglect. In one of the most important decisions involving juvenile offenders and the juvenile courts, the 1967 case *in re Gault,* the Supreme Court ruled that juveniles subject to commitment to a state institution are entitled to advance notice of charges against them as well as the right to legal counsel, the right to confront witnesses, and protections against self-incrimination.[76]

At the same time, the nation's courts and state legislatures took government out of the business of regulating private sexual behavior and defining the sexual norms according to which citizens were supposed to live. In 1957 the Supreme Court narrowed the legal definition of obscenity, ruling that portrayal of sex in art, literature, and film was entitled to constitutional protections of free speech unless the work was utterly without redeeming social value. In 1962 Illinois became the first state to decriminalize all forms of private sexual conduct between consenting adults. Since 1970, twenty states have decriminalized private consensual sexual conduct, and in four other states judicial decisions have invalidated statutes making such conduct a crime. In addition, two-thirds of the states have repealed statutes prohibiting fornication, adultery, and cohabitation outside of marriage. Beginning in 1965, the Supreme Court, declaring in *Griswold v. Connecticut* that the Constitution created a right to privacy, struck down a series of state statutes that prohibited the prescription or distribution of birth control devices or limited circulation of information about contraception. In *Eisenstadt v. Baird* (1972) the high court extended access to contraceptives to unmarried persons. In *Roe v. Wade* (1973) the high court decriminalized abortion, and in *Planned Parenthood v. Danforth* (1976) the Court has held that a "competent" unmarried minor can decide to have an abortion without parental permission.[77]

Recent transformations in family law have been characterized by two seemingly contradictory trends. On the one hand, courts have modified or struck down many traditional infringements on the right to privacy. On the other hand, courts have permitted government intrusion into areas traditionally regarded as bastions of family autonomy. Shocked by reports of abuse against children, wives, and the elderly, state legislatures have strengthened penalties for domestic violence and sexual abuse while greatly expanding foster-care programs for children who have been abused or neglected. Courts have reversed traditional precedents and ruled that husbands can be prosecuted for raping their wives. A 1984 federal law gave states new authority to seize property, wages, dividends, and tax refunds from parents who fail to make court-ordered child-support payments. Other court decisions have relaxed traditional prohibitions against spouses testifying against each other.[78]

What links these two apparently contradictory trends is a growing sensitivity on the part of the courts and state legislatures toward the individual, even when family privacy is at stake. Thus, in recent cases, the courts have held that a husband cannot legally prevent his wife from having an abortion because it is she who must bear the burden of pregnancy; courts have also ruled that a wife's domicile is not necessarily her husband's home. Court decisions on marital rape reflect a growing recognition that a wife is not her husband's property.[79]

One ironic effect of these legal decisions has been a gradual erosion of the traditional conception of the family as a legal entity. In the collision between two sets of conflicting values—individualism and the family—the courts have tended to stress individual rights. Earlier, the law was used to reinforce relationships between spouses and parents and children, but the current trend is to emphasize the separateness and autonomy of family members. The Supreme Court has repeatedly overturned state laws that require minor children to receive parental consent before obtaining contraceptive information or an abortion, and lower courts have been unwilling to grant parents immunity from testifying against their own children. Similarly, state legislatures have weakened or abolished earlier laws that made children legally responsible for the support of indigent parents, while statutes that hold parents accountable for crimes committed by their minor children have been ruled unconstitutional.[80]

SHIFTING MODES OF LEGAL DISCOURSE ABOUT THE FAMILY

It is helpful to think about family law in terms of a discourse involving four broad themes. At each period, one finds a different balance in the dominant ideology. One theme involves the law's functions: pedagogical, prescriptive, and protective of individual rights. A second theme involves the broader values of society. At certain times, law has tended to emphasize marital unity and family solidarity; at other times, personal choice and responsibility; and at still other times, family privacy and autonomy or individual rights. A third theme represents the relative responsibility of private individuals and the broader society for enforcing values. A fourth and final theme is the form of legal regulation of the family, including nonintervention, implicitly ratifying socially assigned family roles and power relationships, the explicit extension of legal rights, criminalization of certain acts, or state-ordered mediation of familial disputes.[81] In colonial New England, many laws dealing with the family were taken word-for-word from the Old Testament, and legal rules reflected the Puritan version of Protestant theology. The law was committed to an organic and hierarchical conception of the family in which family interests were represented by the father. Despite the Puritans' intrusive reputation, the function of Puritan law was in certain important respects pedagogical or symbolic. Enforcement rested largely with individual families or other informal community mechanisms. Local governments allowed individuals a surprising degree of latitude except for repeated or particularly disruptive offenses. Punishments, in turn, were designed to reinforce communal norms and reintegrate the offender back into the community.[82]

During the early nineteenth century, family law was radically revised as legislators codified and jurists created new doctrines governing marriage formalities, divorce, alimony, marital property, child custody, adoption, child support, and child abuse and neglect. The law's functions remained largely pedagogical, but instead of upholding a hierarchical and patriarchal conception of the family and using household unity, jurists and legislators came to think of the family as an institution consisting of distinct members, each with his or her own rights and identity. New emphasis was also attached to personal responsibility. Informal marriages were transformed into common-law marriages, which had binding obligations. Divorce was discussed in terms of espousal fault, and child custody decisions increasingly rested on a judicial determination of the moral fitness of parents.[83]

In the late nineteenth century, legal priorities shifted away from individual choice, voluntary consent, and reciprocal duties to a heightened emphasis on public regulation of the family. New notions of "child welfare" and "state interest" were invoked to justify increasing government supervision of marriage, new restrictions on contraception and abortion, and the creation of new institutions to take care of homeless and ill-treated children and juvenile delinquents. Through law, government articulated a series of moral ideals of family life—that marriage was a lifelong commitment (by permitting divorce only on grounds of serious fault); that sexual relations should be confined to monogamous marriage (by prohibiting fornication, cohabitation, adultery, and polygamy); and that the purpose of sexual relations was procreation (by criminalizing sodomy and restricting access to contraceptives and abortion).[84]

During the late nineteenth and early twentieth centuries, legal discourse continued to shift from moral discourse and toward medical and psychological discourse. Conceptions of "child welfare" and "children's rights and needs" received new resonances and connotations in light of clinical and academic research. Despite the shift in language, however, older legal ideals persisted. Expert opinion tended to discourage divorce, especially when children were involved; stress the importance of keeping families intact, even in cases of abuse and violence; and favor granting child custody to mothers.[85]

Today, jurists and legislators are hesitant to discuss family issues in moral terms. In addressing questions of divorce or child custody, courts tend to avoid issues of fault or moral fitness. In cases of child abuse or neglect, the trend in legal opinion is away from broad statutes that allow the state to intervene on behalf of a child's moral welfare and instead allow intervention only in cases in which a child has suffered or risks severe physical or mental injury. Today, family regulators are little concerned about questions that preoccupied their predecessors, such as family formation and dissolution (including such questions as limitations on marriage, common-law marriage, legitimacy, and grounds for annulment of divorce) or the obligations of spouses. The new view presupposes diversity in the characteristics and functioning of families and rejects the view held earlier that certain specific family characteristics (such as the natural capacity of mothers for child-rearing) were rooted in moral, religious, or natural law. Replacing the older view is a discourse emphasizing equality and individual rights.[86]

Declining state interest in regulating moral conduct has not meant withdrawal from private affairs by the state. In recent years, courts have become increasingly willing to mediate disputes between family members. In the past, judges tended to subscribe to a tradition of noninterference in the family's internal functioning except in extreme circumstances on the grounds that intervention would embroil the courts in endless disputes and that legal intervention in many cases would be futile or even counterproductive. In recent years, the tradition of noninterference has broken down as courts have tried to determine the rights of wives and mothers, fathers, children, grandparents, cohabiting couples, handicapped children (and fetuses), and surrogate mothers.[87]

State involvement in nonmarital relations has also increased. Courts in many states have begun enforcing oral contracts and implied contracts between couples cohabiting outside of marriage, reversing the legal tradition of not enforcing "a contract founded upon an illegal or immoral consideration." Further, government has grown increasingly concerned about such issues as enforcement of child-support duties, supervision of pre- and postnuptial agreements, domestic violence, and contracts among unmarried cohabitants.[88]

State intervention in the lives of children has also undergone certain important changes. Although the state has surrendered some of its powers of *parens patriae,* it has gained the legal means to treat juveniles as adults, fully responsible for their actions. Although it has become more difficult to strip parents of their parental rights and remove children from their natural parents permanently, temporary foster-care services have expanded. In cases of child abuse, legislatures have mandated reports from professionals working with children and have tried to abrogate patient-client privilege to make reporting more effective.[89]

To say that the drift in family law is away from explicit moral judgments is not to suggest that the law does not make implicit moral judgments. Before the adoption of no-fault divorce statutes, the law of marriage implicitly upheld a marital ideal involving lifelong support and marital fidelity. Divorce was obtainable only on grounds of serious fault, and the family breadwinner could be required to pay lifetime support in the form of alimony. Because divorce was available only on the grounds of fault, the spouse who was opposed to a divorce had an advantage in negotiating a property settlement. The tendency now is to avoid questions of fault or responsibility in dissolving a marriage or dividing marital assets. Among the messages conveyed by divorce law today is that either spouse is free to terminate a marriage at will, that after a divorce each spouse is expected to be economically self-sufficient, and that termination of a marriage frees individuals from most economic responsibilities to their former dependents.[90]

Earlier in American history, one of the basic functions of family law was to articulate and reinforce certain widely held standards and norms about the family. Few people questioned the legitimacy of using law to express broader social values regarding the family. In recent years, jurists and legislators have tended to back away from using law and family policy to enunciate family standards and norms. Yet value judgments remain implicit in the law, and the values that the law tends to stress today, such as the ease with which family relationships and obligations can be terminated, tend to decontextualize individual family members from a broader family context and to erode the traditional view of the family as a legal entity. With the triumph of individualistic, egalitarian, and contractual values, the law tends to reinforce broader individualistic and therapeutic currents in the culture, stressing self-fulfillment and individual happiness as ultimate social values. As a result, we have almost precisely inverted the values and mode of discourse of our Puritan forebears.

Notes

This essay is reprinted, with minor editorial changes, from the *Journal of Family History* 4 (1989): 387–408.

1. Marylynn Salmon, *Women and the Law of Property in Early America* (Chapel Hill, 1986), 185–93.

2. Marylynn Salmon, "The Legal Status of Women in Early America: A Reappraisal," *Law and History Review* 1 (1983): 129–51; Salmon, *Women and the Law of Property*, 3–13.

3. Mimi Abramovitz, *Regulating the Lives of Women: Social Welfare Policy from Colonial Times to the Present* (Boston, 1988), 53–54.

4. Edmund Morgan, *The Puritan Family: Religion and Domestic Relations in Seventeenth-Century New England* (New York, 1966), 30–34, 83–84.

5. Maxwell Bloomfield, *American Lawyers in a Changing Society* (Cambridge, Mass., 1976), 93–94.

6. Salmon, *Women and the Law of Property*, 185–93.

7. Henry S. Cohn, "Connecticut's Divorce Mechanism, 1636–1969," *American Journal of Legal History* 14 (1970): 35–55; Nancy F. Cott, "Divorce and the Changing Status of Women in Eighteenth-Century Massachusetts," *William and Mary Quarterly* 3d ser. 33 (1976): 586–614; Lyle Koehler, *A Search for Power: The "Weaker Sex" in Seventeenth-Cen-*

tury New England (Urbana, 1980), 49–50, 77–79, 151–53; Salmon, *Women and the Law of Property,* 58–80; D. Kelly Weisberg, "Under Great Temptations Here: Women and Divorce Law in Puritan Massachusetts," in *Women and the Law: The Social Historical Perspective,* vol. 2: *Property, Family and the Legal Profession,* ed. D. Kelly Weisberg (Cambridge, Mass., 1982), 2:117–131.

8. Elizabeth Pleck, *Domestic Tyranny: The Making of American Social Policy against Family Violence from Colonial Times to the Present* (New York, 1987), 17–33.

9. Morgan, *The Puritan Family,* 78, 130–31, 148; Pleck, *Domestic Tyranny,* 25–28; John R. Sutton, *Stubborn Children: Controlling Delinquency in the United States, 1640–1981* (Berkeley, 1988), 10–42; Lee E. Teitelbaum and Leslie J. Harris, "Some Historical Perspectives on Governmental Regulation of Children and Parents," in *Beyond Control: Status Offenders in the Juvenile Court,* ed. Lee E. Teitelbaun and Alden R. Gough (Cambridge, Mass., 1977), 8–14; Lee E. Teitelbaum, "Family History and Family Law," *Wisconsin Law Review* (1985): 1147–48.

10. Teitelbaum and Harris, "Some Historical Perspectives," 9–11; Morgan, *The Puritan Family,* 27, 78, 148.

11. Pleck, *Domestic Tyranny,* 27–32; John D'Emilio and Estelle Friedman, *Intimate Matters: A History of Sexuality in America* (New York, 1988), 15–38; Linda Auwers Bissell, "Family, Friends, and Neighbors: Social Interaction in Seventeenth-Century Windsor, Connecticut," Ph.D. diss., Brandeis University, 1973, 106–29; Roger Thompson, *Sex in Middlesex: Popular Mores in a Massachusetts County, 1649–1699* (Amherst, 1986), 169–89; Koehler, *A Search for Power,* 136–65; Henry Banfield, "Morals and Law Enforcement in Colonial New England," *New England Quarterly* 5 (1932): 443–47.

12. Morgan, *The Puritan Family,* 88, 100, 146–48; Teitelbaum and Harris, "Some Historical Perspectives," 12–14; Pleck, *Domestic Tyranny,* 29; Bernard Bailyn, *Education in the Forming of American Society: Needs and Opportunities for Study* (Chapel Hill, 1960), 15–36; David H. Flaherty, "Law and the Enforcement of Morals in Early America," *Perspectives in American History* 5 (1971): 207–44; George Lee Haskins, *Law and Authority in Early Massachusetts: A Study in Tradition and Design* (New York, 1960), 79–93.

13. Koehler, *A Search for Power,* 136–65; Pleck, *Domestic Tyranny,* 23–25.

14. Pleck, *Domestic Tyranny,* 23–25, 28–31.

15. D'Emilio and Friedman, *Intimate Matters,* 31, 38.

16. Koehler, *A Search for Power,* 136–65.

17. Ibid.; Pleck, *Domestic Tyranny,* 29–31; D'Emilio and Friedman, *Intimate Matters,* 31, 38.

18. Pleck, *Domestic Tyranny,* 25, 29–31.

19. Ibid., 29–31; Koehler, *A Search for Power,* 137–42.

20. Bissell, "Family, Friends," 106–29; Pleck, *Domestic Tyranny,* 30–31; D'Emilio and Friedman, *Intimate Matters,* 27–32.

21. Bissell, "Family, Friends," 106–29; D'Emilio and Friedman, *Intimate Matters,* 37–38.

22. Pleck, *Domestic Tyranny,* 29, 31–33; D'Emilio and Friedman, *Intimate Matters,* 32–34; William E. Nelson, *Americanization of the Common Law: The Impact of Legal Change on Massachusetts Society, 1760–1830* (Cambridge, Mass., 1975), 110–11; William E. Nelson, *Dispute and Conflict Resolution in Plymouth County, Massachusetts, 1725–1825* (Chapel Hill, 1981), 23–44; David Thomas Konig, *Law and Society in Puritan Massachusetts: Essex County, 1629–1692* (Chapel Hill, 1979), 121–35, 152–55.

23. Bloomfield, *American Lawyers,* 99–104; Abramovitz, *Regulating the Lives of Women,* 75–79.

24. Abramovitz, *Regulating the Lives of Women,* 79–83; Bloomfield, *American Lawyers,* 99–104.

25. Bloomfield, *American Lawyers,* 103–4.

26. Ibid.; David Rothman, *The Discovery of the Asylum: Social Order and Disorder in the New Republic* (Boston, 1971), 3–56.

27. Michael Grossberg, *Governing the Hearth: Law and the Family in Nineteenth-Century America* (Chapel Hill, 1985), ix–xii; Norma Basch, "Invisible Women: The Legal Fiction of Marital Unity in Nineteenth-Century America," *Feminist Studies* 5 (1979): 346–66; Norma Basch, *In the Eyes of the Law: Women, Marriage, and Property in Nineteenth-Century New York* (Ithaca, 1982), 70–112; Bloomfield, *American Lawyers,* 91–135.

28. Jay Fliegelman, *Prodigals and Pilgrims: The American Revolution against Patriarchal Authority, 1750–1800* (New York, 1982); Carl Degler, *At Odds: Women and the Family in America from the Revolution to the Present* (New York, 1980), 3–25; Mary Ryan, *Cradle of the Middle Class: The Family in Oneida County, New York, 1790–1865* (Cambridge, Mass., 1981): 18–59; Steven Mintz and Susan Kellogg, *Domestic Revolutions: A Social History of American Family Life* (New York, 1988), 43–65.

29. Mintz and Kellogg, *Domestic Revolutions,* 17–23.

30. Grossberg, *Governing the Hearth,* 64–83.

31. Degler, *At Odds,* 16, 165; Robert Griswold, *Family and Divorce in California, 1850–1890* (Albany, 1982), 18–38; Michael S. Hindus and Lynne E. Withey, "The Law of Husband and Wife in Nineteenth-Century America: Changing Views of Divorce," in *Women and the Law: The Social Historical Perspective,* vol. 2: *Property, Family and the Legal Profession,* ed. D. Kelly Weisberg (Cambridge, Mass., 1982), 2:133–53; Nelson Manfred Blake, *The Road to Reno: A History of Divorce in the United States* (New York: 1962), 34–63.

32. David Brion Davis, *Antebellum American Culture: An Interpretive Anthology* (Lexington, Mass., 1979), 96.

33. Griswold, *Family and Divorce in California,* 39–140.

34. Basch, *In the Eyes of the Law,* 200–223.

35. Bloomfield, *American Lawyers,* 199–220.

36. Michael Grossberg, "Guarding the Altar: Physiological Restrictions and the Rise of State Intervention in Matrimony," *American Journal of Legal History* 26 (1982): 197–226; Michael Grossberg, "Who Gets the Child?" *Feminist Studies* 9 (1983): 235–60.

37. Michael Grossberg, "Crossing Boundaries: Nineteenth-Century Domestic Relations Law and the Merger of Family and Legal History," *American Bar Foundation Research Journal* (1985): 834–40; Grossberg, *Governing the Hearth,* 196–228; Jamil S. Zainaldin, "The Emergence of Modem American Family Law: Child Custody, Adoption, and the Courts, 1796–1851," *Northwestern University Law Review* 73 (1979): 1041–84.

38. John Demos, *A Little Commonwealth: Family Life in Plymouth Colony* (New York, 1970), 182–86.

39. Christopher Lasch, *Haven in a Heartless World: The Family Besieged* (New York, 1977), 3–8, 12–21; Barbara Laslett, "The Family as a Public and Private Institution: An Historical Perspective," *Journal of Marriage and the Family* 35 (1973): 480–92; Teitelbaum, "Family History and Family Law," 1135–81.

40. Davis, *Antebellum American Culture,* 4.

41. Joel Prentiss Bishop, *The Law of Marriage and Divorce* (Boston, 1852), 517–18, as quoted in Lee M. Teitelbaum, "Family History and Family Law," *Wisconsin Law Review* (1985): 1156.

42. Sutton, *Stubborn Children,* 43–89; Rothman, *The Discovery of the Asylum,* 257–62;

Robert Mennel, *Thorns and Thistles: Juvenile Delinquents in the American States, 1825–1940* (Hanover, 1973), 11–12; Robert S. Picket, *Houses of Refuge: Origins of Juvenile Reform in New York State, 1815–1857* (Syracuse, 1969), 74–75; Steven Schlossman, *Love and the American Delinquent: The Theory and Practice of "Progressive" Juvenile Justice, 1825–1920* (Chicago, 1976), 124; Steven Schlossman, "Juvenile Justice in the Age of Jackson," *Teacher's College Record,* 76 (1974): 119–33; Negley G. Teeters, "The Early Days of the Philadelphia House of Refuge," *Pennsylvania History* 27 (1960): 165–87.

43. Teitelbaum and Harris, "Some Historical Perspectives," 20; Sutton, *Stubborn Children,* 45–49; Joseph M. Hawes, *Children in Urban Society: Juvenile Delinquency in the Nineteenth Century* (New York, 1971), 41, 57.

44. Schlossman, *Love and the American Delinquent,* 33–54.

45. Bloomfield, *American Lawyers,* 134–35; Stephen B. Presser, "The Historical Background of the American Law of Adoption," *Journal of Family Law* 2 (1971): 443–516.

46. Allan M. Brandt, *No Magic Bullet: A Social History of Venereal Disease in the United States since 1880* (New York, 1987), 7; Lasch, *Haven in a Heartless World,* 8–9; Peter Gabriel Filene, *Him-Her-Self: Sex Roles in Modern America* (New York, 1976), 36–39; David M. Kennedy, *Birth Control in America: The Career of Margaret Sanger* (New Haven, 1970), 36.

47. Morton Keller, *Affairs of State: Public Life in Late Nineteenth Century America* (Cambridge, Mass., 1977), 468; Grossberg, *Governing the Hearth,* 103–52; Grossberg, "Guarding the Altar," 197–226; Mintz and Kellogg, *Domestic Revolutions,* 126.

48. Grossberg, *Governing the Hearth,* 153–95; C. Thomas Dienes, *Law, Politics, and Birth Control* (Urbana, 1972); James C. Mohr, *Abortion in America: The Origins and Evolution of National Policy* (New York, 1978).

49. Elaine Tyler May, *Great Expectations: Marriage and Divorce in Post-Victorian America* (Chicago, 1980), 4–7; J. P. Lichtenberger, *Divorce: A Social Interpretation* (New York, 1972), 154–86; Keller, *Affairs of State,* 471.

50. Michael B. Katz, "Child-Saving," *History of Education Quarterly* 26 (1986): 413–24; Michael B. Katz, *In the Shadow of the Poor House* (New York, 1986); Leroy Ashby, *Saving the Waifs: Reformers and Dependent Children, 1890–1917* (Philadelphia, 1984); George K. Behlmer, *Child Abuse and Moral Reform in England, 1870–1918* (Stanford, 1982); Miriam Langsam, *Children West: A History of the Placing Out of the New York Children's Aid Bureau* (Madison, 1964); Anthony M. Platt, *The Child Savers: The Invention of Delinquency* (Chicago, 1969); David Rothman, *Conscience and Convenience: The Asylum and Its Alternatives in Progressive America* (Boston, 1980); Susan Tiffin, *In Whose Best Interest? Child Welfare in the Progressive Era* (Westport, 1982); Walter I. Trattner, *Crusade for the Children: A History of the National Child Labor Committee and Child Labor Reform in America* (Chicago, 1970).

51. Donald K. Pikens, *Eugenics and the Progressives* (Nashville, 1968); Paul Boyer, *Urban Masses and Moral Order in America, 1820–1920* (Cambridge, Mass., 1978), 18–120; David Pivar, *Purity Crusade: Sexual Morality and Social Control, 1868–1900* (Westport, 1973), 50–73, 78–121.

52. Katz, "Child-Saving," 413–24.

53. Pleck, *Domestic Tyranny,* 69–121.

54. Linda Gordon, *Heroes of Their Own Lives: The Politics and History of Family Violence, Boston, 1880–1960* (New York, 1988).

55. Pleck, *Domestic Tyranny,* 125–63; Behlmer, *Child Abuse and Moral Reform,* 11, 52, 136, 213; Wini Breines Behlmer and Linda Gordon, "The New Scholarship on Family Violence," *Signs* 8 (1983): 490–528.

56. Keller, *Affairs of State*, 465–67; Sutton, *Stubborn Children*, 121–53; Douglas Rendleman, "*Parens Patriae* from Chancery to the Juvenile Court," *Southern California Law Review* 23 (1971): 233–36.

57. Mintz and Kellogg, *Domestic Revolutions*, 129; Leslie Woodcock Tentler, *Wage-Earning Women: Industrial Work and Family Life in the United States, 1900–1930* (New York, 1979), 161–65.

58. Mintz and Kellogg, *Domestic Revolutions*, 129–30.

59. Sutton, *Stubborn Children*, 142; Grossberg, *Governing the Hearth*, 248–50, 281–85.

60. Frank W. Nicholas, "History, Philosophy, and Procedures of Juvenile Courts," *Journal of Family Law* 1 (1961): 151–52; Roger C. Algase, "The Right to a Fair Trial in Juvenile Court," *Journal of Family Law* 3 (1963): 292–320; Homer W. Sloane, "The Juvenile Court: An Uneasy Partnership of Law and Social Work," *Journal of Family Law* 5 (1965): 170–89; Lynne Halem, *Divorce Reform: Changing Legal and Social Perspectives* (New York, 1980), 220; Sutton, *Stubborn Children*, 121–53.

61. Mintz and Kellogg, *Domestic Revolutions*, 126–27.

62. Halem, *Divorce Reform*, 116–28, 220–21, 241–51, 280.

63. Ibid., 129–57.

64. Ibid.; Lasch, *Haven in a Heartless World*, 37, 43, 107–10; Paula Fass, *The Damned and the Beautiful: American Youth in the 1920s* (New York, 1977), 71–95; James Reed, *The Birth Control Movement and American Society: From Private Vice to Public Virtue* (New York, 1978), 62.

65. Halem, *Divorce Reform*, 158–232.

66. Ibid., 136; May, *Great Expectations*, 5–6, 30, 104.

67. Halem, *Divorce Reform*, 158–232; Sara A. Levitan and Richard S. Belous, *What's Happening to the American Family?* (Baltimore, 1981), 69–72.

68. Pleck, *Domestic Tyranny*, 164–81.

69. William Binchey, "Book Review: Cases and Materials on Family Law," *Journal of Family Law* 15 (1970): 315–17; Mary Ann Glendon, *The New Family and the New Property* (Toronto, 1981), 1–7; Stephen J. Morse, "Family Law in Transition: From Traditional Families to Individual Liberty," in *Changing Images of the Family*, ed. Barbara Myerhoff (New Haven, 1979), 320–21.

70. Morse, "Family Law in Transition," 322–25; Eva R. Rubin, *The Supreme Court and the American Family: Ideology and Issues* (Westport, 1986), 143–61.

71. Lee M. Teitelbaum, "Moral Discourse and Family Law," *Michigan Law Review* 83 (1985): 430–34.

72. Lenore Weitzman and Ruth B. Dixon, "The Transformation of Legal Marriage through No Fault Divorce: The Case of the United States," in *Marriage and Cohabitation in Contemporary Societies: Areas of Legal, Social, and Ethical Change*, ed. John M. Eekelaar and Sanford N. Katz (Toronto, 1979), 143–53; Halem, *Divorce Reform*, 233–83.

73. Weitzman and Dixon, "The Transformation of Legal Marriage," 143–53; Lenore Weitzman, *The Divorce Revolution: The Unexpected Social and Economic Consequences for Women and Children* (New York, 1985); Halem, *Divorce Reform*, 233–83.

74. Mintz and Kellogg, *Domestic Revolutions*, 229–30.

75. Glendon, *The New Family*, 47, 52–55; Mintz and Kellogg, *Domestic Revolutions*, 229–30.

76. Mintz and Kellogg, *Domestic Revolutions*, 231–32; Martha Schecter, "Juvenile Case Law after Gault," *Journal of Family Law* 8 (1968): 416–17.

77. Morse, "Family Law in Transition," 325–27, 349–50; William Manchester, *The Glory and the Dream* (Boston, 1974), 1035–36.

78. Glendon, *The New Family,* 43.

79. Ibid., 11, 38, 49, 71–73.

80. Ibid., 61; W. Walton Garret, "Filial Responsibility Laws," *Journal of Family Law* 18 (1979): 804–8.

81. Glendon, *The New Family,* 7–9, 112–42; Frances E. Olsen, "The Family and the Market: A Study of Ideology and Legal Reform," *Harvard Law Review* 96 (1983): 1510–12.

82. Bissell, "Family, Friends," 106–29.

83. Teitelbaum, "Moral Discourse," 430–31.

84. Grossberg, *Governing the Hearth,* 103–52; Keller, *Affairs of State,* 461–72.

85. Halem, *Divorce Reform,* 114–57.

86. Carl Schneider, "Moral Discourse and the Transformation of American Family Law," *Michigan Law Review* 83 (1985): 1803–79; Teitelbaum, "Moral Discourse," 430–31.

87. Schneider, "Moral Discourse," 1835–39.

88. Ibid., 1814–19.

89. Walter O. Weyrauch and Sanford N. Katz, *American Family Law in Transition* (Washington, D.C., 1983), 496–98; Eva R. Rubin, *The Supreme Court and the American Family: Ideology and Issues* (Westport, 1986), 156.

90. Glendon, *The New Family,* 108–11.

PART 2

Early America

The term *early America* refers to the period from the time of the original European outposts of the early seventeenth century to the growth of commercialization in the first third of the nineteenth century. It is a period characterized by a myriad of family arrangements existing within Native American and European cultures, modified by interaction between them, and adapted to particular environments. In the interests of continuity, however, this section will concentrate on the English, East Coast settlements because the European family model became the dominant form in subsequent years.

This time span is long enough to reveal the changes families underwent in response to growing commercialism and specialization within society. Among preindustrial Europeans who first settled in the Colonies, a family was viewed as a little kingdom that produced most of the goods and services required by its members. Providing sustenance, shelter, job training, religious instruction, and care for the young, sick, and elderly was the collective responsibility of each unit. Individual preferences were subsumed under that which would benefit the whole. The family was considered to be both a microcosm and building block of society and as such was organized in a hierarchical manner that promoted order and reflected the larger society.

The husband-father, or patriarch, enjoyed sole authority over all family members, matters, and property. Women were assumed to be lustful and to possess a weaker intellect and character, thus requiring as much supervision as children did by a man of rationality and strength of character. Both ruler of the family unit and ambassador for it, the husband-father represented its collective interests in the larger society. Because he bore responsibility for the welfare of the family through succeeding generations, he owned or controlled all the property that would ensure its survival. Such power reinforced his authority and allowed the patriarch to exercise control over individual members and govern in the best interests of the household. So important was the family, however, that its regulation could not be left solely in the hands of its members. The boundary between family and society was a very porous one, and the distinction between public and private often was blurred. Village leaders intervened when conflicts erupted within families, and individuals came to the aid of kinfolk in other families.

Patriarchy under community supervision, however, was stronger in the New England than in the Chesapeake settlements in the seventeenth century. Puritans came in family units, entered a healthy geographical area that was conducive to long-lived families, and settled in towns committed to the good of the community. The majority of Chesapeake inhabitants, in contrast, were individual males intent on economic gain. They settled in a malaria-ridden environment on isolated plantations. The skewed sex ratio made it difficult for a man to acquire a wife, and a high mortality rate disrupted family units formed and then reconfigured after the death of a parent. This made it difficult for a patriarch to retain the subservience of his children by the promise of property and status or even to control a wife who might have to manage the estate for his children should he die. As mortality rates fell in the Chesapeake, and as land became more scarce in the towns of New England, the two areas gravitated toward a common, moderate patriarchy by the end of the eighteenth century.

As society began the process of modernization in the late eighteenth and early nineteenth centuries, families responded by becoming more private, often separated from kin and distancing themselves from interfering outsiders. Within the unit, the hierarchy softened, and more affective bonds developed among its members. Families were more prone to assign some of their functions to external institutions, sending children to schools or for specialized training and supporting orphanages, hospitals, and almshouses. They began to purchase more household items such as cloth, which had been woven at home.

These general changes, however, operated primarily among the more urban middle class, which also left records for later historians to consult. Readers will note that the essays in this section, insightful though they are, focus on the white middle and upper class. We know something about the treatment of the working classes but little about the family strategies they adopted for coping with their circumstances. We have some indication that Native Americans, as a group, reassigned general family roles to facilitate working relations with Europeans but know little about the internal dynamics of this reassignment among particular tribes and clans. Historical accounts of the family structure of Africans have homogenized the wide variety of family patterns practiced in the old world into one generalized "American" form. The same can be said for accounts of the families of European immigrants.

One of the most controversial topics in family history revolves around strategies to acquire, augment, and preserve the property used to ensure support for the future family tree. In her study of women and property in South Carolina (chapter 2), Marylynn Salmon injects some complexity into the easy generalization that a married woman, as a *feme covert,* had virtually no control over her property under English common law and looked to equity law for some release from this subservience. Each colony and state applied the principles of common and equity law differently. Salmon's account of who used marriage settlements (and for what family purposes) at any given time provides an example of how one colony balanced these two sets of laws.

In chapter 3, Susan Branson presents a case study of Elizabeth Meredith, who, during her lifetime, moved from the role of an artisan "helpmeet" to that of a "republican mother" in contributing to the economic success of her family in a changing economy and society. Her timely shifts in strategy highlight the flexibility of family units in assigning specific responsibilities to particular family members as the need arose.

Urbanization and commercialization decreased the necessity for large numbers of family members who could produce all of the household's necessities. Smaller families allowed increased attention to each individual child, who now acquired value in their own right rather than for their productive role within the family. John Locke's emphasis on the importance of molding a child's character was reinforced by a Revolutionary ideology that proclaimed that the future of the Republic rested on a virtuous citizenry whose socialization increasingly became the responsibility of the mother. This was part of a continuum that started in the mid-eighteenth century as women began to dominate church membership and assume a mantle of moral superiority that qualified them to impart religious sensibilities to their offspring. Because the attributes of a moral Christian were quite similar to those of a virtuous citizen, the transition from the concept of "religious mother" to "republican mother" was easy. Such concentrated attention on the individual child might also have motivated the family limitation that Jan Lewis and Kenneth A. Lockridge explore in "Sally Has Been Sick" (chapter 4). Their use of literary sources offers one explanation for declining birth rates at the turn of the nineteenth century.

The growing privatization of families and individualization of their members are described by Karin Calvert in "Children in American Family Portraiture, 1670–1810" (chapter 5). By illuminating the changing view of the nature of childhood, Calvert also casts light on the concomitant alteration in the interrelations between wives and husbands and mothers and fathers. Such insightful use of material culture continues to refine our understanding of families.

2

Women and Property in South Carolina: The Evidence from Marriage Settlements, 1730–1830

MARYLYNN SALMON

During the eighteenth and early nineteenth centuries, two distinct sets of legal principles—those of the common law and equity law—governed the status of women in the British-American colonies and the American states. Complications arose when the rules contradicted each other, as they did, for example, with regard to property ownership. Under the common law, a married woman (*feme covert*) could not own property, either real or personal. All personalty a woman brought to marriage became her husband's. He could spend her money, sell her stocks or slaves, and appropriate her clothing and jewelry. He gained managerial rights to her lands, houses, and tenements and decided whether land was to be farmed by the family or leased.[1] He also controlled the rents and profits from all real estate. With regard to conveyances, however, women held a single note of power. No husband could sell real property without the consent of his wife. The common law sanctioned conveyances only when wives freely agreed to them, although "free" consent was sometimes quite difficult to determine in court.[2]

Because women could not own property under the common law, they could not exercise legal controls over it. A feme covert could not make a legally binding contract. She could not sell or mortgage property that she brought to the marriage or that she and her husband acquired. She possessed no power to execute a deed of gift or write a will unless her husband consented, and even then her power was restricted to personal property. During widowhood, the law allowed women only a life interest in one-third of the family's real property, no matter what proportion of that property had been hers before marriage. With regard to personal property, widows could claim absolute ownership of one-third, but only if the estate were free of debts. If a husband died heavily indebted or insolvent, his wife lost all her personal property (and in some jurisdictions her real property as well) even though she had exercised no control over the accumulation of her husband's debts. Regarding property then, women were virtually powerless under the common law.[3]

Equity law as administered by the British and American courts of chancery was not similarly harsh. Through formal contracts called marriage settlements, femes covert owned and controlled property.[4] In their various forms, marriage settlements allowed women full or partial managerial rights over property. Separate clauses gave women the right to sell or mortgage property, give it away, or write wills. Some marriage settlements stated explicitly the traditional rights that men relinquished by signing them. Many settlements barred husbands from "intermeddling" with their wives' estates in any way and, perhaps most important, stated that settlement property could not be taken by creditors to pay a husband's debts. Separate estates for women also frequently included clauses guaranteeing the inheritances of children. Once women or their relations protected property from the possible business misfortunes of a husband, it could safely be passed through the maternal line.

Marriage settlements were designed, then, to serve several functions: They gave women a measure of financial security during marriage and widowhood. They protected a portion of family property from creditors. They provided grandparents with the assurance that family fortunes would not be spent before grandchildren came of age. Historians of aristocratic society in seventeenth- and eighteenth-century England have tended to emphasize this last function of marriage settlements. They have found that beginning in the late sixteenth century, fathers created trust estates for their daughters in an effort to prevent sons-in-law from controlling, and perhaps squandering, family fortunes. For a man who wanted to guarantee the inheritances of his grandchildren, a trust presented an alternative to turning property over to an outsider—his daughter's husband. According to this interpretation, the primary purpose of English marriage settlements was to create and preserve large family estates.[5]

Historians of early America have tended to discount the importance of the British perspective on trust estates. Instead, scholars such as Richard B. Morris and Mary R. Beard stressed the utilitarian function of settlements for the feme covert. Pointing to the existence of equity law and trust estates, Beard and Morris claimed that in America (Beard also applied the argument to England), women functioned virtually on a legal par with men. If a woman could own property, make contracts, and write wills under equity law, then commonlaw restrictions on her activities lost meaning.[6] Thus the most generally accepted interpretation of equity law in America has emphasized its ability to elevate the legal status of women from subservience to relative independence.

Historians of women in early America have relied on this interpretation of equity law to help define the status of the feme covert. The hypothesis of equality has contributed to the assumption that colonial women enjoyed a legal and social status superior to that of both their English contemporaries and their nineteenth-century descendants.[7] For if, as Morris claimed, marriage settlements were "widely employed" in America, and if, as Beard believed, they were interpreted liberally, then women of all classes in the colonies enjoyed the rights of wealthy Englishwomen. In the view of these historians, the common use of settlements in the eighteenth century reflected a beneficial legal climate for American women. Similarly, the decline of equity law in the nineteenth century demonstrated the advantages enjoyed by eighteenth-century matrons.[8]

Neither Morris nor Beard studied marriage settlements in detail. They knew that equity law contained rules allowing women to own property and that some marriage settlements existed, but they did not know how frequently settlements were employed or what specific powers women exercised through them. Historical understanding of equity law and the use of marriage settlements has been based on scant research and impressionistic evidence. The current lively debate over the nature of women's legal and social status in the colonial and early national periods makes it important, however, to understand equity law more precisely.[9] We must learn who used marriage settlements, how often they were used, and for what purposes. Such information should reveal the degree to which settlements provided women with financial security and whether they were written to benefit women, or children and grandchildren, or all three groups.

Before the role of equity law in America can be understood, many separate studies must be conducted, because each colony and state handled principles of equity law differently.[10] Large numbers of settlement deeds must be scrutinized, even though the informality of American recording practices frequently makes such analysis difficult. This essay reports findings for South Carolina, for which a wealth of information is available. The extent of the documentation makes South Carolina a good place to begin an investigation into the nature of equity law. The legal record reveals remarkably liberal attitudes toward women's property rights—quite possibly the most liberal of all the colonies and states, although that supposition must be tested by comparative study.[11]

In 1720 the colony established a court of chancery that handled cases concerning marriage settlements in a sophisticated manner, imitating the English Chancery Court in style and decisions.[12] The court kept good records and remained active throughout the colonial and early national periods. The legislature did not require registration of marriage settlements until 1785, but before that date prudent persons frequently recorded their settlements with the secretary of state in Charleston. After 1785, all settlements had to be recorded within three months of their creation to be considered valid.[13]

Altogether, some two thousand settlements have survived from the colonial and early national periods.[14] For this study, an attempt was made to discover and analyze all recorded marriage settlements for the colonial and Revolutionary periods. For the period from 1785 to 1830, when the law required settlements to be recorded and the number increased accordingly, a sample consisting of all deeds registered in Charleston totaled 638 (table 2.1). Each settlement gives the names of the parties, the dates of the type of creation and recording of property settled, and the terms of the settlement. Also frequently noted are the occupations of the parties, their residences, their marital status, the name of the owner(s) of the property, and the location and amount of the property.

Proper marriage settlements were complicated documents, usually made in the form of trusts. Before the English case of *Rippon v. Dawding* (1769), all valid settlements were required to include trustees who nominally owned the property in the name of the feme covert (the *cestui qui* trust).[15] After 1769, in England and in some American jurisdictions, simple marriage settle-

Table 2.1. Marriage Settlement Sample Size

	Number	Percent of Total
1730–1740	23	4
1741–1750	35	5
1751–1760	55	9
1761–1770	107	17
1771–1780	107	17
	327	52
1781–1790	88	14
1791–1800	51	8
1801–1810	54	8
1811–1820	49	8
1821–1830	69	11
	311	49%
Total	638	101[a]

a. Total exceeds 100 due to rounding.

ments—contracts made directly between a man and a woman without the intervention of trustees—also created separate estates.[16] In their handling of simple marriage settlements, equity courts initially referred to the husband as trustee for his wife. This language soon disappeared from most cases, however, perhaps as the courts realized the irony of naming husbands trustees for their wives' separate estates. In South Carolina, judges disliked simple agreements, and trusts remained the most common form for separate estates. Trust estates composed 91 percent (582) of the deeds studied. Only 9 percent (56) were simple marriage settlements, indicating the reluctance of South Carolinians to abandon the formality of trusts.[17]

To create a trust estate in the normal fashion, the man, woman, and trustee(s) all joined in the execution of an "indenture tripartite," a contract stipulating the terms of the settlement. This form guaranteed the knowledge and consent of the parties, as required by law. In cases involving separate estates, equity standards demanded that men be fully apprised of the terms of their wives' settlements. Judges refused to support a woman who deceived her fiancé or husband into expecting property at marriage only to secure it to herself through a trustee.[18] They viewed such action as a fraud against the husband's marital rights and held that "he [or she] that hath committed Iniquity, shall not have Equity."[19]

Settlements granting women separate estates could be written either before or after marriage, but most couples executed them prior to marriage. For the period under study, 87 percent (552) of the settlements were prenuptial. There was no significant change in that pattern over time, indicating the constancy of women's desire to secure separate property at the point when they exercised the greatest bargaining power over men.[20] Postnuptial settlements usually resulted when a wife inherited property unexpectedly or when her husband encountered financial difficulties that made it necessary to secure some family property against creditors.

For understandable reasons, creditors disliked trust estates, particularly those made after marriage. They resented the ability of a feme covert to deny them access to her separate estate and argued that husbands as well as wives could find protection under the terms of marriage settlements. A man who lost his own estate through business misfortunes or extravagant living, they claimed, could fall back on income from his wife's trust property. Indebted or insolvent husbands might even attempt to preserve a portion of their own fortunes by fraudulently settling property on their wives.[21]

Evidence from South Carolina undermines the argument that settlements commonly benefited husbands rather than wives. Women who wrote marriage settlements usually wanted to control the property they brought to their marriages, not their husbands' property. Eighty-two percent (523) of the settlements studied included only the wife's estate; 11 percent (68), only the estate of the husband; and 5 percent (35), property from both the husband and wife. (In twelve cases, 2 percent, it is unknown who owned the property.) No man put his entire estate into a trust for his wife. These figures demonstrate no general attempt by men to protect their property through marriage settlements. They benefited, of course, when women held property that could not be confiscated for family debts, but they did not usually safeguard their own estates. The need for credit in money-scarce economies gave men reasons to avoid trusts. In addition, by the end of the eighteenth century, strict recording requirements made deceit difficult, for creditors could easily discover the status of a family's estate and refuse to extend credit on settled property.

Cases of fraudulent trusts demonstrate judicial solicitude for the rights of creditors. The recording statute of 1785 served primarily as a means of informing creditors about separate estates. In addition, chancellors refused to enforce trusts made to deny creditors their just claims.[22] But the South Carolina court of chancery also demonstrated sensitivity to the needs of debtors who wanted to create trust estates. A debtor could execute a valid settlement for the benefit of another person if he possessed assets to repay his debts above the value of the trust property.[23]

In the case of *Tunno v. Trezevant* (1804), to take a well-documented example, we find that a man consented to the marriage of his niece only after her fiancé agreed to create a settlement, including all her property and some of his own.[24] The young man was a merchant whose credit appeared to be good at the time of his marriage (the uncle made inquiries), but within a year he became an insolvent debtor hounded by creditors who demanded payment out of both his business and his private property. From testimony, the court found that he had not created his marriage settlement with any fraudulent purpose in mind. Both he and his bride-to-be had honestly believed that their financial position was secure when they executed the deed. In situations such as theirs, when a settlement was created for the "valuable consideration" of marriage, the court of chancery enforced it against the claims of creditors. In this instance the judges regarded the settlement as a "*bona fide* discharge of a moral duty" and refused to "weigh it too nicely." They did not attach the settlement property to discharge the husband's debts, acting on the fundamental principle that "marriage is not only a *bona fide* and valuable consideration, but the very highest consideration in law; this Court will therefore always support marriage settlements, if there is no particular evidence of fraud made out, showing an intention to deceive or defraud creditors."[25]

Tunno v. Trezevant clearly demonstrates the advantages of separate estates for women and their children. Through marriage settlements, families possessed a source of income that was free from obligations of the male head, either business or, if the estate were so designed, personal. Because separate estates could prove so beneficial, it is important to know how many women actually employed them. In that regard, the documentation for colonial South Carolina is sadly limited. Before 1785, the absence of a recording statute makes it impossible to discover the total number of settlements. For the period from 1785 to 1810, however, when virtually all marriage settlements were recorded in Charleston and when accurate census records are available for the state, it is possible to arrive at a rough estimate of the number of couples with settlements. During those years, approximately 1–2 percent of marrying couples created separate estates.[26] Settlements apparently were far from the common occurrence that some historians have believed, at least in South Carolina. Few women had either means or reason to utilize them.

Who, then, did create marriage settlements? Perhaps the small number of deeds indicates use of settlements only among the wealthy landed families of South Carolina in the manner of the English aristocracy. Fortunately, the detailed information available in the deeds allows us to discover something about the status of couples who employed trust estates and marriage settlements. This can be done by analyzing the value of settled property and by noting the occupations of husbands. (We cannot consider the occupations of wives, because few identified themselves by occupation.) The following discussion investigates property values first and then turns to male occupations.

Analysis of property values presents some difficulty. Many settlements do not specify the amount or type of property but refer to it as "everything" or "all her property both real and personal." When these deeds are excluded, 456 (71 percent) remain for analysis, but even these, while listing specific types of property such as slaves, cattle, or land, rarely give property values. Consequently, only broad, comparative categories will be considered here and not specific property valuations.[27]

The upper ranks of South Carolina society relied on settlements more often than people of middling status. It appears that 69 percent (316 of 456) of the estates that specified types of property included property worth more than £500 sterling, or more than five slaves, or more than one town lot with appurtenances, or a plantation of more than three hundred acres.[28] Settlements of more than ten slaves and hundreds of pounds sterling were common. One settlement included one hundred slaves, another £50,000 sterling, and still another forty-four slaves and more than four thousand acres of land. A number of settlements included more than ten slaves, land, and at least one town lot with appurtenances—the traditional estate of a wealthy South Carolina planter family.

Although the elite employed marriage settlements most often, persons with small amounts of property also used them. Settlements sometimes included only one or two slaves, a few articles of household furniture, or the woman's clothing and household goods. Approximately 9 percent (41 of 456) of the settlements included property estimated worth less than £150 sterling, or included only one slave, or a part of a house. Another 22 percent (99) included property estimated at £151–500 sterling, or contained two to five slaves, or one house, or 100 to 299 acres of land. The settlement of John Darrell and Elizabeth Legeaux is typical of contracts made by persons from the middling ranks of society:

> This is to certify to all whom it may concern that I John Smith Darrell of the city of Charleston and State aforesaid Mariner being now about to be joined in the holy Bond of Wedlock to Miss Elizabeth Browne Legeaux conceiving it just and right that she should continue after marriage to hold what property she might at that time I do therefore by this Instrument Secure to her and the heirs of her body for ever all right and title to Two Negroes left to her by her Father (Vizt.) the Woman Named Constant and her son Caesar together with any other Issue that the said Constant may have. I do also secure to her Bed Bedding and the household furniture that she now posseses reserving to myself the Services of the said Negroes during my Natural life.[29]

Elizabeth Legeaux's estate of two slaves might have been enviable by eighteenth-century standards, but it was hardly that of an heiress. The motivation for creating a trust estate of small value undoubtedly stemmed from more than a desire to protect the inheritances of future generations. A woman who went to the trouble and expense of creating a separate estate for her household furniture was concerned about herself and her own position in life at least as much as with the well-being of her children. Although the desire to protect family property for future generations may have motivated some of the wealthy couples with settlements, the preservation of family status was not the dominant consideration for all. Given the wide range of individuals with separate estates—from a woman with one slave to an heiress with one hundred—we cannot rely on the traditional English interpretation of settlements.

Most women who made settlements owned personal rather than real property. Very few settlements included real estate to the exclusion of personalty (10 of 456), and only one-third (147) included some real estate. The other two-thirds (301) involved only personal property. In South Carolina, women's marriage settlements most often included slaves, money, cattle, and household goods but not land. Such a pattern may indicate that fathers gave their land to sons, while daughters received slaves or money. In the absence of comparative probate materials, it is impossible to be sure. What is clear, however, is that settlements consisting entirely of personal property appeared twice as often in the sample as settlements including any real property. Given the fact that under the common law men acquired absolute ownership of their wives' personal estates at marriage, although they exercised only managerial rights over real property, this is not surprising. Settlements were more useful to women who owned personal property.

This consideration may explain why a substantial number of settlements involved slaves. Eighty-two percent (372) of the deeds that specify the nature of the property included at least some slaves, and 28 percent (129) included only slaves. No other type of property appears so frequently in the settlements. Moreover, settlements including only a few slaves appeared in the sample as often as those with many slaves. When settlements including only slaves are singled out, we learn that fully 32 percent (41 of 129) contained five slaves or fewer and that an additional 19 percent contained six to ten slaves. Women who had slaves appreciated the importance of protecting their property.

More may be learned about the function of settlements by studying the occupational status of the men who made them. Of the whole number of deeds analyzed, 68 percent (434) noted the husband's occupation (table 2.2). More than half of these (228) involved planters (30 percent, $n = 131$) or gentlemen (22 percent, $n = 97$). From the settlements, we can learn no more about the status of these men than the words they used to describe themselves. We do not know, for example, how many of the planters were large landowners and therefore considered members of the social elite. The word *planter* stood for all farmers and landowners in South Carolina, large and small. The fact that 22 percent of the sample referred to themselves as "gentlemen," however, reveals the high social standing of a significant portion of settlement-holders.

Merchants composed the next largest group of men with settlements, 13 percent (58 of 434). Perhaps the volatile fortunes of merchant families gave them special incentives to protect their property from creditors. Indentures tripartite involving merchants frequently alluded to the financial risks of trade. The settlement of William Edwards and Elizabeth Moore in 1774, for example, gave the couple joint control over her property—seven slaves and a £6000 current money bond—"unless it shall happen that the said William Edwards shall become Bankrupt or meet with losses or misfortunes in Trade or Business so as to be unable to support himself and family."[30] In that case, Elizabeth Edwards would have full managerial rights, free from "interference"

Table 2.2. Male Occupations

Title	Number	Percentage[a]
Planter	131	30
Gentlemen and professionals		
Gentleman, esquire	97	22
Merchant	58	13
Physician	30	7
Lawyer, judge	13	3
Minister	6	1
Schoolmaster	2	
Shipmaster	1	
Officials		
Military officer	6	1
Government official	3	1
Shopkeepers and innholders		
Shopkeeper	5	1
Factor	5	1
Clerk	5	1
Innholder, tavernkeeper	3	1
Trader	1	
Indian trader	1	
Grocer	1	
Artisans		
Carpenter	10	2
Cordwainer	9	2
Tailor	8	2
Blacksmith	4	1
Cabinetmaker	4	1
Baker	3	1
Bricklayer	3	1
Butcher	1	
Cooper	1	
Breechesmaker	1	
Watchmaker	1	
Frame mole knitter	1	
Carver	1	
Spinner	1	
Saddler	1	
Coachmaker	1	
Wheelmaker	1	
Perriwigmaker	1	
Shipwright	1	
Painter	1	
Distiller	1	
Mariner	10	2
Free black	1	
Total	434	

a. Percentage not given if less than 1. Therefore, percentages do not add to 100.

by her husband. In 1787 James Stephenson and Elizabeth Scott were equally careful. Their settlement stated that if James became insolvent "by losses in trade or otherwise by accumulation of debts by accident or misfortune," the trustees would give Elizabeth £350 current money for her separate use, "to the intent that the said Elizabeth may have a resource left."[31] The overseas expeditions of merchants could place wives and children in precarious financial situations. Before Josiah Smith left on a "sea voyage," he took out the 1789 equivalent of flight insurance. He settled six slaves on his wife for her sole and separate use, free from his debts, if he never returned.[32] The case of *Tunno v. Trezevant*, discussed earlier, suggests that it was wise for a woman to be wary when entering marriage with a South Carolina merchant.

Almost as many artisans, innkeepers, and mariners made marriage settlements as gentlemen—20 percent (86 of 434). Although we cannot learn the economic standing of these men from the settlements (and some of them may have owned considerable amounts of property), the fact that they identified themselves by trade rather than status indicates that they were not a part of the South Carolina elite. Even persons at the lowest social level could make use of equity law, as demonstrated by the appearance of a free black man in the sample. On the basis of male occupations, then it is possible to state that marriage settlements were not made exclusively by the South Carolina aristocracy. Couples from the middling and even the lower ranks of society also sometimes took the precaution of establishing separate estates for wives.

It is easy to understand why the wife of a merchant or a mariner might want a separate estate, yet not all merchants' wives utilized equity provisions, and not all mariners followed in the footsteps of John Darrell. Moreover, it is not as obvious why a planter's wife, or a physician's, or a cordwainer's might desire this special protection. Why did a particular gentleman and his fiancée step into the office of the secretary of state to register a settlement, given the fact that most genteel families did not? The motivations of individuals cannot be conclusively established but by investigating the provisions for control and descent of settlement property and analyzing the court cases concerning specific disputes over settlement terms we may learn more about the use of separate estates.

Each marriage settlement contained various clauses for delineating control over settlement property. Couples could place property under the management of trustees or they could give trustees no managerial powers at all, reducing them to figureheads. Some husbands retained control over their wives' estates, and in many cases femes covert managed their own property. The powers retained by women became significant for determining women's level of independence. Some trusts gave women extensive authority over their own property, whereas others gave them none at all but instead directed trustees to pay them the rents and profits of their estates. Some settlements gave women one privilege of control while denying others. For example, if a deed granted a feme covert the right to devise, she could not also sell or mortgage her estate; those powers had to be granted in a separate clause. In the same vein, a woman whose settlement gave her rights to the rents and profits of her property could not regulate the principal, which remained in the hands of trustees who made all investment decisions.[33]

Although most South Carolina settlements were trust estates, trustees rarely managed property. Only 3 percent (16) of the deeds gave trustees sole powers of control. In 93 percent (591), trustees were either vested with minimal powers, such as the right to approve a property sale initiated by the feme covert, or were not employed at all. In 5 percent of the settlements (31), control was shared by the trustee and the couple, or else the arrangement is unknown. Settlement terms demonstrate that many creators of separate estates, whether parents, relatives, or the women themselves, wanted women rather than trustees—or husbands—to manage their own property. Over the entire period studied, 40 percent (254) of the women administered their estates alone. In 28 percent (180) of the deeds, husbands and wives managed settlement property together, and in 25 percent (157), men possessed exclusive managerial rights (table 2.3).

Some change in this division of authority occurred over time (figure 2.1). There was a small but steady decline in the number of women who managed their own estates, offset by an increase in the number of husbands and wives

Table 2.3. Control of Settlement Property

	Women		Men		Couples		Trustees		Mixed/Unknown		Number of Deeds
	No.	%	No.	%	No.	%	No.	%	No.	%	
1730–1740	12	52	7	30	4	17	0	0	0	0	23
1741–1750	20	57	6	17	6	17	0	0	3	9	35
1751–1760	29	53	12	22	9	16	3	5	2	4	55
1761–1770	44	41	25	23	32	30	2	2	4	4	107
1771–1780	44	41	25	23	31	29	4	4	3	3	107
1781–1790	34	39	28	32	22	25	1	1	3	3	88
1791–1800	14	27	18	35	16	31	2	4	2	4	51
1801–1810	19	35	13	24	18	33	2	4	2	4	54
1811–1820	17	35	8	16	16	33	1	2	7	14	49
1821–1830	21	30	15	22	26	38	1	1	6	9	69
	254	(40%)	157	(25%)	180	(28%)	16	(3%)	31	(5%)	638

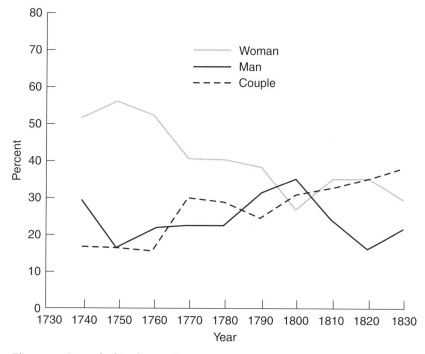

Figure 2.1. Control of Settlement Property

who shared control. With the exception of a slight rise between 1780 and 1800, the number of men who managed settlement property alone remained fairly constant at about 22 percent. What we see is a pattern that shifts away from exclusive privileges for women and toward joint privileges for couples.

A plausible explanation for this pattern may be found in Mary Beth Norton's study of marital relationships in the eighteenth and early nineteenth centuries. Norton discovered that before the American Revolution, wives rarely played an active role in family business beyond the sphere of domestic concerns. They deferred to their husbands on most questions and relied on men to manage family finances. By the end of the century, however, that deferential relationship was changing. Marriages became more egalitarian as wives abandoned passivity to participate in broader decisions concerning family affairs. The need for female autonomy in regulating separate estates would decrease as relationships between spouses became more equal over time. Femes covert might no longer desire total independence in managing their own estates precisely because they exercised more authority over the general fund of family property.

For the 180 settlements involving coadministration, we cannot know who actually managed the property. Perhaps men dominated in all cases and the figure should be combined with that for sole male control. Total freedom for all husbands in this category is unlikely, however, for many of the joint-control settlements restricted husbands in various ways. Some required that the wife consent to all conveyances made by her husband (16 percent, $n = 29$). In others, either the trustee or both the trustee and the wife had to consent to all transactions (5 percent, $n = 9$). More important, the fact that a feme covert wielded authority with her spouse says a great deal about the way she wanted the property handled—under her management as well as her husband's. Because many women did possess managerial rights, we can assume they wanted to take part in decisions concerning their property. At the very least, they exercised veto power over sales and investments stronger than that provided by the common law, which offered only weak protection in the form of private examinations.

Most important for limiting the degree of power exercised by men in joint-control settlements were clauses restricting creditors' interests. Although the principal sums of settlements could never be taken to pay husbands' debts, rents and profits could be so applied if settlement terms gave men access to them. To avoid this danger yet still allow husbands the use of separate estates, many couples relied on clauses that explicitly denied creditors' rights. Martha Baker and Allen Bolton wrote such a settlement in 1765. They agreed that Allen, a planter, could "have Receive and take the use enjoyment profits and interest" of Martha's £5000 estate as long as he continued "in good Circumstances." If his affairs suffered, however, Martha would be permitted to take over management of her own estate. The settlement specified her right to act "without the Controul or Intermeddling of the said Allen Bolton or any Creditors of his in the same manner as if she were sole and unmarried and no part [of her estate] thereof or the interest thereof shall be thereafter liable to any Debts Contracts or engagements of the said Allen Bolton."[34]

Another woman and her fiancé took similar precautions. Although Thomas Bee considered himself a "gentleman," he and Susanna Holmes thought it wise to place £1000 of her money in a trust as protection against future insolvency. The settlement terms allowed the couple full use of the money, unless "by misfortunes or losses (which God avert) the present occupation calling or business of him the said Thomas Bee as a Planter or otherwise, shall fail or decline very considerably, and there shall be manifest danger, or probability, that he will be reduced and obliged to surrender quit or deliver up his Estate and Effects for the Satisfaction of his Creditors."[35] In that case, the money would go into the hands of the couple's trustees, who were directed to pay them the annual interest, safe from creditors' demands. Similar stipulations commonly appeared in settlements throughout the period. More than half (51 percent, $n = 326$) of the women demanded this explicit protection. Without clauses denying creditors' claims on settlement property, husbands' debts, poor business decisions, fraud, or, simply, financial misfortunes could destroy the utility of a separate estate.

Carefully constructed settlements specified each restriction or power of control separately and included sections allowing or disallowing certain basic changes in the settled property. For example, when creating trusts for the benefit of daughters or other female relatives, some individuals perceived a need to forbid future changes in the settlements. They feared the power of their beneficiaries to annul the protective function of their trusts by conveying them to their husbands or making use of the principal.[36] To protect women from male coercion or prevent them from making damaging business decisions, creators of settlements sometimes employed clauses forbidding changes or certain kinds of potentially harmful dispositions. A deed of settlement might state that it could not be altered in any way, or it might include provisions allowing a feme covert control over the rents and profits but not the principal of her estate.

When settlements did not include provisions restricting the right of a woman to control her own property, she could change or even dissolve her marriage settlement at any time.[37] Although some women wanted to alter settlement terms for the benefit of their husbands, more often wives acted to transfer controls from husbands to themselves. At the time of marriage it might seem appropriate for a woman to give her husband powers of active control over her property without any reference to contingency arrangements in the event he encountered difficulties. Many women, unlike Martha Baker and Susanna Holmes, did not express publicly their fears for the future. But if a husband later suffered financial setbacks threatening his wife's estate, she might want to rescind his powers. By inserting a clause in her settlement allowing unspecified changes in her trust, a woman who initially wanted to leave property in her husband's hands could do so, confident that at a future date she could use her power to restrict his managerial capacity.

Such was the case for Charlotte Poaug, whose prenuptial settlement gave her husband control over the rents and profits of her real property.[38] John Poaug was a merchant who became indebted several years after his marriage. In 1771, to prevent John's creditors from seizing their estate, the Poaugs changed the terms of their settlement. In the new document, Charlotte retained all powers of control for herself. Clearly, a safety valve of this nature was invaluable for families with uncertain fortunes.

Unfortunately, some individuals did not understand the importance of precision. They wrote loose documents, failing to delineate specific powers of control. Occasionally, friends or relatives failed to clarify the fact that they were creating a separate estate for a feme covert through a deed of gift or a devise. They gave a woman property, meant for her separate use, but failed to say so explicitly. In South Carolina, when settlements were vague and disputes brought couples into court, judges in equity did everything in their power to protect women. The intent of settlements, gifts, or wills, however haphazardly designed, governed judicial decisions.

Court records indicate that by the early nineteenth century, South Carolina jurists interpreted unclear words in a deed of gift or marriage settlement consistently for the benefit of women. For example, following the English Chancery case of *Tyrrel v. Hope* (1743), the South Carolina court ceased requiring the specific words "to her sole and separate use" for the creation of a separate estate.[39] Instead, chancellors began to assume that any conveyance to a married woman was meant for her own use, whether the donor said so explicitly or not. If it appeared from other evidence, either oral evidence concerning the donor's intent or the wording of the document in question, that the property was intended for the sole use of a woman, the standard phrase could be omitted.

The South Carolina case of *Johnson v. Thompson* (1814) exemplifies judicial practice in this regard.[40] Here a father made a bequest of personal property to his married daughter. Her husband claimed the property and disposed of it. After the woman's death, her children contested his disposition. They stated that their grandfather had intended the property to descend to his daughter as a separate estate, free from the control of her husband. In deciding favorably for the children, the court of appeals noted that because the devise was made to a feme covert, its wording had to be examined closely to determine intent. Here the words "fairly inferred" that the estate was designed to be a separate one, and therefore the woman's husband possessed no right to dispose of it. The implementation of this liberal policy in South Carolina indicates strong support for marriage settlements as a legal form.

South Carolina chancellors also interpreted unclear words in settlements for the benefit of married women. When coercion was not an issue, judges assumed that the absence of restrictive clauses meant freedom to exercise control.[41] In *Lowndes' Trustee v. Champneys' Executors* (1821), the chancellor declared that it was "immaterial in what form or phrase a trust of this nature creating a seperate [*sic*] estate for the Wife is described—technical language is not necessary—All that is requisite is that the intention of the gift should appear manifestly to be for the wife's separate enjoyment."[42] An inference, or the circumstances of a gift or devise, could induce the court to rule in favor of separate estates.

The favorable perspective on marriage settlements in South Carolina equity courts is also demonstrated by acceptance of the doctrine called "equity to a settlement." Settlements became so respectable, and chancellors supported them so wholeheartedly, that by the mid-eighteenth century in England and by 1762 in South Carolina equity courts regarded them as a positive right for all married women.[43] Under certain circumstances, chancellors ordered men to give wives separate estates. Most often, chancellors made such orders when the executor of an estate refused to give a woman her proper inheritance under a will, thereby forcing her and her husband to sue in Chancery for possession. Before awarding them the property, the chancellor would order the husband to settle all or part of it on his wife. The amount of the settlement depended on the man's financial situation. In that way, chancellors knew that they were not giving property to men who could take it for themselves, providing their wives—the rightful owners—no benefits from it.

South Carolina equity courts closely followed English law on the wife's equity to a settlement. Chancellors maintained that any man who sued in an equity court for the property of his wife assumed a moral obligation to settle at least a part of it on her as a separate estate. Thus in *Mathewes and Others v. the Executors of Mathewes et al.* (1762), the court ordered the creation of a trust for Mary Lloyd.[44] Her husband Thomas had refused to appear in court for hearings concerning the execution of his father-in-law's estate. What other transgressions Thomas may have committed are unclear, but the court refused to give him Mary's inheritance. The chancellor ordered division of the deceased's estate and distribution among the heirs, "except the Share and proportion claimed by the Defendant Thomas Lloyd in right of his said Wife Mary." His share was ordered invested, and the proceeds paid to Mary "for her own and separate use, and after her Death the said Money to go to and become the property of the said Thomas Lloyd the Son, if he be then living, if not, then the Interest of said Money shall be paid to the said Thomas Lloyd the Defendant during his Natural Life."[45]

Chancellors ordered the creation of a separate estate when the financial situation of a husband caused them concern for his wife's well-being. Men of good standing in the community were not usually handled as harshly as Thomas Lloyd. When William Henry Drayton, a prosperous planter, member of the Governor's Council, and subsequently chief justice of South Carolina, won a chancery suit against his father-in-law's executors, he did not have to place the property into a trust.[46] Undoubtedly the court believed that his respectable position, added to the fact that his wife already possessed a settlement, made the order unnecessary.

In another similar case, the court ordered no settlement for Mrs. Postell, a plaintiff with her husband in the suit of *Postell and Wife, and Smith and Wife v. the Executors of James Skirving* (1789).[47] The chancellor explained his omission carefully for the record. "The court having in private examined Mrs. Postell, who has attained twenty-one years of age, and the said Mrs. Postell being very desirous that no settlement should be made on her; and it appearing to the court that Mr. and Mrs. Postell have constantly lived together in the greatest harmony; and he being a gentleman of fortune in his own right, it is not requisite that he should make any settlement on his said wife."[48] With regard to the other plaintiff, Mrs. Smith, the court was not so trusting of the husband. She received a settlement, and the words of the chancellor demonstrate his opinion about the importance of female separate estates: "With regard to Mr. O. B. Smith," he wrote, "his wife is not of age to make such request as Mrs. Postell has done, (although the court entertains a similar opinion of him as of Mr. Postell), they find themselves bound to order that the said O. B. Smith do make the usual settlement on his wife, of the fortune she is entitled to from her father."[49] The "usual" settlement gave the Smiths joint control over her property, with descent to the survivor and then to their children. Presumably in a case of this nature, Mrs. Smith could void her own trust upon reaching her majority. Such action could be taken under the law and occasionally was.

On one point South Carolina chancellors were not willing to make liberal interpretations. Unless a settlement explicitly gave a feme covert power to write a will, she could not do so.[50] Women and their benefactors were careful, therefore, to include this right as a clause in settlements. It appeared frequently, particularly during the first two decades under study, when 62 percent (36 of 58) of the women specified the power to make a will. The figure rises to 71 percent if we include those who possessed the right to bequeath in the event they outlived their husbands. Over the course of the eighteenth century this figure fell, but until 1800 more than half of the women with settlements possessed testamentary powers. After the turn of the century, the figure declined until fewer than one-third of all femes covert could write wills under the stated terms of their settlements. From 1801 to 1830, 26 percent (45 of 172) of the settlements sampled gave women this privilege, while 29 percent (50 of 170) gave it to either the feme covert or the survivor of the marriage (table 2.4). As the number of settlements allowing women to write wills declined, those arranging for automatic descent to children increased (figure 2.2).

Table 2.4. Descent of Settlement Property

	Women Control		Survivors Control		Subtotal (cols. 1–2)		Automatic to children		Mixed/Unknown		Number of Deeds
	No.	%	No.	%	No.	%	No.	%	No.	%	
1730–1740	12	52	4	17	16	70	3	13	4	17	23
1741–1750	24	69	1	3	25	71	10	29	0	0	35
1751–1760	26	47	3	5	29	53	24	44	2	4	55
1761–1770	37	35	9	8	46	43	52	49	9	8	107
1771–1780	50	47	6	6	56	52	45	42	6	6	107
1781–1790	39	44	6	7	45	51	43	49	0	0	88
1791–1800	20	39	1	2	21	41	29	57	1	2	51
1801–1810	15	28	2	4	17	31	30	56	7	13	54
1811–1820	14	29	1	2	15	31	27	55	7	14	49
1821–1830	16	23	2	3	18	26	47	68	4	6	69
	253	(40%)	35	(5%)	288	(45%)	310	(49%)	40	(6%)	638

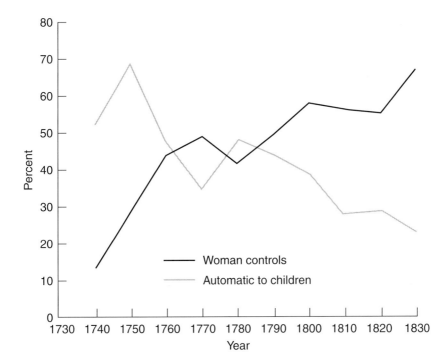

Figure 2.2. Descent of Settlement Property

The reasons for this decline are not clear. One explanation may lie in the increasing standardization of settlements. As the chancellor noted when ordering creation of a trust for Mrs. Smith, there was a "usual" settlement. It consisted of joint control for husband and wife, with descent to their children. Over the period studied, we have seen an increase in settlements allowing for joint control, as well as descent to children. Chancellors ordered this kind of settlement in most cases coming under their jurisdiction, and the increasing use of automatic descent provisions may demonstrate female acceptance of a standard form on this point. Moreover, as marriages became less patriarchal over the period, women may have regarded the right to make wills as less vital to their financial autonomy. The desire to exert control after death dwindled as more women possessed authority during life. Most mothers, even when they did write wills, undoubtedly divided their estates equally among children. The change to automatic descent probably represents little difference in the way estates were administered but does demonstrate a weakening of women's desires for explicit protection and control.

Some mothers were fully aware of the potential power of testamentary rights. Mary Ladson, marrying for the first time in 1760, included a clause in her settlement allowing her to write a will. She wanted her estate to be divided among her children "in such shares and proportions and at such times as the said Mary by her last Will and Testament shall give Limit." The widow Jane Wilkie was equally explicit about her desire to decide what property should go to her children. In 1774 she wrote in her settlement, "All such Child or Children shall possess & enjoy all such part & proportion in the manner & form as she the said Jane Wilkie shall point out & direct." Even after the turn of the century, when fewer women possessed the legal ability to write wills, some still realized the power they held. Elizabeth Legare wrote in 1825 that she intended to use her estate during her lifetime for the provision of her children "at her own discretion" and not otherwise.[51]

Women who had already experienced married life, such as Jane Wilkie and Elizabeth Legeaux, took special care to protect their property rights in marriage settlements. Most single women were not so careful. Comparison of settlements made by widows and single women proves valuable for understanding some individuals' needs for separate estates. A woman's marital status frequently acted as a motivating force for the creation of a settlement and for the inclusion of female managerial and testamentary powers.[52]

Of the 638 settlements sampled, 532 recorded a marital status for the woman. From 1730 to 1780, widows appeared in more than half of the settlements giving status, 56 percent (159 of 286); single women constituted 44 percent (127) of the sample. Even taking into account the high mortality rate in colonial South Carolina and the use of the state as a Revolutionary battlefield, the high percentage of widows is surprising. After 1780 the number declined, but widows still made settlements in 40 percent (98 of 246) of the sample.

When we compare the powers of control exercised by widows with those held by single women, it becomes clear that experienced matrons were more emphatic about managing their own property than were women marrying for the first time (table 2.5). Widows held complete managerial powers and specified the right to make wills at more than double the rate of first brides. Rather than directing settlement property by themselves, most single women divided between giving their husbands authority and arranging for coadministration. They also provided for automatic descent of settlement property in fully two-thirds of their deeds, whereas widows did so less than one-third of the time. The settlements of first brides thus demonstrate a less protective attitude than those of experienced matrons. Moreover, after 1740 there was remarkably little change in that pattern, either for control or descent (figures 2.3 and 2.4).

Clearly, the experience of marriage affected the attitudes of women toward property control and management. Before entering a second union, many women demanded the right to administer their own property. Widows' desire for active control may have reflected the fact that their estates were no longer simply gifts from parents and friends but property they had worked

Table 2.5. Widows and Single Women Compared

	Widows		Single Women	
	Number	Percentage	Number	Percentage
Control				
Women	133	52	59	21
Men	50	19	90	33
Couples	55	21	107	39
Trustees	3	1	10	4
Mixed/Unknown	16	6	9	3
Total	257	99	275	100
Descent				
Women control	150	58	53	19
Survivors control	10	4	19	7
Subtotal	160	62	72	26
Automatic to children	79	31	185	67
Mixed/unknown	18	7	18	7
Total	257	100	275	100

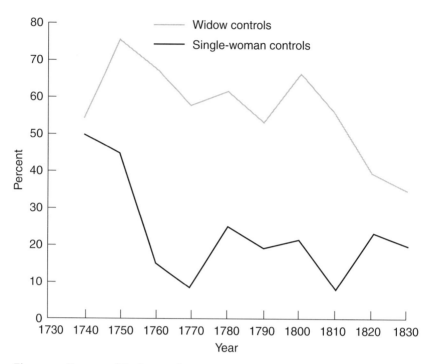

Figure 2.3. Descent of Settlement Property

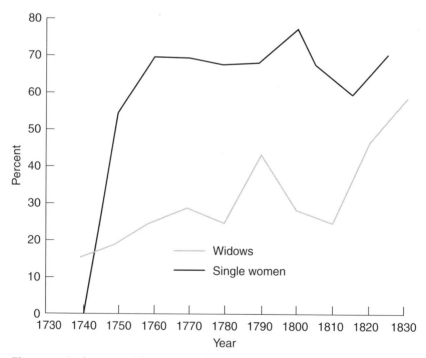

Figure 2.4. Settlements with Provisions for Children

for themselves, either alone or with their former husbands. Parents who initiated the settlements of new brides concerned themselves primarily with protecting property from husbands' creditors. They did not seek to provide daughters with the power to control and devise property as much as they created a fund for family income.

Widows, however, frequently demanded the right to manage property they had obtained themselves. Elizabeth Meshaw's settlement in 1736 observed, "The said Elizabeth Meshaw since the Death of her said Husband hath by her great pains care Labour and Industry acquired a considerable addition to the Estate and Interest so left her. . . . [P]articularly [she] hath purchased a Tract of Land containing Two Hundred and Fifty Acres." Elizabeth retained the right to devise her estate as she saw fit, without the interference of her new husband. When Christiana Hoff purchased a slave through her own labor, she wrote a settlement in 1772 explicitly denying her husband any rights to it. The case of Elizabeth Baxter may be the most revealing. Before Elizabeth, a "merchant," consented to marry Thomas Robinson, a "mariner," in 1771, she executed a settlement of all her personal estate and business property. She reserved absolute control over the property for herself "in order the better to enable her to support & maintain her & her children & which the said Thomas Robinson is at present rendered incapable of doing."[53] Elizabeth was taking no chances. If Thomas could not support her, she would arrange to do so herself. Women such as Elizabeth, who knew the dangers of marriage and widowhood, took special care for their own and their children's futures.

Although the number of widows who provided for children in their settlements increased throughout the period, widows remained less likely than young brides to arrange for automatic descent. Widows such as Elizabeth Baxter had the responsibility of caring for the children of previous marriages and undoubtedly felt pressure to include protective clauses for children in their settlements yet did so at half the rate of single women. Thus Mrs. Baxter retained the right to devise her estate. Although she clearly was concerned with providing for her children, she did not think it necessary to arrange for their inheritances when she wrote her settlement. Such dispositions could be made later, when she was closer to death. For the moment, she worried primarily about living in a male-dominated world with a new husband who could not support her. The failure to arrange for automatic descent implies that many widows did not view settlements primarily as a means of guaranteeing the inheritances of their children. More than anything else, they wanted absolute control over management decisions and the right to bequeath to whomever they pleased. When they chose to remarry, they did so with strings attached.

Although the comparative powers of widows and single women remained largely the same throughout the eighteenth and early nineteenth centuries, one development in the settlements of single women may indicate an increasing desire on their part to exercise authority. There was a gradual but steady increase in the number of settlements allowing couples joint powers of administration. Single women did not feel the need to exercise sole control to the same degree as widows, but they did become less willing to give husbands absolute managerial rights. From 1730 to 1780, only 32 percent (41 of 127) of their settlements gave couples joint powers of administration, whereas 45 percent (66 of 148) did so from 1781 to 1830. The number of men with sole powers fell from 39 percent (49 of 127) to 28 percent (41 of 148). With regard to the management of property, therefore, settlements of widows and single women became slightly more uniform over time, with both groups favoring partnerships in managing separate estates.

Widows, heiresses, merchants' wives, the wives of debtors, and women whose parents had warned them about the dangers of married life—these were the South Carolina matrons with trust estates. They were frequently women of wealth with a great deal to lose if their husbands proved wasteful or unfortunate in business. Sometimes they were women of small fortunes and intent on protecting what little they had. They were intelligent, or experienced, or protected by concerned parents. Above all, given the legal status of women under the common law, they were fortunate.

Courts of chancery in South Carolina offered liberal support for marriage settlements. Judges regarded separate estates as the right of every feme covert, necessary for women's security in many cases and helpful to society in providing some families with economic support. Judges consistently ruled in favor of the creation of separate estates and enforced liberal precedents for administering them. Realizing the delicate position of married women under the common law, chancellors acted to mitigate legal hardships by wholeheartedly supporting women's rights to separate estates. Judicial acceptance of settlements increased during the period studied, demonstrating expansion of women's property rights under equity law. As seen in the cases of *Postell and Smith v. Surviving's Executors, Johnson v. Thompson,* and *Lowndes' Trustee v. Champneys' Executors,* equity law promoted the legal rights of South Carolina women. Historians of colonial American law may have been overly optimistic in positing wide use of settlements among femes covert, but they were correct in stressing the legal importance of equity law. Women with separate estates in eighteenth- and early-nineteenth-century South Carolina enjoyed many of the legal rights of men. It remains to be seen if other jurisdictions duplicated this pattern.

Although chancellors supported the use of separate estates, settlements were rare, used either by wealthy women with valuable family interests to protect or by women with an uncommon perspective on their legal status. Equity proved invaluable to women such as the widow Elizabeth Holson, who wanted to enjoy her own estate without "the Least or Smallest Controul or intermeddling" of her husband, but Elizabeth was one of only a small number of women with marriage settlements.[54] We still do not know why so few women relied on separate estates. Either they were satisfied with their common-law status, or they did not regard equity law as a viable alternative. In South Carolina, it may be important that settlements were not necessary to confer *feme sole* trader status. Independent businesswomen functioned under the common law as long as their husbands demonstrated tacit consent to their activities. But more important, the majority of women apparently regarded equity law protections as superfluous to their needs. For women without much property, or for those who perceived their legal status as secure, separate estates served no purpose.

We must learn more about the application of common-law principles before we will fully understand the meaning of equity law. Perhaps the harshness of common-law rules was mitigated in practice, making separate estates largely unnecessary. If most women did not feel a need to use equity law, then we must reevaluate the effect of common-law restrictions on women's lives. We must also consider an alternative possibility—that social custom so oppressed women that they did not consider the possibility of employing separate estates. Community scorn or family opposition may have prevented women from acting on their desire for separate estates. There is some evidence to show that the fear and distrust women exhibited by creating settlements antagonized men. The wording of settlements, for example, occasionally reveals attempts to appease men's feelings. Some women wrote that their desire for separate estates arose from a fear of the system, not the individual. Such public statements relieved men of responsibility for the anxiety women experienced and thus saved them face in the community. Otherwise, the mere existence of a settlement attested to the insecurity of a particular woman.

At this point it is impossible to be sure whether male antipathy to settlements prevented most women from making them. Final conclusions await further research on the social customs of families in the South and on the use of common-law rules pertaining to the rights of women. Perhaps the words of Sarah Ann Binnikes demonstrate, as well as anything we now have, the attitude of women who wrote settlements. Sarah's settlement stated that its object was to protect her separate interests so that she would not be "defeated or defrauded" out of her property "by the collusive act or device" of her husband. The job of Sarah's trustees was to sue her husband in case he "bargained, sold, or inveigled away" her lands and to demand damages from the court "for any waste which he may commit upon the said lands or injury he may commit upon the said personal or any of the said personal property."[55] There can be no doubt that Sarah Ann did not trust her husband-to-be. It is unlikely that most couples began married life with such distrust. Undoubtedly, women as well as men preferred to demonstrate hope, rather than fear, on the day of their marriage. But if experience proved women naive, then we can understand why so many widows insisted on the creation of settlements, and we can also comprehend why they carefully reserved managerial rights for themselves.

Notes

This essay is reprinted, with minor editorial changes, from *William and Mary Quarterly* 39 (Oct. 1982): 655–85.

1. William Blackstone, *Commentaries on the Laws of England,* 4 vols. (Oxford, 1765–69), 2:132, 2:136, 2:255, 2:293, 2:355; Thomas Smith, *De Republica Anglorum: A Discourse on the Commonwealth of England,* ed. Leonard Alston (Cambridge, 1906), 127; William Holdsworth, *A History of English Law,* 5th ed., 16 vols. (London, 1903–66), 3:193, 3:195–96, 3:249; *An Essay on the Nature and Operation of Fines and Recoveries* (London, 1728), 68–69; *The Laws Respecting Women . . .* (London, 1777, repr. Dobbs Ferry, 1974), 181; James Kent, *Commentaries on American Law,* 4 vols. (New York, 1826–30), 2:151–54; Samuel Church, "Lectures on Law by Tapping Reeve, Esq." (1806), unpublished notebook, Cornell University Law Library, Ithaca, N.Y.

2. Tapping Reeve, *The Law of Baron and Femme, of Parent and Child, of Guardian and Ward, of Master and Servant, and of the Powers of Courts of Chancery . . .* (New Haven, 1816), 98; *The Laws Respecting Women,* 70–72; Marylynn Salmon, "The Property Rights of Women in Early America: A Comparative Study," Ph.D. diss., Bryn Mawr College, 1980, 27–84.

3. No comprehensive study of the legal status of early American women has yet been written. The best general discussion is still Reeve, *The Law of Baron and Femme. Laws Respecting Women,* a good survey of English law, is available in a reprint edition. Holdsworth's impressive overview of the history of English law is also helpful. The most commonly cited discussion of the legal rights of early American women is Richard B. Morris, *Studies in the History of American Law, with Special Reference to the Seventeenth and Eighteenth Centuries* (New York, 1930), ch. 3. This should be used with care, however, because it is only a cursory study and unreliable.

4. Holdsworth cited *Avenant v. Kitchen* (1581), the first case in which an equity court supported the right of a woman to hold property separately from her husband by the force of a prenuptial contract. Within a short period, the Chancery Court permitted women to exert active control over settlements. Decisions recognized the right of women to enter into binding contracts (1582), write wills (1594), make presents to their husbands (1614), and convey to strangers (1619). Holdsworth, *A History of English Law,* 7th rev. ed., 1:494,

5:303, 5:310–15; Richard Francis, *Maxims of Equity . . .* (London, 1728), 5; Reeve, *The Law of Baron and Femme,* 222–23, 238; *The Laws Respecting Women,* 179; Zephaniah Swift, *A System of the Laws of the State of Connecticut: In Six Books,* 2 vols. (New Haven, 1795–96), 1:200–201.

5. Christopher Clay, "Marriage, Inheritance, and the Rise of Large Estates in England, 1660–1815," *Economic History Review,* 2d ser., 21 (1968): 503–18; H. J. Habakkuk, "Marriage Settlements in the Eighteenth Century," [Royal Historical Society] *Transactions,* 4th ser., 31 (1950): 15–31; Lawrence Stone. *The Crisis of the Aristocracy, 1558–1641* (Oxford, 1965).

6. Morris, *Studies in the History of American Law,* 126–55; Mary R. Beard, *Woman as Force in History: A Study in Traditions and Realities* (1946, repr. New York, 1962).

7. In fact, historians usually depict the colonial period as a golden age for women. In addition to Morris's legal study, books by Elisabeth Anthony Dexter (*Colonial Women of Affairs: Women in Business and the Professions in America before 1776* [Boston, 1924]) and *Career Women of America, 1776–1840* [Francestown, N.H., 1950]) and Mary Sumner Benson (*Women in Eighteenth-Century America: A Study of Opinion and Social Usage* [New York, 1935]) helped build the theory of a liberal legal and social climate for colonial women. More recently, the theory has been supported by the work of John Demos (*A Little Commonwealth: Family Life in Plymouth Colony* [New York, 1970]); Roger Thompson (*Women in Stuart England and America: A Comparative Study* [London, 1974]); Mary P. Ryan (*Womanhood in America: From Colonial Times to the Present* [New York, 1975]); Ann D. Gordon and Mari Jo Buhle ("Sex and Class in Colonial and Nineteenth-Century America," in *Liberating Women's History: Theoretical and Critical Essays,* ed. Berenice A. Carroll [Urbana, 1976], 278–300); and Joan R. Gundersen and Gwen Victor Gampel ("Married Women's Legal Status in Eighteenth-Century New York and Virginia," *William and Mary Quarterly,* 3d ser., 39 [1982]: 114–34). In her pathbreaking study of American women between 1750 and 1800, Mary Beth Norton revises significantly the old interpretations, for she concludes that women possessed both a low status and a low self-image during the colonial period. The status of women changed as a result of the American Revolution, improving on some points such as self-esteem but remaining ambiguous in the areas of politics and law. Norton, *Liberty's Daughters: The Revolutionary Experience of American Women, 1750–1800* (Boston, 1980). Linda K. Kerber has also demonstrated that women's lives changed after the American Revolution, but she emphasizes points on which women lost rights, especially in the law. Kerber, *Women of the Republic: Intellect and Ideology in Revolutionary America* (Chapel Hill, 1980). Kerber's contention that the legal status of women deteriorated in the nineteenth century has not been proved. For a revisionist study of the legal rights of women, see Salmon, "The Property Rights of Women."

8. Morris, *Studies in the History of American Law,* 138; Beard, *Woman as a Force,* 151.

9. There appears to be a growing split among women's historians concerning the changing status of women after 1800. Scholars such as Norton, and Kerber to a lesser degree, see a widening of the female sphere during the early national period, away from the subservience and dependency of colonial women. Other historians still maintain that colonial women occupied a privileged position compared to nineteenth-century women, who lost status and economic power with the rise of industrialism. Gerda Lerner has made the latter argument in a review of the Norton and Kerber books: "What the Revolution Meant for Women," *Washington Post Book World,* Jan. 4, 1981, 9.

10. Some colonies, such as Massachusetts, Connecticut, and Pennsylvania, did not have separate courts of equity in the English fashion. On the problem of equity law in early

America, see Stanley N. Katz, "The Politics of Law in Colonial America: Controversies over Chancery Courts and Equity Law in the Eighteenth Century," *Perspectives in American History* 5 (1971): 257; and Swift, *A System of the Laws*, 2:419–60. For a full discussion of regional comparisons on the administration of marriage settlements, see Salmon, "The Property Rights of Women," 150–234.

11. Salmon, "The Property Rights of Women," 150–256.

12. Anne King Gregorie, ed., *Records of the Court of Chancery of South Carolina, 1671–1779* (Washington, D.C., 1950), 5–7.

13. "An Act to oblige persons interested in Marriage Deeds and Contracts, to record the same in the Secretary's office of this state," in *The Statutes at Large of South Carolina*, ed. Thomas Cooper and David J. McCord (Columbia, 1836–41), 4:656–57.

14. Marriage Settlements, vols. 1–10 (1785–1830); Records of the Register of the Secretary of the Province, vol. A–1 (1721–33); and Miscellaneous Records of the Secretary of State, Charleston Series, vols. AB, BB–20 (1735–89). All manuscripts cited are located in the South Carolina State Archives, Columbia, unless noted otherwise.

15. *Rippon v. Dawding*, Ambler, 565 (1769).

16. Reeve reported in 1816 that settlements without trustees had become "no uncommon thing" (*The Law of Baron and Femme*, 163). One of the earliest American cases dealing with a simple marriage settlement appeared on the docket of the Pennsylvania supreme court in 1793. See *Barnes Lessee v. Hart*, 1 Yeates 221 (1793). The case is analyzed in Marylynn Salmon, "Equality or Submersion? *Feme Covert* Status in Early Pennsylvania," in *Women of America: A History*, ed. Carol Ruth Berkin and Mary Beth Norton (Boston, 1979), 91–113.

17. South Carolina courts preferred women to use formal trusts rather than direct agreements with their husbands. In *Barret v. Barret*, 4 S.C. Eq. (4 Des.) 491 (1814), and *Dupree v. McDonald*, 4 S.C. Eq. (4 Des.) 209 (1812), the judges noted their disapproval of settlements made without trustees. See also the arguments of counsel in *Executors of Smelie v. Executors of Smelie*, 2 S.C. Eq. (2 Des.) 72 (1802).

18. Holdsworth, *A History of English Law*, 5:313; George W. Keeton and L. A. Sheridan, *Equity* (London, 1969), 442–43; Reeve, *The Law of Baron and Femme*, 236. In the South Carolina case of *Cape v. Adams*, 1 S.C. Eq. (1 Des.) 567 (1797), a man tried to create a settlement of his wife's property for his own benefit without her knowledge or consent. The court disallowed his deed.

19. Francis, *Maxims of Equity*, 5.

20. Reeve noted the significant role of parents and guardians in bargaining with the suitors of young women. *The Law of Baron and Femme*, 174.

21. Some men did attempt to settle property on their families after contracting debts. Examples of cases involving fraudulent trusts include *Drayton v. Pritchard* (1816), Charleston District Equity Decrees, 3:161; *Peigne v. Snowden*, 1 S.C. Eq. debts. (1 Des.) 591 (1800); *Peace v. Spierin*, 2 S.C. Eq. (2 Des.) 500 (1807); and *Croft v. Townsend's Administrators*, 3 S.C. Eq. (3 Des.) 223 (1811).

22. The preamble to the recording statute of South Carolina noted the problem. It read, "The practice prevailing in this State of keeping marriage contracts and deeds in the hands of those interested therein, hath been oftentimes injurious to creditors and others, who have been induced to credit and trust persons under a presumption of their being possessed of an estate subject and liable to the payment of their just debts." Cooper and McCord, eds., *The Statutes at Large of South Carolina*, 4:656.

23. Reeve, *The Law of Baron and Femme*, 176. In *Croft v. Townsend's Administrators,* Chancellor Desaussure ruled against a settlement that included too much of an indebted man's property (see especially his comments on page 2). In *Taylor v. Heriot*, 4 S.C. Eq. (4 Des.) 227 (1812), a legal opinion noted that indebted men were fully justified in creating settlements of their future wives' estates before marriage.

24. *Tunno v. Trezevant,* 2 S.C. Eq. (2 Des.) 264 (1804).

25. Ibid., 269–71.

26. There are no accurate marriage rates for South Carolina in the period under study. Population figures are available, however, and by applying the earliest available marriage rate, that of 1860 (1 in 115), we can arrive at a rough percentage of marrying couples with settlements. Thus in 1790, when the white population was 140,000, the estimated number of marriages was 1,610. Twenty-two settlements were written in that year, and therefore 1.4 percent of marrying couples had settlements. The next federal census (1800) revealed a population figure of 196,000, making the estimated number of marriages 2,254. Because twenty-eight settlements were written in 1800, 1.2 percent of marrying couples had settlements. *The Statistical History of the United States: From Colonial Times to the Present* (New York, 1976), 1168; *Population of the United States in 1860* (Washington, D.C., 1869), xxxvi.

27. For determining the approximate values of property included in marriage settlements, the work of Alice Hanson Jones was indispensable. See *American Colonial Wealth: Documents and Methods,* 2d. ed., 3 vols. (New York, 1977). Equally useful for determining exchange rates for South Carolina in the eighteenth century was John J. McClusker, *Money and Exchange in Europe and America, 1600–1775: A Handbook* (Chapel Hill, 1978), 223–24. Throughout the eighteenth century, approximately £7 South Carolina currency equaled £1 sterling.

28. For the purpose of making comparative statements concerning settlement property, I assigned estimated values to certain types of property based on information provide in Jones, *American Colonial Wealth,* vol. 3. A slave was valued at £85, one acre of improved land at £1, one head of cattle at £10, one riding horse at £75, one town lot with appurtenances at less than £500, and more than one town lot with appurtenances at more than £500. Settlements with a single slave were all classified as containing property of a value less than £150, as were settlements containing only part of a house. Settlements including only slaves, numbering two to five, were all classified in the £150–500 range. All pounds are pounds sterling. Although estimated valuations such as these are extremely unreliable for determining absolute wealth, they enable us to distinguish between individuals of great and middling wealth.

29. Marriage Settlement between Elizabeth Legeaux and John Smith Darrell (1809), Marriage Settlements, 5:522–23.

30. Marriage Settlement between Elizabeth Moore and William Edwards (1744), Miscellaneous Records of the Secretary of State, RR:212–13.

31. Marriage Settlement between Elizabeth Scott and James Stephenson (1787), Marriage Settlements, 1:338.

32. Marriage Settlement between Mary Smith and Josiah Smith (1789), Marriage Settlements, 1:446–47.

33. Reeve, *The Law of Baron and Femme*, 162–63, 170–73; *Price v. Michel* (1821), Charleston District Equity Decrees, 3:377; Kent, *Commentaries on American Law,* 2:164–65.

34. Marriage Settlement between Martha Baker and Allen Bolton (1765), Marriage Settlements, 1:110.

35. Marriage Settlement between Susanna Holmes and Thomas Bee (1761), Marriage Settlements, 1:170.

36. In any case in which it appeared conclusively that a man forced his wife to transact a certain agreement against her will, she was not held liable for the agreement. Reeve, *The Law of Baron and Femme*, 165; *Bethune v. Beresford*, 1 S.C. Eq. (1 Des.) 174 (1790). The evidence had to be positive, however, for once a woman possessed separate property, jurists defined her as a feme sole rather than a feme covert and did not regard her as susceptible to coercion. In the mid-nineteenth century, a debate arose in Maryland and South Carolina over the need for women with trust estates to undergo private examinations when conveying their property. Maryland decided that women did not need private examinations because they were legally femes sole. South Carolina decided just the opposite. See *Tiernan v. Poor* 1 G. & J., 216 (1829); *Brundige v. Poor* 2 G. & J., 1 (1829); and *Ewing v. Smith* 3 S.C. Eq. (3 Des.) 467 (1811), 1. The South Carolina stance indicates concern with protecting women from male coercion. See Marylynn Salmon, "Life, Liberty, and Dower: The Legal Status of Women after the American Revolution," in *Women, War and Revolution*, ed. Carol R. Berkin and Clara M. Lovett (New York, 1980), 85–106.

37. Reeve, *The Law of Baron and Femme*, 162–63; *Curtis v. Duncan* (1821), Charleston District Equity Decrees, 3:468; *Price v. Michel* (1821), Charleston District Equity Decrees, 3:377; *Garner v. Garner's Executors*, 1 S.C. Eq. (1 Des.) 477 (1795); *Dupree v. McDonald* 4 S.C. Eq. (4 Des.) 209 (1812). In *Garner,* the court corrected nonsensical words in a deed of settlement that had the effect of denying a woman all rights to her property until after her own death. The court opinion noted that it was the duty of a chancellor to correct such errors. In *Dupree,* the court interpreted a poorly worded settlement to benefit the feme covert and her son against the claims of the woman's second husband, who attempted to seize all of her property after her death.

38. Marriage Settlement between Charlotte Poaug and John Poaug (1771), Marriage Settlements, 1:78.

39. *Tyrrell v. Hope,* 2 Atkyns 561 (1743); Reeve, *The Law of Baron and Femme,* 164; *Lowndes' Trustee v. Champneys' Executors* (1821), Charleston District Equity Decrees, 3:354.

40. *Johnson v. Thompson,* 4 S.C. Eq. (4 Des.) 498 (1814).

41. During the period under study, only one case indicated a judicial reluctance to support female powers of control, and there the controversial subject of divorce clouded the issue. See *Barret v. Barret* 4 S.C. Eq. (4 Des.) 491 (1814).

42. *Lowndes' Turstee v. Champney's Executors* (1821), Charleston District Equity Decrees, 3:354.

43. Reeve, *The Law of Baron and Femme,* 9:178–79. Favorable decisions include *McPike v. Hughes and Rumph* (1816), Charleston District Equity Court Decrees, 3:175; *Tatnell v. Fendwick's Executors,* 1 S.C. Eq. (1 Des.) 147 (1786); *Greenland v. Brown,* 1 S.C. Eq. (1 Des.) 196 (1791); and *Postell and Smith v. Skirving's Executors* 1 S.C. Eq. (1 Des.) 158 (1789).

44. Gregorie, ed., *Records of the Court of Chancery,* 507–11.

45. Ibid., 510.

46. Ibid., 551–52; Marriage Settlement between Dorothy Golightly and William Henry Drayton (1764), Marriage Settlements, 2:185–92.

47. *Postell and Smith v. Skirving's Executors,* 1 S.C. Eq. (1 Des.), 158 (1789).

48. Ibid., 158.

49. Ibid., 158–59.

50. Women without the right to make wills through marriage settlements could bequeath

personal property if their husbands consented. See *Grimke v. Grimke* 1 S.C. Eq. (1 Des.) 366–82 (1794), and *Smelie v. Smelie* 2 S.C. Eq. (2 Des.) 66–79 (1802). The law on this point is discussed in Blackstone, *Commentaries,* 2:498 and *The Laws Respecting Women,* 178–79. Without valid marriage settlements, however, women could never devise real property. Smith, *De Repubica Anglorum,* ed. Alston, 127; *The Laws Respecting Women,* 149; Holdsworth, *A History of English Law,* 3:185; Kent, *Commentaries on American Law,* 2:130–31.

51. Marriage Settlements between Mary Ladson and Thomas Poole (1760), Miscellaneous Records of the Secretary of State, MM:41–44; Jane Wilkie and Charles Cogdell (1774), Miscellaneous Records of the Secretary of State, RR:314–16; Elizabeth Legare and William B. Legare (1825), Marriage Settlements, 9:185–87.

52. For a discussion of one enterprising widow's experience, see Mary Beth Norton, "A Cherished Spirit of Independence: The Life of an Eighteenth-Century Boston Businesswoman," in *Women of America: A History,* ed. Carol Ruth Berkin and Mary Beth Norton (Boston, 1979), 48–67. Although the woman Norton describes was a Bostonian, the same influences governed her actions in creating a marriage settlement as governed the actions of many South Carolina women.

53. Marriage Settlements between Elizabeth Meshaw and Thomas Snipes (1736), HH:27–28; Christiana Hoff and John Hoff (1772), PP:254; Elizabeth Baxter and Thomas Robinson (1771), PP:6–8, Miscellaneous Records of the Secretary of State.

54. Marriage Settlement between Elizabeth Holson and John Harth (1779), Marriage Settlements, 1:152.

55. Marriage Settlement between Sarah Ann Baxter and Joseph Binnikes (1825), Marriage Settlements, 9:159.

3

Women and the Family Economy in the Early Republic: The Case of Elizabeth Meredith

SUSAN BRANSON

"As we have no clerk, your mother, as usual, officiates in that capacity. Though she is old & weak she still acquits herself with some degree of reputation Especially in the financing business. You know tis hard for any Gentleman to refuse the request of a Lady."[1] These were Elizabeth Meredith's words to her son in 1796. Meredith was then in her middle fifties, and she had been married to her husband, Jonathan, a tanner, for more than twenty years. They had five children (three of them still living at home) ranging from the early teens to early twenties. Between 1794 and 1797 she wrote letters to her son in France that detailed her contribution to the tannery business, a business that by law and custom belonged to her husband. Despite a lack of legally recognized work status, Meredith contributed significantly to her family's financial development: She kept the tannery's account books, borrowed money from the Bank of Pennsylvania, and collected debts from recalcitrant clients. Her letters provide abundant evidence of her economic role within her family and her influence over decisions concerning her family's financial future.

Meredith was one of the many women in the early republic who were hidden investments to their families. If we are to make an accurate assessment of married women's work experiences at the end of the preindustrial era, we must explore the less tangible ways in which women like Elizabeth Meredith contributed to their family's economic prosperity. The work experiences of this Philadelphia woman demonstrate how husbands and wives shared work roles and economic goals, and they allow us to explore the less apparent ways in which women contributed to their family's welfare through social and economic networks.

Furthermore, Meredith's circumstances highlight the effect of economic and social transitions on women and their families at the end of the eighteenth century. As traditional artisan culture began a long and even process of disintegration, upward or downward pressures induced many artisans to become permanent wage laborers while propelling others into the ranks of the developing middle class as capitalist-entrepreneurs. The sons of the new entrepreneurial class had opportunities, which their fathers did not, to become professionals. For men in these economically mobile families, their participation in work and responsibilities associated with the family economy diminished. Old duties were exchanged for new ones that were defined by the developing ideology of "separate spheres," referred to by many historians as the "cult of domesticity." Elizabeth Meredith's circumstances exemplify these economic and social trends.

Elizabeth and her husband Jonathan began married life in the 1770s with a tannery in which Jonathan worked side by side with his journeymen and apprentices. Twenty years later, the Merediths sold the tannery and invested accumulated capital in real estate ventures and mercantile opportunities. Two of their sons became professionals (one a president of the Schuylkill Bank and a founding member of the Pennsylvania Academy of Fine Arts, the other a merchant and landowner). Their two daughters and daughter-in-law, unlike Elizabeth Meredith, were firmly ensconced in a domestic environment as wives and mothers, not participants in the family economy. Thus Meredith was centered between two very different positions for women within the family: that of traditional artisan wives and that of the new, middle-class domesticity. She was not a colonial "goodwife" whose household activities sometimes required the role of deputy husband rather than a partner, nor was she like a nineteenth-century middle-class wife whose identity was shaped by the cult of domesticity (a consumer who no longer participated in the family economy as a producer).[2] Meredith ably abetted her husband in his economic climb to affluence, and she sedulously promoted her daughters' preparation for a life of domestic ease and social and cultural accomplishments.

Meredith's case nicely complements several arguments that labor, economic, and women's historians have made in recent years concerning women and the household economy, the development of a class of capitalist-entrepreneurs from master craftsmen, and the crystallization of the separate spheres ideology in the postrevolutionary era. Elizabeth Meredith and her husband Jonathan shifted from a successful trade to real estate investments and entrepreneurial ventures just as the transition from an urban, craft-based artisan economy to a cash-based, wage-labor urban economy was evolving. This transformation involved capital accumulation and entrepreneurship. The process, which affected some trades much earlier than others (and was still occurring in the mid-nineteenth century), entailed the removal of wives from the workplace and from work-related activities. Those masters who became entrepreneurs sought to create distance between home and work, thus reinforcing a separate spheres ideology.[3]

During this transition, several things happened to women within the household. In laboring families, women continued to contribute to their family's economic welfare. Women were always necessary to the survival of these families.[4] Prosperity relied on cooperation and negotiation among members of the household.[5] In this family strategy in the cooperative ventures between husbands and wives, men were often paid in goods instead of cash. Their wives then opened small stores to sell the goods. Women in the families of such men "linked their productive and reproductive lives, working to provide moral and material support to launch children well in an increasingly difficult world." That continued to be true well into the nineteenth century.[6]

Concomitant with middle-class women's retreat from the workplace was a shift in cultural values that contributed to the perception of productive labor associated with men and wages but not with women. Although working women's contributions remained the same, they were less frequently recognized as valuable contributors to their families' economic welfare. What began as a "gender *division* of labor" became a "gendered *definition* of labor" in the culture of the new republic. Women's work within the household (domestic and financial) began to disappear from view as new social values predominated. The lives of Lynn shoemakers and their wives illustrate this point: Men became identified as wage earners, women did not.[7]

Another consequence of the economic transition was the growing number of women who no longer participated in the workplace. As one historian has noted, "City daughters from well-to-do homes were the only eighteenth-century American women who can accurately be described as leisured." Rural households, even fairly affluent ones, all required the labor of daughters as well as wives. City daughters, on the other hand, were left free to attend school or learn domestic skills such as cooking and child care.[8] By the end of the century, an increasing number of families could afford to allow both mothers and daughters to stop working. At the same time, the ideology of republican motherhood informed the upbringing of these daughters and defined their roles as wives and mothers. Good citizenship became a justification for improving female education; women, as the wives and mothers of citizens, had a duty to be rational and informed. The necessity for female republicans arose through two separate channels: One was the developing emphasis on greater equality in marriage. Women were to be intellectual, as well as emotional, companions to their spouses. The second was the acknowledgment of the significance of maternal influence.[9]

These daughters of the Republic were responsible for child education, moral instruction, and, increasingly in the nineteenth century, benevolent activities outside the home. This is precisely what occurred in the Meredith family; Elizabeth Meredith's daughters did not assist their mother with tannery-related work. Instead, they attended the Young Ladies' Academy, socialized with other young Philadelphians from the middle and elite classes, married, and became part of the culture of domesticity. This was only possible because Elizabeth Meredith, herself a product of traditional artisan culture, embraced a new set of postrevolutionary values for the next generation, which accompanied the family's economic rise to middle-class status. Throughout these changes in the family's financial circumstances, Elizabeth Meredith's participation in the family economy remained constant. Meredith was first involved with the tannery and then in the investments made during the last years of the business, particularly those concerning her son David's mercantile venture in France. Meredith was removed from the workplace when her husband gave up the tannery, but she did not remove herself from participation in their economic interests.

Elizabeth Meredith, like a majority of married women, engaged in undocumented and unpaid economic activities. Evidence of such work is hard to uncover. Without the benefit of Meredith's correspondence with her son in the 1790s, she, like most other married women, would have remained a shadowy background figure in Jonathan Meredith's work history. There is far more evidence (and therefore more emphasis) in the historical record of women's economic productivity through waged labor or through independent market activities as *feme sole* traders.[10]

Historians have not neglected married women's work, but many cases document circumstances where women conducted businesses separate from that of their spouse to supplement family income.[11] A few are known to have had extensive independent economic relationships within their communities. In the seventeenth century, Hannah Grafton ran a shop out of one room in her house in Salem, Massachusetts. She sold hardware, cloth, and sewing supplies procured by her husband on his sailing voyages.[12] Elizabeth Murray, an eighteenth-century Boston woman, arranged a prenuptial agreement with second husband to protect her independent business interests.[13] Married women in the rural area outside Philadelphia conducted extensive dairy businesses, and midwives like Martha Ballard of Maine were working spouses.[14]

All of these women had businesses at least partially separate from their husbands' activities. Income in the form of cash or the exchange of goods or services was independent from any produced in partnership with a spouse. In contrast, Elizabeth Meredith's activities were part of a more hidden economic sector, which was comprised of women with *feme covert* status who worked in a store or craft shop alongside their spouse and children, and contributed to their family's financial prospects without advertising their market activities or appearing independently.

Several factors, including occupation and income, influenced the form and extent of a woman's participation in her family's economic life. Laboring women often contributed necessary income to the family. Yet even with a wife working as a huckster, seamstress, washerwoman or boardinghouse keeper, many urban families, especially in the last decade of the eighteenth century, barely made ends meet.[15] Compelling need, however, was not the reason that wealthy Philadelphia women involved themselves in family businesses and investments. Interest, education, and ownership of property was often the reason upper-class women knew a great deal about their own and their husbands' businesses. Elizabeth Drinker was one of these women. She was married to Henry Drinker, one of Philadelphia's wealthiest Quaker merchants.[16] Prior to her marriage, Drinker and her sister, Mary Sandwith, ran a feather import business in the city. Drinker knew how to keep accounts, a skill she may have acquired as a student, because Quaker schooling for girls in the middle of the eighteenth century sometimes included instruction in mathematics and accounting—skills thought proper and necessary to the running of a household.[17] During her marriage, Drinker participated in discussions of various real estate transactions (some of which involved property she had brought into her marriage).[18]

One method of determining the extent of married women's participation in the family business is to examine the occupations of widows. An examination of Philadelphia city directories and census records has linked the occupations of widows listed as running businesses to that of their deceased husbands. In the case of artisans especially, many widows continued their spouses' businesses. For example, the Philadelphia city directory for 1811 indicates that Anthony Baugier's widow continued his merchant business at 24 South Third; Joseph Galley's widow still ran his tobacco shop at 123 Race; and Madame Fimeton, widow of J. Fimeton, continued to list her husband's carpentry business at 24 South Tenth Street.[19]

Occasionally, widows took the additional step of advertising their intention to continue the family profession. In 1793 Ann Kip, widow of an upholsterer, announced in the New York *Daily Advertiser* that she was carrying on her deceased husband's business.[20] Philadelphia widows continued their husbands' businesses in more than half of all the professional occupations investigated, including merchants, lawyers, doctors, and those listed simply as "gentlemen." The strong inference here is that "many [women] were actively engaged in 'hidden market work' when they were married." In other words, although unseen in legal documents, tax records, or business papers, a wife was an important part of her husband's work. The activities of widows and female heads of households indicate that "the contribution of women to national income was substantial when the home and workplace were unified."[21]

Such proof of wives as silent partners is easier to find after they became widows and resumed feme sole status.[22] Information concerning a woman's economic life prior to becoming a widow is more difficult to unearth. There is an array of anecdotal evidence to support the claim that married women were an integral and often necessary part of the family economy. Benjamin Franklin acknowledged in his autobiography that his wife, Deborah Read Franklin, had been "a good and faithful helpmate [who] assisted me much by attending the shop."[23] Deborah Franklin folded and stitched pamphlets, ran the shop, and purchased printing supplies such as "old linen rags" for the paper-makers. Deborah could only do this because home and work were located together. This family practice of printing husbands and wives continued through Franklin's grandson, Benjamin Franklin Bache, and his wife Margaret Markoe Bache. She successfully ran the *Aurora* while Benjamin toured New England publicizing the Jay Treaty in 1795. Margaret Bache later became the proprietor of the newspaper for a time after her husband's death in 1798.[24]

This physical proximity of household and work allowed wives to acquire skills during marriage that many continued to practice during widowhood. Another woman trained in the printing trade, Anne Greenleaf, took over the New York Democratic-Republican newspaper *Argus* after her husband's death from yellow fever in 1798. She subsequently became the only woman the Federalists targeted with the Sedition Act. Even after she sold the newspaper as a result of her legal difficulties, Greenleaf advertised in the city directory as a bookseller—a sideline that her husband and many other newspaper editors had.[25]

Examples like Elizabeth Drinker, Deborah Franklin, and Margaret Bache, combined with the data on widows, offer limited although tantalizing glimpses into family economic life. The value of Elizabeth Meredith's case is the extensive documentation of her working life in the 1790s contained in letters to her son, David. When added to the information already at hand, Meredith brings us an important step closer to understanding the pervasiveness of family-directed, as opposed to individual, economic goals in preindustrial America. Meredith's activities also show that women within the family economy performed duties, made choices, and held responsibilities beyond those historians have described as "deputy husbands.'"[26] Her letters reveal the breadth of interests and energies that Meredith and her family had as they made the transition from hard-working artisans to affluence and ease through their capital accumulation and new investment opportunities in the early republic.

Elizabeth Meredith directly contributed to her family's economic well-being in two ways. First, she was largely responsible for the daily business in the tannery from 1794 until it closed in 1796. Meredith could not trade in her own right; nevertheless, she made daily decisions regarding the business, including collecting debts from customers and procuring loans from the Bank of Pennsylvania.[27] There is little evidence surviving to document her involvement prior to 1794, when Meredith spent most of her energies in raising their five children and running her household. After 1794, her letters and the account books verify her daily presence in the shop.[28] Whether she had assisted in the tannery before child-care duties claimed her attention is not known, but her extensive knowledge of bookkeeping, clients, and banking practices, evident from her letters, indicates either her participation at some earlier date or a continuing acquaintance with the business even though she was physically removed from the daily running of the tannery. A letter from Meredith to her son David, written in 1788 (when her youngest child was only six), indicates her active involvement. Even then, she advised David to "take orders from good people for leathers" as he traveled home through Virginia.[29] Just before they retired from the tanning business in 1796, Meredith remarked to her son that she and her husband, Jonathan, "have both of us spent many years in labor and it is time we had a little rest."[30]

Meredith contributed to the family in a second way through her care for a boarder who lived with the family until the Merediths moved in 1795. Meredith would have supervised all cooking, cleaning, and possibly washing for this man. There is no indication that the boarder was an employee at the tannery. Because boarding was a way in which "women entered the market economy as producers," Meredith's efforts brought cash into the household rather than labor.[31] That was particularly true of lower-class wives and more frequently widows, some of whom listed themselves in city directories as running boardinghouses.[32] Others, like Elizabeth Meredith, did not advertise this fact. Yet in either instance, "cash from boarders flowed into accumulated savings that could be reinvested in the household trade or additional property."[33] Very likely, that was the situation with Elizabeth Meredith's income.

Despite a reliance on a boarder for extra income, the Merediths were wealthy artisans. They belonged to the rising class of artisan/entrepreneurs in the nation's urban centers. By the 1790s Jonathan Meredith was nearing retirement from the leather business and no longer did physical work at the tannery. By then, Elizabeth and Jonathan had acquired enough capital from their business to fund real estate investments, including new house construction and rentals. In 1796 they gave their eldest son, David, $20,000 for his fledgling mercantile enterprise in France. Still, the Merediths saved money where they could. This close attention to finances prompted Elizabeth's decision to take over the accounting and clerking activities at the tannery during the last two years they kept it. And as we shall see, they were also rather tightfisted landlords, willing to evict tenants by force in order to replace them with higher-paying ones.

Meredith took over as clerk when Jonathan was injured by a fall from a horse in 1794. David, their eldest son, had formerly assisted in the business side of the tannery (taking customers' orders on trips to other states), but was now busy with his own mercantile business. The Meredith's second son, William, although assisting in some way, had been educated as a lawyer. Even though he was so discouraged at his lack of clients that he considered giving it up, William apparently did not have the knowledge to take care of bookkeeping or banking for his parents. Contrary to the trend of separating home and work, the Merediths moved from their separate residence on Third Street to a location on Chestnut Street, a block and a half away, where the business office and residence were located together. This was primarily for Elizabeth. She told her son, "It was very inconvenient for me to be continually at the counting house which has been the case ever since you left us that your father thought it necessary to fall on some plan of getting a situation where the business might be carried on at the place of our residence."[34]

Elizabeth Meredith enthusiastically involved herself in the leather business. She served as clerk, kept the accounts, and, judging from her complaints about the "exorbitant wages of journeymen" and the "dissatisfied insolence of servants," also dealt with both tannery and household workers.[35] She collected on accounts due, paid the workers, and brought order out of Jonathan's chaotic books. Her efforts gave her the satisfaction that she was contributing to her family's financial welfare. Her skills as a businesswoman were also personally fulfilling.

Meredith believed that her contribution to the tannery made a crucial difference to its success. When she took over responsibility for keeping the books in 1794, she noted that they were "so deranged and it was impossible to tell where to begin. I found many of our affairs in a dismal situation but hope assiduity and care will in future prevent such disagreeable consequences."[36] Meredith was confident that she would run the business far better than her husband. A month after she started on the books, she informed her son that she had "got everything in a very good train," and she hoped to conduct their business free from the "loss, blunder or error" that had plagued it before her tenure.[37] Clearly, she was not modest about her business skills. Speaking in the third person, she told her son, "Though she is old & weak she still acquits herself with some degree of reputation Especially in the Financing business." She also referred to a reputation acquired at some earlier period in her life, perhaps before domestic responsibilities required too much of her time and attention to also continue work with her husband in the tannery. Although men controlled the world of banking and finance, Meredith believed that there was some advantage to be derived from the fact that she was a woman. She reminded David, "You know tis hard for any Gentleman to refuse the request of a Lady."[38]

Meredith did more than simply straighten out Jonathan's wayward books. Her activities brought her into direct contact with other businesspeople. During the hard times in the aftermath of the Jay Treaty, local merchants met to discuss their financial prospects. These meetings sometimes were held at Meredith's house on Chestnut Street. Elizabeth Meredith attended these occasions and commented to her son, "I cannot forbear smiling at the profound sagacity worn by every face in the assembly."[39]

She was responsible as well for collecting on bills due from customers and negotiating with the bank. She bragged at one point that she had finally wrung a payment out of a particularly recalcitrant client, Mr. A. B., who owed £100. Meredith billed him and argued for the money until he paid it.[40] The bank proved to be a greater challenge for Meredith's talents than bill collection. Erratic in dispensing loans and discounts, banks played favorites among their customers, granting discounts for some and none to others. On one occasion, Meredith lamented, "Cash remains extremely scarce with us. The banks . . . serve their favorites first. They seem to have taken up a droll idea of the wants of their fellow citizens & have made a resolution, that the men who make the most deposits shall be entitled to the most discounts—did they consider the matter with propriety, they would find that the men who are able to make large cash deposits are in the least want of cash. . . . To be out of debt is an object of great magnitude to me."[41] Meredith sometimes congratulated herself on her financial acumen; at other times she railed against the close-fisted "misers" who denied a discount.[42]

Elizabeth Meredith's detailed knowledge of, and participation in, tannery is explained by the financial goals she and her husband shared. She saw her participation in business as a "step very necessary to our interest."[43] Both husband and wife strove to achieve a genteel competency. That entailed both a sufficient amount of wealth for personal comfort and the ability to aid the next generation on its way to the same goal. The economic decisions made by Elizabeth and Jonathan Meredith about their business and their investments illustrate this approach. When Jonathan decided to retire from the tannery at the age of fifty-seven, he was motivated in part by ill health. Yet he also believed that his accumulated wealth had given him, as David called it, an "independency."[44] Elizabeth Meredith echoed that attitude when she explained why she worked in the tannery office before Jonathan retired: "I do it with a view to promote the happiness of my husband and the interest of my children. I will, while providence blesses me with health and faculty, exert them both in their service."[45]

In addition to the leather business, Meredith had a thorough knowledge of the real estate investments Jonathan undertook to develop their capital. In the 1790s the Merediths attempted to increase their financial security by investing in housing construction in central Philadelphia. Like many other investors, they endeavored to profit from the boom in the building trade connected with both the state and national governments' temporary location in the city.[46] The president's house, in particular, was the cornerstone of a neighborhood in great demand. The Merediths purchased several lots nearby and built rental houses. When Congress voted additional money to finish the presidential residence in 1796, Elizabeth Meredith rejoiced, commenting that "this has added to the value of our lot, as well as to every estate in the vicinity of the neighborhood." Well aware of the "advantages that would accrue to us from finishing the President's house," she assumed the boom would bring them a good income. Meredith explained, "It bids fair to be the most genteel part of the town & consequently our lot must increase in value. The houses your father has begun are large & elegant & the finishing of them is a matter of importance."[47]

Meredith shared with David the good news concerning the progress on their buildings. To William she related the troubles associated with their construction. Their building contractor abandoned the project because the Merediths were not paying him enough to finish the job. Meredith wrote to William that the contractor had told his employers that he could not "even support his own family on the small pittance furnished by us."[48] A picture thus emerges of the Merediths as rather tightfisted business people who squeezed out as much value for their money as they could. Although profitable for the Merediths, this practice was not conducive to good employer-employee relations.

The same month that the contractor quit, another man, John Campbell, who had also worked there but had been fired, burglarized the Merediths' home while they were out of the city. In addition to stealing Jonathan's gold watch and a pair of "yellow olive colored overalls," Campbell and an accomplice broke open a chest containing most of the family's business papers: "[They] took out all the deeds and every paper therein, tied them up in a bundle and carried them into the market house, but fearing they might lead to a discovery they replaced them. They lodged in the house one or two nights. The last they intended to have plundered of everything movable but overleaping themselves they made off without effecting their design." Campbell remained on the loose, and Meredith despaired "of regaining any part of the property."[49]

The Merediths were no more lenient with tenants than they were with employees. Their aggressive determination to profit from investments is starkly revealed in an encounter with a Mrs. Young. Meredith told David, "After a work of several years we have at last got Mrs. Bankson out of the house in Front St. He [Mr. Bankson] died Last fall a Martyr to dissipation which I believe was brought on him by his wife who is a perfect tyrant." This "tyrant" caused problems for the Merediths when she sublet to another party, Mrs. Young. In order to remove this unwanted person, the Merediths decided to occupy the house physically and illegally until means could be found to evict her.

Counseled by two lawyers that physical possession of the property would help them gain legal victory, the Merediths callously plotted to drive Mrs. Young from the house. Jonathan sent several friends "to smoke unmercifully in the room & every place she occupied. She went to the street door as she said to breathe & they shoved her out & locked the door." Mrs. Young regained possession, however, when Jonathan's assistants were fined and jailed for unlawful entry. The next stratagem was partially successful in getting rid of the unwanted tenant. Elizabeth bragged to her son William:

> Your father's mind retains its activity & after 6 or 7 days had pass'd without any alteration he order'd a parcel of dry hides—tan'd leather & to be taken down & put up a signboard the smell offended the ladies & they decamp'd putting in the house two fellows of very bad character to keep possession. They in rotation with a negro girl have kept the house three weeks, they staying above stairs & our people below. But the day before yesterday they all Left it but a little boy. Jon. M. took advantage of their absence, lock'd up the doors & turn'd out the boy. one of the fellows return'd & again broke open the door by order of the justice—took the street door off its hinges & the hinges off the cellar door, the Chief justice was again called upon who issu'd warrants for the Squire & the other ruffians & bound them over to the peace. The other fellow took possession again but yesterday using some very threatening language to J. M., Col. Coats granted a warrant against him & bound him over

also. Your poor father was oblig'd to ride up to Col. Coats, when the business was before him & just before it was concluded rode off, & knowing there was nobody in the house but a little boy, he got a stranger to run down & turn him out, & J. M. was again in possession. This happen'd yesterday & we are still quiet. How long we shall remain so—time must determine!

The Merediths triumphed but not before involving Chief Justice McKean and several officers of the court. Elizabeth Meredith's summary of the situation was that "the revolution in France has not made more noise over the world, than this transaction has created in our city. It has occupied all our conversation & engrossed all our time." Her detailed account of their ruthless practices as landlords confirms Elizabeth Meredith's close connection with this aspect of the family's investments.[50]

Meredith was also involved in David's fledgling mercantile venture in France; Jonathan and Elizabeth invested $20,000 of their capital in his business. During David's stay in France, Elizabeth was his primary family correspondent and kept him informed about business and family interests. He, in turn, kept his mother and the family abreast of the political situation in France and potential business opportunities. Ever on the lookout for new money-making enterprises, Meredith requested that David send them information on new tanning techniques he had seen abroad.

Family investment in David's French business meant that Meredith, out of financial and maternal necessity, paid close attention to political relations among France, Britain, and the United States. Both her son and much of the family fortune were put at risk by entering a country beset by internal revolution and engaged in external wars. The British frequently seized American ships suspected of trade with France. These transatlantic dangers induced many merchants and artisans to support Jay's Treaty. Elizabeth Meredith supported the treaty in the hope that it would resolve a situation that caused the Merediths, and many other investors, financial hardship and economic uncertainty.[51]

Meredith's anxieties concerning international politics turned to personal fears in April 1796, when David's ship, the *Sea Nymph,* was confiscated by the British. David (along with his other business partners) lost the ship and its cargo, and the Merediths lost their $20,000.[52] Elizabeth Meredith was indignant. She remarked that "it appears to me a very strange thing, that a nation with whom we have formed a treaty of amity & commerce, should continue in the almost daily habit of infringing our liberty, destroying our commerce & violently plundering us of our prosperity?—this is most undoubtedly the case."[53] David continued unsuccessfully to seek his fortune in Europe until he returned to Philadelphia late in 1797. Elizabeth and Jonathan never recovered their investment. The financial blow contributed to Jonathan Meredith's bankruptcy in 1805, six years after his wife's death.

Active participation in a variety of business ventures was not the only way in which Elizabeth Meredith worked toward the happiness of her husband and the interest of her children. Her daily involvement in the tannery and the real estate venture was her most tangible contribution. But she aided her family in an indirect but no less important way as well. The early republic was a society in which social, political, and economic relationships were interwoven and interdependent. "Kinship, friendship, and acquaintance" were the basis for much of the capitalist enterprise in the city, and social networks among artisans and merchants were an important means of establishing and maintaining business ties.[54] Philadelphians of all classes and professions resided in close physical proximity to one another. In addition, the heart of the residential area of the city was also the business area. Physically as well as socially, artisan-entrepreneurs like the Merediths were in daily contact with various merchant families and other artisans, with whom they formed social and economic alliances. That was possible because Philadelphia's core was still geographically small, no more than seven or eight hundred households.[55] Families were at the center of networks that combined business and social relationships, and Elizabeth Meredith was the focal point that linked the Merediths to other families and individuals who aided them in the economic sphere.

One way Elizabeth Meredith connected hers to other important families was by forging social relationships for her children. Mary and Betsy Meredith attended the Young Ladies' Academy in the late 1780s, and both David and William received degrees from the University of Pennsylvania. These educational experiences naturally acquainted the young Merediths with other artisan and mercantile families. Ensuing friendships then linked Elizabeth and Jonathan to social networks that assisted them in their immediate financial circumstances and promised to provide long-term benefits to the Meredith children through employment, business connections, and marriage. The two boys became acquainted with William and Sarah Bache's sons William and Benjamin at the college. Through her children, Elizabeth Meredith in turn developed an acquaintance with the elder Baches. She had much to say about the romantic troubles of their daughter Betsy Bache (who spent the winter of 1795 with the Meredith family) and the political opinions of their son, Benjamin Franklin Bache. Meredith also knew Mary Hewson, a close confident of Benjamin Franklin, who sent her sons to the college as well. William Meredith, William Bache, and Benjamin Franklin Bache all received degrees in 1790.

Elizabeth and Jonathan Meredith acquired a degree of wealth through the tannery that surpassed their goal for a "competency." Not only did they intend to retire and live comfortably, but they also strove to provide a financial start for their children. Their eldest son David had ambitions to become a merchant. William took a law degree. The Meredith daughters, provided with a genteel education, were expected to make good marriages. Elizabeth Meredith was conscious of the benefits of education to a woman's behavior (and consequently, to a certain degree, her marriage prospects). She privately criticized William's wife, Gertrude Ogden Meredith, for her "roughness of manners" and was convinced that Gertrude's deficiency in this regard was the result "of an improper education."[56] The Merediths were connected to William Bingham's family, the wealthiest Philadelphians at the time, when Betsy was invited to spend a summer at the Binghams' vacation home in New Jersey. Like Elizabeth Meredith, Anne Bingham helped consolidate her own family's political, economic, and social power in Philadelphia through her network of relationships and acquaintances. Such an acquaintance with the Binghams placed the Meredith family on the periphery of Philadelphia's elite (and Federalist) mercantile circle.[57] Thus social and familial ambitions were achieved at one and the same time.

The various suitors for the hand of Meredith's other daughter, Mary, illustrate the interconnection of the family's social and economic relationships and Elizabeth Meredith's direct involvement. As a parent, it was her responsibility to oversee the upbringing, education, and marriage of her daughters. Mary ultimately married a man whom she probably met through the Merediths' interstate leather business. But during the 1790s, she was courted first by her brother David's business partner, Robert Andrews, and then by Charles Wollstonecraft, whom Meredith described as the brother of "the Lady of that name who wrote the rights of Woman." In 1796, Charles Wollstonecraft resided near the Philadelphia waterfront, in the High Street ward, and the Merediths may have come to know him through mutual merchant acquaintances.[58] Meredith described him as being "much of a gentleman in his deportment a man of good sense & great information." Wollstonecraft's advances on Mary Meredith evoked such jealously in Robert Andrews that "he [Andrews] became the laugh of his acquaintance, he told the most ungenerous falsehoods, & was so impudent as to abuse him [Wollstonecraft] even in his hearing. Mr. W's temper is irritable but not vindictive & he had I imagine determin'd to resent it." This ill-feeling between the competitors for Mary's favors almost led to a duel.[59]

A third suitor, the wealthy merchant and Democratic-Republican Congressman John Swanwick, appeared in 1795. Swanwick wrote a poem to

Mary—"Elegy on the Death of a Favorite Canary Bird, Inscribed to Miss Meredith." He also gave prizes out to the Young Ladies' Academy of Philadelphia in 1787 when Mary Meredith won for "superior knowledge in the catechism of the Protestant Episcopal Church."[60] Here again, Mary's suitor emerged from the web of the Meredith's financial connections. Elizabeth Meredith played a key role in the family's economic well-being by maintaining valuable financial contacts (despite opposition from other family members) with Swanwick. Although Meredith had misgivings about her daughter's possible marriage to Swanwick, she nonetheless defended him against "the current of envy, malice, & detraction" expressed by her husband and younger son William.[61] David encouraged the match, as well he might, considering the value, to a young man setting out to become a merchant, of having Swanwick for a brother-in-law.

Politically, however, the Merediths were at odds with Swanwick. Meredith and her family condemned the Whiskey Rebellion, favored the Jay Treaty, and, despite her children's friendships with the Bache family, increasingly disliked Benjamin Franklin Bache and his Democratic-Republican paper's "smutty pieces."[62] Swanwick, however, had been publicly condemned for his support of the Whiskey rebels. He was a chief instigator of the Jay Treaty protests in Philadelphia (and was believed to have funded them), and in 1794 he was elected as the first Democratic-Republican Congressman for Pennsylvania. Little wonder that Jonathan and William Meredith condemned him. But Elizabeth understood that although politics divided the family from Swanwick, financial affairs united them. Moreover, she reminded her husband and son of their "obligations to him of consequence, such as nothing but pure friendship could dictate." He had used his influence as the director of the Bank of Pennsylvania in 1794 to procure discounts and short-term loans for the Merediths.

On this point, however, she could not persuade the Meredith men change their minds. Their opposition to Swanwick, Elizabeth lamented, was "so Strong as to render my wishes abortive, & counteract my good intentions."[63] Mary Meredith married another young merchant from Maryland, Thomas Hawthorne, and the Meredith family's connection with Swanwick ended upon his death from yellow fever in 1797.[64] Elizabeth Meredith lived only two years longer. She died in July 1799. She may have regretted that David had yet to provide for himself, but she helped three of her children settle in life.

Much of their success was due to their mother's valuable partnership in her family's economic enterprises. Although the value of women like Elizabeth Meredith often remained unarticulated, it was nonetheless taken for granted that wives were important economic partners. In a revealing magazine article entitled "The Plague of the Learned Wife," a tradesman complained that both his wife and daughter spent too much of their time improving themselves through literature and not enough time working in the family business. He offered his opinion that "neither tradesmen, nor tradesmen's wives, nor any body belonging to them, have any business to talk like skolards [*sic*]." He hastened to caution unmarried tradesmen to "take special care how they venture upon a bookish woman."[65] The warning was clear: Choose a wife who will be an asset not a liability, no matter how "accomplished."

Yet the advice offered to tradesmen did not apply to the rising entrepreneurs and professionals like the Merediths' sons or to their sons-in-law, Thomas Hawthorne and Charles Ogden. Elizabeth Meredith and her husband raised their children to become part of a higher social and economic class than that in which they had begun their own working lives. These were timeless ambitions of one generation for the next, but in the Merediths' case parental desires occurred within a new, postrevolutionary framework for familial relationships. Daughters raised in the 1780s and 1790s were more educated in manners and literature but were less able to assist in shops, care for journeymen and apprentices, or give business advice. A new set of social values concerning the activities and responsibilities of wives and mothers shaped the training, education, and expectations of women like Betsy and Mary Meredith. Ironically, part of Elizabeth Meredith's contribution to her family's welfare was the financial security that enabled the next generation of women to exist within a domestic sphere quite different from her own.

These new values determined William Meredith's choice of a wife and dictated the scope of his spouse's responsibilities. The differences are instructive. Gertrude Ogden Meredith, daughter of Samuel Ogden and niece of Gouverneur Morris, led a very different married life than her mother-in-law, Elizabeth Meredith. Whereas Elizabeth Meredith took pride in her abilities to handle banking matters and give advice on financial investments, Gertrude Meredith was not a part of her husband's law practice. And she explicitly articulated her desires to be "an *attentive* wife, and a *good* mother—herein consists my ambition—I feel no other—it is the only pursuit I delight to labor in."[66] Her disengagement from William's business affairs allowed her to make extended visits to family and friends in North Jersey, something Elizabeth Meredith, with her responsibilities associated with Jonathan's tannery, could never have done.

Elizabeth Meredith's upbringing in the 1740s and 1750s prepared her for life as the wife of an artisan; Gertrude's education in the 1780s included encouragement of her literary skills (she contributed to John Fenno's *Portfolio* magazine). This activity, learned in girlhood, was not compatible with the kind of occupational training her mother-in-law had. During a visit to her parents at "The Vale," Gertrude had time between caring for children, attending quilting parties, sewing shirts for her young son Willie, and reading to the children books such as Pope's *Homer,* to pen "Love Elegies, Soliloquies and Sonnets—Serious Meditations and Allegories, Charades, Epigrams, Odes."[67]

William and Gertrude, firmly established in middle-class Philadelphia society, strove for gentility. William Meredith was a founding member of the Academy of Fine Arts, a contribution to Philadelphia culture for which Gertrude Meredith believed William deserved to be "carved in marble."[68]

Despite Elizabeth Meredith's comment on her daughter-in-law's "roughness of manners," Gertrude's desire for culture and sophistication caused her to sometimes judge other women of her class harshly. On a visit to Baltimore she told William, "I should be unwilling to make an uncharitable remark, but I really never have viewed my own sex with so little interest as in this place. They possess not the most common information, less reflection, and very little understanding. The most approved topics of conversation are negroes and cards."[69] On another occasion, after receiving a cold reception from a young Philadelphia bride, Gertrude remarked to her husband that she thanked her stars that she had been "born a lady. . . . I could scarcely keep from assuring her that I was fully sensible of her elevation and considered her now quite my equal."[70] The social environment for her children was no less important than her own. She advised that their son William, Jr., attend Mr. Abercrombie's school rather than Mr. Brown's. The latter's school was made up of "little rag tags and bob tails." She wished that "of all things that William was kept from it."[71] She was even disappointed in her uncle Morris's library at Morrisiania because it contained so few leather bindings. His books appeared "more like the purchases of a great economist than a man of fortune. The editions are few of them elegant and the greater proportion of them very common indeed, and some in boards."[72]

Whether Elizabeth Meredith would have agreed with her daughter-in-law's opinions, the older woman was responsible, at the end of the eighteenth century, for creating an environment in which Gertrude Meredith's activities and desires could flourish in the early nineteenth century. In short, Elizabeth Meredith contributed to the "refinement of America." Through hard work and thrift, the older generation propelled the younger toward a genteel lifestyle, that "favored leisure and consumption over work and thrift."[73]

This transition to new cultural, economic, and familial values occurred as a result of changing market forces, technologies, and ambitions over an extended period. At the end of the eighteenth century, motives and assumptions made by husbands and wives about economic goals, family security, and work relations meant that Elizabeth Meredith shared with her husband the responsibilities, decision-making, and planning necessary for long-term security. Slowly, as work separated from home, class divisions between women became clearer. Laboring women continued to work for their families' welfare, and middle-class women, removed from work, pursued their families' interests through social and cultural activities unconnected with the marketplace. Elizabeth Meredith had much in common with the wife of a poorer artisan. Gertrude Meredith shared almost nothing with either. Not only does Elizabeth Meredith's life offer a detailed understanding of how married women contributed to the family economy, but it also suggests how the economic and social changes occurring in the early republic affected the women who experienced them.

Notes

This essay is reprinted, with minor editorial changes, from the *Journal of the Early Republic* 16 (Spring 1996): 47–71.

1. Elizabeth Meredith to David Meredith, July 2, 1796, Meredith Family Papers, Historical Society of Pennsylvania, Philadelphia. Elizabeth Meredith was born in England in 1742. She and her husband Jonathan migrated from England in the 1760s. In addition to serving local clients, they shipped hides to Virginia, Massachusetts, and New York. During the 1790s, their eldest son, David, attempted a mercantile venture between France and Philadelphia. Elizabeth, David's chief family correspondent, wrote extensively to her son during his absence. Meredith's activities in the family business before that time went unrecorded. Knowledge of her participation comes from letters written between 1794 and 1797. Meredith died in July 1799 in her fifty-seventh year.

2. Laurel Thatcher Ulrich, *Good Wives: Image and Reality in the Lives of Women in Northern New England, 1650–1750* (New York, 1980). Barbara Welter, "The Cult of True Womanhood: 1820–1860," *American Quarterly* 18 (Summer 1966): 151–74, first described the separate spheres ideology. Also see Nancy F. Cott, *The Bonds of Womanhood: "Woman's Sphere" in New England, 1780–1835* (New Haven, 1977). For recent thoughts on how historians should move beyond this conceptual framework, see Linda Kerber et al., "Beyond Roles, Beyond Spheres: Thinking about Gender in the Early Republic," *William and Mary Quarterly* 46 (July 1989): 565–85.

3. Sean Wilentz, *Chants Democratic: New York City and the Rise of the American Working Class, 1788–1850* (New York, 1984); Gary J. Kornblith, "From Artisans to Businessmen: Master Mechanics in New England, 1789–1850," Ph.D. diss., Princeton University, 1983; Lisa Lubow, "Artisans in Transition: Early Capitalist Development and the Carpenters of Boston, 1787–1837," Ph.D. diss., University of California, Los Angeles, 1987.

4. Billy G. Smith, *The "Lower Sort": Philadelphia's Laboring People, 1750–1800* (New York, 1990); Christine Stansell, *City of Women: Sex and Class in New York, 1789–1860* (New York, 1986).

5. Allan Kulikoff's observation for rural households is also true for urban ones: "Ne-

gotiations over the division of labor or resources and [cooperation] in daily life were integral to sustaining the family." Kulikoff, *The Agrarian Origins of American Capitalism* (Charlottesville, 1992), 31.

6. Donna J. Rilling, "Building Philadelphia: Real Estate Development in the City of Homes, 1790–1837," Ph.D. diss., University of Pennsylvania, 1993; Carol Blesser, "Gender, Ideology, and Class in the Early Republic," *Journal of the Early Republic* 10 (Fall 1990): 335; Mary P. Ryan, *Cradle of the Middle Class: The Family in Oneida County, New York, 1790–1865,* (New York, 1981); see also Claudia Goldin, "The Economic Status of Women in the Early Republic: Quantitative Evidence," *Journal of Interdisciplinary History* 16 (Winter 1986): 400; and Lisa Wilson, *Life after Death: Widows in Pennsylvania, 1750–1850* (Philadelphia, 1992), 115.

7. Jeanne Boydston, *Home and Work: Housework, Wages, and the Ideology of Labor in the Early Republic* (New York, 1990), 55; Mary H. Blewett, *Men, Women, and Work: Class, Gender, and Protest in the New England Shoe Industry, 1780–1910* (Urbana, 1991), 17.

8. Mary Beth Norton, *Liberty's Daughters: The Revolutionary Experience of American Women, 1750–1800* (Boston, 1980), 23–26.

9. See also Benjamin Rush, *Thoughts upon Female Education* (Philadelphia, 1787). Another educator, Caleb Bingham, explicitly delineated the proper direction for female education for the rising middle class: "While the sons of our citizens are cultivating their minds and preparing them for the arduous important and manly employment which America offers to the industrious, their daughters are gaining that knowledge, which will enable them to become amiable sisters, virtuous children, and in the event, to assume characters more interesting to the public, and more endearing to themselves." Bingham, "Oration upon Female Education, Pronounced by a Member of One of the Public Schools in Boston" (Sept. 1791), reprinted in Bingham's *American Preceptor* (Boston, 1813), 48–50. In *Liberty's Daughters,* ch. 9, Norton discusses eighteenth-century female education, as does Kerber in *Women of the Republic: Intellect and Ideology in Revolutionary America* (Chapel Hill, 1980), ch. 7. Also see Ann D. Gordon, "The Young Ladies' Academy of Philadelphia," in *Women of America: A History,* ed. Carol Ruth Berkin and Mary Beth Norton (Boston, 1979), 69–91.

10. For example, these women were a numerically significant part of Philadelphia's economic community; in 1791, 28 percent of all shop or storekeepers were female. Goldin, "Economic Status of Women in the Early Republic," 400.

11. Boydston, *Home and Work,* 37.

12. Ulrich, *Good Wives,* 27.

13. Mary Beth Norton, "A Cherished Spirit of Independence: The Life of an Eighteenth-Century Boston Business Woman," in *Women of America: A History,* ed. Carol Ruth Berkin and Mary Beth Norton (Boston, 1979), 48–60.

14. Joan Jensen, *Loosening the Bonds: Mid-Atlantic Farm Women, 1750–1850* (New Haven, 1986); Laurel Thatcher Ulrich, *A Midwife's Tale: The Life of Martha Ballard, Based on Her Diary, 1785–1812* (New York: 1990).

15. Smith, *The "Lower Sort,"* 111–12; Stansell, *City of Women,* ch. 1.

16. Henry Drinker's estimated wealth in 1784 was £35,559, but he was also wealthy by the time of their marriage. The company of James and Drinker made £2,000 a year between 1761 and 1775, the year Drinker retired from business. Thomas M. Doerflinger, *A Vigorous Spirit of Enterprise: Merchants and Economic Development in Revolutionary Philadelphia* (Chapel Hill, 1986), 75, 130.

17. Nancy F. Rosenberg, "The Subtextual Religion: Quakers, the Book, and Public Education in Philadelphia, 1682–1800," Ph.D. diss., University of Michigan, 1991.

18. For example, on March 12, 1794, she wrote in her diary, "HE agree'd this evening, with Daniel King for his plantation on the old York road for which he is to pay him £3146— it is between 5 and 6 miles from the City." *Diary of Elizabeth Drinker*, ed. Elaine F. Crane, 3 vols. (Boston, 1991).

19. Goldin, "Economic Status of Women in the Early Republic," 402; Jane Aitken, *Census Directory for 1811* (Philadelphia, 1811).

20. *New York Daily Advertiser*, Oct. 16, 1793, in Stansell, *City of Women*, 15n.

21. Goldin, "Economic Status of Women in the Early Republic," 401; Claudia Goldin, *Understanding the Gender Gap: An Economic History of American Women* (New York, 1990), 49.

22. Many middle-level craftsmen and shopkeepers trusted their widows with entire estates and businesses. Lisa Wilson's study of widows in Philadelphia and Chester County reveals that middle-income testators, especially shopkeepers and craftsmen, "bequeathed everything to their widows because they valued their wives' business sense. This trust almost certainly grew from years of working together behind the store counter." As Lenore Davidoff found in British households, "Marriage was indeed a 'trade' and as economic actors [women] appear as shadows behind the family enterprise." Wilson, *Life after Death*, 115; Leonore Davidoff, *Family Fortunes: Men and Women of the English Middle Class, 1780–1850* (Chicago, 1987), 273.

23. Benjamin Franklin, *The Autobiography of Benjamin Franklin: A Genetic Text*, ed. J. A. Leo Lemay and P. M. Zall (Knoxville, 1981), 71, 76.

24. James Tagg, *Benjamin Franklin Bache and the Philadelphia* Aurora (Philadelphia, 1991), 395–401.

25. James Morton Smith, *Freedom's Fetters: The Alien and Sedition Laws and American Civil Liberties* (New York, 1956), 399–415; see also New York City directories for 1800 through 1802.

26. Laurel Ulrich used the term *deputy husband* in her study of seventeenth-century New England wives. Subsequently, economic historian Julie Matthaei described the term as referring to wives who "entered and left the masculine sphere as by the needs of her family. Hence, the manly activities of these women did not undermine the sexual division of labor and did not challenge the category of 'men's work.'" Matthaei, *An Economic History of Women in America: Women's Work, the Sexual Division of Labor, and the Development of Capitalism* (New York, 1982), 71.

27. For details on the Meredith family's financial ventures, see Ric Northrup, "Decomposition and Reconstitution: A Theoretical and Historical Study of Philadelphia Artisans, 1785–1820," Ph.D. diss., University of North Carolina, 1989.

28. Christ Church records and Meredith genealogy, Historical Society of Pennsylvania.

29. Elizabeth Meredith to David Meredith, Oct. 9, 1788, Meredith Family Papers.

30. Elizabeth Meredith to David Meredith, May 20, 1795, Meredith Family Papers.

31. Stansell, *City of Women*, 234. This non-labor-related boarding occurred increasingly during the early nineteenth century. Boydston, *Home and Work*, 37. Sharon Salinger's work on journeymen and masters suggests that few journeymen or apprentices continued to board with their masters during this period. Salinger, "Artisans, Journeymen, and the Transformation of Labor in Late-Eighteenth-Century Philadelphia," *William and Mary Quarterly* 40 (Jan. 1983): 62–84.

32. Smith, *The "Lower Sort,"* 185. Some women catered to a particular clientele. Philadelphia directories, for example, list many boardinghouses specifically for the numerous French refugees in the city during the 1790s. See Susan Branson, "'Comme L'Arche de Noe': The French in Philadelphia in the 1790s," given at a meeting of the Pennsylvania Historical Association, Oct. 1994.

33. Elizabeth Blackmar, *Manhattan for Rent, 1785–1850* (New York, 1989), 63; Boydston, *Home and Work,* 17.

34. Elizabeth Meredith to David Meredith, April 25, 1795, Meredith Family Papers. Hides were first cured in calcium oxide and water, then stirred for months in vats filled with the "ooze" of tannin, and finally stretched to dry before being curried and sold to customers. See Leonard Everett Fisher, *The Tanners* (New York, 1966); Harry B. Weiss and Grace M. Weiss, *Early Tanning and Currying in New Jersey* (Trenton, 1959); and *Diderot's Encyclopedia, 1751–1780,* which has detailed illustrations and descriptions of the tanning process contemporaneous with the Merediths' business. Convenience was not all, however. Close proximity to the production of leather meant constant exposure to the smells associated with tanning. In fact, most Philadelphia tanneries had moved out of the city by this time. The Meredith tannery was one of the few leather businesses still located in the central part of town. As early as 1739, Philadelphia ordered three tanneries to relocate to the outskirts to alleviate residents' olfactory discomfort. Why the Merediths were allowed to remain is unclear, particularly because it would have been hard for their neighbors to ignore the odors associated with the transformation of fleshy white hides into brown, supple leather.

35. Elizabeth Meredith to David Meredith, May 20, 1795, Meredith Family Papers.

36. Elizabeth Meredith to David Meredith, March 12, 1795, Meredith Family Papers.

37. Elizabeth Meredith to David Meredith, April 25, 1795, Meredith Family Papers.

38. Elizabeth Meredith to David Meredith, July 2, 1796, Meredith Family Papers.

39. Elizabeth Meredith to David Meredith, Nov. 5, 1795, Meredith Family Papers.

40. Elizabeth Meredith to David Meredith, April 25, 1795, Meredith Family Papers. This was probably Anthony Butler, a lawyer and land agent for the Penn family. He had done business with the Merediths for several years. Northrup, "Decomposition and Reconstitution," 126.

41. Elizabeth Meredith to David Meredith, Jan. 2, 1796, Meredith Family Papers.

42. "Discounting" was the term used when a bank purchased promissory notes, at a percentage of their full value at maturity, from businesspeople. The bank made a small profit when it collected on the note, and bank customers were freed of the worry of collecting payment, as well as having capital free for investment or purchases. For a lucid explanation of these banking practices, see Doerflinger, *A Vigorous Spirit of Enterprise,* 303.

43. Elizabeth Meredith to David Meredith, April 25, 1795, Meredith Family Papers.

44. Northrup ("Decomposition and Reconstitution," 123) has an extended argument for the idea of achieving a competency, which distinguished "between comfort and riches" and "implied limits on the desire to invest capital, superintend business, and accumulate wealth." Northrup emphasizes the financial and psychological worries, over money and losses, of both Elizabeth and Jonathan Meredith; he makes no distinction between husband and wife in these matters. See Ric Northrup, "Speculation and Competence: Case Studies in Capitalist Expansion, 1785–1815," presented at the Philadelphia Center for Early American Studies, May 1985; see also David Meredith to Jonathan Meredith, Feb. 8, 1795, Meredith Family Papers.

45. Elizabeth Meredith to David Meredith, March 12, 1795, Meredith Family Papers.

46. Northrup ("Speculation and Competence," 14) maintains that the Merediths built at least six houses. The Pennsylvania capital relocated to Lancaster in 1799, and the federal government's new facilities in Washington, D.C., were ready for occupation in 1800. For information on building in the city, see Smith, *The "Lower Sort,"* 21, 81; Sam Bass Warner, Jr., *The Private City: Philadelphia in Three Periods of Its Growth* (Philadelphia, 1968); Stuart Blumin, *The Emergence of the Middle Class: Social Experience in the American City, 1760–1900* (New York, 1988); and Doerflinger, *A Vigorous Spirit of Enterprise,* 178. Details on the speculation in property during the 1790s can also be found in Blackmar's study of New York City in this era. She notes that the assessed value on investments between 1795 and 1815 increased more than 700 percent. See Blackmar, *Manhattan for Rent,* 39.

47. Elizabeth Meredith to David Meredith, March 10, Feb. 20, 1796, Meredith Family Papers.

48. Elizabeth Meredith to William Meredith, Sept. 29, 1797, Meredith Family Papers.

49. Elizabeth Meredith to William Meredith, Sept. 23, 1797, Meredith Family Papers.

50. Elizabeth Meredith to David Meredith, July 2, 1796, Meredith Family Papers. The Merediths' ruthless attitude toward tenants was not new. Almost twenty years before the Front Street house fracas, Jonathan Meredith removed another woman, a Mrs. Church, from a farm at Perkiomen Ferry, because, as he argued, "There must be a tavern and ferry kept there and her situation with respect to laborers would not permit her even to work the place properly." Jonathan Meredith, March 20 1779, Meredith Family Papers.

51. Elizabeth Meredith to David Meredith, April 14, 1796, Meredith Family Papers.

52. Ibid. In "Speculation and Competence" Northrup provides details about this situation.

53. Elizabeth Meredith to David Meredith, May 17, 1796, Meredith Family Papers.

54. Northrup, "Decomposition and Reconstitution," 105.

55. Doerflinger (*A Vigorous Spirit of Enterprise,* 304) estimates there were 7,600 heads of household in Philadelphia in 1790, based on his analysis of the 1790 census.

56. Elizabeth Meredith to David Meredith, Jan. 2, 1796, Meredith Family Papers.

57. Robert James Gough, "Towards a Theory of Class and Social Conflict: A Social History of Wealthy Philadelphians, 1775 and 1800," Ph.D. diss., University of Pennsylvania, 1977; Tom W. Smith, "The Dawn of the Urban-Industrial Age: The Social Structure of Philadelphia, 1790–1830," Ph.D. diss., University of Chicago, 1980. For a discussion of Anne Bingham's networks, see Wendy Anne Nicholson, "Making the Private Public: Anne Willing Bingham's Role as Leader of Philadelphia Society in the Late Eighteenth Century," master's thesis, University of Delaware, 1988; Ethel E. Rasmussen, "Democratic Environment-Aristocratic Aspiration," *Pennsylvania Magazine of History and Biography* 90 (April 1966): 155–82; and Robert C. Alberts, *The Golden Voyage: The Life and Times of William Bingham, 1752–1804* (Boston, 1969).

58. Elizabeth Meredith to David Meredith, Feb. 20, 1796, Meredith Family Papers; Emily W. Sunstein, *A Different Fact: The Life of Mary Wollstonecraft* (New York, 1975), 264, 296.

59. Elizabeth Meredith to David Meredith, Sept. 24, 1796, Meredith Family Papers.

60. John Swanwick, *Poems on Several Occasions* (Philadelphia, 1797), 122; John Swanwick, *Thoughts on Education Addressed to the Visitors of the Young Ladies' Academy of Philadelphia* (Philadelphia, 1787), 27.

61. Elizabeth Meredith to David Meredith, Dec. 16, 1795, Meredith Family Papers.

62. Elizabeth Meredith to David Meredith, March 10, 1796, Meredith Family Papers.

63. Elizabeth Meredith to David Meredith, Dec. 16, 1795, Meredith Family Papers; Roland M. Baumann, "John Swanwick: Spokesman for 'Merchant-Republicanism' in Philadelphia, 1790–1798," *Pennsylvania Magazine of History and Biography* 97 (April 1973): 131–82.

64. Mary's husband, Thomas Hawthorne, was not a good financial choice. Hawthorne constantly relied on financial assistance from Jonathan Meredith to keep his Maryland store afloat, and Hawthorne's troubles contributed substantially to Jonathan Meredith's bankruptcy in 1805. The Hawthornes eventually migrated to Ireland.

65. "The Plague of the Learned Wife," *Weekly Magazine of Original Essays* (May 1798).

66. Gertrude Meredith to William Meredith, Sept. 2, 1800, Meredith Family Papers.

67. Gertrude Meredith to William Meredith, Sept. 7, Sept. 24, 1805, Aug. 31, 1800, Meredith Family Papers.

68. Gertrude Meredith to William Meredith, Sept. 17, 1807, Meredith Family Papers.

69. Gertrude Meredith to William Meredith, May 3, 1804, Meredith Family Papers.

70. Gertrude Meredith to William Meredith, Feb. 7, 1805, Meredith Family Papers.

71. Gertrude Meredith to William Meredith, May 3, 1804, Meredith Family Papers.

72. Gertrude Meredith to William Meredith, Sept. 6, 1802, Meredith Family Papers.

73. Richard L. Bushman, *The Refinement of America: Persons, Houses, Cities* (New York, 1992), xvii.

4

"Sally Has Been Sick": Pregnancy and Family Limitation among Virginia Gentry Women, 1780–1830

JAN LEWIS AND KENNETH A. LOCKRIDGE

The great legend that has grown up around them says, among many things, that antebellum southerners were fatalists, women no less than men. Statistics seem to bear that out. The lesson read from census and impressionistic evidence both is that before the Civil War southern gentry women continued to accept the eight to ten children God gave them.[1] Their "traditional" behavior is often contrasted to that of northern women, who by 1860 had already entered the transition to limited fertility within marriage and were bearing perhaps five children apiece. The consensus among southern historians and historical demographers has been that southern gentry women found neither a need nor a way to broach with their husbands so delicate and bold a subject as reduced fertility, even while Yankee couples were, presumably, beginning to carry on a rational and effective dialogue in which a kind of "domestic feminism" gave women an equal role with their husbands.[2]

It is perhaps unfair to fault American historians for not having tested the comparison further. Any demographer will affirm that very little is known about discussions between husbands and wives anywhere about reproduction on the eve of the great transition to lower marital fertility that struck the Western world in the nineteenth century. Little enough is known about actual reproductive behavior. Given that vacuum, it was as easy to go on seeing, in cursory glances at the American evidence, fatalistic and repressed southern wives who lagged far behind their northern sisters in a quest for reproductive autonomy. Our data, in the aggregate, initially seemed to confirm this picture. Our statistics, based on a sample of 298 Virginia gentry women born between 1710 and 1849, indicate that, thus aggregated, married gentry women born in Virginia between 1760 and 1799, and bearing children between 1780 and 1840, bore nearly as many children as their sisters born between 1710 and 1759—just over eight apiece.[3]

Yet a preliminary look at the letters and diaries of hundreds of Virginia gentry women between 1760 and 1830 reveals that at least some after 1790 or 1800 were becoming more articulate and insistent in their complaints about the burdens of repeated pregnancies and childbirths.[4] Their dialogue with their husbands, dwelling as it did on pain and suffering alone, was perhaps not wholly the language of feminine autonomy, let alone rational economic discourse, but it may eventually have been effective. A closer analysis of the childbearing experience of our sample of 298 Virginia gentry women born from 1710 to 1849 and bearing children between 1760 and 1840 indicates that the faint beginnings of the fertility transition were in evidence as early as the 1820s. A definite trend to lower marital fertility had commenced by the 1840s and 1850s, well before the Civil War.

In the letters of Virginia gentry women written between 1760 and 1790 or 1800, childbirth was regarded as a difficult time for a woman. That is hardly surprising; the connection between childbirth and female suffering goes back at least as far as Genesis. The risks and more painful realities of human reproduction made such an association inevitable. What is striking is the relative brevity, directness, and stoicism with which eighteenth-century Virginia women discussed childbirth—when they discussed it at all. Even as late as the 1790s (in some instances, later still), the entire business, including its fears, was discussed in routinized language, as in a letter from Martha Jefferson Carr to Lucy Terrell of August 9, 1794: "[Patsy Randolph will have a child soon] how happy should I be could I repeat my attentions to you on the same occasion but I have not a dou[bt] of your being blest with some good female friend that will act the Mother [and] sooth you with her compassion when the painful hour arrives and soften [you] by her tenderness. The necessary time of retirement may God of his mercy grant you a favorable time." In this letter, the woman's need of companionship can be met by any "female friend" who will fill a standard role by acting "the Mother" in "the painful hour," that is in "the necessary time of retirement." It is still largely the standardized language of the stoical eighteenth century, in which such conventionalized formulas at once expressed and yet controlled the fear and other emotions which, by the use of such language, were assumed to be the inevitable concomitants of childbirth. Childbirth was, in short, frightening, but like all other occasions of emotion it was, in the eyes of the eighteenth century, nothing to make a great fuss about. Men similarly subsumed childbirth's recognized problems under routine formulas. To William Byrd, it was "breeding," as in "my wife is breeding again." To David Meade, his daughter's impending delivery of a child was called "being taken to the Chamber for a season. . . . She will not," he continued, "be without your anxious wishes for her speedy recovery from so critical a state."[5] The recognized dangers were being subsumed under formulas that both expressed and contained human fears.

By the turn of the eighteenth century, however, some Virginia gentry women (and eventually men) were beginning to discuss childbirth much more frequently and to make it ever more clear that they faced childbirth with hesitation, even fear and trembling. Theirs became the standard mode of future discussions. It was not that they did not love their children. If anything, the increasing value that the nineteenth century attached to the individual tended to make a mother more satisfied with a smaller family upon whom she could lavish, proportionately, more affection. Thus, Eleanor Lewis, anticipating the birth of her second child in 1801, could tell a friend, "You say my Dear Mrs. Pinckney, that you shall be pleased to hear I have another little darling to divide my affection with my precious Frances—in August or September [three or four months hence] I expect to inform you of such an event if no accident intervenes—I often think what I shall do with more, when one engrosses me so much."[6] Similarly, Ellen Coolidge, also anticipating the birth of a second child, told her sister, "My present poppet is such a source of hope and comfort to me that I do not allow myself to repine at the thought of another, although I should certainly have preferred to defer the arrival of the little sister another year."[7] Thus, women who had only one child, and one they loved dearly, might express reservations about the impending arrival of a second.

Similar reservations were expressed by women who were, to all indications, happily married. The anxiety women expressed about childbirth cannot be read as a covert protest against marriage itself or against the physical intimacy that was an accepted, indeed welcomed, part of marriage. One euphemism for pregnancy was being "in the way that ladies love to be who love their lords."[8] Because that phrase was used among women rather than with men or in mixed company, it should not be read literally, as an acknowledgement of male mastery, so much as female appreciation of the sexual dimension of marriage. In other words, it is women who love their husbands who will find themselves pregnant. That also is the meaning of the confession to her sister of a woman pregnant for the first time: "Oh my dear Jane how can I ever get through[?] I feel as the time approaches that I would rather die than bear so much pain. What a fool a girl is ever to get married, if I should be so fortunate as to have a daughter my first lesson to her shall be to despise everything that wears breeches."[9] Sidney Carr held herself, not her husband, responsible for her predicament. Ironically, forces that worked in the early

nineteenth century to make marriage more intimate and increase the acceptance of romantic love, the only legitimate basis for marriage, would assure
that the sex attracted to the one who wore breeches would find itself pregnant time and again.[10]

That was the catch. The women who expressed love of their children and
husbands also feared childbirth, so much so that a married woman, gossip-
ing with a female friend about an unmarried woman who had become pregnant, could not comprehend the maiden's lapse: "How ca[n you] account for
a young woman's so far losing all . . . fear of what even *we* dread so much?"[11]
Neither shame nor economic insecurity but pain and danger were what impressed, and these were discussed in the blunt language of fear and dread.
What woman would undertake such risks without the benefits of marriage?
The prospect of pain and the very real possibility of dying in childbirth combined to make women's descriptions of the experience strikingly negative. It
was richly, variously, and sometimes appallingly termed "this dreadful event,"
a "trial," "an affliction," and "one of the evils of this life."[12] The stoicism of
the eighteenth century was being strained to—and beyond—its limits by this
amplifying terminology.

Women approached the moment of childbirth with grave trepidation.
According to one letter writer, a relative was "in miserable spirits at her ap-
proaching confinement, which is to take place next month."[13] Another, even
more despondent, was "in a very gloomy state of Mind . . . she expects the
birth of her child will put a period to her existence as her constitution is far
too exhausted to bear the distresst state to which she is exposed in childbirth."[14]

During the eighteenth century, female mortality rates in the Chesapeake
consistently exceeded those of men, with perhaps 30 percent of women dying before their forty-fifth birthdays. Historians have attributed that lower
life expectancy to the hazards of childbirth.[15] By the beginning of the nineteenth century, women themselves ever more frequently made this association between childbirth and maternal death. Further, their language of dread
was by now seldom rendered in brief formulae alone but was amplified into
such varying chronicles of individual misery and fear.

Women who well knew the hazards of childbirth made it ever more clear
that they dreaded facing the trial, which might, to use a conventional term
(but one seldom used in this context previously), "put a period" to their
existence. They wanted with them not just any female, but their loved ones,
especially their mothers, women whom they knew for a fact had successfully passed through the same danger. Sally Lacy, for example, implored, "What
would I not give if you my dear Mother could be with me or rather if I could
be with you."[16] Similarly, Mary Anderson explained to her brother, "Believe

me Duncan the company of a much loved Mother to comfort & sooth in affliction & pain is a blessing indeed."[17] Any woman who could "act the Mother" would no longer do. These women were not alienated from their husbands. Sally Lacy's was "the best nurse I ever saw," and Mary Anderson described hers as a "kind friend and affectionate husband." Yet even those who believed themselves to be living out the nineteenth century's ideal of an affectionate marriage wanted their mothers with them when they gave birth.

Perhaps women looked to their mothers because they sensed that, as much as they loved their husbands, men could not fully empathize with their increasingly articulated fears. Until perhaps 1820, the letters written by husbands and fathers reveal much less anxiety about the dangers of childbirth than did women's. Few Virginia men after the dawn of the nineteenth century were as patriarchal in their views as David Meade had been in 1799, when he proclaimed to a kinswoman that his "newly married Daughter promises to support the credit of our race by duly answering the most important purpose of her creation—already she discovers strong indications of that disposition."[18]

Meade's circumlocutions are revealing; in his mind, pregnancy was woman's natural state. More characteristic of the attitudes of early-nineteenth-century men is the postscript Sally Lacy's husband appended to the rather anxious letter she wrote to her brother: "Sally intends to give me another little boy, as much finer and smarter than little Ned, as her health and spirits (which are as good as possible) are better now, than previous to Ned's entrance into life."[19] His focus was upon the prospect of another child—indeed, another boy—as much as upon his wife's very real fears.

Much more than women, men tended to regard the pains and dangers of childbirth as necessary and inevitable, and, more than women, they hoped for sons. Thus, Randolph Harrison announced to his good friend John Hartwell Cocke, "Last night at 11 o'clock, my wife presented me with a little Nancy Cocke, instead of a John Hartwell as I expected. I say expected, because after so many daughters I thought I had a right [to] calculate on a son. . . . Poor Dear Soul, she has suffered more than on any former occasion. She was taken slightly on the night of the 16th, lingered for two days, and for several hours before the birth suffered the most excruciating torture that can be imagined." In the long run, Harrison's desire for sons overrode his sympathy for his wife's ordeals. Ten years later, he reported to Cocke that "after two days of pain, generally slow and lingering but lately extremely violent, my wife at 11 last night was made the happy mother of the 8th daughter, and 10th child. She is now Thank God (who has always dealt with me more bountifully than I deserve), as well as I could reasonably expect."[20] Tellingly, Harrison deemed himself, not the mother of his ten children, the beneficiary of God's mercy.

At least until about 1820, women appear to have been considerably more anxious about childbirth than were their husbands, Thus, any woman who wanted to limit her fertility would have to devise or discover her own means. That, at least, is what women seemed to have believed. Ann Barraud, for example, repeated to her married daughter a kinswoman's observation "about Women's being with child, unless they chose it."[21] (The daughter would die six years later in 1816, shortly after giving birth to her sixth child in fourteen years of marriage.) Such a comment suggests that women believed that they, and they alone, could exercise some control over their own fertility. Such also is the conclusion to be drawn from the letter of another mother. "I was not surprised," Peggy Nicholas wrote to her daughter, "nor would I have been grieved to hear that you were again in the family way; but I must acknowledge to hear that your confinement was to take place next Month, dashed me not a little. I had hoped that you had got into a confirmed habit of an intervall of two years, that there was no doubt of your continuance in this, and that [there] might be some reasonable guide in calculating your number. But now that you have got into your old habits, there is no saying where will be the end."[22]

Between 1815 and 1839, Peggy Nicholas's daughter Jane Randolph bore thirteen children at an average interval of twenty-three months, an experience that virtually duplicated her mother's twelve children, also at a rate of one every twenty-three months.[23] Both women had several more than the average of 8.32 for their age cohort. Although neither woman suggested what an ideal number of children might have been, the mother clearly believed, to put it in demographers' terms, that some control of fertility might be achieved by effective spacing and that the ideal birth interval was no less than twenty-four months. Such maternal advice is significant for several reasons. First, it suggests that Virginia women in this period may have tried to limit the frequency of births if not the size of their families. Second, it suggests that without some conscious effort, a birth interval shorter than two years would be the usual result. And third, that goal—and, presumably, the means by which it could be accomplished—was part of a women's tradition, passed from mother to daughter. Peggy Nicholas had learned of her daughter's pregnancy from her son-in-law, but she addressed her complaint not to him but to her daughter.[24]

In fact, our evidence suggests that Virginia gentry wives had long been successful in maintaining the modest goal of the average two-year interval espoused by Peggy Nicholas and practiced by her and her daughter. Thus the median birth interval for women in our sample born between 1710 and 1759 was twenty-three months; that for women born between 1760 and 1799 increased slightly, to between twenty-three and twenty-four months.[25] What means were at a woman's disposal to assure that she could give birth, on the average, at two-year intervals? The most likely was breastfeeding. Not only does lactation seem to retard ovulation, but there is also some evidence that Virginia women realized that prolonged breastfeeding might extend the interval between pregnancies.[26] The two-year interval for gentry women born between 1710 and 1799, which was Peggy Nicholas's ideal, is consistent with the practice of breastfeeding.

We would expect women who were not breastfeeding and were instead using a wet nurse to give birth every eighteen to twenty-four months and, as a consequence, to bear a greater number of children than women who did breastfeed. Frances Tasker Carter, who used a wet nurse for many of the sixteen children to whom she gave birth between 1757 and 1784, delivered a child about every seventeen months (median, on an average of eighteen and a half months).[27] Our figures, which indicate a longer median birth interval and a lower fertility rate among Virginia gentry women, provide additional confirmation for the assertions of Daniel Blake Smith and Sally McMillen: The vast majority of southern women breastfed their own infants.[28]

It is likely that the women born between 1760 and 1799, like their predecessors, relied upon breastfeeding as a strategy to space their children and possibly as an effort, albeit one with feeble effect, to limit fertility. The method was perhaps not totally ineffective, but it still meant that a married woman born between 1760 and 1799 and who survived her childbearing years could expect to give birth to an average of 8.3 children, as had her predecessors in the earlier generation. The figure, characteristic of the high fertility of colonial American women, represents the limits of female-controlled, breastfeeding-based, fertility limitation—and very feeble limits they were.[29] Without the cooperation of her husband, a woman could accomplish no more.[30]

To put it another way, further limitation of fertility on the part of early-nineteenth-century women would require the participation of husbands. How might men, who regarded frequent pregnancies with more equanimity than their wives, be persuaded to extend spacing further or in another way unquestionably to limit family size? One might think that economic considerations would be important and that men who could not afford to support in independence large families would be inclined to control fertility. By that logic, the group that was born from 1760 to 1799 and bore children from roughly 1780 to 1840 should have borne fewer children than the earlier cohort (those born from 1710 to 1759). The post-Revolutionary decades in Virginia were characterized by serious economic woes. Soil exhaustion, falling tobacco prices, a series of depressions, and land pressures combined to undermine the economic security of the gentry. Yet only in the letters of women was the connection between economic pressures and a large family confronted.[31] Men, in contrast, never seemed to consider family limitation as a strategy for coping with hard times. In fact, family size for the cohort of women born from 1760 to 1799 fell almost insignificantly (from an average of 8.37 to 8.33).

The only instances in which men accepted some form of family limitation were those when the wife's life clearly would have been endangered by pregnancy. Thus one Virginian explained to a kinswoman, "It is not probable that I shall ever have a numerous family, if any. My wife has been accidentally unfortunate last winter in a miscarriage, which has rendered her health very delicate." Similarly, James Parker noted that his son's "poor Wife has lost another Little One. It lived only two days, so Dr. Currie writes me. & he thinks that absence from her husband and another climate are the only chances she has of ever doing better."[32] In such cases, the husband would, presumably, avoid intercourse with his wife or would separate from her in order to spare her health. To be sure, not every husband with a delicate wife was willing to forego sexual relations with her. Thomas Jefferson is a case in point. It is worth noting, however, that the doctor's remedy of a woman's "absence from her husband" strongly suggests that the practice of coitus interruptus, often regarded by historical demographers as the most common pre-twentieth-century method of family limitation, was not used by Virginians.[33] Instead, abstinence was recommended, a remedy so difficult that it was thought to require the separation of husband and wife.

That, apparently, was the conclusion reached by Ellen Coolidge and her husband Joseph, who announced the birth of their sixth child to his mother-in-law: "Only think of it—four sons, the oldest of whom is but two years and eight months! I can hardly realize it, and as for Ellen what a melancholy idea of suffering does it give to be told that—with six children she has barely been married six years; take out the weary months of pregnancy, and nursing, and how little is left to restore her strength of mind a[nd] body. . . . If we could but feel that we had come to the end of the chapter, I should soon be reconciled, and so would she, to our present number,—which the loss of one would so painfully diminish, (and can we hope to go through life and never lose a child?)."[34] A year later, in 1832, Coolidge, who was a merchant, departed for Canton, China. He was not permanently reunited with his family until his wife has passed out of her childbearing years.[35] If loving couples had to resort to separation, it is unlikely that they had at their disposal less drastic means of birth control. Abstinence, although surely effective, was no easy solution, and it was accepted only by husbands who had grave fears for their wives' health and well-being.

These examples suggest that men may have proved more susceptible to a feminine reason for birth control, fear of maternal death in childbirth, than to the more "masculine" one of economic necessity, which does not appear in their correspondence. In order for such a rationale to become a spur to widespread family limitation, however, it would be necessary for men as a class to perceive pregnancy as dangerous, in the way their wives already had come to do. In other words, most men would have to consider all women, and not merely particular husbands their exceptional and obviously ill wives, as delicate. Pregnancy would have to become an acknowledged pathology in which childbirth was dangerous to all women. (And, presumably, means less drastic than abstinence would have to be adopted.)

Perhaps Virginia women somehow knew that this was the only appeal that would persuade their husbands to engage in a mutual program of family limitation. Whether or not that was the case, slowly after the turn of the century Virginia men as well as women began to describe pregnancy as an illness, using a language of pathology that had been uncommon earlier to describe it. In 1728, for example, William Byrd II exploited his wife's impending confinement to display his wit: "I wonder any Mother shoud be affraid of dying in child-bed; considering tis dying in obedience to the first command, and consequently in the best cause in the world. . . . I fancy if there were any such thing as seeing into Female hearts we shoud find this is the reason the whole Sex wants to be married, that by being with child they may have a chance to dye Martyrs."[36] Pregnancy was no cause for concern.

By the early nineteenth century, however, women and men both were beginning to describe pregnancy and childbirth as something unnatural, a disruption of a woman's health. Of course, it is not unusual that miscarriage should have left one man's wife "a good deal indisposed & much debilitated," nor that childbirth left another's "as well as I could reasonably expect."[37] What is exceptional is the use of the language of pathology to describe pregnancy itself. Thus one man alluded to his wife's impending confinement by saying that she was "indisposed." Another Virginian, searching for the right words to inform his daughter of a kinswoman's pregnancy, said merely, "Laura looks very badly." The adjectives of ill-health—"indisposed," "unwell," "sick"—became euphemisms for pregnancy. Sally Lacy, for example, described herself as "restless" and "generally . . . unwell at night."[38] By a process of cultural synecdoche, its discomforts became the part that stood for the whole of pregnancy. As one woman put it, using terms whose meaning was quite clear, "Sally S— has been sick almost since she went down, she is in the way to increase her family." Such an "illness," of course, lasted nine months. Another woman, using a similar terminology, was "delighted to hear of her [sister's] improved health, I pray it may continue; and that she may indeed have had her quantum of children."[39]

The gradual redefinition of pregnancy as disease, in evidence by the beginning of the nineteenth century, did not immediately result in family limitation. Instead, it was a prelude to the very different demographic experience of women born between 1800 and 1839. Although a slight lengthening occurred of the median birth interval for women born at the end of the eighteenth century, and a small (4 percent) drop in fertility among women born in the 1790s, it is only for the women born after the turn of the century that we see an unmistakable decline in family size.[40] For these women, born between 1800 and 1839, there was a slight further increase in median birth interval (to just over twenty-four months). The most important factor leading to limited family size was the sharp drop in the fertility of women in their thirties, which resulted in an average completed-family size of 5.81 for women born between 1800 and 1839, compared to 8.37 for the 1710 to 1759 cohort and 8.33 for the 1760 to 1799 cohort.[41]

Our preliminary calculations suggest that men agreed to limit family size only when their wives had entered their thirties and given them a healthy male heir or two. Although our figures for women born between 1800 and 1839 show some drop in fertility for women aged twenty to twenty-four, the fertility rate is consistent with effective spacing—a child born every two and a half years or so—whereas the rate for women twenty-five to twenty-nine remains consistent for all Virginia gentry women born from 1710 to 1839. Yet the sharp decline in the fertility rate of women in the 1800 to 1839 cohort aged thirty-five to thirty-nine and forty to forty-four (along with data for later cohorts) suggests strongly that after 1830 many married women stopped, or tried to stop, bearing children after they had reached age thirty-five and delivered what they considered their "quantum" of children.

We do not know what means these families used. It is unlikely that many Virginia men joined Joseph Coolidge in Canton. Perhaps after a certain number of births Virginia's husbands and wives resorted to shorter periods of separation or agreed to abstinence when they were together. Our sources are mute on this subject. What they do tell us is that an inchoate desire for family limitation was voiced first among women and that the description of pregnancy as pathological by both women and men preceded a clear and irreversible drop in fertility.

Most historians of the South and historical demographers have assumed that antebellum southern couples did not attempt to limit family size, and that, in contrast to the North, no demographic transition took place in the pre–Civil War South.[42] Our statistics, although preliminary, may indicate otherwise. Virginia gentry women born in the first five decades of the nineteenth century seem to have borne progressively fewer children, especially after age thirty-five, than their mothers, even if their fertility did not drop as early and as sharply as that of northern women. Their success in limiting family size might in some sense be considered a southern instance of the domestic feminism that Daniel Scott Smith has found among northern women. It seems possible that in Virginia as well, control of fertility depended upon a woman persuading her husband to accede to her desire for a smaller family.[43]

Still, the victory for Virginia's elite women was not necessarily proof of—as Smith puts it—"women's increasing autonomy within the family."[44] Family limitation may have had its costs. It could be purchased only by sacrificing the physical intimacy that the nineteenth-century's cult of romantic love had awakened. It may also have required that women depict themselves as weak, frail, and too delicate to endure the rigors of repeated pregnancies. Women themselves and not, as some have suggested, their physicians may have played the leading role in medicalizing pregnancy and describing it as a pathology.[45] In this way, ironically, women themselves may have encouraged the belief that they were frail and that the essence of their femininity posed a grave, unnatural threat to their health. Such a view perhaps gave them leverage over husbands, a sort of "domestic feminism," but it was possibly as the "weaker vessel" and not as autonomous equals that Virginia gentry women finally prevailed on their husbands to liberate them from the pain of childbirth.

The Virginia evidence, aside from being seen as strictly preliminary, should not be rendered too pessimistically. The great attitudinal changes of the early nineteenth century—evangelical religion, romanticism, and emerging medical "science"—had all helped free these women to express more eloquently than ever what was certainly an ancient concern—indeed, an ancient slavery—for women. From all the evidence, once they expressed this concern, Virginia gentry women prevailed upon their husbands (at whatever cost in their own self-images) to help liberate them. By the cohort born in 1800, Virginia gentry women were having seven rather than nine children. By the cohort born in 1840, that number was probably closer to five—four by the turn of the twentieth century. Further, because our research in the correspondence of this class of women does not extend to cover many of the letters of the cohorts born after 1800 and bearing children chiefly after 1830 (i.e., those who finally succeeded in limiting their families), it is entirely possible that a more optimistic construction could be placed upon the evident adoption of family limitation practices among the later generations of women. These women and their husbands, born after 1800 and growing up in the 1800s, 1810s, and 1820s, heard on their parents' lips the ample language of suffering and pathology used to describe pregnancy and childbirth. And they saw their parents fail, by and large, to limit their families substantially. This experience may have led the women and the men of these younger generations born after 1800 quietly to agree not to endure such extensive suffering and "sickness" as a part of their own marriages. Swedish research indicates that such a sober, mutual resolution "not to have ten children like our mothers," reached by young women and men alike, lay behind the advent of family limitation in far northern Sweden in the 1930s and 1940s.[46] The desperate, almost demeaning, frustrations of Virginia mothers who bore children between 1800 and 1830 and did not generally succeed very well in having fewer may have become a quieter, more mutual, resolution of daughters—and sons—born after 1800 who did succeed in having fewer children. In these younger and more successful generations, the net product could have been something closer to Daniel Scott Smith's "domestic feminism"—a quiet, mutual, and effective decision to change reproductive behavior.

Which model is characteristic of the advent of fertility limitation elsewhere in America—the desperate appeal to weakness characteristic of Virginia gentry women at least up to 1830; a more quiet mutual decision not to prolong such suffering, as was possibly found in later generations in Virginia and probably in northern Sweden a century later; or the classic "domestic feminism" posited by Daniel Scott Smith—is anyone's guess.[47] Wally Seccombe of the Ontario Institute for Studies on Education has completed a study of working-class women in Britain from around 1910 to 1930 that is remarkably similar to this one in its sources and conclusions. His investigation implicitly suggests that each social class employed all three models, perhaps in the order specified, across several generations, and could have entered into a fertility transition that was generally led by women's concerns.[48]

These questions and possibilities aside, the only certainty is that our theories of the advent of family limitation in Western society, some relating it more closely to structural change and others to attitudinal revolutions, must all take greater cognizance of the varied conversations of women, both among themselves and with their husbands.[49] These conversations and the views they embodied were the final lens through which both structural change and attitudinal modernization were focused into radically changed behavior.[50]

Notes

This essay is reprinted, with minor editorial changes, from the *Journal of Social History* 22 (Fall 1988): 5–19.

1. Richard H. Steckel, *The Economics of U.S. Slave and Southern White Fertility* (New York, 1985), esp. 176; Catherine Clinton, *The Plantation Mistress: Woman's World in the Old South* (New York, 1982), 152–53; Bertram Wyatt-Brown, *Southern Honor: Ethics and Behavior in the Old South* (New York, 1982), 205.

2. Daniel Scott Smith, "Family Limitation, Sexual Control, and Domestic Feminism in Victorian America," *Feminist Studies* 1 (1973): 40–57.

3. We have drawn our demographic sample from unpublished genealogies of Virginia gentry women available at the Virginia Historical Society and published genealogies of the same group, from the collection of the Virginia Historical Society and from *The William and Mary Quarterly*, 1st ser., and the *Virginia Magazine of History and Biography*. "Gentry" is defined throughout as slave-owning families with possessions and pretensions indicating, and in many cases with self-identification confirming, membership in the planter elite of Virginia. It should be noted that this was often an upper-middle-class elite, however, hence the term *gentry*, which many at the time preferred. We have not used genealogies that appear to be "tainted," that is, ones that appear to have excluded children who died young or did not themselves produce issue, as well as those that in other ways seem incomplete or unreliable. As a result, our figures for completed family size may be shaded toward the high side; our age-specific fertility rates, particularly for women over twenty-five, may likewise be slightly high. That is, in trying to make certain that we excluded from our sample all genealogies in which the compiler chose to follow only those individuals who achieved adulthood or those lines that produced issue, we may have eliminated a very few women who bore relatively few children. But most cases of data tainted in this way are clearly tainted and thus must be excluded from the sample. We have divided our demographic sample into three cohorts: women born between 1710 and 1759 ($n = 44$); those born between 1760 and 1799 ($n = 121$); and those born between 1800 and 1839 ($n = 97$). We also have data on thirty-six women born in the 1840s. Whenever possible, we have included in this sample the actual fertility histories of those women from whose correspondence we have quoted. It is this demographic sample that provides the evidence cited here in the text.

Live births per married woman surviving to age 45:

Women born 1710–59	8.37 ($n = 24$)
Women born 1760–99	8.33 ($n = 38$)

4. The women whose correspondence is to be used in developing this argument come from the primary sample used in this essay. That "sample" is nothing more, or less, than a reading of the letters of hundreds of Virginia gentry women between 1760 and 1830, more than half (and as much as two-thirds) of all such letters surviving in Virginia archives. In general, although the majority of such letters surveyed are not articulate about the issues of childbirth and pregnancy, they are nonetheless, in tone and often language, consistent with, and often implicitly or explicitly support, the more articulate minority of women who wrote in some detail on these issues and who are quoted here. This articulate minority within Virginia gentry women's culture around 1760 to 1830—perhaps a hundred

women in all—might therefore be seen as the voice of their feminine culture on fertility issues—the voice of a given sex, class, culture, and milieu. The fertility histories of these more articulate women have been traced wherever possible (in a majority of cases) and are included. In all cases they are consistent with the fertility histories of the women of their generation in the appropriate and larger demographic subsample of women of the same class (i.e., those cited in note 3, born between 1710 and 1759 and 1760 and 1799) analyzed to check for actual fertility behavior among the various generations of Virginia gentry women of the era. In this pilot study, the correspondence sampled is therefore and perforce not strictly identical with the demographic behavior sampled in women of the same class and generations. For some women, we have only correspondence; for others, only demographic behavior, as is inevitable from the nature of the surviving sources. But all of the most vital examples, from correspondence where demographic information is available, show demographic behavior consistent with that of the larger demographic samples invoked.

5. Martha Carr to Lucy Terrell, Aug. 9, 1794, Terrell-Carr Papers, Alderman Library, University of Virginia; William Byrd, in *The Correspondence of the Three William Byrds of Westover, Virginia* (Charlottesville, 1977), 1:391; David Meade to Ann Randolph [1799?], Bolling Papers, Perkins Library, Duke University.

6. Eleanor P. Lewis to Mrs. Pinckney, May 9, 1801, Custis Family Papers, Library of Congress.

7. Ellen Wayles Coolidge to Virginia Trist, March 20, 1827, Ellen W. Coolidge Papers, Alderman Library, University of Virginia.

8. Sarah Nicholas to Jane H. Randolph, Jan. 1, 1830, Edgehill-Randolph Papers, Alderman Library, University of Virginia; see also Martha J. Randolph to Ellen W. Coolidge. Nov. 16, 1825, Coolidge Papers.

9. Sidney Carr to Jane Randolph, Dec. 31 [1825], Edgehill-Randolph Papers.

10. Jan Lewis, *The Pursuit of Happiness: Family and Values in Jefferson's Virginia* (New York, 1983), ch. 5; Ellen W. Rothman, *Hands and Hearts: A History of Courtship in America* (New York, 1984), ch. 1.

11. F. H. Allison to Margaret Coalter, July 15, 1797, Brown, Coalter, and Tucker Papers, Earl Gregg Swem Library, College of William and Mary.

12. Betsy Carrington to Ann Fisher, Nov. 22, 1799, Carrington-Ambler Papers, Alderman Library, University of Virginia; Virginia Trist to Ellen W. Coolidge, March 23, 1827, Coolidge Papers; Peggy Nicholas to Jane H. Randolph, May 25, 1827, Edgehill-Randolph Papers. See also Peggy Nicholas to Jane H. Randolph, April 28, 1828, Edgehill-Randolph Papers, and William Shepard to Ebenezer Pettigrew, Aug. 5, 1818, Pettigrew Papers, Southern Historical Collection, University of North Carolina.

13. W[ilson] J. Cary to Virginia Cary, July 21, 182 1, Carr-Cary Papers, Alderman Library, University of Virginia.

14. Ann Barraud to Ann Cocke, May 18 [1812], Cocke Deposit, Alderman Library, University of Virginia.

15. Allan Kulikoff, *Tobacco and Slaves: The Development of Southern Cultures in the Chesapeake, 1680–1800* (Chapel Hill, 1986), 63. Approximately 30 percent of the women in our sample born between 1710 and 1799 died before age forty-five; only about 10 percent of the women in that cohort were preceded in death by their husbands (men who were, typically, several years older than their wives). The higher female mortality rate may well be related to childbirth, in particular to the debilitating effects of malaria. Darrett B.

Rutman and Anita H. Rutman have hypothesized that Chesapeake women of childbearing age were weakened by malaria. See Rutman and Rutman, "Of Agues and Fevers: Malaria in the Early Chesapeake," *William and Mary Quarterly,* 3d ser., 33 (1976): 51–52. For women's fear of childbirth, see also Judith Walzer Leavitt and Whitney Walton, "'Down to Death's Door': Women's Perceptions of Childbirth in America," from *Childbirth: The Beginning of Motherhood, Proceedings of the Second Motherhood Symposium* (Madison, 1982), in *Women and Health in America,* ed. Judith Watzer Leavitt (Madison, 1984), 155, 165; and Judith Watzer Leavitt, *Brought to Bed: Childbearing in America, 1750–1950* (New York, 1986), 20–35.

16. Sally Lacy to [Margaret Graham], July 21, 1817, Graham Family Papers, Perkins Library, Duke University.

17. Mary Anderson to Duncan Cameron, Aug. 17, 1798, Cameron Papers, Southern Historical Collection.

18. David Meade to Ann Randolph [1799?], Bolling Papers; see also David Meade to Ann Randolph, May 6, 1798.

19. Sally Lacy to William A. Graham, Feb. 7, 1819, Graham Family Papers.

20. Randolph Harrison to John Hartwell Cocke, Feb. 19, 1819 and Feb. 1829, Cocke Deposit.

21. Ann Barraud to Ann Cocke, Aug. 13 [1810?], Cocke Deposit. See also Milton Rugoff, *The Beechers: An American Family in the Nineteenth Century* (New York, 1981), 237, quoting Catharine Beecher's letter to her sister Mary about their sister Harriet, who "says she shall not have any more children, *she knows for certain* for one while. Though how she found this out I cannot say, but she seems quite confident about it."

22. Peggy Nicholas to Jane H. Randolph, April 28 [1828?], Edgehill-Randolph Papers; see also Peggy Nicholas to Jane H. Randolph, Feb. 18, 1829.

23. Both married younger than the average of their cohort. The average age at first marriage for women born from 1710 to 1759 is 20.9; for those born from 1760 to 1799, 20.3; and for those born from 1800 to 1839, 21.46. Peggy Nicholas married at nineteen, and her daughter Jane at seventeen.

24. Peggy Nicholas to Jane H. Randolph, April 28 [1828?]; see also Peggy Nicholas to Jane H. Randolph, Feb. 18, 1829.

25. Smith has found a typical birth interval of twenty-four to thirty months. Daniel Blake Smith, *Inside the Great House; Planter Life in Eighteenth-Century Chesapeake Society* (Ithaca, 1980), 27.

26. Catherine M. Scholten, *Childbearing in American Society* (New York, 1985), 14; Smith, *Inside the Great House,* 36–37. Smith believes that most women breastfed for about eighteen months.

27. Smith, *Inside the Great House,* 51.

28. Ibid., 36–37; Sally McMillen, "Mothers' Sacred Duty: Breast-feeding Patterns among Middle- and Upper-Class Women in the Antebellum South," *Journal of Southern History* 51 (1985): 333–56.

29. See note 3. John Demos, for example, found an average of 9.3 births to third-generation Plymouth families. Demos, *A Little Commonwealth: Family Life in Plymouth Colony* (New York, 1970), 192.

30. There is some evidence that Virginia women of this period may have been aware of some methods of abortion and could even imagine infanticide, but both were considered the remedies of desperate women and certainly inappropriate for married women.

See F. H. A[llison] to Margaret Coalter, July 15, 1797, Brown, Coalter, and Tucker Papers; and Francis Biddle, "Scandal at Bizarre," *American Heritage* 12 (Aug. 1961): 10–82, esp. 79, for knowledge of abortifacients. We have found no evidence, however, that artificial means of birth control such as syringes, which Joan Jensen has found were available in Philadelphia by the 1790s, could be obtained in Virginia. Jensen, *Loosening the Bonds: Mid-Atlantic Farm Women, 1750–1850* (New Haven, 1986), 29.

31. Cary Ann Smith to Jane H. Randolph, June 16, 1819, Edgehill-Randolph Papers; Peggy Nicholas to Jane H. Randolph, Sept. 19, 1829, Edgehill-Randolph Papers; Virginia Trist to Ellen W. Coolidge, March 23, 1827, Coolidge Papers. For problems in the Virginia economy, see Lewis, *Pursuit of Happiness*, ch. 4.

32. Gideon Fitz to Elizabeth Fitz, Sept. 22, 1808, George Carr Manuscripts, Alderman Library, University of Virginia; James Parker to Charles Steuart, April 21, 1791, Steuart Papers, Research Archives, Colonial Williamsburg Foundation.

33. In ten years of marriage to Thomas Jefferson, Martha Wayles Skelton (a widow with an infant son at the time of their marriage in 1772) bore six children, only two of whom survived infancy. Throughout her marriage, Martha Jefferson suffered from poor health, and she never recovered from the birth of her last child. Dumas Malone, *Jefferson the Virginian* (Boston, 1948), 214, 241, 245–46, 393–96, 434. Among those who have argued that coitus interruptus was the most common method of birth control are Carroll Smith-Rosenberg and Charles Rosenberg in "The Female Animal: Medical and Biological Views of Woman and Her Role in Nineteenth-Century America," *Journal of American History* 60 (1973): 332–56.

34. Joseph W. Coolidge to Martha J. Randolph, Aug. [28, 30], 183, Coolidge Papers. Note that Coolidge first mentions his four sons and only later that his wife is the mother of six children in all. His calculation that at least one of these children will fail to survive to adulthood suggests strongly that his desire for a male heir has entered into his reckoning. Fathers seemed to consider limiting family size only after they were assured of a male heir. See also Cary Ann Smith to Jane H. Randolph, June 16, 1819, Edgehill-Randolph Papers.

35. Walter Muir Whitehall, "Eleanora Wayles Randolph and Joseph Coolidge, Jr.," in *Collected Papers to Commemorate Fifty Years of the Monticello Association of the Descendants of Thomas Jefferson* ed. George Green Shackelford (Princeton, 1965), 89–99.

36. William Byrd II to Cousen Taylor, July 28, 1728, Letter Book 1:23–24, Colonial Williamsburg Foundation (original in the Virginia Historical Society).

37. Larkin Smith to Littleton Tazewell, Oct. 16, 1804, Tazewell Papers, Colonial Williamsburg Foundation (original in the Virginia State Library); Randolph Harrison to John Hartwell Cocke, Feb. 1829, Cocke Deposit; see also Mary Anderson to Duncan Cameron, Aug. 17, 1798, Cameron Papers.

38. Jean Cameron (quoting her brother Duncan) to Rebecca Cameron, Jan. 6, 1804, Cameron Papers; W. H. Cabell to Louisa Carrington, May 21, 1829, Cabell-Carrington Papers, Alderman Library, University of Virginia; and Sally Lacy to Margaret Graham, July 21, 1817, Graham Family Papers; see also Sarah Preston to Mrs. Susanna McDowell, Feb. 27, 1826, Papers of the Carrington and McDowell Families of Virginia, Library of Congress. Abigail Adams used similar terminology in describing pregnancy, once referring to it as "*her old* sickness." See Paul C. Nagel, *The Adams Women: Abigail and Louisa Adams, Their Sisters and Daughters* (New York, 1987), 97.

39. S[ally] Faulcon to Ann Cocke, May 14, 1810, Cocke Deposit; Agnes Cabell to Louisa

Cabell, Feb. 16, 1819, Cabell-Carrington Papers. Randolph Trumbach notes that an influential midwifery manual, published in French in 1672 and available in England in the eighteenth century, described pregnancy as an illness, albeit a necessary and unavoidable one. Trumbach, *The Rise of the Egalitarian Family: Aristocratic Kinship and Domestic Relations in Eighteenth-Century England* (New York, 1978), 176. We have no evidence that this work or its assumptions were shared by early Virginians.

40. See p. 101 for birth intervals. We have subdivided our post–1759 cohorts and obtained the following completed-family sizes:

1760s	8.43	(number of women with completed families = 10)
1770s	9.26	($n = 3$)
1780s	8.41	($n = 12$)
1790s	7.98	($n = 13$)
1800s	6.54	($n = 16$)
1810s	6.31	($n = 16$)
1820s	5.39	($n = 22$)
1830s	5.47	($n = 31$)
1840s	5.17	($n = 24$)

Because the numbers in each cohort are small, these calculations are rough. They show a rather steady decline in family size beginning in 1790, with the clearest drop for women born after 1800. We also have broken down the cohort because those born at the end of it (after 1830) would have been of childbearing age during and after the Civil War. One would assume that the difficulties of that period would have encouraged family limitation, yet the trend toward a smaller family size was well under way before that time, as was the sharp drop in fertility for women thirty-five and older.

41. Although the average age of marriage for women increased by 1.2 years for the cohort born between 1830 and 1839, that increase is insufficient in accounting for such a sharp drop in fertility. (For age at first marriage, see note 23.) Our calculations of age-specific marital fertility rates are preliminary. They suggest a drop in fertility for women born after 1800: 22 percent for women thirty to thirty-four and just over 50 percent for those thirty-five to thirty-nine and forty to forty-five. We hope to refine these data and then apply to them Coate and Trussell's *m* to obtain a more precise measure of the possible presence of family limitation. In general, this sort of decline in fertility over age thirty-five is one indication of such limitation. So is the irreversibility of the trend to smaller family size, also found in this data.

42. Steckel, *The Economics of U.S. Slave and Southern White Fertility;* Clinton, *The Plantation Mistress;* Wyatt-Brown, *Southern Honor.*

43. Smith, "Family Limitation."

44. Ibid.

45. See, in particular, G. J. Barker-Benfield, *The Horrors of the Half-Known Life: Male Attitudes toward Women and Sexuality in Nineteenth-Century America* (New York, 1976), pt. 2. Barker-Benfield argues that nineteenth-century physicians were hostile to their female patients; hence, he believes, the medicalization of pregnancy and childbirth represented "the male drive to take control of women" (61). Analyses of the medicalization of pregnancy and childbirth that are more sympathetic to physicians and recognize the desire of at least some of them to alleviate feminine suffering are provided by Scholten, *Childbirth in American Society,* ch. 2, and Regina Markell Morantz-Sanchez, *Sympathy and*

Science: Women Physicians in American Medicine (New York, 1985), 26, 222–31. Both note as well that the medicalization of childbirth was associated with the professionalization of medicine. In her study of childbearing among the British aristocracy, Judith Schneid Lewis has found that women were the first to question the inevitability of maternal suffering. They, not their physicians, were the first to insist upon medical intervention in childbirth. Lewis, *In the Family Way: Childbearing in the British Aristocracy, 1760–1860* (New Brunswick, 1986). See also Martin Pernick's fascinating discussion of the use of anesthesia for childbirth in the nineteenth century. Because women were thought to be especially sensitive to pain, they were among those most often afforded anesthesia. Hence, the availability of relief from pain, including that associated with childbirth, depended upon the cultural assumption of feminine frailty. Pernick, *A Calculus of Suffering: Pain, Professionalism, and Anesthesia in Nineteenth-Century America* (New York, 1985), 149–54 passim.

46. Unpublished interview-based research by Sune Ackeman, Department of History, University of Umeå, Umeå, Sweden.

47. Although the demographic transition in the North may have preceded that in the South, the experience of women in the two regions may otherwise have been similar. In *The Adams Women,* Paul C. Nagel provides evidence from correspondence of a family of Massachusetts women of a pattern strikingly similar to that observed in Virginia. By the end of the eighteenth century, the Adams women were worrying, in letters to each other, about the burdens and dangers of repeated pregnancies. They cautioned and commiserated without providing specific advice about techniques for family limitation. (Nagel hypothesizes that the preferred method was absence from their husbands.) Not until well into the nineteenth century did men in the family voice the sorts of concerns that women had expressed for several decades (see, for example, 80, 96–97, 265–71). It was apparently only at (or after) this point that effective fertility limitation within marriage began in this context as well, suggesting a generational effect like that hypothesized for Virginia.

48. Wally Seccombe, *Weathering the Storm: Working-class Families from the Industrial Revolution to the Fertility Decline* (New York: Verso Press, 1993); see also J. Caldwell, "Demographic Change in Rural South India," *Population and Development Review* (1982): 689.

49. Kenneth A. Lockridge, *The Fertility Transition in Sweden: A Preliminary Look at Smaller Geographic Units, 1855–1890,* report no. 3 from the Demographic Data Base, University of Umeå, 0349–5132 (Umeå, Sweden, 1983), S-901 87.

50. As another recent approximation of this goal, see John Knodet, "Fertility Transition in Thailand: A Qualitative Analysis," *Population and Development Review* 10 (June 1984): 297–328.

5

Children in American Family Portraiture, 1670–1810

KARIN CALVERT

In 1670 three children of the Mason family, David, Joanna, and Abigail, posed for an unknown limner in Massachusetts (figure 5.1). As artists had always done, the painter emphasized those things that his patrons considered important. He focused on the faces and intricate costumes of the children by reducing the setting to a suggestion of tiled floor and a black void and by positioning his subjects across the very front of the canvas. Their rigid, full-length, and nearly full-frontal positions overlap one another so slightly that no detail of costume is lost. All three children display expensive white linen, lace, ribbons, and jewelry. Eight-year-old David wears the voluminous petticoat breeches, slashed sleeves, and shoulder-length hair that were then the height of adult fashion and carries the kid gloves and silver-handled walking stick of a gentleman. His hand-on-hip pose was commonly employed for adult men to suggest authority and elegance. His younger sisters, Joanna and Abigail, exhibit the costumes, hairstyles, and accessories popular with all women of their station. The portrait emphatically presents the sex and social status of its subjects. Their stiff postures, solemn expressions, and adult accouterments made the young Masons seem the very image of the seventeenth-century child as miniature adult. They suggest a social system in which the sexes and classes were clearly differentiated but age groups were not.

Although social and cultural historians have often used paintings such as this one for illustration and example, few have attempted to examine large numbers of these visual artifacts.[1] This essay is based on the study of 334 family portraits painted between 1670 and 1810.[2] These include 476 children—49 percent boys, 33 percent girls, and the remainder primarily infants and unclassified as to sex (table 5.1). Thirty-one percent of the children come from New England, 43 percent from the middle colonies or states, and 18 percent from the South, but the portraits exhibit no significant regional differences.

Figure 5.1. *The Mason Children: David, Joanna, and Abigail, 1670.* Attributed to the Freake-Gibbs painter, Massachusetts. Courtesy of the Fine Arts Museums of San Francisco. (Gift of Mr. and Mrs. John D. Rockefeller 3rd, 1979)

Such regional characteristics as existed in the seventeenth century consisted more of style than of substance. Early painters in New England practiced two-dimensional medieval limning, while those in the southern colonies imitated the Jacobean baroque style of portraiture. Even that distinction disappeared during the first half of the eighteenth century, due, in part, to the fact that artists traveled widely in search of commissions.

The study from which this essay is derived compares the presentation of children younger than seven, the age at which seventeenth-century boys customarily adopted adult clothing, with that of children aged seven to fourteen.[3] Because few American portraits of children date from before the mid-eighteenth century, all that could be located have been included in the data. Paintings from the second half of the century are sufficiently abundant, however, to justify a random selection of approximately one-third of those ex-

Table 5.1 Children in Portraits

	Boys		Girls		Sex Undetermined		Totals
1670–1689	3		6		1		10
1690–1709	5		2		2		9
1710–1729	12		7		4		23
1730–1749	27		26		8		61
1750–1769	43		33		14		90
1770–1789	47		30		21		98
1790–1809	98		53		35		185
	235	(49%)	157	(33%)	85	(18%)	476

amined.[4] Well over half of all the portraits date from the last four decades of the period under consideration. Because of the smaller number from the years before 1750, conclusions drawn from that portion of the evidence must be regarded as tentative.

This body of material yields significant insights into early American perceptions of family structure and the nature of childhood. It complements, and in some respects is superior to, literary evidence in that it reveals beliefs and attitudes—for example, about age, sex, social status, and intrafamilial relationships—that were so well understood and accepted that they were rarely verbalized.[5] Through collective study of portraits of children we may gain a fuller understanding of the cultural norms of family life, of variations within the norms, and of changes in values and attitudes over time.

In interpreting this material, one should remember that it is plainly biased as to social class. Early on, only the very affluent could afford to have their children's portraits painted. Itinerant and amateur artists became more numerous after about 1750, and decreasing costs brought portraiture within the reach of the middling sort, but at no period do we find representations of children of the lower classes.[6] In addition, it should be noted that the portraits are cultural constructs and therefore cannot be read as though they are photographs. A photograph captures a real moment in a real world, for photographers have only a limited ability to edit their work. They may select and pose subjects and add, rearrange, or remove objects, but no matter how contrived the scene, it represents a real moment in time. A painting, however, is the creation of an artist, who has nearly unlimited ability to alter or invent. Artists usually attempted to render a good likeness of the face of each subject but felt free to improve on costume or setting.[7]

Furthermore, because originality was not considered essential to a successful painting, artists were expected to build on the successes of their predecessors. Thus settings, props, costumes, and poses were often borrowed from other paintings or, more commonly, from the numerous European prints available after at least the mid-seventeenth century.[8] A print could be available in America within months of the completion of the original painting, and American artists were therefore able to keep abreast of the latest artistic fashions in London. Like their provincial English counterparts, however, colonial painters did not necessarily discard old traditions while embracing new ones but added the new forms to their repertoire to produce an art that reflected a composite of influences. For example, as a young artist John Singleton Copley relied on prints of works by Peter Lely and Godfrey Kneller half a century after the originals were created while at the same time employing a very up-to-date rococo palette.[9]

At the same time that American artists clung to the past, they adopted, or adapted from, the latest styles those elements of costume, pose, or setting that seemed appropriate for their purposes. American art was thus sensitive to and heavily influenced by the fashionable art of London but was never merely imitative. Artists also employed a set of stock conventions. A portrait of a baby with one shoe off, for example, did not represent an impulsive act of a particular infant but was rather standard piece of stage business. The painting of children could thus be a complex combination of reality, local or borrowed motifs, and imagination.

The connotations of certain objects have changed over the last three hundred years, making it easy to overlook or misinterpret the importance of what we see in the paintings. For example, the depiction of a seventeenth- or eighteenth-century gentleman in his dressing gown or nightcap was not an attempt at informality but a convention signifying a man of letters or artistic talents.[10] The cut of a wig or coat could identify a man's profession and social status.[11] For children, the shape of a collar or the presence of buttons were clear indications of sex, whereas wearing lace, velvet, and rosy pastels was not. Portraits, then, contained conventionalized visual idioms that we must learn to recognize and to distinguish from our own.

Psychological examination of the painted subject is always hazardous, because a painting is not a literal representation. A small child, for example, could be portrayed standing next to the mother rather than in her arms, not from any lack of maternal affection but because the pose was borrowed from a print of a Raphael Madonna and Child or one of Kneller's formal portraits of the English nobility.[12] Similarly, the stiffness of many portraits does not necessarily reflect a personal character trait. Sitting for a portrait was a time-consuming, often once-in-a-lifetime event, totally lacking the spontaneity of a modern snapshot. Ill-trained artists added to the illusion of coldness by awkward attempts to convey a subject's dignity and respectability. The result was less a portrayal of character than a composite of European motifs, accepted conventions, personal preferences of the sitters, and skill of the painter.[13]

Whatever fabrication and fancy an artist might employ, a portrait had to conform to the type of presentation considered appropriate for each sitter's age, sex, and social position. Because artists worked on commission, their portraits had to fit patrons' perception of themselves and their children.[14] A portrait was thus a visual representation of society's expectations, with the subject tidied up for public viewing. Precisely for that reason, a study of the accepted models is instructive. The formal costumes and stereotypical artifacts that appear in portraits served important emblematic and hierarchical functions. An artist described an individual's position in his or her world through the idioms of costume, prop, and pose. Such conventions gradually changed to reflect changes in social mores.

The image of the American family as depicted in portraits changed significantly between 1750 and 1770. Before 1750, portraits presented the family as having two complementary components, one dominant over the other. This dichotomy was expressed in a polarized vocabulary of artifacts and conventions. As the exemplary portrait of the Mason children suggests, only two basic forms of costume were available in the seventeenth century. One consisted of knee breeches, the other of ankle-length petticoats. The division, however, was not solely a sexual one. For his portrait at four-and-a-half years of age, Robert Gibbs (figure 5.2) wore petticoats and pinafore very similar to those of the Mason sisters.[15] Dress distinguished a dominant group of men and breeched boys from a subordinate group of women and children in petticoats. After about 1770, the image of the family became far more complex, albeit still hierarchical. A portrait of the last quarter of the eighteenth century could contain six separate types of family members, each distinguished by costume, artifacts, and conventions. The rather crude symbolism of the first century of this study that set breeched males apart from all other family members was replaced by an intricate pattern that more precisely indicated each individual's position in the family. This elaborate visual vocabulary appeared in nuclear family portraits that became common in America after 1770, suggesting a new emphasis on the family as a unit and a new fascination with the matrix of relationships within that unit.

Colonial portraiture commissioned from the mid-seventeenth to the mid-eighteenth century reveals a succession of changing fashions without any significant change in substance. Colonists fought the stigma of provincialism with a determination to stay abreast of the latest styles from London. However, the basic portrayal of the family remained essentially unchanged

Figure 5.2. *Robert Gibbs, Age Four and a Half.* Artist unknown, Massachusetts, 1670. (M. and M. Karolik Fund, courtesy, Museum of Fine Arts, Boston)

from 1670 to 1750. Thus, although the cut of a frock coat or the width of a petticoat would be adapted to prevailing fashion, the family remained polarized between the breeched leaders (and potential leaders) and their subordinates in petticoats.

Until the middle years of the eighteenth century in the Colonies, nonambulatory infants of both sexes were dressed in clouts (diapers) and a long petticoat that extended well below the feet.[16] A walking child was "short-coated" in petticoats reaching to the ankles. Nothing was worn under the petticoat so that the child could urinate on open ground. Small boys and girls alike wore petticoats; this garb, like the swaddling clothes of European infants, was a sign not of sex but of subordination and submission.[17]

It is therefore significant that female costume underwent only modest changes from childhood to adulthood. Because a girl would never rise above the subordinate position into which she was born, the costume of an adult woman remained essentially that of a toddler but with a few small variations. A little girl wore a bodice that laced up the back, which she would exchange when she was old enough to dress herself for one that fastened in front. She might wear a pair of hanging sleeves that looked like two wide ribbons suspended from the shoulders. These were the atrophied remnants of the false sleeves that had been popular in the fifteenth and sixteenth centuries. Adults had long since abandoned them, but they were retained for both boys and girls as a symbol of immaturity.[18] Essentially, a girl dressed like a woman, carried the same props, and assumed the same poses. If a girl could be viewed as a miniature adult, a grown woman could be viewed as a more advanced child. Subordination, femininity, and childishness were tightly intertwined.[19]

A boy, by contrast, would outgrow his subordinate position and take his place among ruling adult males. His development was underscored by changes in his costume. Even in infancy, however, boys were frequently distinguished from girls by details of dress. Only boys wore the large square collar, or falling band, that Robert Gibbs and David Mason display. The falling band made a costume of petticoats appear masculine to seventeenth-century eyes just as the color pink makes a toddler's overalls appear feminine today.

The metamorphosis of boy into man occurred as he gradually gave up childish and feminine artifacts and acquired dominant, masculine ones; the concepts of masculinity, maturity, and authority shared a visual vocabulary. Robert Gibbs, although not yet five, has already begun the transformation. His younger brother, one-and-a-half-year-old Henry, who appears in another portrait painted in the same year, is dressed in every detail like the Mason sisters except for his falling band.[20] He wears petticoats, pinafore, and bonnet, has coral jewelry, and carries a feminine prop. Robert also retains the short petticoat and pinafore but has given up the bonnet for an adult-male hairstyle. He carries a pair of gloves, a common male prop, and stands in the conventional hand-on-hip pose of masculine authority. No contemporary would have mistaken young Robert for a little girl, but he would have been recognized by his petticoats as still a member of the dependent class of women and children.

The dePeyster boy (figure 5.3) has progressed a step beyond Robert Gibbs. He wears a robe that closely resembles an adult's frock coat but falls to the ankles.[21] As Philippe Ariès has pointed out, the robe was the gown worn by all men in the Middle Ages.[22] When men abandoned it for breeches, it was retained for boys and students to signify their subordinate status. The American robe had the buttons, cuffs, and cut of a frock coat and was quite different from anything worn by women.[23] Nevertheless, it was still a skirt and hence a mark of a boy's immaturity and dependency.

Figure 5.3. *DePeyster Boy, with a Deer.* By an unidentified artist, ca. 1730–35. (© Collection of The New-York Historical Society)

By the age of six or seven, a boy was breeched, gave up petticoats forever, and dressed, like David Mason, as a little replica of adult men. This rite of passage marked the beginning of a period of training and preparation for manhood.[24] The junior status of boys in their mid-teens or younger can be read in portraiture, for artists commonly depicted breeched youths in conventional feminine poses, surrounded by a flutter of drapery (a device used for women's portraits) or holding a feminine prop. Boys of this age were never depicted with such standard male props as an account ledger, military baton, or Bible, which indicated occupation or achievement, although they did carry artifacts that symbolized masculinity and social status, such as gloves, a walking stick, or a sword. A third of the boys between the ages of seven and fourteen posed with a feminine prop such as fruit, flowers, or pets—a last tie to the subordinate class from which they were emerging.[25]

Before the middle of the eighteenth century, portraiture offered a very meager vocabulary with which to express childishness without resorting to feminine idioms. Except for hanging sleeves and the boy's robe, all articles of dress were miniature replicas of adult fashions. Portraits before 1750 contain no distinctive childish artifacts such as toys, children's furniture, or schoolbooks. The stock poses give no signs of play or playfulness, and the faces of children are as solemn as those of their elders. Childhood had no positive attributes of its own considered worthy of expression. A child was merely an adult in the making, and childhood, as a period of physical and spiritual vulnerability, was a deficiency to be overcome.[26]

As late as the mid-eighteenth century, women and children still dressed as members of the same subordinate group within the family. In 1753 Mrs. Henry Tucker sat for a portrait with her children, Nathaniel and Elizabeth (figure 5.4). Three-year-old Nathaniel, like his mother and older sister, wears the fashionable petticoat, bodice, and corset of the time.[27] The style of costume is quite different from that worn by the Mason and Gibbs children eighty years before, but the social implications remain the same. Nathaniel's sex is suggested only by the fact that he has given up his bonnet and appears bareheaded.

The mid-eighteenth-century family continued to place less emphasis on the development of daughters than on that of sons. Elizabeth Tucker's dress differs little from that of her mother and brother. In a portrait of 1750 (figure 5.5), Lucy Grymes, seven, is similarly dressed, while her brothers, aged two, three, and four, display three quite different stages in the recognized devel-

Figure 5.4. *Mrs. Henry Tucker and Children, Nathaniel and Elizabeth.* By Joseph Blackburn, South Carolina and Bermuda, n.d. (Courtesy of the Bermuda National Trust Collection)

Figure 5.5. *The Grymes Children: Lucy, John, Philip, and Charles.* Attributed to John Hesselius, Virginia, 1750. (Courtesy of the Virginia Historical Society)

opment of a boy. The artist portrayed Philip, aged four, as already an adult in every detail of dress, while his three-year-old brother John wears an ankle-length robe and carries, like his sister, a sprig of cherries.[28] The artist did not depict baby Charles, two, in a petticoat like his sister's, however, but shows him barefoot and wearing only a shift, wielding a toy pony whip and riding in a two-wheeled baby cart drawn by Philip.[29]

This portrayal of Charles Grymes marks an important break from artistic tradition. His costume and pose are startlingly informal and unrestricted, and the props relate specifically to his infancy. Furthermore, the artist expressed the youthfulness of the mature-looking Philip not with a feminine prop or pose but by a somewhat awkward attempt to show him playing with his little brother. The new elements of informality and playfulness, and the inclusion of childhood artifacts, had not appeared before in extant American portraiture.

Before 1750, a young boy's childhood symbolically ended at about the age of seven, when he adopted adult male dress. After mid-century, the costume and hairstyle of breeched boys differed in certain particulars from those of adult men. The introduction of an intermediate stage between childhood and maturity is apparent in the 1757 portrait of Mann Page, pictured at age eight with his sister, Elizabeth, six (figure 5.6). He wears breeches, frock coat, and fashionable hairstyle, but unlike Philip Grymes or David Mason, he is not a miniature adult. A grown man of fashion in 1757 would have powdered his hair or worn a wig and would have wrapped a white cravat about his throat. Mann, however, wears his hair quite innocent of powder, and, instead of a cravat, only the ruffle of his shirt fastened with a black ribbon shows above his coat. The modest alterations were less restrictive and more comfortable than cravat and wig. Boys over the age of seven were permitted a simplicity of dress denied adult males.[30] This appearance of a stage between childhood and adulthood became more striking after 1770 as the costumes of boys over seven underwent further modification.

Between 1750 and 1770, artists began to develop a new vocabulary to express the characteristics of childhood. They portrayed children as free from

Figure 5.6. *Mann Page and His Sister Elizabeth.* By John Wollaston, Virginia, ca. 1757. (Courtesy of the Virginia Historical Society)

some of the constraints of the fashionable, formal dress of adults. Less strik-ing are evidences of playfulness and informality. A few painters began to depict artifacts of childhood such as the baby cart of Charles Grymes and the doll of Elizabeth Page, but less than 10 percent of the children sampled between 1750 and 1770 were portrayed with such artifacts.[31]

Perceptions of the nature and duration of childhood during the last quar-ter of the eighteenth century changed drastically from those of the previous hundred years. Increased geographic mobility weakened patriarchal control in New England and encouraged greater reliance on relationships within the nuclear family. Lengthened life expectancy in the southern colonies fostered a more stable family life. The security that came with improved infant mor-tality rates, particularly in Maryland and Virginia, allowed parents to make strong emotional investments in their offspring. The growing affluence and increased leisure of the upper and upper-middle classes encouraged parents to indulge their children and enjoy their antics. Reflecting these trends, the portraits reveal changes in perceptions of children and principles of child-rearing along lines projected by John Locke, who stressed the natural inno-cence and nurturable potentialities of the young.[32]

Costume provides the leading signs of changing custom. The stiff cor-sets and bodices, high-heeled shoes, and restrictively tight sleeves of gowns and frock coats were abandoned. In their place, young children such as three-year-old Henry Tallmadge (pictured with his mother and year-old sister Maria in figure 5.7) wore loose, white muslin frocks and soft slippers.[33] The new frock represented a dramatic break with previous conventions of dress in America because it was quite different from the costume worn by adult women. Simpler, lighter, and looser than a woman's gown, it suggests great-er freedom, activity, and comfort for children. By distinguishing children from women and thus breaking the link between femininity and childish-ness, it visually announced that women and children were now viewed as distinct although still subordinate groups. The muslin frock also signified a greater emphasis on the development of a young girl, for she now had a cos-tume different from the one she would assume as an adult.[34] Her transition from one dress to the other marked her passage into maturity. The distinc-tions between women and children were further accented by the adoption of a new hairstyle worn by both boys and girls but not by either men or women. Until this period, children had adopted the adult hairstyle appro-priate to their sex as soon as their hair grew long enough to dress. Now, chil-dren of both sexes began to wear their hair loose to the shoulders and cut in bangs across the forehead (figures 5.7, 5.8, 5.9). This style identified the wearer as a member of a specific age group without reference to gender.

The breaking of the link between femininity and childishness meant that society could permit boys a greater sense of masculinity before they attained adulthood. Boys aged three to ten began wearing a new costume that was not like anything that had been worn before by adult men or women of the upper classes (table 5.2). Called a "skeleton suit," it consisted of long trousers and a short, attached jacket over a wide-collared shirt. William Smith Tallmadge wore the new style for his portrait in 1790 (figure 5.8), while his father posed in the traditional attire of breeches.[35] The skeleton suit was not an American innovation but appeared on young boys in English and European portraits at about the same time that it first appeared in America. Trousers were the common uniform of some subordinate classes of men, including laborers, sailors, and European peasants. A young boy's trousers therefore symbolized his subordination to the men of the family, but the vocabulary of submission was now borrowed from the dress of lower-class males rather

Figure 5.7. *Mrs. Benjamin Tallmadge and Children.* By Ralph Earl, Connecticut, ca. 1790. (Collection of the Litchfield Historical Society, Litchfield, Conn.)

Figure 5.8. *Colonel Benjamin Tallmadge and Son William.* By Ralph Earl, Connecticut, ca. 1790. (Collection of the Litchfield Historical Society, Litchfield, Conn.)

Figure 5.9. *The Angus Nickelson Family.* Attributed to Ralph Earl. New England, ca. 1790. (Gift of Robert L. Munson, courtesy of the Museum of Fine Arts, Springfield, Mass.)

Table 5.2. Boys' Costumes

	Number	Adult Female Petticoat	White Frock	Robe	Skeleton Suit	Modified Adult Male	Adult Male
Ages 0–7 years							
1670–1689	2	100%					
1690–1709	1			100%			
1710–1729	5	40		60			
1730–1749	8	13		62			25%
1750–1769	20	30		30	5%	30%	5
1770–1789	27		22%	7	37	27	7
1790–1809	64		20	5	33	19	3
Ages 7–14 years							
1670–1689	1						100
1690–1709	4						100
1710–1729	7						100
1730–1749	19						100
1750–1769	23					48	52
1770–1789	20					80	20
1790–1809	34				15	64	21

than that of upper-class women. Boys as young as three or four were dressed in skeleton suits, recognizing their masculinity long before they reached maturity. The new costume separated young boys from the mass of women, girls, and very small children in petticoats and placed them in a separate category. The skeleton suit drew equal attention to the wearer's age and sex, for it was worn neither by miniature men nor by asexual children but by boys.[36] It also divided the development of a boy into three clear stages: three or four years of infancy in frocks, about six years of boyhood in the skeleton suit, and another four or five years of youth in a modified adult costume.

After 1770, family groupings presented in portraiture changed markedly. Americans had always commissioned portraits of individuals, sibling groups, and mothers and children. Nuclear family portraits, however, were a different matter. No portrait of a nuclear family has yet to come to light from the years before 1730, and for the next forty years such portraits constituted fewer than 1 percent of those studied. By contrast, for the period from 1770 to 1810, nuclear family portraits make up 27 percent of the sample.[37] That figure may actually underrepresent the popularity of the new style, for some artists painted one portrait of the mother, youngest children, and daughters and another of the father and sons, to be hung side by side as in the case of the Tallmadge family. A third alternative involved a portrait of the mother and children and a companion piece of the father alone. Unfortunately, over the years many such companion portraits have been separated and are no longer recognized as parts of a set.

Whatever the form, nuclear family portraits increasingly became the composition of choice as families became more private and insular. One reason for this trend was the increased availability of painters capable of executing complex compositions. Numerous young men followed Benjamin West to England, where they were exposed to the expertly executed domestic scenes of such artists as George Stubbs and Arthur Devis. From the time of John Smibert's arrival in Newport, Rhode Island, in 1729, there had always been a few artists capable of group portraiture.[38] That they were rarely called on for large compositions suggests a lack of interest in that type of presentation. After 1770, nuclear family portraits were commissioned not only from professionally trained artists but also from provincial limners. The preferences of patrons were changing, and painters of all degrees of skill sought to comply.

Very rarely do portraits of this period include members of the extended family; one catches few anticipatory glimpses of the large, multigenerational groups so characteristic of Victorian paintings.[39] Rather, the family was depicted as consisting of one couple and their offspring. Typically, the portraits, commissioned while the family was still young, contain infants and small children. Although a handful show as many as six or seven children, the mean number is three. (That figure, however, should not be used as evidence of family size, for a portrait was often commissioned before the wife had ceased to bear children or after older children were sent away to school.) The 1790 painting of the Angus Nickelsons is exemplary of portraits of large nuclear families and of the conventions of such portraits (figure 5.9).

The scene is a comfortably appointed parlor or library. Previously, artists and patrons had preferred more grandiose, less realistic settings, usually involving a column, draperies, and garden vista. A growing preference for realistic interior settings—the family's natural habitat, as it were—was part of the new fashion. Another departure placed the father in intimate relations with one of his sons.[40] For at least a century, it had been conventional to portray the head of the house as provider; the shelves of account books, the desk, and the letters in hand attest to Angus Nickelson's standing as a prosperous businessman. Now portraits began to accent the paternal role as well, showing the father sharing with the mother in nurturing and protecting the children. Almost always we find the mother with the youngest child, and the father is usually with the youngest or second-youngest son but only rarely with a daughter unless the family had only daughters.

The Nickelsons' costumes indicate their positions and interrelationships. Should a family portrait of, say, 1690 ever come to light, it would depict no more than two visually distinct groups, one consisting of men and boys in knee breeches, the other of women and children in petticoats. The Nickelson family displays a more complex set of alignments. The sexes are plainly set apart by costume. All the females (and the infant) wear gowns; all the males wear pants. Hairstyles, however, divide the family by age. The children have bangs and shoulder-length hair, and the adults wear more complicated styles.

Six positions within the family hierarchy are defined by this vocabulary of costume and hairstyle. The most subordinate group consists of the baby and the little daughter dressed in the sexless white frocks of infancy and posed closest to their mother. The girl holds an open book, an allusion to childhood as a time of learning. The small boy leaning against his father's knee is younger than the daughter just mentioned, but his sex gives him the right to abandon the white frock at an earlier age in favor of the skeleton suit. He holds a very boyish prop, a toy drum. The wide, white collar of his shirt is modeled after the fashionable white kerchief that women wore, but nothing else about his dress, pose, or placement visually connects him with the world of women. His older brother poses in a transitional costume that combines the frock coat and waistcoat of manhood with the long trousers and hairstyle of childhood.[41] Like his younger sister, he grasps an open book. The next-eldest daughter, standing near the center, is also in a transitional phase of development.[42] Her gown is quite grown-up, but her hairstyle is that of a child. The two eldest daughters wear the formal, elaborate gowns and hairstyles of adults but without the matronly mobcap and wide kerchief that symbolize the mother's age and position. At the pinnacle of family hierarchy, Angus Nickelson himself appears in frock coat and knee breeches.

Toys had previously been included in only a handful of portraits; now they became quite popular. Between 1770 and 1810, thirty-one boys (21 percent of those sampled for that period) carry a toy, but only nine (11 percent) of the girls do. While artists portrayed boys with pony whips, pull-toys, drums, and the implements of games such as battledores, marbles, balls, hoops, and skittles, the toys of little girls are almost always dolls.[43] The few exceptions are either doll-oriented (doll clothes or furniture) or quiet games. Toys are thus sharply differentiated by sex. The only toy depicted with children of both sexes is a ball on a string, with which to amuse a pet dog. Toys of girls are domestic; they signify play of a quiet, even solitary kind. Those of boys suggest active, noisy games, outdoors and in groups. Another popular prop is the book, again with a sexual distinction: 23 percent of the boys but only 5 percent of the girls are shown holding or reading a book. Most girls, but very few boys, carry the traditional feminine emblems of fruit or flowers. In addition, children's furniture makes an appearance. Artists posed children in or near high chairs, small children's chairs, little wagons, and cradles, or they appropriated adult footstools as child-size seats. The toys, furniture, costumes, hairstyles, and informal or playful poses represent a visual lexicon for expressing the positive attributes of childhood. Not one but two perceptions of childhood, however, were evident during the last quarter of the eighteenth century. Childhood for boys was a time of active, boisterous play; for girls, an introduction to the domestic arts. Boys were permitted to be boys; girls were regarded as little women.

On the evidence of portraits, we may suggest that four major changes occurred in perceptions of the family between 1670 and the beginning of the nineteenth century. First, the length of visually expressed childhood doubled. In 1670 a boy wore petticoats for six or seven years before dressing as a man. Although not accepted as an adult at that age, he was viewed as an apprentice adult or an adult in the making. A girl of the seventeenth century passed almost imperceptibly from childhood into the world of adult women. Because she would never outgrow her subordinate status but only advance within it, only slight alterations in her gown at the age of seven or eight marked the entry into womanhood. After 1770, boys exchanged the frock for long trousers and then for a modified adult costume over a childhood that now lasted about fourteen years and was clearly divided into periods of infancy, boyhood, and youth. Girls also exchanged the frock for a modified adult costume, but childhood for them lasted about twelve years and was divided into only two stages, suggesting that girls were still seen as developing within a narrower range, their limitations set by nature.

Second, the number and composition of visually distinctive groups within the family changed twice during the second half of the eighteenth century. Until mid-century, portraiture recognized only a dominant group of men and breeched boys, who literally wore the pants, and a subordinate group of women and children in petticoats. Between 1750 and 1770, the dominant group split in two, and adolescent boys became a second subordinate subdivision. After 1770 the original subordinate group also split; a family portrait of that period could contain as many as six separate subgroups, each with its own vocabulary. The father still stood at the peak of the family hierarchy, but the hierarchy itself had become more complex.

Third, a vocabulary of childhood developed by the last quarter of the eighteenth century, breaking the link between femininity and childishness. The perception of childhood, as reflected in portraiture, became increasingly distinct and positive, with virtues, activities, and artifacts of its own. Art portrayed the new freedom accorded children and a new fondness for, or at least acceptance of, childish behavior. Significantly, women in the closing years of the century adopted the simple white empire dress based on the white muslin frock young girls had worn for thirty years. Soon thereafter, men assumed the long trousers that had previously been worn by their sons. For the first time in America, children set the fashion and adults followed. Before 1750, when the third and fourth decades of life were prized as the age of ability and power, there was no desire to emulate the fashions of callow youth, but by 1800 adults adopted forms of dress that had previously been reserved for the young. This by no means represented a general worshiping of youth. Rather, it indicated a lifting of the stigmatic perception of children as unfinished, imperfect adults. Soon after men began wearing trousers, boys were put into knee breeches (knickers) in order to maintain the distinction of age. Adult women also gained a more distinctive identity from the new acceptance of children expressed in portraiture. Children of the early eighteenth century dressed like miniature women, but it was also true that women dressed like grown-up children. With a new lexicon of simplified costumes for girls and special artifacts for children, much of the old feminine idiom became by default the exclusive property of the adult woman and therefore could be used to express both her sex and maturity.

Finally, a new interest in the nuclear family as a unit appeared in portraiture after 1770. An increasing percentage of patrons chose to have the whole family presented on one canvas. Such portraits, while fulfilling the traditional purposes of preserving likenesses and displaying worldly success, stressed the inner life of the family itself. Artists replaced conventional backgrounds of fantastic draperies and baroque gardens with personal domestic interiors and strove to demonstrate the relationships between family members and, to some extent, even the individuality of children. The rising demand for such pictures after the Revolution may be said to reflect the growing sense of the family as a unit sufficient unto itself.

Notes

This essay is reprinted, with minor editorial changes, from *William and Mary Quarterly* 39 (Jan. 1982): 87–113.

1. The most successful interpretations of portraiture as primary data have been made by Philips Ariès, *Centuries of Childhood: A Social History of Family Life,* trans. Robert Baldick (New York, 1962), and Philip Greven, *The Protestant Temperament: Patterns of Child-Rearing, Religious Experience and the Self in Early America* (New York, 1977). Others who have dealt with visual images as primary data include Stephen Brobeck, "Images of the Family: Portrait Paintings as Indices of American Family Culture, Structure and Behavior, 1730–1860," *Journal of Psychohistory* 5 (1977): 81–106, and Ilene H. Forsyth, "Chil-

dren in Early Medieval Art: Ninth through Twel[f]th Centuries," *Journal of Psychohistory* 4 (1976): 31–70.

2. The research from which this article is drawn covers nine hundred American portraits depicting 1,330 children and dating from 1670 to 1870. Three distinct periods in the perception of childhood in American emerge: 1670–1750, 1750–1830, and 1830–70.

3. Biographical data, including age, are available for slightly less than 50 percent of the children. The rest are assigned to age groups on the basis of physical appearance. A test with thirty children whose ages are known but were hidden for the purposes of the test resulted in an 80 percent accuracy rate in assigning children to age categories. Inevitably, some six-, seven-, and eight-year-olds have been misassigned. Because the age of seven as a dividing point is somewhat arbitrary, errors of a year should not affect the major conclusions.

4. In order to be eligible for selection, a painting had to reveal enough of the child so that type of costume and hairstyle could be determined. Once a painting was selected, all the children depicted in it were included in the study.

5. The search for nonverbalized social assumptions is perhaps best expressed by Ariès: "But how was I to discover, in the documents of the past, references to things which were too ordinary, too commonplace, too far removed from the memorable incident for contemporary writers to mention them?" *Centuries of Childhood,* 10.

6. Artists who painted for middle-class patrons included Joseph Badger, John Singleton Copley (during his early years), John Greenwood, Ralph Earl, John Durand, and Ammi Phillips.

7. Not all painters were skilled at capturing the individuality of each client. Robert Feke and John Wollaston were but two successful painters who relied on standard formulas to produce a face, especially for female subjects.

8. The use of European prints by American artists has been most thoroughly researched by Waldron Phoenix Belknap, Jr., *American Colonial Painting: Materials for a History* (Cambridge, 1959).

9. Copley's 1739 portrait of Jane Clark (Massachusetts Historical Society), for example, includes a costume and pose borrowed from a print after Godfrey Kneller's portrait of Lady Essex Mostyn (1680) yet employs the rococo palette of the 1730s.

10. See, for example, Joshua Reynolds's portrait of Sir Joseph Banks (Parham Park) and Charles Wilson Peale's portraits of Benjamin Rush (Henry Francis Du Pont Winterthur Museum, Wilmington, Del.) and Benjamin Franklin (Historical Society of Pennsylvania, Philadelphia).

11. For example, an early-eighteenth-century American parson's wig was parted in the center and fell in curls to just above the shoulders, while a doctor's or "physick's" wig replaced the curls with a fluffy, teased effect known as a "thatched" or "natty" bob. These and other categories of wigs are illustrated in Richard Corson, *Fashion in Hair: The First Five Thousand Years* (New York, 1965). The importance of a cuff is illustrated in John Smibert's 1729–31 portrait *Dean Berkeley and His Entourage* (Yale University Art Gallery, New Haven, Conn.), in which two men who worked with their hands, the artist and the secretary, wear the cuffless coats of artisans, whereas the intellectuals wear the deep cuffs of gentlemen.

12. See, for example, the Virginia portrait [artist unknown], *Mrs. William Goldsborough and Grandson* (ca. 1763), Maryland Historical Society, Baltimore, based on a print of Kneller's *Duchess of Ormonde and Earl of Ossory* (1693).

13. Examples of attempts at psychologizing portraits are found in Brobeck, "Images of the Family," and Rosamond Olmsted Humm, *Children in America: A Study of Images and Attitudes* (Atlanta, 1978), 16.

14. Only commissioned portraits are included in the study, except for a few portraits of the artists' own families that adhered to the same conventions as commissioned works. Anomalies never meant for public display, such as C. W. Peale's *Rachel Weeping* (Philadelphia Museum of Art), have been excluded. Paintings created for other purposes, such as Copley's portraits of Peter Pelham (Museum of Fine Arts, Boston) and Mary Warren [?] (Toledo Museum of Art) are not included because they are exhibition pieces.

15. Other portraits of young boys in petticoats were painted before 1750 and include: [artist unknown)], *Henry Gibbs* (1670, Massachusetts), in the collection of Mrs. David M. Giltiman; [artist unknown], *The Barclay Children* (ca. 1700, New York), Ten Eyck Powell Collection; Justus Engelhardt Kuhn, *The Frank Child* [misidentified as Elizabeth Frank], (ca. 1710, Maryland), Milwaukee Art Center; Justus Engelhardt Kuhn, *Ignatius Diggs* (1710, Maryland), Philip Carroll Collection; Francis Berkely, from John Smibert, *Dean Berkeley and His Entourage* (1729–31, Massachusetts), Yale University Art Gallery; [artist unknown], *Mrs. Mann Page and Her Son* (ca. 1745, Virginia), College of William and Mary; and Charles Bridges, *Mann Page* (ca. 1738, Virginia), College of William and Mary.

16. Representations of infants in long petticoats were painted before 1750 and are included in the following portraits by unknown artists: *Mrs. Freake and Baby Mary* (1674, Massachusetts), Worcester Art Museum, Worcester, Mass.; *The Barclay Children* (ca. 1700, New York), Ten Eyck Powell Collection; and *Mrs. Patteshall with Her Baby* (1764, Massachusetts), collection of Miss Isabella Curtis.

17. Greven persuasively demonstrates the concern in what he terms "evangelical" and "moderate" families for instilling submissiveness and obedience in their small children. He also argues that the years spent in gowns had a feminizing effect on young boys. Greven, *The Protestant Temperament*, 32–55, 151–91, 46.

18. The significance of hanging sleeves was first pointed out by Ariès, see *Centuries of Childhood*, 54–56.

19. Portraits of young girls of the period ending 1750 include: [artist unknown], *Alice Mason* (1670, Massachusetts), Adams National Historic Site, Quincy Mass.; [artist unknown], *Elizabeth Eggington* [?] (ca. 1680, Connecticut), Wadsworth Atheneum, Hartford, Conn.; [artist unknown], *Margaret Gibbs* (1670, Massachusetts), collection of Mrs. Alexander Quarrier Smith; [artist unknown], *Christina Ten Broek* (1720, New York), Mrs. Ledyard Cogswell Collection; Justus Englehardt Kuhn, *Eleanor Darnall* (1710, Maryland), Maryland Historical Society; [artist unknown], *Girl of the Schuyler Family* (ca. 1730, New York), collection of Mrs. W. Leland Thompson; [John Smibert], *Joanna and Elizabeth Perkins* (1749, Massachusetts), Paul M. Hamlen Collection; and [artist unknown], *Catherine Van Alstyne* (1732, New York), Albany Institute of History and Art.

20. [Artist unknown], *Henry Gibbs* (1670, Massachusetts), Mrs. David M. Giltiman Collection.

21. Other examples of boys wearing robes from portraits before 1750 are: [artist unknown], *Boy with Fawn* (ca. 1700, region unknown), collection of Edgar William and Bernice Chrysler Garbisch; [artist unknown], *The Barclay Children* (ca. 1700, New York), Ten Eyck Powell Collection; and Frederick Tellschaw, *Thomas Lodge* (1745, New York), New York Historical Society.

22. Ariès, *Centuries of Childhood*, 55–56.

23. The one major exception was the feminine riding habit, which, with a masculine tricorn hat and frock coat, expressed the horsewoman's mastery over her mount.

24. The distinction between adult and youth is ably demonstrated through conventional documentary sources by Ross W. Beales, Jr., "In Search of the Historical Child: Miniature Adulthood and Youth in Colonial New England," *American Quarterly* 27 (1975): 378–98.

25. Pre–1750 portraits of breeched boys holding feminine or childish props include the following paintings by unknown artists: *Pau de Wandelaer* (ca. 1725, New York), Albany Institute of History and Art (flowers); *Edward Jacquelin* (ca. 1722, Virginia), Virginia Museum of Fine Arts, Richmond (pets and drapery); *Jonathan Benham* (ca. 1710, region unknown), Garbisch Collection (pet and flower); *Edward Brodnax* (ca. 1720, Massachusetts), Virginia Museum of Fine Arts (pet); *Matthew Ten Eyck* (1733, New York), collection of Mrs. Frank H. Nowaczek (flower); *Adam Winnie* (ca. 1710, New York), Winterthur Museum (fruit); *John Van Cortlandt* (ca. 1730, New York), Brooklyn Museum (pet); and *Two Boys with Pets* (ca. 1730, region unknown), Garbisch Collection (pets, fruit, and flowers).

26. For discussions of childhood as a vulnerable period in which the child had to be forcibly adapted to parental authority see John Demos, *A Little Commonwealth: Family Life in Plymouth Colony* (New York, 1970), 131–45; and Greven, *The Protestant Temperament,* 32–43.

27. Other examples of boys wearing petticoats from portraits painted between 1750 and 1770 are: Jeremiah Theus, *Charles Cocran* (ca. 1754, Maryland), Museum of Early Southern Decorative Arts, Winston-Salem, N.C.; and C. W. Peale, *Child with a Toy Horse* (1768, Pennsylvania), Museum of Fine Arts, Houston. Portraits of little girls of the period include: John Wollaston, *Mrs. Perry and Her Daughter Anna* (ca. 1758, Pennsylvania), Philadelphia Museum of Art; Jeremiah Theus, *Sarah White* (1753, Maryland), Mrs. John Campbell White Collection; John Singleton Copley, *Two Sisters of Christopher Gore* (ca. 1755, Massachusetts), Gore Place, Waltham, Mass.; John Singleton Copley, *Mary and Elizabeth Royall* (1758, Massachusetts), Museum of Fine Arts, Boston; John Durand, *Catherine Beekman* (ca. 1768, New York), Beekman Family Association; Jeremiah Theus, *Peggy Warner* (ca. 1750, South Carolina), Telfair Academy of Arts and Sciences, Savannah, Ga.; and Joseph Blackburn, *The Four Children of Governor Saltonstall* (1762, Connecticut), New Haven Historical Society.

28. Examples of portraits of boys wearing robes from the period from 1750 to 1770 are: John Singleton Copley, *Boy of the Appleton-Greenleaf Family* (1755–58, Massachusetts), collection of Mr. and Mrs. J. H. Joynt; Joseph Badger, *Two Children* (1752, Massachusetts), Abby Aldrich Rockefeller Folk Art Collection, Williamsburg, Va.; John Singleton Copley, *Thomas Aston Coffin* (ca. 1759, Massachusetts), Munson Williams Proctor Institute, Utica, N.Y.; John Singleton Copley, *Brothers and Sisters of Christopher Gore* (1755, Massachusetts), Winterthur Museum; Joseph Badger, *Benjamin Badger* (ca. 1760, Massachusetts), Winterthur Museum; Joseph Badger, *James Badger* (ca. 1760, Massachusetts), Metropolitan Museum of Art; and William Williams, *The William Denting Family* (ca. 1750, New York), collection of Ettie Shippen.

29. Portraits of small children presented with similar informality of pose and dress include: [artist unknown], *Child in Blue* (ca. 1750, New England), Waldron Phoenix Belknap Collection; John Hesselius, *Gustavus Hesselius* (ca. 1767, Pennsylvania), Baltimore Museum of Art; and John Singleton Copley, *Mrs. Daniel Rea and Her Daughter* (1757,

Massachusetts), Butler Institute of American Art, Youngstown, Ohio. A few examples of portraits of mothers holding infants dressed only in a bit of drapery appeared earlier in the century. They lack the playfulness and informality of the Grymes baby and were probably based on European paintings of the Madonna and Child. A typical painting of this sort is John Smibert, *Mrs. Samuel Vetch and Child* (1732, Massachusetts), Museum of the City of New York.

30. Among portraits of breeched boys in modified adult dress between 1750 and 1770 are: John Singleton Copley, *Master Hancock* [?] (1758–59, Massachusetts), Alvan T. Fuller Collection; John Durand, *Robert Ray* (1765, New York), Museum of the City of New York; John Singleton Copley, *Jonathan Mountfort* (ca. 1753, Massachusetts), collection of Lendall Pitts; William Williams, *David Hall* (ca. 1750, New York), Winterthur Museum; and John Hesselius, *Charles Calvert* (1761, Maryland), Baltimore Museum of Art.

31. Toys and other childish artifacts are rare in English portraits before 1750. Occasionally, a portrait of a royal child contains a toy, an elaborate piece of children's furniture, or a fancy dress costume, but such anomalies had little or no effect on provincial portraiture and did not reflect popular views of the appropriate presentation of children. American portraits of children with toys of the period from 1750 to 1770 include: John Wollaston, *Mrs. Perry and Her Daughter Anna* (ca. 1758, Pennsylvania), Philadelphia Museum of Art (rattle); John Singleton Copley, *Master Hancock* [?] (1758–59, Massachusetts), Alvan T. Fuller Collection (battledore and shuttlecock); Joseph Badger, *Two Children* (1752, Massachusetts), Abby Aldrich Rockefeller Folk Art Collection (rattle); Joseph Badger, *John Joy, Jr.* (1758, Massachusetts), Maryland Historical Society (ball); John Singleton Copley, *Thomas Aston Coffin* (ca. 1758, Massachusetts), Munson Williams Proctor Institute (battledore and shuttlecock); John Wollaston, *Rebecca Calvert* (1754, Maryland), Baltimore Museum of Art (doll); and John Hesselius, *Charles Calvert* (1761, Maryland), Baltimore Museum of Art (toy drum).

32. For a discussion of the effect of mobility on the family, see Philip J. Greven, Jr., *Four Generations: Population, Land, and Family in Colonial Andover, Massachusetts* (Ithaca, 1970). The effect of changing demographic patterns on southern family life is discussed in Daniel Blake Smith, *Inside the Great House: Planter Family Life in Eighteenth-Century Chesapeake Society* (Ithaca, 1980), esp. 40–41, 282–85; see also James L. Axtell, ed., *The Educational Writings of John Locke* (Cambridge, 1968).

33. Portraits of small boys in frocks depicted in portraits dated after 1770 include: C. W. Peale, *The James Gittings Family* (ca. 1773, Maryland), Maryland Historical Society; Matthew Pratt, *William Randolph* (1773, Virginia), Colonial Williamsburg Foundation; C. W. Peale, *Mrs. Richard Tilgham and Sons* (1789, Maryland), Maryland Historical Society; Joseph Wright, *Self-Portrait of Artist and His Family* (1793, Pennsylvania), Pennsylvania Academy of Fine Arts; R. Earl, *Mrs. William Taylor and Son* (1790, Connecticut), Albright-Knox Art Gallery, Buffalo, N.Y.; James Earl, *Charlotte Rhoda and Moses Brown Ives* (1795, Rhode Island), collection of Mr. and Mrs. R. H. Ives Goddard; and John Brewster, Jr., *Francis O. Watts with Bird* (1805, New York or New England), New York State Historical Association, Cooperstown.

34. Examples of young girls in muslin frocks depicted in portraits after 1770 are: Henry Benbridge, *The Bulloch Family* (1776, Georgia), Georgia Historical Society, Savannah; C. W. Peale, *Peale Family Group* (1773, Pennsylvania), New-York Historical Society; [artist unknown], *Miss Proctor* (ca. 1775, Maryland), Harmon-Harwood House, Annapolis, Md.; Henry Benbridge, *The Morel Family* (1776, Georgia), National Portrait Gallery;

R. Earl, *Child with Pet Dog* (1776, region unknown), collection of I.B.M. Corporation, New York; and Ezra Ames, *Lucretia* (ca. 1800, New York), Albany Institute of History and Art.

35. Between 1770 and 1830, most small boys between the ages of three and ten wore trousers. During the 1830s, both boys and girls were put into knee-length dresses and long white trousers; both sexes had either cropped hair or long curls. The white trousers would later acquire the name *pantalettes* and be remembered as feminine attire, but at the time of their introduction they were worn by both sexes. The explicit purpose of the new costume was to blur sexual distinctions and preserve the innocence of children as long as possible. Although the costume fell from general fashion in the 1870s, some families continued to put dresses on little boys well into the twentieth century.

36. Among portraits of boys wearing skeleton suits are: R. Earl, *Mrs. William Moseley and Son Charles* (1789, Connecticut), Yale University Art Gallery; [artist unknown], *James Fitzgerald* (1785, Virginia), collection of Mrs. Walter Gray; C. W. Peale, *Mrs. Richard Tilgham and Sons* (1789, Maryland), Maryland Historical Society; [Brother of the Moravian Society], *Samuel and Sarah E. Franks* (1798, Pennsylvania), collection of Mrs. Harold B. Starkey; John Trumbull, *James Gore King* (1801, New York), Joseph Larocque Collection; John Trumbull, *John Vernet and Family* (1806, New York), Yale University Art Gallery; and John Brewster, Jr., *James Prince and Son William* (1802, Massachusetts), Historical Society of Old Newburyport.

37. Examples of nuclear family portraits after 1770 are: Edward Savage, *The Washington Family* (1789, Virginia), National Gallery of Art; Henry Benbridge, *The Bulloch Family* (1776, Georgia), Georgia Historical Society; C. W. Peale, *The James Gittings Family* (ca. 1773, Maryland), Maryland Historical Society; Henry Benbridge, *The Morel Family* (the father was later cut out of the portrait; 1776, Georgia), National Portrait Gallery; William Wilkie, *Nathan Hawley and Family* (1801, New York), Albany Institute of History and Art; and Ezra Ames, *The Fondey Family* (1803, New York), Albany Institute of History and Art.

38. Among them (in addition to John Smibert) were John Wollaston, Joseph Blackburn, and John Greenwood.

39. Some portraits of grandparents and grandchildren do exist. The most striking exception to the general form of the nuclear family portrait, however, is *The Peale Family Portrait* (1773) in the New-York Historical Society. In it, C. W. Peale has included himself, his wife and children, two of his brothers, his mother, and the children's nurse.

40. Other portraits after 1770 that depict an affectionate relationship between father and young son are: C. W. Peale, *The Goldsborough Family* (1789, Pennsylvania), Baltimore Museum of Art; R. Earl, *Family Portrait* (1804, Connecticut), Garbisch Collection; and [artist unknown], *The Colden Family* (1795, region unknown), Abby Aldrich Rockefeller Folk Art Collection. Portraits of fathers posed with young daughters include: James Peale, *Paul Ambrose Oliver and Daughter* (ca. 1800, Pennsylvania), collection of Mrs. Elizabeth Brownell; and C. W. Peale, *The Edward Lloyd Family* (1771, Maryland), Winterthur Museum.

41. Other portraits of boys in transitional costumes are: Joseph Badger, *Master Stephen Crossfield* (1775, Connecticut), Metropolitan Museum of Art; William Wilkie, *Nathaniel Hawley and Family* (1801, New York), Albany Institute of History and Art; John Singleton Copley, *Daniel Verplanck* (1771, Massachusetts), Metropolitan Museum of Art; C. W. Peale, *The Johnson Brothers* (ca. 1774, Maryland), Maryland Historical Society; Winthrop Chandler, *John Paine* (ca. 1780, Massachusetts), Worcester Art Museum; C. W. Peale, *Mrs.*

Isaac Hite and James Madison Hite, Jr. (1799, Maryland), Maryland Historical Society; and R. Earl, *William Carpenter* (1779, Connecticut), Worcester Art Museum.

42. Examples of portraits containing girls in transitional costumes are: [artist unknown], *Phoebe Denison* (1792, region unknown), National Gallery of Art; [artist unknown], *Matilda Denison* (1792, region unknown), collection of the descendants of Matilda Denison; and R. Earl, *John, Charlotte, and Nathaniel Taylor* (1796, Connecticut), C. Goodhue Huntington Collection.

43. Portraits depicting children with toys, books, or children's furniture include: Joseph Badger, *Master Stephen Crossfield* (1775, Massachusetts), Metropolitan Museum of Art (battledore and shuttlecock); Henry Benbridge, *The Bulloch Family* (1777, Georgia), Georgia Historical Society (book); Henry Dawkins, *The Burroughs Family* (1775, region unknown), Henry Shaw Newman Gallery (toy drum); [artist unknown], *Miss Proctor* (ca. 1780, Maryland), Hammond-Harwood House, Annapolis, Md. (doll); [artist unknown], *The Domino Girl* (ca. 1775, region unknown) Garbisch Collection (dominoes); John Wollaston, *Mother and Daughters* (ca. 1770, New York), Montclair Museum, Montclair, N.J. (doll); Rembrandt Peale, *Franklin Peale* (1808, Maryland), Pennsylvania Academy of Fine Arts (bubble pipe); [artist unknown], *Sally Ann Bond and Her Brother* (ca. 1805, region unknown), Colonial Williamsburg Foundation (doll, toy wagon, and child's chair); and [artist unknown], *The Sargent Family* (ca. 1800, region unknown), National Gallery of Art (ball).

PART 3

The Nineteenth Century

By the middle of the nineteenth century, increasing privatization, individualization, specialization, and reassignment of attributes to its members had transformed the family ideal from a little kingdom into a miniature republic where a "true woman" presided over the domestic sphere. To her ascribed innate spiritual and moral superiority were added the equally natural attributes of purity, beauty, sensitivity, emotionalism, and cooperativeness, which allowed her to rise above the base aggression, competition, rationality, and materialism of the commercial world in which the father operated and to which he was supposedly suited by his masculine nature.

As the "republican mother" became the "true woman," her responsibilities within the domestic sphere evolved and became a mirror image of the father's growing involvement in the public sphere of business on whose financial returns the family had become dependent. Fathers became more dissociated from routine household activities. The focus of the family shifted from producing goods and services to socializing children who could succeed in a commercial society. Both spheres were necessary and equal, albeit separate, in fulfilling this familial task.

The separation of spheres was reflected in the changing physical configuration of the family dwelling. Homes that were large, afforded more privacy for family members, and separated from the outside world became the ideal. The boundaries between public and private hardened so the softer virtues of women could be protected and the character of children molded into the proper form, free from outside influences. Dwellings were set back from public thoroughfares, surrounded by yards and fences, encased in porches, and centered around interior entrance hallways that served as buffer zones between the private family and visitors from the outside. The appearance of streetcars allowed some to escape to suburbs, not only away from the noise, violence, and unsavory influences of cities but also farther from kinfolk. This trend fueled an even greater separation of the domestic and public spheres.

Seminole family in dugout. (LC-801095-D4-72410, courtesy of the Library of Congress)

Southern family. (Sarah Daniel Collection, courtesy of Special Collections, Mitchell Memorial Library, Mississippi State University)

In Grandfather Juan Romero's room. (LC-USW3T01-17809-E, courtesy of the Library of Congress)

Mississippi family. (Sarah Neilson Collection, courtesy of Special Collections, Mitchell Memorial Library, Mississippi State University)

Accompanying this assignment of separate and complimentary spheres for which mother and father were responsible was the appearance of a rough equality in the internal dynamics of the family. Wifely submission to a husband was still expected and economic and political inequality persisted in the public realm, but within her family, a wife's ascribed nature and duties accorded her some status and respect. Society now conceived of marriage as more of a freely chosen contract and based on mutual affection.

That new context, however, also provided husbands with a psychological weapon with which to assert authority over wives. By maligning the character of his spouse, Robert Griswold contends (chapter 6), a middle-class husband could inflict a telling blow to her sense of self-worth and her reputation and standing in the community. Griswold deftly charts the response of courts and legislatures to these subtle attacks and the concomitant rise of the concept of mental cruelty.

This more egalitarian and privatized middle-class family model served as the ideal if not the practice within rural areas as well. Southern planter families, for instance, subscribed to the nature of a "true woman" but not to the practice of operating private and nuclear families within a separate domestic sphere under her direction. Planters remained in their homes and maintained some control over the more hierarchical society that the institution of slavery seemed to require in the interest of order. Long visits from members of extended kin networks both diluted the nuclear nature of the family and its privacy.

Non-Europeans in America selectively adapted those facets of middle-class families that complimented their traditional arrangements or proved especially valuable to them. In his classic *Death and Rebirth of the Seneca*, Anthony Wallace argued that once the Seneca had accepted the need to reform their society along European lines, their families became nuclear in structure and in residence. On closer inspection, however, Nancy Shoemaker has discovered that as late as 1900 the Seneca lived in complex households that resembled the residential patterns of the longhouses of the eighteenth century (chapter 7). Such "log-house" households were complex, and most who lived in the newer log houses were related to each other. Her findings underline the need to approach the study of families with a finely honed lens that can discern subtleties of change and persistence as subcultures creatively adjusted to the dominant culture.

In chapter 8, Peggy Pascoe graphically portrays the "gender systems in conflict" that played out between traditional Chinese marriage practices and those of late-nineteenth- and early-twentieth-century America. Although both were patriarchal, the total powerlessness of the Chinese wife until she became a mother-in-law was mitigated in American marriages by the moral authority residing in the wife from the outset of the marriage. Chinese immigrant women, and even men, recognized the practical advantages that middle-class, companionate marriages could offer and were willing to accept the conversion efforts and moral supervision by San Francisco Presbyterian Home Mission matrons who could arrange and police such marriages. In this case, the Home Mission filled the role of absent kin as supporters of domestic arrangements radically different from those in China because they granted some individual autonomy to a "true woman" of any ethnic background.

6

Law, Sex, Cruelty, and Divorce in Victorian America, 1840–1900

ROBERT L. GRISWOLD

In 1874, Justice John M. Scott of the Illinois Supreme Court described the damage a husband inflicted upon his wife by his false allegations of infidelity: "Cruel treatment does not always consist of actual violence. There are words of false accusation that inflict deeper anguish than physical injuries to the person—more enduring and lacerating to the wounded spirit of a gentle woman, than actual violence to the person, though severe."[1] Sometime later, the Oregon Supreme Court addressed the same issue and underscored the dire impact such accusations had on innocent wives: "To charge a woman, in the presence and hearing of others, with the commission of the crime of adultery, is to render her subject to the gross insults of lustful men who may hear and believe the rumor, which, whether true or false, tends to rob her of her good name, alienate her friends and acquaintances, and deprive her of their society and companionship."[2] Both justices then proceeded in each case to sunder the bonds of matrimony, the very foundation of Victorian social order.

Their decisions, although restrained and wedded to precedent, nevertheless directly or obliquely reflected contemporary debates over family stability, marital cruelty, conceptions of manhood, woman's place in nineteenth-century society, and Victorian attitudes about sexuality. The two judges were no more immune to these issues than anyone else—probably less so, for they held the responsibility of reconciling middle-class hopes for family cohesion with changing sex roles, marital expectations, and legal definitions of domestic cruelty.[3] These two appellate decisions, supplemented by about a hundred others dealing with sexual cruelty, thus provide a way to investigate the complicated connections among Victorian ideology, sexual behavior, and acceptable marital conduct. If judges were not always consistent, if they sometimes favored marital indissolubility over freedom from objectionable marriage

bonds and at other times preferred the reverse, their ambivalence or incon-
sistency surely reflected wider confusion over the competing claims of family life and personal autonomy.[4] Despite this ambivalence, judges during the
nineteenth century nevertheless grew more sensitive to the issue of sexual
cruelty and more willing to break a marriage when either spouse, especially
husbands, offended the sexual sensibilities of their mate.

The history of sexual cruelty and divorce is inextricably linked to the
interrelated histories of the meaning of marriage in general and matrimonial cruelty in particular. In the century after 1750, middle-class family life
increasingly became the realm of affection, mutuality, expression, and sentiment. Although the economic aspects of marriage did not vanish—romantic marriages, in fact, obscured the fundamental economic dependence of
wageless wives upon breadwinning husbands—the growing emphasis on
compassionate love shifted the balance of marital motivation away from
instrumental concerns and toward matters of the heart. As part of this development, gender ideals changed. For women, the emergence of domestic
ideology, the ideology of passionlessness, and the apotheosis of motherhood
inflated their moral and spiritual standing while simultaneously identifying
them ever more closely with a separate female sphere centered in the home.
For men, compassionate family relations included the traditional requirement that husbands support their wives economically—now increasingly in
a location removed from the home—and new demands that they respect their
mates' moral superiority, control their sexual urges, and make a more profound psychological commitment to their wives and children.[5]

This shifting balance in the meaning of marriage brought more rather
than less marital discord. Changes in sex roles and family life prompted thousands of Americans to demand more of their marriages than ever before.
When expectations did not meet with reality, many of these same Americans
sought relief in divorce court. By today's standards, the figures on divorce in
the late nineteenth and early twentieth centuries are quite low, but they
seemed alarmingly high to contemporaries. From 1867 to 1886, U.S. courts
granted 328,716 divorces; in the next twenty years, the number jumped to
945,625, far outstripping the proportionate rise in population. At the center
of this increase was a giant rise in the number of cases on the grounds of
cruelty. From 1867 to 1906, wives received 218,520 divorces because of cruelty, and husbands received 39,300. Next to nonsupport, cruelty cases rose more
sharply than cases based on any other cause in these years. Comparing the
years 1902–6 with 1867–71, divorces granted to wives on the ground of cruelty jumped 960 percent; to husbands, 1,610 percent. Between 1867 and 1871,
18 percent of divorces granted to wives were on the ground of cruelty; that

figure for the years 1902–6 was 29 percent. The same comparison for husbands reveals a jump from 4 percent to 12.5 percent.[6]

The surge in divorces brought on the ground of cruelty suggests a transforming marital relationship. Couples quite clearly expected more of marriage than ever before and showed an increasing willingness to use the courts for redress, a point especially true for women, who received more than 80 percent of divorces on the ground of cruelty. Whether guilty of physical or more subtle forms of psychological abuse, almost a quarter of a million husbands found themselves successfully accused of matrimonial cruelty between 1867 and 1906. Pressed by these changing ideas about marriage, jurists after midcentury expanded the legal definition of marital cruelty to embrace behavior once considered endurable, albeit unfortunate. No longer did American courts insist on violence or threats of violence to prove cruelty sufficient for a divorce. Inspired in part by a new disposition toward sexual epithets and sexual excesses, jurists began to find mental torment sufficiently cruel to warrant the breakup of a marriage. Helped by vague statutes and equally vague but flexible appellate decisions, husbands, and especially wives, found in cruelty complaints a convenient repository for their marital discontents.

The transformation of the legal definition of marital cruelty was a slow process that took the better part of a century to accomplish. Until the 1840s, American interpretations of matrimonial cruelty remained closely aligned with English theories. All English libels for separation on the ground of cruelty included actual violence, and not until the landmark case of *Evans v. Evans* in 1790 were threats of violence and a "reasonable apprehension of bodily hurt" deemed sufficient to justify legal separation.[7] This narrow definition underlay the statutory laws that appeared in the new American states in the late eighteenth and early nineteenth centuries. Unlike England, which technically had no absolute divorce, however, some American states granted absolute divorces on the ground of cruelty. For example, New Hampshire laws included cruelty as a ground for absolute divorce in 1791, Vermont and Rhode Island in 1798, Ohio in 1804, Kentucky in 1809 (to the wife only), Pennsylvania in 1815 (to the wife only and in 1854 to both the wife and husband), Delaware and Michigan in 1832, Iowa in 1839, Texas in 1841, and Kansas in 1855.[8] Other states, especially in the South, passed laws that permitted legal separations for cruel behavior but continued to limit grounds for absolute divorces to adultery or, in some cases, to incurable impotency, confinement in a penitentiary, premarital pregnancy by someone other than the groom, or desertion. By 1886 only six states did not grant an absolute divorce on the ground of cruelty.[9]

Not until the 1840s did American judges draw away from the English insistence on violence or threats of violence as the basis for a partial or total divorce.[10] This reluctance stemmed from the belief that individual happiness was less important than social order and that instrumental aspects of marriage should take precedence over emotional matters. Certainly, cruelty did not warrant a divorce simply because such behavior caused unhappiness or signified the absence of love.[11] The family unit was far too important to be dissolved for such capricious reasons; better to endure bickering, coldness, and insensitivity than to threaten the foundation of society.[12]

Yet after 1850, faults and slippages developed within this traditional legal landscape. The granite of conservative doctrine began to crack ever so slowly as new views of family life, sexuality, the female psyche, and manhood emerged.[13] Although courts continued to insist that only "grave and weighty" reasons warranted legal dissolution of a marriage, the definition of "grave and weighty" expanded to include behavior that posed a serious threat to the health of the spouse yet offered no physical violence or even threat of such violence. By the late nineteenth century, even the emphasis on bodily health disappeared in some states as jurists began accepting mental cruelty as a justifiable ground for divorce.[14]

One area that figured prominently in jurists' deliberations about cruelty was sexuality, specifically sexual epithets, sexual excesses, and sexual deprivation. The first two played key roles in prompting more expansive definitions of matrimonial cruelty that redounded to woman's benefit; the third revealed that jurists were as yet unwilling to see sexual satisfaction as essential to marriage. To jurists, companionate family relations did not necessarily include mutually satisfactory sexual relations. Although a husband's sexual epithets or excessive carnal demands became divorceable offenses, sexual deprivation by either party did not.

SEXUAL EPITHETS, SOCIAL CHANGE, AND THE TRANSFORMATION OF MATRIMONIAL CRUELTY

As the meaning of marriage in the nineteenth century shifted from a less instrumental to a more affective basis, and as the status of women within the home rose, the image of an uncontrollable, brutish husband falsely impeaching the sexual fidelity of his innocent, passionless wife troubled the Victorian conscience. Although there is no direct evidence that the use of such epithets was increasing in frequency, husbands could not have been oblivious to the realization that such accusations could cause overwhelming pain. What better way to wound a wife than to challenge her fidelity to prevailing conceptions of sexual decorum?[15] If such accusations went unchallenged, a wife stood to lose not only her sexual reputation but also any claim to respect. Although the risks for a woman seeking a divorce were great—what she gained in peace of mind she might lose due to social ostracism and economic vulnerability—thousands found the prospect of new dependencies less troubling than the prospect of remaining with a man who defiled all that gave meaning to nineteenth-century marriage. Against the backdrop of these moral and ideological changes in family life and womanhood, American courts began to acknowledge that a husband's false allegations of adultery justified a divorce. In short, legal leverage shifted in directions more favorable to women.[16]

Sexual epithets had not always possessed such power. Reflecting older English interpretations of cruelty and traditional views of marriage, an 1845 Connecticut decision deplored the husband's "vulgar, obscene, and harsh" epithets and his false allegations of adultery but found them insufficient for divorce unaccompanied by acts of actual menace or violence. Although his jealousy caused her great sorrow and prompted pity, "The law furnishes no remedy for conduct like this. It may be intolerable, but [it] is not intolerable cruelty."[17] So, too, the Missouri Supreme Court in 1847 made a similar argument and worried that "too great a facility in obtaining divorces is exceedingly injurious to the good morals and happiness of domestic life." How, the court asked, could mere words qualify as cruelty without some scale or standard of refinement for estimating the degree of offense to female sensibilities?[18] In fact, courts repeatedly stumbled over the difficulty of assessing the impact of cruel behavior on women of different social classes; most jurisdictions, however, agreed that a refined, sensitive woman could endure less cruelty than a woman of "coarse" or "rough" background.[19]

After the 1840s, false allegations of adultery began to carry increasing weight in divorce suits. More traditionally inclined courts insisted that false adultery allegations must also create fears of bodily harm or actual damage to health to be sufficient for a divorce, but a divorce was at least possible. Others suggested that such allegations, accompanied by even the slightest threat of personal violence, met statutory definitions of cruelty, for only a husband consumed by hatred—and hence a physical threat to his wife— would make such charges. A third group of interpretations emphasized that such accusations, if made publicly, exposed wives to "the contempt of the world and the insults and assaults of the worst of mankind." The courts' fear that predatory, lascivious males might stalk and victimize their innocent, unjustly accused wives reveals Victorian suspicions, shared by conservatives and feminists alike, of male sexual aggression. Finally, some courts underscored the mental suffering caused by such accusations or, in states recognizing indignities as a ground for separation or divorce, the fact that false adultery accusations "make life burdensome" and the "discharge of marital obligations impossible."[20] The new perspectives on sexual epithets came about in large part because of changing judicial attitudes about the nature of family life.

Although statutory laws, the interpretation of such laws, and the analyses of precedent varied from state to state, judges in mid-century sexual cruelty cases began offering less traditional definitions of the family that reflected long-developing changes in courtship, romance, and child-rearing. In so doing, they acknowledged that personal happiness and a woman's claim to sexual self-respect outweighed traditional commitments to marital stability. In 1854 the Indiana Supreme Court delineated this modern view of the family by noting that marriage was not simply a physical or sensual relation but a bond that ideally promoted "social happiness and mental enjoyments." Moreover, people's social, moral, and intellectual natures subjected them to both pain and pleasure, and "if they can be wounded and healed, as well as the physical part, with accompanying suffering and delight, then, we think, that conduct which produces perpetual sorrow, although physical food be not withheld, may well be classed as cruel, and entitle the sufferer to relief." The court added that cold neglect "has sent broken-hearted to the grave hundreds of wives, where the dagger, poison, and purposed starvation have sent one."[21] Likewise, the Kansas Supreme Court in 1883 criticized older interpretations for "taking too low and sensual a view of the marriage relation. . . . The tendency of modern thought," Justice Daniel M. Valentine added, "is to elevate the marriage relation and place it upon a higher plane, and to consider it as a mental and spiritual relation, as well as physical relation."[22]

Although state courts continued to struggle with the weight of traditional doctrine, and not all jurisdictions embraced such modern interpretations of the family and marital misconduct, enough did so by 1895 to inspire legal commentator William Nelson to concoct a zoological metaphor to describe modern marriage: "Marriage is not, in our time, regarded as the imprisonment of two beasts in a cage for the purpose of breeding, to be separated, if they quarrel, only when the weaker languishes in fear. It is an intellectual and spiritual union for the happiness and welfare of the parties, for nurturing and training of children under the most favorable circumstances, for the promotion of health, virtue, and morality of the parties and their children, and for the preservation of their homes."[23] Emphasizing the companionate aspects of modern marriages, these decisions helped to heighten the emphasis on individual fulfillment within marriage and to make possible the shift to broader definitions of cruelty.

In addition, a more complex view of human emotion and physical health after mid-century promoted a more expansive view of cruelty. Concurring with doctors', domestic moralists', and popular writers' assertions that American women were by nature frail, sensitive, nervous, and subject to a host of "female complaints," judges increasingly recognized that physical well-being could be injured by behavior far more subtle than physical blows.[24] Such was the argument in an often-cited case from Pennsylvania in 1849. After reviewing earlier English cases, the court reiterated the view that mere insults did not justify divorce, that marital stability was necessary for social order, and that couples must practice forbearance when problems arose. Judge Edward King followed these hoary truisms, however, by staking out new ground. Surely, he argued, violence or threats of violence were not the only behavior that threatened a spouse's health: "Again a husband may, by a course of humiliating insults and annoyances, practiced in the various forms which ingenious malice could readily devise, eventually destroy the life or health of his wife, although such conduct may be unaccompanied by violence, positive or threatened." He added that the court's concern should be with the consequences of the cruel behavior not its particular shape and that "whatever form marital ill-treatment assumes, if a continuity of it involves the life or health of the wife, it is legal cruelty."[25]

The shape of cruelty, as jurists began to recognize, could take a myriad of forms, but what gave an especially sharp edge to sexual epithets was not only the redefinition of family life and female health underway in the nineteenth century but also, and more important, the contradiction between such calumnies and the image of female sexual passionlessness that had taken root in the late eighteenth and early nineteenth centuries. Inspired largely by the rise of evangelical religion and an oblique facet of the ideology of domesticity, passionlessness was both a prescription for women and a critique of male licentiousness. By inflating women's moral standing and downplaying their sexual characterization, the male and female architects of this ideology transformed sexual thought. Men were now the more carnal sex, women the more spiritual gender; men were the sexual predators, women the victims; men were in need of sexual reeducation, women in need of respect and protection.[26]

It was an ideology, as Nancy Cott has noted, that offered women a way to assert control in sexual matters, to inflate their moral stature, and to create homosocial solidarity among women; moreover, it was an ideology that legitimated female efforts to control the sexual behavior of men. Secure in the knowledge that females occupied the high moral ground, women found in the ideology of passionlessness a set of assumptions and a vocabulary to check traditional male prerogatives as well as justification for organized efforts to defend themselves against male transgressions of female purity. In prescriptive literature, domestic fiction, and temperance, religious, and sexual purity campaigns, women (and some men) set forth a new standard of manhood that asked of men greater psychological commitment to their wives and children. The new man—kind, affectionate, and attuned to his wife's sensitivity and refinement—respected and even deferred to her keener domestic, religious, and moral judgment. To do otherwise, to treat her as a menial or, worse, to impeach her sexual integrity and thereby expose her to the lascivious desires of undomesticated men, branded the husband a social deviant undeserving of the benefits of marital life.[27]

This interplay between the ideology of female passionlessness and the fear of male licentiousness gave rise in the years after 1830 to a variety of female reform groups and a blizzard of literature intent on controlling male sexual behavior. Although feminists after 1860 began to attack passionlessness—they decried both the medical community's efforts to establish a somatic rather than a spiritual basis for the ideology and the confusion of sexual passionlessness with prudery—the belief in Victorian women's sexual indifference only slowly receded, and not before American jurists had incorporated the assumptions of Victorian sexual ideology into legal interpretations of marital cruelty.

In conjunction with changing conceptions of family life and female health, such assumptions moved many courts after mid-century away from the insistence that marital stability take precedence over individual happiness. Writing in 1883, for example, the Texas Supreme Court left no doubt that malicious accusations of infidelity had the power to destroy a wife's life. After noting that some states did not accept the false charge of unchastity against the wife as a ground for divorce whereas others found it almost sufficient, the judge boldly stated that Texas courts found it not an *almost* but an *altogether* sufficient ground: "And why should it not be so held? What are wounds to the person as compared with those that affect the mind? The former may be healed; the latter endure for a life-time. Of all the treasures cherished by a woman, her reputation for chastity is the dearest. 'It is the immediate jewel of her soul'; and when an attempt is made by her husband, who should be her protector, to rob her of it; cruelty has reached its utmost limit."[28]

False accusations of adultery not only degraded wives and rendered happiness unobtainable but also heightened female vulnerability to lustful men, a vulnerability that obsessed those reformers who hoped to channel male sexual energy into more constructive pursuits. Men, viewed as predatory, needed control, and both social reformers and feminists hoped to furnish the institutions, the moral instruction, the social pressure, and the laws necessary to end male sexual aggressiveness and female sexual vulnerability. Reformers hung their hopes on "white life" campaigns in the Women's Christian Temperance Union, on antiprostitution, antipornography, and anticontraception campaigns, and on proper moral instruction of husbands and sons by mothers and wives. Feminists adopted some of these strategies and in the three decades after the Civil War also pursued a far-reaching effort to reduce the frequency of crimes against women. Fornication, seduction, visits to prostitutes, adultery, connubial lust, rape, and incest—these and other manifestations of aggressive male sexual behavior and the double standard came under attack as feminists tried to protect women victimized by men.[29] The concern about false allegations of adultery should be seen in the context of these reform efforts.

When a husband falsely accused his wife of adultery, he not only defiled her reputation but also increased her vulnerability to sexually profligate, unreconstructed males. Such a husband became, in short, a deviant. In 1880 the Wisconsin high court, for example, chided a husband for failing to protect his wife's honor from the advances of a hired man. Worse yet, when the husband found the hired man crying by the roadside because his attempt to have sex with his employer's wife had failed, the husband took the man home and paid him his back wages before dismissing him. Such perverse solicitousness did not go unnoticed, "for surely no husband with the feelings of a man, and who entertained for his wife proper love and affection," wrote the judge, "could but resent in some way such a deadly insult and indignity offered to his wife."[30]

The hired hand, despite his abject failure in this instance, represented the uncontrolled male lust that so troubled Victorians. The asymmetry of nineteenth-century sexuality meant that good husbands protected pure wives; deviant husbands exposed their good wives to the lascivious desires of untamed men. A decision in the Texas Supreme Court in 1884 illustrated this dynamic. The judge first argued that a husband must protect his wife's reputation from the "imputations and aspersions of others"; not to do so branded the husband "a poltroon," worthy of universal contempt. But when the husband went further, when he falsely disgraced and degraded his wife, cruelty reached its peak, for she now stood exposed "to the contempt of the world and the insults and assaults of the worst of mankind."[31] When a husband impeached his wife's chastity, the protector became the assailant and she became "subject to the gross insults of lustful men who may hear and believe the rumor."[32] Judges, for their part, increasingly recognized the saliency of sexual complaints in cruelty suits, thereby expanding the range of legally unacceptable male behavior.

Despite the difficulty of defining marital cruelty, something of a rough consensus developed after the 1850s. Most American courts accepted some variant of the argument that cruelty could indeed occur without violence or threats of violence, but the behavior must somehow impair the health of the wronged spouse.[33] By the last quarter of the nineteenth century, an even more expansive interpretation of cruelty challenged this consensus as some judicial interpretations and even statutory laws began to recognize the reality of mental cruelty free from observable impact upon the body. It was, of course, a perilous step. Physical cruelty, or threats thereof, was more tangible than the slipperiness of mental cruelty, for how could the courts, as the famous English jurist Lord Stowell asked in 1790, "gauge the quantum of injury done and felt" to women of different temperaments and social backgrounds? How could marital stability—so crucial to social order—be maintained if something so vague as mental cruelty was permitted? Nevertheless, several states explicitly included "mental cruelty" as a ground for divorce, and other states passed laws permitting divorces when "indignities, excesses, or outrages" rendered living conditions intolerable or made "the discharge of marital obligations" impossible.[34] Still, the issue remained clouded, and most jurisdictions insisted that mental cruelty—like false allegations of adultery—be shown to cause physical harm before a divorce could be granted. Therefore the secure divorce ground continued to maintain some connection between verbal cruelty and the declining personal health of the wife.

Courts were far less certain about the status of men unfairly accused of adultery. Some states recognized no distinction. Nevada and Michigan shared the Oregon court's opinion: "If either party to the marriage contract falsely charge the other with the commission of the crime of adultery, such false accusation is a sufficient cause for divorce."[35] Other states, however, quite clearly discriminated against men. The reluctance to grant divorces in such cases likely stemmed in part from the judges' awareness of the devastating consequences for a woman if she were the unsuccessful defendant in a divorce suit. Without hope of alimony, faced with the possibility of loss of child custody, and confronted by a job market that had little room for her, the guilty wife in such a case faced a perilous future indeed.

In addition to such paternalistic, protective considerations, there were other reasons why judges were reluctant to grant husbands a divorce when falsely accused of adultery. Despite increasing psychological demands made upon husbands over the course of the nineteenth century, despite the fact that restraint, sexual fidelity, and emotional commitment comprised elements of proper manhood as well as womanhood, some states maintained that the damage inflicted upon men by false adultery allegations paled compared to the harm done to women. The Texas Supreme Court, for example, found the male psyche far less vulnerable to malicious accusations of infidelity. In 1886 the court averred that a wife's false allegations did not endanger her husband's life, limb, or health, nor did they cause him mental anguish. Indeed, the court clearly supported a double standard: "Taking the gravity of the offense when made against the wife with the comparative levity of it when against the husband, we are of opinion that the mere charge of adultery on the part of the husband made by the wife, though the charge be often repeated and be false, is not, under our laws, a sufficient ground for divorce."[36]

No, this issue was peculiarly women's. Although changing family values prompted both husbands and wives to take advantage of less restrictive definitions of cruelty, women likely benefited more than men from these changes. Courts found the female psyche, not the male, especially vulnerable to false charges of sexual impurity and men, more than women, far more likely to make such charges. The burden of fidelity fell upon both women and men but more heavily upon women, a sexual asymmetry that increased women's power to break free of insensitive, hateful men.

The heightened legal significance given to sexual aspersions suggests a broader paradox: More companionate marital relations increased a wife's vulnerability to psychological abuse but simultaneously stimulated transformations in legal thinking especially helpful to women. Given changing definitions of gender and family relationships, women may well have expected more psychologically from their marriages than men. Unlike men who divided their time between home and work, nineteenth-century middle-class housewives invested almost all of their emotions and energies into their family relationships. When an insensitive husband cruelly assaulted his wife's sexual fidelity, her entire life might well be ruined unless she could end the marriage and start anew. Even if we acknowledge that many late-nineteenth-century cruelty suits were consensual rather than adversarial in nature (a point made by legal historian Lawrence Friedman), wives likely gained more than husbands from this development.[37] As the patriarchal fiction of marital unity slowly gave way to the recognition that two individuals made up a marriage, wives no longer had to suffer at the hands of cruel, domineering husbands. Mutually miserable couples could now find legal redress by filing a "consensual" cruelty petition.

In addition to freeing wives from psychologically oppressive husbands, new definitions of cruelty signified a legal redefinition of family power relationships. The inflation of women's moral standing and the redefinition of family life brought women—bereft of most other forms of power—the leverage to expect and even demand higher standards of treatment from their husbands. A modicum of kindness and material support were no longer enough. Husbands now had to build relationships that were not only economically secure but also morally, psychologically, and emotionally fulfilling.[38] Such, at least, was the message to the white middle class, a message that had special meaning for husbands. For the ideal to become a reality, husbands had to give up the traditional prerogatives of patriarchy, for no truly companionate marriage could take root in the soil of domestic oppression. Some husbands willingly gave up such prerogatives in return for a higher degree of emotional companionship; others were more reluctant, a reluctance reflected both in increasing divorce rates and in a variety of female reform groups that sought to change male behavior.

The changing significance of false allegations of adultery symbolized this transformation in a rather dramatic way. The legal meaning of what had always been a damning epithet clearly changed under the impact of new ideas about family life and gender ideals. Men, of course, could ignore these developments and castigate their wives unmercifully, but if they did so, they took the chance of encountering a judiciary increasingly disposed to more expansive definitions of matrimonial cruelty and a wife increasingly willing to file for a divorce. Wives, after all, received 85 percent of the burgeoning number of divorces granted on the ground of cruelty, a fact all the more remarkable in light of the difficulties unmarried women faced in the nineteenth century. With few economic opportunities available and alimony virtually nonexistent, an unmarried woman, especially if she had children, encountered an uninviting world once she left the home of her husband. Yet statistics suggest that thousands of women found the risks worth the trouble; a life of economic dependence or poverty may have been bad, but life with an abusive husband was worse.

DIVORCE LAW AND THE REGULATION OF SEXUAL BEHAVIOR

Although false charges of adultery were the most common type of sexual abuse, they were by no means the only form. When spouses complained of too much or too little sex, jurists had to struggle not with character defamation but with the more complicated problem of regulating sex within marriage. They were not alone. Moralists, ministers, physicians, feminists, freelovers, and utopians all offered contradictory ideas about regulating marital sex, but only judges had to decide exactly what constituted deviant sexual behavior sufficient to dissolve a marriage. Conservative middle-class social thinkers and religious utopians might counsel abstinence while others advocated male control, but judges had to consider sexual behavior in light of legal precedent, their commitment to stable families, and their belief in personal autonomy.[39] Complicating the matter was the lack of consensus about sex in general. Was it a drain on one's vital systems or an expression of intense, even spiritual affection between a husband and wife? Were sexual desires something that men could barely control and that women should scarcely recognize, or were such desires for both genders healthy and natural?[40]

Answers to these questions varied, but almost all agreed that marriage properly disciplined, regulated, and channeled sexuality to a socially desirable end: procreation. Although medical opinion remained divided on the question of female sexuality and some feminists insisted that women had sexual desires equal to men (health reformer Mary Gove Nichols claimed in 1854, for example, that "a healthy and loving woman is impelled to material union as surely, often as strongly, as man. . . . The apathy of the sexual instinct is caused by the enslaved and unhealthy condition in which she lives"), many American husbands and wives surely subscribed to the belief that the ideal woman had little interest in sex. The emphasis on passionlessness had become the reigning orthodoxy by 1850. The ideology was not necessarily antifemale; wives, hopeful of inflating their moral standing, controlling male sexual aggression, and limiting their fertility, had their own reasons for supporting the ideal of female passionlessness. Even writers who recognized the importance of sexual expression to women underscored the necessity of restraining male lust and establishing sexual relations based on mutuality.[41]

That emphasis on sexual restraint did not bode well for husbands who had sex with their wives despite the wives' protestations. Just as nineteenth-century sexual ideology increased the legal impact of false allegations of adultery, the same ideas subjected husbands' sexual behavior to new standards of judgment. Sexual restraint within marriage became the goal, restraint that would, in the hopes of moralists like Henry Wright and William Alcott, direct marriage away from sensuality and toward spirituality.[42] Certainly, no truly companionate relationship could develop if a husband disregarded his wife's sexual desires. Husbands did not have an unlimited right to their wives' bodies, a point made by conservative moralists, voluntary motherhood advocates, and progressive feminists. All agreed that husbands' sexual control would enhance women's autonomy, promote good health, and establish marriages based on mutuality not coercion. Such ideas ultimately led to the formation of various organized efforts to control sexuality by increasing the age of sexual consent and eliminating prostitution and the double standard.

These campaigns converged with other efforts to control male aggression and violence within the family. In the 1860s, feminists like Elizabeth Cady

Stanton and Susan B. Anthony linked crimes against women—bigamy, seduction, wife-beating, rape, incest, and pornography—to male sexual privilege and aggression. Only when husbands stopped treating wives as property and adhered to a single standard of sexual morality, argued Stanton and
Anthony, would such outrages end. In the short run, divorce must be made
more accessible to women; in the long run, marriage must become a true
spiritual, emotional, and physical partnership that guaranteed a wife's right
to say no to her husband's sexual advances.[43] In the 1870s, conservative feminists like Lucy Stone and Henry Blackwell also turned attention to crimes
against women and, like Stanton and Anthony, hoped that social purity campaigns would foster male continence and end brutality toward women. Three
times, Stone proposed legislation to protect wives from husbands' assaults;
three times, her bill failed. Frustrated by these failures, Stone turned in the
mid–1880s to supporting the establishment of a whipping post for wife-beaters and, when that failed, to suffrage as the panacea for domestic violence.[44]
Victoria Woodhull's bold declaration in 1873 that she "would rather be the
labor slave of a master, with his whip cracking continually about my ears than
the forced sexual slave of any man a single hour" expressed in extreme form
the sentiments of less radical women as they joined the battle to tame male
sexuality.[45]

Although jurists' personal reactions to these reform efforts cannot be
gleaned from the case reports, their decisions reflected a growing belief that
the control of male sexuality within marriage was within the regulatory powers of the state. At a time of unparalleled debate on male and female sexuality, fertility control, and the need for male sexual control, jurists after the Civil
War had to decide what composed acceptable marital sexual misconduct
sufficient to justify a divorce. Legal confusion regarding the general definition of a cruelty compounded their problems as did changing conceptions
of family life and gender roles. Finally, the fact that millions of American
couples evidently cooperated on sexual matters—witness the dramatic decline in nineteenth-century fertility—likely intensified judges' difficulty in
reconciling their desire to keep families together with their hope of protecting women's right to sexual self-possession.

Two important cases involving sexually abusive husbands reveal the resolution of this issue in favor of marital stability. In 1845 the Connecticut Supreme Court of Errors excused Daniel Shaw's sexual indulgence, not because
his wife failed to tell him that his sexual demands endangered her health (she
had done so) but because he supposedly did not know that his behavior actually harmed her health. (The court determined that it did so.) Not willing
to stop with ignorance as an excuse, the court added words that later judges

would reject and feminists and purity reformers would surely deplore. Acknowledging that she had indeed informed her husband of the danger his behavior posed to her health, the court asked, "But are we to allow nothing to the innocent opinions of a man mad with jealousy? Are we to allow nothing to the frailty of human nature, excited by passion? Are we to couple an act of this kind with an act where a violent blow was given, which must greatly injure or endanger, and which was so intended?"[46] No, the court inferred, such issues had to be taken into consideration, and in this case the judges decided that his jealousy, uncontrollable passion, and ignorance of his wife's real condition undercut her allegations of cruelty. Therefore, they dismissed her suit.

The difficulties purity reformers and feminists faced in redefining and controlling male sexual behavior appeared even more tellingly in an 1876 New Jersey case. The wife, Abigail English, received a separation in chancery court on the basis of her husband's "gross abuse of marital rights." Despite her affliction with a uterine disease that made intercourse painful, he insisted on having sex every night, sometimes two or three times, and used force when she resisted. Somehow enduring two years of such abuse, she finally left her husband and moved to her father's home. After considering the evidence, the lower court granted her a separation on the ground that his behavior rendered it "unsafe for her, under existing circumstances, to cohabit with him or to be under his dominion or control."[47]

Several months later, the case appeared on appeal in the New Jersey Court of Errors and Appeals. The high court began by reaffirming the importance of family stability and then chipped away at her case by drawing on the testimony of a doctor who averred that although Abigail did indeed suffer pain during intercourse, "a large proportion of married women assent under exactly those circumstances." The judge followed that cheerless view of marital sex with a brief history of the couple's married life, emphasizing how they had overcome class and religious differences to establish a marriage friends and relatives characterized as "remarkably affectionate." But the deciding point was the judge's attitude. His wife's departure, wrote the judge, left John English miserable, remorseful, and "willing to make any reasonable concessions if she will return." Tender letters, entreaties to ministers, Christmas presents for the children, and promises of self-denial and forbearance all impressed the court with the husband's contrition and desire to reunite his family. Convinced that John posed no further threat to Abigail, the court dismissed her suit but warned her husband that a resumption of his past transgressions would bring a permanent separation.[48] Faced with a choice between preserving a marriage or chastising a husband for sexual incontinence, the New Jersey court chose the former on the ground that the husband, filled with guilt and properly repentant, no longer threatened his wife, That decision came despite the fact that he answered her protestations with a chilling reply: "You have stood it before and you will stand it again; you know I cannot help it."[49]

Such were the legal attitudes that purity reformers, feminists, and voluntary motherhood advocates strove to overcome in the late nineteenth century. For all of its traditionalism, however, the case involving Abigail and John English was less hostile to women than the Connecticut case of 1845. In the earlier case, the court excused the husband's actions because of his passion, jealousy, and ignorance. In the latter decision, the court emphasized not only the husband's ignorance but also his affection, contrition, and fervent desire to reunite his family. Despite the decision against Abigail English, the court hinted at the kind of reasoning that would prompt later American courts to grant divorces on such grounds. John English's behavior had run badly afoul of Victorian attitudes about male sexual control and female sexual vulnerability. He had also trampled upon mid-century attitudes about the importance of family relations built upon domestic morality and mutual respect. Given the enormity of these transgressions, the court in no way excused his sexual profligacy. What it did do, however, was to accept John's promises of reform. He had shown, to the court's satisfaction, his new allegiance to the companionate ideal. He was properly repentant, he loved his wife and children, he was brokenhearted without their company, and he would control his lust. At least in 1876, such promises prompted the New Jersey court to give the marriage one more chance. The adherence to the traditional reluctance to break up families, however, did not stop the court from warning John that a resumption of improper behavior would bring a permanent separation. In essence, the court placed John English on notice—curb his sexual aggression, control his passion, or face the consequences of state intervention in his family life.

Courts could not long sustain such reasoning in the face of widespread sentiment that men needed to control their sexual impulses. That sentiment developed largely as a corollary to the ideology of domesticity, and although not all women accepted some of the assumptions of domesticity (feminists, for example, criticized the identification of women with the home), most women, whatever their political persuasion, agreed that restraining male sexual aggression was a laudable goal. This consensus, in turn, prompted a reevaluation of cruelty cases involving sexual incontinence more favorable to reformers hoping to check male lust by redefining the nature of manhood.

The decision that best illustrates the shift in sentiment on this issue came in a Connecticut case of 1891. Emily Mayhew's successful lower-court suit alleged that her husband insisted on sex despite his knowledge that such behavior undermined her health. In considering his appeal, the high court began by admitting that "what may or may not constitute intolerable cruelty by a husband towards his wife in the exercise of the marital rights is a difficult and delicate question." After that truism, the court moved well beyond the decision rendered by the same court almost fifty years earlier in *Shaw v. Shaw.* Now the court underscored not husbandly passion and jealousy as an explanation and excuse for uncontrolled sexuality but rather the importance of mutual rights and duties regarding sex. Although not endorsing the feminist contention that wives alone decide when intercourse occurs, the court certainly emphasized that cooperation and reciprocity lay at the heart of sexual relationships. Marital sex, opined the court, required "the duty of forbearance on the part of the husband at the reasonable request of the wife, as well as the duty of submission on the part of the wife at the reasonable request of the husband."[50]

Despite the Victorian diction—husbands were the sexual aggressors, wives the submissive partners—the court emphasized that control, reasonable requests, and cooperation govern sexual relations. This emphasis on mutuality also appeared in the court's emphatic declaration that men's forbearance was as important as women's "reasonable" submission in regulating sexuality: "Any decision of what constitutes intolerable cruelty in these matters that should leave out of consideration the duty of the husband and look only to the duty of the wife, would be manifestly erroneous."[51] Wives had duties but so, too, did husbands; past interpretations of cruelty, implied the court, had placed too much emphasis on wifely responsibilities and not enough on husbandly forbearance. That courts were moving, by the end of the nineteenth century, to correct that imbalance suggests that the efforts to promote female autonomy and alter the meaning of manhood within the family were bearing fruit.

The regulation of excessive sexuality was one thing; sexual indifference was quite another. Husbands and wives who charged that their mates' refusal to have sexual relations justified a divorce received little sympathy and no legal redress in court. Time after time, judges insisted that the absence of sex constituted neither cruelty nor desertion. Although such behavior was lamentable, it did not warrant the breakup of a family. The ideal Victorian family, after all, was built on moral and emotional commitment and sexual restraint. Gross, insensitive sexual indulgence clearly violated the tenets of Victorian sexual ideology, and justices responded by subsuming such behavior under the rubric of matrimonial cruelty. An unwillingness to have sex, on the contrary, was simply an overzealous extension of mainstream Victorian thought.

Marriage involved love, affection, respect, economic support, child-rearing, and, yes, carefully regulated sexual relations that led to procreation and, for a few progressives, a spiritual union of husband and wife. The cultural meaning given to sexual control within the compassionate family, therefore, worked against the interest of husbands and wives dissatisfied with their spouse's unwillingness to have sex.

Although it is perhaps noteworthy that litigants considered sexual denial sufficiently grave to include in divorce suits, judges believed otherwise. To their minds, sex was an important part of the marriage relationship but not essential for the perpetuation of the conjugal bond.[52] In 1891 the Illinois Supreme Court, for example, first alluded to legal commentator Joel Prentiss Bishop's claim that denial of sex for two years constituted desertion and then brusquely swept aside that view as one not "sustained by well considered authorities." Such a claim rested on the assumption that sexual intercourse was "the central element of marriage to which the rest is but ancillary," but the judges rejected such an emphasis: "We think that the willful desertion here referred to was intended to mean the abnegation of all the duties of the marital relation, and not one alone."[53]

The New Jersey Court of Chancery eloquently expressed the assumptions behind such findings in an 1894 decision dismissing a husband's desertion allegations. After twenty years of marriage, the wife in this case withdrew to the front room and insisted that she would never sleep with her husband again. She continued to care for their rooms, however, and the couple continued to eat together and to consult about their two daughters away at school. This continued interaction typified to the court the many elements that made up the marital bond: "It would, I think, degrade the marriage relation," wrote the New Jersey judge, "to hold that it is abandoned when sexual intercourse ceases. The lawfulness of that intercourse is perhaps a prominent and distinguishing feature of married life, but it is not the sum and all of it." Marriage involved far more than a physical bond. It was a relationship that also satisfied emotional, psychological, and day-to-day needs and deserved to continue even in the absence of sexual relations: "The higher sentiment and duty of unity of life, interest, sympathy, and companionship have an important place in it, and the thousand ministrations to the physical comforts of the twain by each in his or her own sphere, in consideration of the marriage obligation and without thought of pecuniary recompense, fill it up. These latter factors may possibly, to some extent, exist in other relations of life, but not in completeness. They are all necessary to the perfect marriage relation."[54] That emphasis on the reciprocity, mutuality, and multifunctional character of marriage, in combination with the general interest in promoting marital stability and controlling sexuality, sorely circumscribed the power of divorce complaints based on sexual disinterest. In a culture obsessed with fear of sexual excess, cries of sexual deprivation received little sympathy.

Even the avoidance of sex to limit fertility did not constitute legal cruelty of desertion. Motherhood certainly was a key element of nineteenth-century womanhood, but so, too, was women's growing right to control their fertility, a right that left husbands with little recourse when wives refused sex in order to avoid pregnancy. Surely, as scholars have suggested, the great fertility decline in the nineteenth century came not without considerable cooperation on the part of couples, but divorce evidence offers hints that marital tension may have accompanied this demographic earthquake as well. Against a husband's claims to the contrary, an 1866 Pennsylvania decision asserted that a wife's refusal to have sex, and her simultaneous declaration that she would have no children, did not comprise cruelty.[55] The next year, the Supreme Court of Massachusetts likewise rejected Jonathan Southwick's claim that his wife deserted him when she withdrew from his bedroom in 1861 because he had permitted their eldest son to enlist in the Union Army. Despite her bold assertion that she "didn't intend to have any more boys for Mr. Southwick to send to the war," that she "had no love for him," and that she was now "nothing but a boarder," the court insisted that legal desertion was more encompassing than denial of sex and that it involved the cessation of cohabitation and abnegation of all the duties and obligations of marriage.[56] In short, refusing sex was wrong, but it was not a divorceable wrong. It was not cruelty because cruelty must threaten bodily health, and it was also not desertion because the marriage bond involved far more than sex.[57]

In fact, a mate's concern for his or her own health might well outweigh the duty to perform sexually. While Julia Disborough charged her husband with cruelty, she included among her allegations the fact that her sixty-seven-year-old husband refused to have sex with her. He defended himself by claiming that intercourse threatened his health, a point the New Jersey Court of Chancery evidently found convincing because it dismissed her cruelty suit in 1893. Although Victorian suspicions of sex made it difficult to prove that its absence caused bodily injury, these same suspicions, as this case reveals, meant that courts were ready to accept the idea that indulgence might threaten one's health. After all, how could courts chastise Isaiah Disborough for practicing, albeit perhaps to excess, the kind of sexual control that was the hope of feminists and purity reformers in the late nineteenth century?[58] If he carried it to extreme, they were extremes with which the court could live.

The decisions on sex and marital cruelty after mid-century reflected a wider nineteenth-century debate on the meaning of family and gender. Jurists in these years found themselves poised between two eras, forced to reconcile older, traditional views of marriage—a product of the patriarchal world of the common law—with newer assumptions about family life and sex roles so determinedly pressed by domestic moralists and reformers. Their resolution of this conflict in terms more favorable to divorce-seekers—especially to female petitioners—reflects two important developments. First, it reflects the power of changing family and gender ideals to change traditional legal assumptions about the virtual indissolubility of marriage. The contradictions within domesticity—itself an ideology of social order—heightened the very breakdown in family stability so feared by domestic theorists. The celebration of women's moral stature, the valorizing of women's domestic contributions, the assertion that women had a right to control sexuality and fertility, the emphasis on female sexual purity, and the insistence that men soften their patriarchal grip—all of these corollaries of domesticity increased the likelihood of marital dissolution.

Second, jurists' increasing willingness to grant divorces represents a facet of what historian Michael Grossberg has called nineteenth-century "judicial patriarchy."[59] No matter how much religious leaders agitated for uniform divorce laws and tougher legal restrictions on divorce, no matter how much conservative state legislators tinkered with statutory laws, jurists continued to grant divorces to the small army of petitioners who sought an end to their marital woes. In doing so, judges not only staked out new powers for the bench—they were the ones who gave legal meaning to vague statutory language—but also expanded the powers of the state to protect weaker members of the family who were physically or psychologically harmed by stronger members. Most of the time, that meant legal intervention to protect wives, an intervention that eroded male patriarchy and simultaneously increased the discretionary powers of the judicial patriarchy.

Jurists gained such discretionary power by capitalizing on suspicions directed toward both the power of traditional patriarchs—now suspect within the context of nineteenth-century family and gender ideals—and the power of statutory regulation, power suspect because of wider suspicions about centralized government authority in general. As the "primary domestic-relations agents of the expanding republican state," trial and appellate judges in divorce trials (as in other areas of family law) were uniquely situated to examine domestic relations on a case-by-case basis. Only judges, not distant legislators, had the ability to assess a couple's situation, listen to the testimony, weigh the facts, and then grant or withhold a divorce. This power, "an expression of the nation's persistent localism," meant that jurists, pushed by changing cultural currents, interpreted and reinterpreted the meaning of unacceptable marital behavior, and they did so in a way that expanded the judiciary's protection of weaker family members.[60] Cruel treatment, once deemed merely unfortunate but insufficient for divorce, became acceptable as a basis for a divorce suit. Injury to the body and the psyche appeared possible without direct physical violence. By the end of the century, increasing numbers of jurisdictions even found "mental cruelty" sufficiently harmful to justify a divorce.

Sexual cruelty played a crucial role in legitimating this expanded conception of cruelty. Family life provided the terrain on which passionless, domesticated women encountered the insensitivity of carnal, undomesticated men, and out of this encounter between Victorian symbols of virtue and vice came a new definition of marital cruelty. What could be more cruel, judges asked, than for a husband to question falsely the fidelity of his wife or to insist on sex against her wishes? As an answer, judges moved to protect wronged women who had upheld their domestic responsibilities; in so doing, jurists substituted one form of patriarchal protection for another. Quite clearly, divorce law had become a part of the domain of sexual politics, part of the multifaceted struggle over definitions of gender and the regulation of family life and sexuality.

This struggle not only broadened and redefined legal conceptions of marital cruelty but it also helped set the stage for the "divorce crisis" at the turn of the century. Confident that their cruelty petitions would receive sympathetic treatment in most American courts, thousands of late-nineteenth- and early-twentieth-century Americans petitioned for divorce. The upward trend continued until the Great Depression, fueled by changes in family life produced by urbanization, increased leisure and consumption, a cult of youth, and heightened marital sexual expectations. Paradoxically, the expanded conceptions of cruelty that owed so much to the assumptions of nineteenth-century domesticity were even more appropriate to the culture of the twentieth century as domesticity began to crumble and a heightened emphasis on personal autonomy and individual fulfillment began to take shape.[61]

From a late-twentieth-century viewpoint, it is tempting to assess the legal developments discussed in this essay in much the same way contemporary proponents did—that is, as the triumph of "advanced civilization" over the "barbarism of the past." And this perspective may have made sense to the husband who found himself legally yoked to a cruel, ill-tempered, insensitive wife or, more commonly, to the woman publicly humiliated by her husband or forced against her wishes to have sexual intercourse. Yet we should not forget that divorce for women was still a perilous step. What a wife gained in peace of mind or physical well-being she may have lost because of social ostracism and economic vulnerability. In a society with so few economic options for women, divorce meant not general liberation but the advent of different dependencies. The fact that thousands of women were willing to take such a step illustrates how powerfully new conceptions of family and gender resonated in the lives of late-nineteenth-century Americans.

Notes

This essay is reprinted, with minor editorial changes, from the *American Quarterly* 38 (Winter 1986): 721–45.

1. *Farnham v. Farnham, 73 Illinois Reports* 500 (1874).

2. *Crow v. Crow, 29 Oregon Reports* 394 (1896).

3. Although the historical literature on women and domestic violence is quite slim, three provocative articles by Elizabeth Pleck have begun to examine the issue: "Feminist Responses to 'Crimes against Women,' 1868–1896," *Signs* 8 (Spring 1983): 451–70; "The Whipping Post for Wife Beaters," in *Essays on the Family and Historical Change,* ed. Leslie P. Much and Gary Stark (College Station, 1983), 127–49; and "Wife-Beating in Nineteenth-Century America," *Victimology* 4 (Fall 1979): 62–74. Jane T. Censer explores the expansion of legal definitions of marital cruelty in the antebellum South in "'Smiling through Her Tears': Ante-Bellum Southern Women and Divorce," *American Journal of Legal History* 25 (Jan. 1981): 24–47. For English reform efforts to punish wife-beaters and help their victims, see Margaret May, "Violence in the Family: An Historical Perspective," in *Violence and the Family,* ed. J. P. Martin (Chichester, Sussex, 1978), 135–67. Two works on late-nineteenth- and early-twentieth-century divorce use county court records to examine changing family values, rising marital dissolution, and changing conceptions of proper behavior—including changing perceptions of cruelty among California couples: Elaine T. May. *Great Expectations: Marriage and Divorce in Post-Victorian America* (Chicago, 1980) and Robert L. Griswold, *Family and Divorce in California, 1850–1890: Victorian Illusions and Everyday Realities* (Albany, 1982). Lynne Halem examines divorce law and divorce reform in *Divorce Reform: Changing Legal and Social Perspectives* (New York, 1980); also see Michael S. Hindus and Lynne E. Withey, "The Law of Husband and Wife in Nineteenth-Century America: Changing Views of Divorce," in *Women and the Law: The Social Historical Perspective,* ed. D. K. Weisburg (Cambridge, 1982), 2:133–53. An older survey is provided by Nelson Blake, *The Road to Reno: A History of Divorce in the United States* (New York, 1962). William O'Neill examines the battle between liberals and conservatives over divorce in *Divorce in the Progressive Era* (New Haven, 1967), and Lawrence M. Friedman briefly discusses divorce law in *A History of American Law* (New York, 1973), 179–84, 434–40. The most complete discussion of family law in the nineteenth century is Michael C. Grossberg, *Governing the Hearth: Law and the Family in Nineteenth-Century America* (Chapel Hill, 1985).

4. For an extended analysis of the competing claims of family life and personal autonomy as it affected women, see Carl Degler, *At Odds: Women and the Family in America from the Revolution to the Present* (New York, 1980). Most of the evidence in this essay is based on appellate decisions, and although such evidence is not without limitations—it

may, for example, suggest a legal clarity and consistency that did not actually exist at the local level—such cases can function as a kind of survey of legal thinking on important questions. The other major drawback with the use of appellate records is the tendency to treat the law as if it existed in a social vacuum, but my intention is to do precisely the opposite. Another methodological point also bears mention: although nineteenth-century divorce law was almost wholly a statutory creation, statutory law offers little insight into legal thinking about divorce. Most states, as Lawrence Friedman has noted, "compiled hackneyed list of grounds: adultery, cruelty, impotence, desertion" (*A History of America Law,* 440). What so vague a term as *cruelty* actually meant had to be determined by local and appellate courts. My research in local California divorce records, those from 1850 to 1890, analyzes petitioners' complaints and witness testimony and confirms the general trends discussed in this essay. See Griswold, *Family and Divorce in California,* 72–75, 114–16. Whether using local or appellate-level records, care must be taken to avoid confusing legal interpretations and constructs with actual behavior. Finally, the cases cited in this essay, with a few exceptions, originated as cruelty complaints, although a few involved desertion petitions. The category "sexual cruelty" is my own, one that admittedly links both allegations about sexual activity (or the lack thereof) with allegations about verbal assault concerning sexuality. On the use of appellate records, see G. Edward White, "The Appellate Opinion as Historical Source Material," *Journal of Interdisciplinary History* 1 (1971): 491–509.

5. Among many fine books on nineteenth-century family history, two of the best are Degler, *At Odds,* and Mary Ryan, *Cradle of the Middle Class: The Family in Oneida County New York, 1790–1865* (Cambridge, 1981).

6. These statistics are from Carroll D. Wright, *A Report on Marriage and Divorce in the United States, 1867–1886* (Washington, D.C., 1889), 169, and U.S. Bureau of the Census, *Special Reports: Marriage and Divorce, 1867–1906* (Washington, D.C., 1908–9), 1:11, 1:26–27.

7. On the history of English legal definitions of matrimonial cruelty, the most helpful work is John Biggs, *The Concept of Matrimonial Cruelty* (London, 1962). Nineteenth-century legal commentaries are also useful in tracing the history of cruelty and indispensable for locating relevant cases in state appellate reports. Among the most complete are Joel Prentiss Bishop, *Commentaries on the Law of Marriage and Divorce,* 4th ed. (Boston, 1864), 1:586–632; Joel Prentiss Bishop, *New Commentaries on Marriage, Divorce, and Separation as the Law; Evidence, Pleading, Practice; Forms and the Evidence of Marriage in All Issues on a New System of Legal Exposition* (Chicago, 1891) 1:629–85; and William T. Nelson, *A Treatise on the Law of Divorce and Annulment of Marriage* (Chicago, 1895), 260–318. Also helpful is Irving Browne, "Oral Cruelty as a Ground of Divorce," *Central Law Journal* 46 (Jan.–June 1898): 81–86.

8. George Elliot Howard, *A History of Matrimonial Institutions* (Chicago, 1904), 3:11, 3:14–15, 3:53, 3:71, 3:109, 3:111, 3:113, 3:120, 3:126–28.

9. Howard, *A History,* 3:31–95; Wright, *A Report on Marriage and Divorce,* 114.

10. *Wright v. Wright,* 6 *Texas Reports* 6–7 (1851). Jurists repeatedly emphasized the importance of the family for social order, see, for example, *Gordon v. Gordon,* 48 *Pennsylvania Reports* 232–33 (1864); and *Latham v. Latham,* 30 *Grattan* (Virginia) 329 (1878).

11. Bishop, *New Commentaries,* 629–30.

12. In the 1790 English case of *Evans v. Evans,* Sir William Scott (Lord Stowell) elegantly describes what was and was not marital cruelty under the law. No case comes remotely

close to being as often cited as this one. Lengthy excerpts appear in many case reports, and Bishop includes much of the Evans text in both his 1864 commentary (589–90) and in his 1891 commentary (632–33). On ill-treatment that does not constitute cruelty, see Bishop, *New Commentaries,* 668, and James Schouler and Arthur Blakesmore, *A Treatise on the Law of Marriage, Divorce, Separation and Domestic Relations,* 6th ed. (Albany, 1921), 2:1811–14, 2:1818–19. *Scott v. Scott,* 61 *Texas Reports* 12 (1884), discusses the importance of forbearance, as does *Gordon v. Gordon,* 48 *Pennsylvania State Reports* 232–33 (1864): "But it is better that individual hardships should be borne by the party whose folly or passion has caused them," wrote the Pennsylvania court, "than that the great interests of society should be periled by tampering with the marriage tie."

13. I have analyzed the history of "mental cruelty" in American divorce elsewhere; see Robert L. Griswold, "The Evolution of the Doctrine of Mental Cruelty in Victorian American Divorce, 1790–1900," *Journal of Social History* 19 (Fall 1996): 127–48.

14. Such changes came at a time when conservative thinkers sought to arrest the trend toward more liberal divorce laws. From pulpits, newsrooms, and legislatures, post–Civil War moralists struggled to shore up family stability in the face of disorder inspired by immigration, industrialization, urbanization, and, more directly, soaring divorce rates. Their efforts met with limited success. In the face of attempts by post–Civil War feminists to liberalize divorce laws, state legislatures began to limit the grounds of divorce, abolish open-ended omnibus clauses, restrict the right of remarriage, impose more stringent residency requirements, and establish stricter provisions for notice. Despite these conservative efforts at divorce reform, the late-nineteenth- and early-twentieth-century divorce rate continued to rise, in part, as statistics suggest, thanks to a great expansion in the number of cruelty suits. Clearly, the cultural currents pushing the surge in divorce, especially divorce due to cruelty, were considerably more powerful than the currents pushing conservative efforts to strengthen family stability. On conservative reforms, see Halem, *Divorce Reform,* 27–40.

15. Conceivably, some husbands made such accusations with the express purpose of gaining a divorce; the records, however, do not yield such devious designs.

16. The image of nineteenth-century women as sexually passionless is discussed in Nancy Cott, "Passionlessness: An Interpretation of Victorian Sexual Ideology, 1790–1850," *Signs* 4 (Winter 1978): 219–36. On the effort to check predatory male sexuality, see Carroll Smith-Rosenberg, "Beauty, the Beast, and the Militant Woman," *American Quarterly* 23 (Fall 1971): 562–84.

17. *Shaw v. Shaw,* 17 *Connecticut Reports* 194 (1845); also see *Poor v. Poor,* 8 *New Hampshire Reports* 308–9, 319 (1836).

18. *Cheatham v. Cheatham,* 10 *Missouri Reports* 296–99 (1847). Several cases during the 1850s linked false accusations of adultery with other allegations of misbehavior to prove a defendant's cruelty. See *Sharp v. Sharp,* 34 *Tennessee Reports* 495–500 (1855); *Cook v. Cook,* 11 *New Jersey Equity Reports* 195–201 (1856); and *Cartwright v. Cartwright,* 18 *Texas Reports* 626–44 (1857). During the 1850s, however, courts began to move away from the tendency to combine malicious charges of infidelity with other evidence of cruelty to prove the husband's unworthiness; words alone began to be sufficient.

19. The issue of social class and cruelty is discussed in Bishop, *New Commentaries,* 663–64; see, too, *Berry v. Berry,* 88 *North Western Reporter* 1076 (Iowa, 1902); *Cline v. Cline,* 10 *Oregon Reports* 476 (1882); *Rahn v. Rahn,* 62 *Texas Reports* 518 (1884); *Scoland v. Scoland,* 4 *Washington Reports* 122–23 (1892); *Whispell v. Whispell,* 4 *Barbour* (N.Y.) 220 (1848).

20. Nelson, *A Treatise on the Law,* 303; *Jones v. Jones,* 60 *Texas Reports* 460 (1883); *Crow v. Crow,* 29 *Oregon Reports* 394 (1896). In his study *A Report on Marriage and Divorce in the United States, 1867 to 1886* (Washington, D.C., 1889), Commissioner of Labor Carroll D. Wright summarized divorce legislation, noting that Arkansas, Missouri, Oregon, Pennsylvania, Tennessee, Washington, and Wyoming all included "indignities rendering condition intolerable or life burdensome" as a ground for absolute divorce. Louisiana included "public defamation" as a ground for divorce (114–15). Wright's important document (77–122) and a later, even more comprehensive, government report (U.S. Bureau of the Census, *Special Reports,* 1:264–328) offer detailed compilations of divorce laws in the various states. Also see the compilation in *Humaker v. Humaker,* 65 *American Decisions* 708–25 (1911). See note 34 herein for a discussion of mental cruelty. Jane T. Censer found that several southern states in the antebellum period included "indignities" as a ground for divorce, and women falsely accused of adultery secured divorces on that ground. With one exception from 1849, the cases she cites to make that point all appeared during the 1850s, thus supporting the periodizations put forth in this essay. Censer, "'Smiling though Her Tears,'" 27–33.

21. *Rice v. Rice,* 6 *Indiana Reports* 85 (1854).

22. *Carpenter v. Carpenter,* 30 *Kansas Reports* 744 (1883). This case is repeatedly cited among judges taking a more expansive view of marital cruelty than that suggested by English precedent. Also see *Elmes v. Elmes,* 9 *Pennsylvania State Reports* 167 (1848).

23. Nelson, *A Treatise on the Law,* 262. On the law and "modern" family relations, also see Schouler, *A Treatise on the Law of Marriage* (1805), and *Scoland v. Scoland,* 4 *Washington Reports* 118–24 (1892).

24. The literature on women and health in the nineteenth century is sizable, but a good starting point is Carroll Smith-Rosenberg and Charles Rosenberg, "The Female Animal: Medical and Biological Views of Woman and Her Role in Nineteenth-Century America," *Journal of American History* 60 (Sept. 1973): 332–56. John S. Haller, Jr., and Robin M. Haller discuss neurasthenia in *The Physician and Sexuality in Victorian America* (1974, repr. New York, 1977). chs. 1, 2.

25. *Butler v. Butler, Parsons* (Pennsylvania) 337, 334–46 (1849). Another antebellum case of the 1850s put the issue even more bluntly: "And what to a virtuous woman can be more contumelious," asked the North Carolina Supreme Court in 1856, "than a charge made by her husband of infidelity to her marriage vow?" *Coble v. Coble,* 55 *North Carolina Reports* 395 (1856).

26. Cott, "Passionlessness," 219–36. Passionlessness was an ideology that offered protection to vulnerable women and provided a powerful critique of male behavior. The behavioral reality of nineteenth-century female sexuality is another matter. In an important revisionist essay on Victorian sexuality, Carl Degler argues that prescriptive literature and sexual behavior were less uniform and more complex than commonly assumed. Many nineteenth-century doctors, for example, recognized the legitimacy of women's needs and desires; moreover, the only survey of nineteenth-century American sexual behavior suggests that women were far from uninterested in sex. Cott's data, however, is from the first half of the century, and Degler's is from the second half. What Degler may be finding is the unraveling of the ideology of passionlessness due to countervailing ideas and behavior. Nevertheless, legal records suggest that the ideology retained sufficient power after 1850 to play an important role in reshaping interpretations of sexual cruelty. See Degler, "What Ought to Be and What Was: Women's Sexuality in the Nineteenth Century," *American Historical Review* 79 (Dec. 1974): 1467–90.

27. On organized efforts to reform men, see Smith-Rosenberg, "Beauty, the Beast and the Militant Women," passim, and David J. Pivar, *Purity Crusade: Sexual Morality and Social Control, 1868–1900* (Westport, 1973), passim. On domestic fiction and its critique of aggressive men, see Mary Kelley, "The Sentimentalists: Promise and Betrayal in the Home," *American Studies* 19 (Fall 1978): 23–40. Glenda Riley discusses the power of domestic ideology to rebuke and reform men in her analysis of nineteenth-century magazine editor Sarah Hale: "The Subtle Subversion: Changes in the Traditionalist Image of the American Woman," *The Historian* 32 (1970): 210–27.

28. *Jones v. Jones,* 60 *Texas Reports* 460 (1883). In this case the court added, "The law looks with much indulgence upon the conduct of a woman who is unjustly charged by her husband with the highest offense she can commit against his conjugal rights, and excuses any outbursts of resentment on her part under such accusations." Also see *Graft v. Graft,* 76 *Indiana Reports* 138 (1881).

29. Pleck, "Feminist Responses to 'Crimes against Women,'" passim.

30. *Beyer v. Beyer,* 50 *Wisconsin Reports* 255–56 (1880).

31. *Bahn v. Bahn,* 62 *Texas Reports* 518–20 (1884).

32. *Crow v. Crow,* 29 *Oregon Reports* 394 (1896). Husbands' duty to protect wives is discussed in *Straus v. Straus,* 22 *New York Supplement* 567–70 (1893).

33. As of 1886, six states still did not allow an absolute divorce on the ground of cruelty: Maryland, New Jersey, New York, North Carolina, Virginia, and West Virginia. These states did, however, permit legal separations due to cruelty. In Alabama, Kentucky, and Tennessee, only wives could receive a divorce on the ground of cruelty. Wright, *A Report on Marriage and Divorce,* 114, 116.

34. The key case in the development of the concept of "mental cruelty" is probably *Carpenter v. Carpenter,* 30 *Kansas Reports* 744 (1883); also see Justice McFarland's dissent in *Waldron v. Waldron,* 24 *Pacific Reporter* 754 (California, 1890), and *Barnes v. Barnes,* 30 *Pacific Reporter* 299 (California, 1892), wherein the California Supreme Court explicitly recognized mental cruelty in divorce suits. Also of interest are *Whitmore v. Whitmore,* 49 *Michigan Reports* 417–18 (1882); *Avery v. Avery,* 5 *Pacific Reporter* 418–22 (Washington, 1885); and *Mason v. Mason,* 131 *Pennsylvania State Reports* 161–65 (1840). Irving Browne noted in 1898 the elasticity of the definition of marital cruelty as it appeared in divorce statutes. "Ungovernable temper," "cruel treatment, outrages, or excesses," "such indignities as render life burdensome," "intolerable severity," "inability to live in peace and union," and "settled aversion ends to destroy all peace and happiness" are but a few of the many statutory efforts to define cruelty. Browne, "Oral Cruelty," 84.

35. *Crows v. Crows,* 29 *Oregon Reports* 393 (1896); also see *Smith v. Smith,* 8 *Oregon Reports* 101 (1879); *Kelley v. Kelley,* 18 *Nevada Reports* 53 (1883); and *Whitmore v. Whitmore,* 49 *Michigan Reports* 417–18 (1882).

36. *McAlister v. McAlister,* 71 *Texas Reports* 696–97 (1886); also supporting a double standard, see *Hart v. Atlantic Reporter* 431 (New Hampshire, 1896).

37. Lawrence M. Friedman, "Rights of Passage: Divorce Law in Historical Perspective," *Oregon Law Review* 63, no. 4 (1984): 649–69.

38. Griswold, *Family and Divorce in California,* ch. 6.

39. Linda Gordon, *Woman's Body, Woman's Right: A Social History of Birth Control in America* (New York, 1977) discusses efforts to regulate nineteenth-century sexuality in the interests of birth control. On utopians, see Louis J. Kern, *An Ordered Love: Sex Roles and Sexuality in Victorian Utopias* (Chapel Hill, 1981), and Lawrence Foster, *Religion and Sexuality: Three American Communal Experiments of the Nineteenth Century* (New York, 1981).

40. For a review of the literature on nineteenth-century sexuality, see Estelle B. Freedman, "Sexuality in Nineteenth-Century America: Behavior, Ideology, and Politics," in *The Promise of American History: Progress and Prospects,* ed. Sanley Katz and Stanley Kutler (Baltimore, 1982), 196–215.

41. Nichols, as quoted in Cott, "Passionlessness," 236; Degler, *At Odds,* 249–78.

42. Degler, *At Odds,* 270–71.

43. Peck, "'Crimes against Women,'" 452, 454–55, 457.

44. Ibid., 457, 459–62; also see Pleck, "The Whipping Post," 127–29. Stone's bill gave wives the power to apply at the local police court for a legal separation, provided an order requiring the husband to support his estranged wife and children, and included a custody award to the wife. Opponents feared the bill would make marital separations too easy to obtain.

45. Woodhull quoted in Degler, *At Odds,* 276.

46. *Shaw v. Shaw,* 17 *Connecticut Reports* 196 (1845). Western courts tended to be more flexible than those in the East, a point made by the Nebraska Supreme Court in 1898 when it criticized the *Shaw* decision for finding that false adultery allegations, husbandly tyranny, and excessive intercourse was "such cruelty as 'can be borne.'" Said the Nebraska court, "But we confidently say that no rule of law as announced by the court in the Shaw case exists west of the Allegheny Mountains." *Walton v. Walton,* 77 *Northwest Reporter* 398 (Nebraska, 1889).

47. *English v. English,* 27 *New Jersey Equity Reports* 71–75 (1876). This action was for a legal separation, not an absolute divorce.

48. *English v. English,* 27 *New Jersey Equity Reports* 580–86 (1876). The court divided nine to five on this decision. An earlier 1864 New Jersey case held that a "gross abuse of marital rights" may constitute cruelty, although the court found the wife's complaint unconvincing in this suit. The court suspected that she had fled her husband simply to avoid "the pains of childbearing," especially given the pain that her last pregnancy had caused her. See *Moores v. Moores,* 16 *New Jersey Equity Reports* 1 (C. E. Greene) 275–83 (1863).

49. *English v. English* 27 *New Jersey Equity Reports* 72 (1876). The complete text of these two decisions and a brief introduction can be found in Robert L. Griswold, "Sexual Cruelty and the Case for Divorce in Victorian America," *Signs* 11 (Spring 1986): 529–41.

50. *Mayhew v. Mayhew,* 61 *Connecticut Reports* 235 (1891); also see *Melvin v. Melvin, Hampshire Reports* 571 (1879), and *Walsh v. Walsh,* 61 *Michigan Reports* 557 (1886). Nevertheless, traditional decisions continued to be voiced, notably in Illinois where the court held that, to constitute cruelty, excessive sexual indulgence must be against the will of the wife, and in addition the husband must know that his actions harm her health. See *Young v. Young,* 33 *Illinois Appellate Reports* 225 (1889).

51. *Mayhew v. Mayhew,* 61 *Connecticut Reports* 235 (1891). In *Grant v. Grant,* 53 *Minnesota Reports* 181–82 (1893), the court held that excessive sexual demands were legally cruel when they rendered it "unsafe and improper for her to cohabit with him." Bishop argued that sexual demands that endangered health comprised cruelty; see *New Commentaries,* 675.

52. There were exceptions. In two New Hampshire cases, spouses who joined a Shaker community and thereafter renounced sex found successful divorce complaints lodged against them: *Dyer v. Dyer* 5 *New Hampshire Reports* 271–74 (1830); and *Fitts v. Fitts,* 46 *New Hampshire Reports* 184–85 (1871).

53. *Fritz v. Fritz,* 138 *Illinois Reports* 438–40 (1891); also see *Stewart v. Stewart,* 78 *Maine Reports* (1887). Bishop's claim that denial of sex for two years or more constituted deser-

tion was supported by *Stein v. Stein,* 5 *Colorado Reports* 55–57 (1879) and explicitly by *Steele v. Steele,* 8 *Washington D.C. Reports* 505–08 (1874). Drawing on English precedents, the Pennsylvania Supreme Court in 1854 and again in 1864 maintained, "The fact that a husband sleeps in a different bed from that occupied by his wife and declines to exercise his marital privileges respecting the enjoyment of conjugal endearments is not sufficient." *Eshback v. Eshback,* 23 *Pennsylvania State Reports* 343 (11 Harris) (1854); *Gordon v. Gordon,* 49 *Pennsylvania State Reports* 228 (1864). The English precedent is *D'Aquilar v. D'Aquilar,* 1 *Haggard* 776 (1794).

54. *Watson v. Watson,* 52 *New Jersey Equity Reports* 350–51 (1894).

55. *Magill v. Magill,* 3 *Pittsburgh Review* 25 (1866). This case is discussed in William H. Browne, *A Commentary on the Law of Divorce and Alimony* (Philadelphia, 1890).

56. *Southwick v. Southwick,* 97 *Massachusetts Reports* 327–29 (1867). In an 1870 Massachusetts case, the court included denial of sex as part of its desertion findings, but in this case the husband had also physically left home, leaving his wife impoverished and thus forcing her to go to work: *Magrath v. Magrath,* 103 *Massachusetts Reports* 579 (1870).

57. *Reid v. Reid,* 21 *New Jersey Equity Reports* 332–33 (1871); *Cowles v. Cowles,* 112 *Massachusetts Reports* 298 (1873); *Segelbaum v. Segelbaum,* 39 *Minnesota Reports* 258–62 (1888); *Latham v. Latham,* 30 *Grattan* (Virginia) 328 (1878); *Schoessaw v. Schoessaw,* 83 *Wisconsin Reports* 553 (1892). Although most argued the contrary, a few judges did suggest that the absence of sex constituted cruelty. The Maine Supreme Court in 1887 held that the refusal of sex did not constitute desertion, whereas cohabitation continued, but it may amount to cruelty. To justify this position, the opinion noted that impotence was a cause of divorce and then suggested that there was no meaningful difference between a spouse that cannot or will not assent to sex: *Stewart v. Stewart,* 78 *Maine Reports* 553 (1887). Bishop argued that the refusal of sex in conjunction with other facts may constitute cruelty, especially if the "health of the woman has suffered from her being obliged to sleep with a male person without any proper gratification of passions thereby excited." Bishop, *New Commentaries,* 660–61.

58. *Disborough v. Disborough,* 26 *Atlantic Reporter* 853 (New Jersey, 1893).

59. Grossberg, *Governing the Hearth,* 289–307.

60. Ibid., 290, 295.

61. In *Great Expectations,* May discusses (chs. 3–6) how urban life created new expectations in marriage that often could not be met.

7

From Longhouse to Log House: Household Structure among the Senecas in 1900

NANCY SHOEMAKER

Anthony Wallace's *The Death and Rebirth of the Seneca* has been in use for more than two decades. To this day, it stands as the definitive interpretation of how the Seneca Indians responded to European colonization. Although the book's brilliance will never be questioned, some of its conclusions beg for a long-overdue revision. Wallace argued that early-nineteenth-century Seneca society, particularly Seneca families, made an adaptive transition in the midst of social chaos. Using a structural-functionalist model, Wallace characterized early Seneca Indian reservations as dysfunctional "Slums in the Wilderness" and claimed that the Senecas quickly accommodated new social values to become a functional society once more. In his words, "The combined effect of the new settlement pattern . . . and of the social gospel preached by Handsome Lake [a Seneca prophet], emphasizing the focal moral importance of the nuclear household, had within a generation been able to complete the transition from the ancient matrilineal household to the nuclear family."[1] There is little empirical support for Wallace's contention that the Seneca family transformed itself so completely and so quickly. We know that some form of matrilineage must have survived, because tribal membership is based on it. Less is known, however, about transformations of household structure.

Certainly, in the early 1800s, when Handsome Lake "revitalized" the Iroquois, the Senecas were facing enormous changes in their economy and lifestyle. The Revolutionary War disrupted the continuity of their subsistence patterns, and confinement to ever-shrinking reservations required a new, less mobile economy. One significant change in the Senecas' material culture was the widespread adoption of Euro-American housing styles, an event that William Fenton has called the Senecas' first housing revolution.[2] Quaker missionaries introduced the new housing style to the Senecas at Allegheny around 1798 when they built a two-story house on mission grounds. By 1803, according to Halliday Jackson's account, "seventeen new houses with shingled roofs, were observed neatly built, with square logs, most of them two stories high, with stone chimneys and glass windows."[3] Other Seneca communities approached the Quakers for sawmill tools, and log houses quickly began replacing bark houses on all the Seneca reservations.

What effect did the changed structure of houses have on the structure of families living inside the houses? A precise history of the longhouse—its prevalence, chronology, family composition, and relationship to defense and stockaded villages—has yet to be written, so it is difficult to compare the nineteenth-century log house to the more obscure longhouse of earlier times. The Iroquois longhouse has typically been described as a long, bark-covered building containing one big extended family, within which nuclear families lived in distinctly divided and yet still open compartments.[4] Although this multifamily living arrangement had a nuclear component, non-nuclear relatives lived close by and no doubt greatly influenced the ways in which family members interacted. Seneca household structure needs to be examined to see whether close ties between non-nuclear relatives persisted and to measure the impact that new housing styles had on Seneca society. As with the products of other Euro-American technologies—guns, iron kettles, and glass beads—the Senecas could have borrowed the technology of the log house without interrupting cultural traditions.

Unfortunately, the earliest available censuses collected among the Senecas say little about household composition. The only measure available before 1900 is family size. Figures were compiled from a variety of sources to show a decrease in the size of families between 1789 and 1900 (table 7.1). *Family* is an ambiguous term, however, and the possibility of shifting definitions of "family" obscures whether these figures represent a significant change. Census enumerators of nineteenth-century populations may each have had a different sense of what was meant by the word *family*. By 1900 the U.S. Census Bureau had become bureaucratized enough to give its enumerators explicit criteria for determining who lived in a family.[5] Earlier censuses, however, have left fewer clues about what the word *family* meant, whether residence or blood relationships or some mixture of both. Another problem with using family size is that differences in fertility could create large differences in family size; nuclear families are not necessarily smaller than more complex families.

The 1900 U.S. federal census is the earliest available resource for analyzing Seneca household structure in detail. Although the Senecas were enumerated in censuses many times throughout the nineteenth century, these data

Table 7.1. Mean Family Size for the Senecas
(excluding Tonawanda Senecas), 1789–1900

1789	7.7	1865	4.8
1845	4.7	1875	4.8
1855	5.3	1900	3.9

Sources: "Census of Six Nations Giving Names of Tribes and Heads of Families, October 20, 1789," Kirkland Papers, Hamilton College, Clinton, N.Y.; Henry Schoolcraft, *Notes on the Iroquois; or, Contributions to American History, Antiquities, and General Ethnology* (Albany, 1847), 32 (an enumeration of the Iroquois for the 1845 New York State census); New York State, *Census of the State of New York for 1855* (Albany, 1857), 500; Franklin B. Hough, *Census of the State of New York for 1865* (Albany, 1867), 603; New York State, *Census of New York State for the Year 1875* (Albany, 1877); manuscript schedules from the 1900 U.S. census for Allegheny and Cattaraugus reservations, National Archives, microfilm collection T623, reels 1011 and 1034.

are either inadequate for analyzing household composition or the manuscript forms are no longer extant.[6] For this study, I collected data from the 1900 U.S. census for the two Seneca Nation reservations, Allegheny and Cattaraugus, located in western New York state.[7]

Although the problems related to defining family are not completely resolved by using the 1900 census, at least we know that enumerators put people into the same family if they lived in the same "dwelling place or part of the same dwelling place" and if they used the same table for eating.[8] By that definition, the term *family* at the end of the nineteenth century is roughly equivalent to what most of us would call "household." Here, "family" does not refer to all of one's relatives, and therefore residence patterns and relationships occurring beyond the household will not be discussed. In part, this approach is limited by the nature of the data. Census-takers grouped individuals according to living arrangements and did not ask other, potentially interesting, questions such as, "Who are all your relatives?" "Who taught you your social values?" and "With whom do you have reciprocal relations and bonds of obligation?" Household, however, is in itself important because it is a critical arena for family interaction.

There is one possible problem with using census data for analyzing American Indian household structure. Census-taking is a modern, Western phenomenon, a fact that could bias the results of a census of a non-Western society. One group's cultural and linguistic schema for organizing relationships, for example, might not translate accurately onto census forms. When analyzing census data for a different Indian group, the Ojibway, I noticed several women with more children listed as theirs in a household than cited in the column marked "children-ever-born." Because in the Ojibway language *daughter* and *niece* are often the same word, as are *sister* and *cousin,* presumably the translation from one language to another could not as easily translate Ojibway relationships into equivalent Euro-American concepts. I did not notice similar discrepancies in the Seneca data. Because practically all Senecas could speak English in 1900, perhaps they referred to relatives using the Euro-American system.

There are, however, several other potential problems. Indian societies might have more fictive kin than Western society, but a census enumerator would not be able to detect fictive kin from kin related by blood or marriage. Also, nineteenth-century enumerators clearly expected men to be household heads, because corrections and the rearranging of family members are evident on the manuscript forms. There could also be seasonal variation in household composition that would not be detectable with census data because censuses catch people at one point in time. The 1900 census, taken in June, might have revealed a different household composition if taken in December. Thus, although the 1900 census manuscripts for Indians seem complete and accurate, the extent of cultural bias within them cannot be determined.

To provide a context for interpreting Seneca household structure, I compared the Senecas to three other groups in 1900: the U.S. population, the Yakima Indians of Washington State, and the Ojibway Indians of Red Lake Reservation in Minnesota.[9] The Ojibwas and Yakimas represent two extremes in their family types. The anthropological and historical literature on the Ojibwas has demonstrated the importance of the nuclear family in their social and economic activities.[10] In contrast, the Yakimas historically have preferred extended families. Like the Senecas, they at one time lived in multi-family longhouses. Also like the Senecas, the longhouse survived in symbolic form as the meeting place for the Yakimas' longhouse religion, even after Yakima housing styles changed.[11]

If family structure was influenced by acculturation of American values— by the Senecas' adapting to a nuclear-family structure in response to their new environment—one would expect a Seneca family to most resemble a U.S. family. Almost all Senecas could speak English, their children regularly attended schools, and their houses and farms looked little different from those of their white neighbors. In contrast, the Yakimas and Red Lake Ojibwas had had much less contact with whites. Fewer than half spoke English, and many lived in traditional houses.[12]

The Senecas did, however, live in very complex households in 1900 (table 7.2). To distinguish nuclear from complex families, I used a simple system based on the relationship-to-head variable. An "extended relative" is any relative of the head other than wife or children. The extended relatives and those who live with them will all be referred to as "individuals living in extended families." In all three Indian groups, the number of individuals living in extended families is very high compared to that of the U.S. population. According to historical research in U.S. family history, the United States likely experienced a rise in the number of extended families during the nineteenth century. Thus, the figure of 21.3 percent, extended for the U.S. population, is fairly high in the context of the history of the Western family.[13] The much higher figures for Indian groups suggest that Indian families, no matter how assimilated they may have appeared, had different, decidedly non-Western living arrangements.

Differences between the Indian groups confirm that the Seneca family had not adopted a nuclear family structure but in 1900 seems to have been much more like the Yakima family, perhaps reflecting the extended family ideal present in both cultures. The Yakima family, however, was much more complex. In several Yakima households, siblings and cousins lived together with their spouses and children, and in other households both the wife's and the husband's relatives were coresident. The especially high lateral extension among the Yakimas also indicates a stronger preference for multifamily households than among the Senecas. The Senecas were not living in multifamily households in 1900, but neither can it be said that Seneca social structure became organized primarily around the nuclear family unit.

One aspect of the Indian groups' family structure contributing to high family extension is that almost all Indians lived with relatives. Among the Senecas, Yakimas, and Ojibwas, the percentage of individuals living without relatives ranged from 1.2 to 2.7 percent, whereas 9.1 percent of the U.S. population lived without relatives. Presumably in the Indian groups, individu-

Table 7.2. Individuals Living in Extended Families, 1900

	Seneca	Yakima	Ojibway	United States
Vertically extended	29.2%	28.0%	23.1%	12.4%
Laterally extended	6.9	17.4	5.1	7.3
Both	5.0	13.6	3.3	1.6
	41.1	59.0	31.5	21.3
Number of cases	2,017	1,645	1,347	9,984

Sources: 1900 U.S. Census manuscript forms and one-in-ten sample of the 1900 public use sample.

als who had no immediate family still managed to live with relatives of one kind or another.

Perhaps the most significant difference between the Indian groups and the U.S. population, however, is the high percentage of individuals living in vertically extended families. These were members of three-generation families or families of grandparents and grandchildren with the middle generation absent, often, no doubt, due to mortality. The high percentage of individuals living in vertically extended families suggests that young married couples stayed in their parents' homes instead of immediately setting up their own households and their own nuclear families. To see if that was the case for the Senecas, I isolated young married couples (arbitrarily set at married people with spouse present who were less than thirty years old). If married for five years or less (table 7.3), that subpopulation of young married for all Indian groups was especially likely to live in vertically extended families. In the United States, young people married for five years or less did not differ from the rest of the population. In all these populations, the percentage of individuals married more than five years was lower in vertically extended families than was typical for the population as a whole.

Considering the demographic constraints under which individuals made residence decisions, the prevalence of vertically extended families among Indian groups is even more remarkable. Marriage age and mortality are the two demographic parameters essential to understanding family structure (table 7.4). A young age at marriage leads to young parents and a short generation length. High mortality, however, limits the number of vertically extended families, because many parents will have died before their children marry and start new families.[14] In 1900, Indian populations had a low age at marriage, which

Table 7.3. Individuals Living in Vertically Extended Families: Young Married People Compared to Total Population, 1900

	Seneca	Yakima	Ojibway	United States
Percentage of total population	34.2	41.6	26.4	14.0
Married individuals less than thirty years old Percent married for five years or less	47.0	50.5	31.5	14.0
Percent married for more than five years	32.8	29.5	12.2	7.3
Number of young marrieds	199	153	114	916
Total population	2,017	1,645	1,347	9,984

Sources: 1900 U.S. Census manuscript forms and one-in-ten sample of the 1900 public use sample.

Table 7.4. Demographic Characteristics, 1900

	Seneca	Yakima	Ojibway	United States
Singulate mean age at marriage for women (synthetic cohort, women ages 15–49)	20.5	19.6	21.9	23.4
Singulate mean age at marriage for men (synthetic cohort, men ages 15–49)	26.8	22.5	25.6	27.0
Estimated life expectancy at birth (using children-born and children-surviving variables for women ages 20–44)	30.7	LT 25	29.7	48.8
Number of cases				
Women ages 15–49	468	415	304	2,556
Men ages 15–49	508	369	283	2,630
Women ages 20–44	355	316	211	1,866

Sources: 1900 U.S. Census manuscript forms and one-in-ten sample of the 1900 public use sample.

Note: The methods for arriving at mean age at marriage are described in Henry S. Shyrock and Jacob S. Siegel et al., *The Methods and Materials of Demography* (San Diego, 1976), 167. The method for arriving at life expectancy using the children-ever-born and children-surviving variables from the 1900 census was developed by Brass and is described in Shyrock and Siegel, 499–500, and in William Brass et al., *The Demography of Tropical Africa* (Princeton, 1968). The figures were arrived at using United Nations software. Population Division, United Nations, "Mortpak: The United Nations Software Packages for Mortality Measurement," Sept. 20, 1986, fitting Model West of the Coale-Demeny regional model life tables to the mortality experience of children born to women ages 20–44.

is conducive to extended-family formation. Indians also had extremely high mortality in 1900, however. Because many Senecas lived in vertically extended families despite the devastating effects of high mortality, probably most lived with parents unless the parents (and the spouse's parents) were dead.

Seneca family structure in 1900, characterized by complex families and especially high vertical extension, was more like that of other Indian groups than like U.S. family structure. Consistent with their histories and traditions, the Senecas and Yakimas showed a clear preference for living in extended families in 1900. Even among the Ojibwas, who had a nuclear-family orientation, there was an unusually high number of extended families compared to the experience of the Western family.

There are many possible explanations for why Senecas preferred to live in extended families in 1900, including the "huddling together in poverty" thesis. However, recent research on the Western family—some of which has used data drawn from the county surrounding the Cattaraugus Reservation—has demonstrated that extended families in the late nineteenth century were concentrated among the upper classes.[15] If Senecas formed extended families for the same reasons as their neighbors, we would have to assume that the Senecas were well-off—somewhat better off than the Ojibwas but not nearly as well-off as the Yakimas. Clearly, economic conditions in themselves are not a satisfactory explanation.

The economic context of family life, however, may be important. Family historians, whose work has focused on the Western family, have been especially concerned with how new families form. To what extent did marriage have to wait until sons inherited their fathers' farms or earned an independent livelihood? How prevalent was the stem family, where one married son stayed in the home with his parents in anticipation of an eventual inheritance? Did newly married couples tend to start separate households?[16] The questions family historians have asked are rooted in the economic context of the Western family, with such values as accumulating land and attaining individual self-sufficiency. The Seneca economy in 1900 was partly integrated with the American market economy, and the Seneca Nation allowed land to be bought and sold, bequeathed and inherited, so long as all parties to these transactions were Senecas. Despite such elements of Western capitalism in Seneca society, however, the Senecas were not completely engaged in the economic life of western New York state. The differing economic context for Indian societies perhaps encouraged young married couples to stay with parents instead of immediately setting up new households.

Culture as well no doubt had an impact on Seneca family structure. Seneca cultural values—attitudes toward parents and elders and traditional living patterns—could have survived despite the new physical surroundings of reservations and log houses. The role of the Handsome Lake prophecies in Seneca family life remains unclear. The innovations Handsome Lake introduced to Seneca society were revived in the 1830s out of a conservative impulse to preserve traditional values. Over time, the longhouse religion could have conveyed values conducive to extended families and not small, nucleated ones.

If the Senecas adapted to the new conditions of reservation life, it is unclear how they adapted and why. Writing about Seneca families in the 1960s, Anthony Wallace naturally used the context of his times. Structural functionalism and modernization theory, both in vogue in the 1950s and 1960s, propagated the myth that all premodern societies had extended family structures and adapted to the nuclear family as they modernized.[17] Since the 1960s, however, research on the history of the Western family has thoroughly revised most commonly held notions about it. In the early 1970s, English historian Peter Laslett and others questioned the model of an adaptive transition in family type and showed that the Western family had always been predominately nuclear.[18] Wallace's use of this model in his history of the Senecas deserves a similar reevaluation, but with one difference. The nuclear family of industrial America and Europe has been shown to be a continuation of preindustrial living arrangements. In contrast, the extended family provided continuity for the Senecas in their transition from prereservation to reservation conditions.

Notes

This essay is reprinted, with minor editorial changes, from the *American Indian Quarterly* 15 (Summer 1991): 329–38.

1. Anthony F. C. Wallace, *The Death and Rebirth of the Seneca* (New York, 1969), 312.

2. William N. Fenton, "From Longhouse to Ranch-type House: The Second Revolution of the Seneca Nation," in *Iroquois Culture and Prehistory: Proceedings of the 1965 Conference on Iroquois Research,* ed. Elisabeth Tooker (Albany, 1967), 11–22.

3. Halliday Jackson, *Civilization of the Indian Natives* (Philadelphia, 1830), 48.

4. Lewis Henry Morgan, *Houses and House-Life of the American Aborigines* (1881, repr. Chicago, 1965), 65; Dean R. Snow, "Iroquois Prehistory," in *Extending the Rafters: Interdisciplinary Approaches to Iroquoian Studies,* ed. Michael K. Foster, Jack Campisi, and Marianne Mithun (Albany, 1984), 241–57.

5. Robert G. Barrows, "Instructions of Enumerators for Completing the 1900 Census Population Schedule," *Historical Methods Newsletter* 9 (Sept. 1976): 201–8.

6. Like other Indian groups living on reservations, the Senecas were first enumerated by the federal government in 1890, the manuscripts for which were lost in a fire. The 1900 and 1910 U.S. census manuscripts are available to the public on microfilm; the 1910 census for Allegheny Reservation is nearly entirely illegible. New York State censuses enumerated the Senecas beginning in 1845. The 1845 census still survives in manuscript form, but because it is a household-level census it says little about family members within the household. Unfortunately, the 1855, 1865, and 1875 New York State censuses, which did enumerate individuals, have only partially survived. The forms for Indians do not seem to be available and were probably lost when the bulk of New York State records burned in a 1911 fire. The 1915 and 1925 state censuses survive intact, and future analysis of the Indian data should prove fruitful because the state enumerations include variables unheard of in federal censuses, such as religious affiliation and clan.

7. The Seneca dataset for 1900 consists of all 2,017 residents of Cattaraugus and Allegheny reservations except for those children living at the Thomas Indian Orphan Asylum, a state institution for Indian orphans from all New York State reservations. The data were collected from National Archives microfilm collection T623, 1900 Federal Census, reels 1011 and 1034. Other Iroquois (Cayugas, Onondagas, and Oneidas) and intermarried whites who resided on Seneca Nation reservations were thus included as part of the population.

This essay focuses on residents of the Seneca Nation reservations, Cattaraugus and Allegheny. Tonawanda Senecas were excluded from the analysis because of their separate political identity. The 1789 and 1845 figures include Indians from Buffalo because most Buffalo Creek émigrés resettled at Cattaraugus. For every census year, the Cayugas, Onondagas, and Oneidas living on the Seneca Nation reservations were included in the analysis, because many of them were intermarried with, and in other ways related to, Senecas.

8. Barrows, "Instructions of Enumerators," 204.

9. The Yakima and Red Lake datasets consist of all residents of the Yakima Reservation in Washington State and the Red Lake Reservation in Minnesota. The data come from the manuscript schedules National Archives microfilm collection T623, 1900 Federal Population Census, reels 1756 (Yakimas) and 756 (Ojibways). The U.S. data is a one-in-ten sample of the 1900 public use sample. See Stephen N. Graham, *1900 Public Use Sample: User's Handbook* (Seattle, 1980).

10. Robert E. Ritzenthaler, "Southwestern Chippewa," in *Northeast*, ed. Bruce Trigger, vol. 15 of *Handbook of North American Indians* (Washington, D.C., 1978), 743–71; Ruth Landes, *The Ojibwa Woman* (1938, repr. New York, 1969).

11. Helen Hersh Schuster, "Yakima Indian Traditionalism: A Study in Continuity and Change," Ph.D. diss., University of Washington, 1975.

12. Thomas Donaldson, *Extra Census Bulletin, Indians: The Six Nations of New York* (Washington, D.C., 1892); Department of the Interior, U.S. Census Office, *Report on Indians Taxed and Indians Not Taxed in the United States* (Washington, D.C., 1894), 603–16.

13. Steven Ruggles, *Prolonged Connections: The Rise of the Extended Nineteenth-Century Family in England and America* (Madison, 1987).

14. Ruggles, *Prolonged Connections*, Appendix D.

15. Ibid., 42–48.

16. Michael Anderson, *Approaches to the History of the Western Family, 1500–1914* (Cambridge, 1980); Lutz Berkner "The Stem Family and the Developmental Cycle of the Peasant Household: An Eighteenth-Century Austrian Example," *American Historical Review* 77 (1972): 398–418; Peter Laslett, ed., with the assistance of Peter Richard Wall, *Household and Family in Past Time* (Cambridge, 1972).

17. See W. J. Goode's critique, "Industrialization and Family Change," in *Industrialization and Society*, ed. B. F. Hoselitz and W. E. Moore (Paris, 1963); also see Talcott Parsons, "The Social Structure of the Family," in *The Family: Its Function and Destiny*, ed. Ruth Nanda Anshen (New York, 1949); Neil Smelser, *Social Change in the Industrial Revolution* (Chicago, 1959); and Ferdinand Tonnies, *Community and Society*, trans. and ed. Charles P. Loomis (East Lansing, 1959).

18. Laslett and Wall eds., *Household and Family in Past Time*.

8

Gender Systems in Conflict: The Marriages of Mission-Educated Chinese American Women, 1874–1939

PEGGY PASCOE

As soon as Wong Ah So entered the United States in 1922, she was sold into prostitution. Her owner, a Chinese woman who moved her from one town to another, took most of her earnings, but Wong Ah So scraped up extra money to send to her impoverished family in Hong Kong. When the man who had helped smuggle her into the country demanded $1,000 for his services, Wong Ah So, who was afraid of him, borrowed the money to pay him. Shortly afterward, she developed an illness, apparently venereal disease, that required daily treatment and interfered with her work as a prostitute.

In February 1924, Protestant missionaries raided the residential hotel in Fresno, California, where Wong Ah So was staying. Wong Ah So was frightened. Her owner had tried to keep her away from missionaries by telling her that their leader, Donaldina Cameron, "was in the habit of draining blood from the arteries of newly 'captured' girls and drinking it to keep up her own vitality."[1] But Wong Ah So was also tired, sick, and afraid that she could not repay her heavy debts. She agreed to enter Cameron's Presbyterian Mission Home in San Francisco. Wong Ah So would live in the Mission Home for only a little more than a year, but the course of the rest of her life would be changed by her contact with missionary women.[2]

From the late nineteenth century to the present, accounts like that of Wong Ah So fed the white American taste for exoticism and formed a unique genre in the popular mythology of American race relations. Missionary women called them "rescue" stories and saw them as skirmishes in a righteous battle against sexual slavery. Newspaper reporters exploited the stories for sensational copy, attracting readers with provocative headlines such as "Slave Girls Taken in Raid on Chinese" or "Woman Tells of Traffic in Slave Girls."[3] Anti-Chinese politicians relied on images of "Chinese slave girls" to bolster their successful 1882 campaign to restrict the immigration of Chinese laborers.

In the rescue genre, sensational images of victimized Chinese women were accompanied by equally sensational portrayals of nefarious Chinese organizations—the tongs—that kidnapped, enslaved, and exploited prostitutes. Because rescue stories suggested that every Chinese organization thrived on organized vice, they left scandalized readers ignorant of the distinction between the tongs, which controlled prostitution, and the Chinese family and district associations that had little connection to the trade.[4]

In order to counter these racially based stereotypes, scholars of Chinese America writing in the 1960s and 1970s tried to desensationalize the Chinese American past by shifting attention away from organized vice. Trying to convince readers that Chinese immigrants were model Americans, they depicted tongs as misunderstood benevolent institutions and did their best to ignore prostitution altogether.[5]

Their silence on the subject of prostitution came at the same time that another group of historians was mounting a trenchant critique of American racism. In these writings, Protestant missionaries were, for the first time, given their full share of the blame for American racism and ethnocentrism. Historians of race used rescue stories like that of Wong Ah So to demonstrate the racist attitudes and cultural condescension of Victorian missionaries, with the term *rescue* used skeptically and in quotation marks.[6] From their efforts, we have come to a much fuller understanding of the ways in which missionary adoption of racial stereotypes helped maintain white American dominance over minority groups.

The alternatives available to Chinese immigrant women in American Chinatowns were conditioned by Victorian racial hierarchies, and they were also affected by the conflict between gender systems revealed in the contact between Chinese immigrant women and Protestant women reformers.[7] Because rescue stories illuminate both race relations and gender systems, missionary records are an ideal source for exploring the complexity of race *and* gender relations between dominant groups and minority groups in American society.[8] To explore these issues, I will use the case files of the Presbyterian Mission Home that Wong Ah So entered in 1924 as a window on gender relations in San Francisco's Chinatown at the turn of the twentieth century.

Specifically, I want to do three things: first, describe the two different gender systems idealized in China and in nineteenth-century America; second, show how the immigrant context made Chinese women in San Francisco particularly vulnerable to exploitation yet at the same time put some of them in a particularly opportune position to challenge traditional male prerogatives; and, finally, show how Chinese immigrant women used the conflict between traditional Chinese and Victorian American gender systems to shape one set of possibilities for a distinctive Chinese American culture.

Let's begin with the gender system of traditional China, the set of ideals Wong Ah So and many other immigrant women were raised to emulate.[9] In traditional China, families provided the social glue of society, and families focused their energies on the importance of raising male heirs to carry on the lineage.[10] For this reason, young girls were considered to be less important than young boys from birth. Especially—but not only—in impoverished families, young girls might be sold to pay debts or expected to demonstrate filial piety by working for wages. Something like that happened to Wong Ah So when her mother bargained with a young man who told them that in San Francisco Wong Ah So could make money to support her family as an entertainer at Chinese banquets. When the young man offered the mother $450 for her daughter, Wong Ah So went to California.[11]

Although historians should be cautious in equating cultural ideals with individual behavior, there is little doubt that Wong Ah So understood and accepted her subordinate position in this traditional gender system. Even after she awoke from her dreams of fancy entertaining to the harsh reality of prostitution in immigrant California, Wong Ah So's letters to her mother in Hong Kong were framed in traditional terms. "Daughter is not angry with you," she wrote in one letter later found and saved by missionary women. "It seems to be just my fate." Dutifully reciting familiar stories of Chinese children renowned for their filial piety, she promised her mother that "after I have earned money by living this life of prostitution, I will return to China and become a Buddhist nun. . . . By accomplishing these two things," she ended rather hopefully, "I shall have attained all the requirements of complete filial piety."[12]

The full weight of the gender system of traditional China descended on young women at the time of marriage. Matches were generally arranged by go-betweens, with little personal contact between prospective mates. In and of themselves, new brides held little status until they produced male heirs; until then, they were expected to serve their mothers-in-law. Whether mothers or daughters-in-law, women were expected to display female submission to male authority. Thus Wong Ah So knew by heart what she called the "three great obediences": "At home, a daughter should be obedient to her parents; after marriage, to her husband; after the death of her husband, to her son."[13]

The subordination of young wives was ensured by a series of social sanctions. Wives who did not produce male heirs might find their husbands taking concubines; there was a highly stratified system of prostitution from which such concubines could be chosen.[14] Furthermore, wives who did not behave according to custom might find themselves divorced and sent back to their families in disgrace.[15] Even young wives' most forceful weapon of complaint—committing suicide to protest bad treatment—brought social judgment on their in-laws only at the cost of their own lives.[16]

Young women who adapted to the constraints of this traditional patriarchal system, however, could achieve significant social status later in life as mothers and mothers-in-law. As Wong Ah So noted, evidently trying to resign herself to her situation, "Now I may be somebody's daughter, but some day I may be somebody's mother."[17] Wives who gave birth to sons could look forward to becoming mothers-in-law, a position of some authority within the patrilineal lineage.[18]

By the late nineteenth century, when Chinese immigration to the United States was in full swing, the traditional system of patriarchal control was beginning to lose some of its power in China. In Kwangtung, the area from which most immigrants to America came, some young women who were able to find employment in the sericulture industry were mounting a "marriage resistance" movement and entering all-women's houses rather than living with parents or in-laws.[19] Their relative freedom was based on a unique combination of economic circumstances that allowed them to support themselves outside of marriage.

It appears that most Chinese women who immigrated to America were more impoverished and less able to challenge the traditional ideals of marriage head-on than the marriage-resisters of their native land. Yet when immigrant women reached the United States, they encountered a Victorian gender system that contrasted with the traditional gender system of late-nineteenth-century China. Victorian Americans held up an ideal that some historians have called "companionate" marriage. According to these historians, companionate marriage differed from traditional marriage in significant respects. Companionate unions were based on attraction between spouses rather than parental arrangement, and in them, at least according to the ideal, women were idealized as nurturant mothers and sexually pure moral guardians.[20]

Yet as feminist historians have pointed out, Victorian marriages also reflected an unequal arrangement of gender power.[21] Companionate marriage may have differed from traditional marriage, but women who held to the Victorian ideal gained affection and moral influence at the cost of legal and economic powerlessness. Throughout the nineteenth century, middle-class American women had to fight for such basic rights as the chance to be considered legal guardians of their own children. Often deprived of formal control over their property, women were expected by society to be the economic dependents of men, a status that sharply limited their alternatives in and outside of marriage.

The ideal of compassionate marriage was the rhetorical panacea put forth by the middle-class women who established the Presbyterian Mission Home that Wong Ah So entered in San Francisco. Yet the Mission Home matrons who espoused companionate marriage were themselves single women devoted to professional careers in missionary work, women who had encountered in their own lives few of the daily restraints of Victorian marriage and who occupied a somewhat marginal place within the Victorian gender system.[22] Their single status and their public activism combined, not always smoothly, with their advocacy of compassionate marriage to offer a striking example to the Chinese immigrant women with whom they came in contact.

Thus, while both the Victorian American and traditional Chinese gender systems were patriarchal, the two forms of patriarchy were significantly different. In the Victorian gender system, women's status rested not on their position as mothers-in-law but on their ability to parlay their supposedly "natural" nurturing influence into a form of moral authority recognized by white Americans. To Victorians, a display of female moral authority rooted in sexual purity was the only sure measure of women's standing in society. As a result, missionary women believed that women who did not fit Victorian definitions of female morality were oppressed and subjugated examples of the victimization of women. Thus Donaldina Cameron, the Presbyterian Mission Home matron, was fond of saying that Chinese prostitutes were the "most helpless and oppressed group of women and children who live within the borders of these United States of America."[23]

Clearly, this Victorian analysis of women's position rested in part on an ethnocentric—at times even racist—belief in the superiority of American culture. Victorian assumptions can be seen in the words of Presbyterian Mission Home workers, who had long insisted that "the first step upwards from heathenism to civilization is the organization of a home on Christian principles."[24] In ideological terms, missionary women equated the emancipation of women with the adoption of middle-class Victorian marriages in which husbands' traditional powers could be reduced by wives' moral influence, conveniently ignoring the legal and economic powerlessness Victorian women endured. Further, as long as they held to the assumptions of the Victorian gender system, missionaries could not disentangle their critique of the treatment of women in traditional societies from their assumption of racial and cultural superiority.

The cultural ideas of these two distinct gender systems clashed in American Chinatowns, where a unique pattern of immigration rendered Chinese immigrant women easily exploitable even as it held before them the promise of unprecedented opportunity. At the root of this unique social context was an extreme numerical imbalance between male immigrants (who formed the vast majority of the Chinese population in America) and the much smaller number of female immigrants. The number of Chinese women who traveled to the United States in the nineteenth century was so small that by 1882, when American exclusion legislation cut Chinese immigration drastically, the sex ratio in Chinese immigrant communities was already sharply skewed. In 1890 there were twenty-two Chinese men in California for every Chinese woman, and by 1920 there were still five Chinese men for every Chinese woman.[25]

That population imbalance created a demand for sexual services that sustained a thriving network of organized prostitution in Chinese immigrant communities.[26] Only a few married Chinese women traveled to America, because respectable young wives were expected to remain with in-laws in China.[27] Most of the female immigrants were young women who, like Wong Ali So, were placed into prostitution. They entered prostitution by a variety of means. Very few Chinese prostitutes were independent entrepreneurs. Many had been enticed into dubious marriages in China only to be sold into the trade on their arrival in America; others had been purchased from their poverty-stricken parents; still others had been kidnaped by procurers and smuggled into American ports.

Compared to white American prostitutes of the same period, Chinese prostitutes were particularly powerless; in fact, many were kept in conditions that render some truth to the sensational stereotype of the Chinese slave girl.[28] Some were indentured and had few hopes of paying off their contracts; others were virtually enslaved. Most were under the control of tong leaders and their henchmen, many of whom operated with the collusion of white officials.

Thus, the skewed sex ratio of immigrant Chinatowns increased the vulnerability of Chinese immigrant women to sexual exploitation. At the same time, however, the extreme sexual imbalance also offered unusual opportunities for those immigrant women who could find a way to take advantage of them. As Lucie Cheng Hirata has noted, both the skewed sex ratio and the absence of established in-laws created unique opportunities for immigrant prostitutes to marry in order to leave prostitution behind.[29]

That is where the rescue homes founded by Protestant women came in. Rescue homes gave missionary women space and time to impose the Victorian gender system and its ideal of compassionate marriage on Chinese immigrant women. Even the term *rescue home* is a significant clue to their intentions and conveyed the twin goals of Protestant women. On the one hand, they wanted to "rescue" Chinese women who had been sold or enticed into prostitution; on the other, they wanted to inculcate in all women their particular concept of the "Christian home." Protestant women believed that their institutions would separate women victims from the men who preyed on them, providing space for the supposedly natural virtues of Victorian "true womanhood"—purity and piety—to come to the surface.[30] These Victorian ideals clashed with the more traditional gender system held by Chinese women. Nowhere was the conflict between gender systems more intense than in the Presbyterian Mission Home for Chinese women, founded in San Francisco in 1874 and in operation until 1939.[31]

Support for Victorian female values was built into the institutional routine of the Presbyterian Mission Home. The Victorian conception of female purity, for example, was ensured by drawing strict boundaries between the rescue home and the surrounding community. Such a strategy seemed like mere common sense to missionary women who believed that the Chinese women who entered the institution were the innocent victims of predatory men. Mission Home officials had been threatened by tong members and local white gangs so frequently that they saw every venture outside the Home as potentially dangerous.[32] In their view, structured isolation was a necessary protection. As a result, Mission Home residents were never allowed outside the institution without escorts; in the early years, they were even hidden behind a screen at church services.[33]

Further, the Home had trusted doorkeepers whose job it was to screen visitors—men in particular—and keep them away from the women within.[34] Contact with people outside the Mission Home was limited to those approved by the staff: schoolteachers, employers judged suitable for domestic servants, and young men of "good" character who had been scrutinized by staff members. Matrons read all incoming and outgoing mail and confiscated letters they thought would prove detrimental to the residents' journey toward true womanhood.[35]

Victorian female piety was encouraged in the Mission Home by continual attempts to convert residents to Protestant Christianity. Morning and evening prayers, with more extended sessions on weekends, were the rule. Because matrons were determined that the "Bible shall be deeply implanted within [residents'] minds" in case they were "ever again surrounded with heathen influence," Protestantism permeated institutional educational activities.[36] Training in scripture was thought to be such a fundamental part of the Mission Home education that managers once canceled an arrangement with the Board of Education to provide a teacher for the Home because "the staff felt that she did not give the religious influence necessary," even though the decision meant that they had to finance a replacement themselves.[37]

Along with the emphasis on purity and piety came a routine of constant business, which was desired both as a means of training in domesticity and as a way of keeping rescue home residents from looking longingly at their old lives. The day began with 7 A.M. prayers, followed by breakfast, an hour of supervised housework, morning and afternoon school classes, dinner, a 7 P.M. prayer meeting, a study session, and then lights out.[38] Each resident cleaned her own room and did her own laundry in addition to the shared household tasks. Pairs of women were assigned each day to special tasks—cooking the Chinese and American meals perhaps, or caring for the few babies in residence at any one time, a favorite assignment. The staff depended on the most trusted residents to translate, for most missionaries did not speak Chinese. Older residents also assisted in rescue work, litigation, and the critical initial encounters with new entrants. Younger ones recited lessons or performed skits at the monthly public fund-raising meetings held at the Home.

The capstone to all this training in purity, piety, and domesticity was the marriage of a rescue home resident. Missionary women believed that by separating "degraded" women from their unsuitable liaisons with male "betrayers" and allowing them to regain their supposedly natural moral purity, Christian homes would be formed in which moral wives and mothers would preside, their womanhood respected and honored by kindly Protestant husbands. Accordingly, matrons kept count of the number of "Christian homes" formed by residents and considered them the surest measure of institutional success. They lavished praise on young married couples, orchestrated elaborate wedding celebrations, and published photographs accompanied by society-page-style descriptions of the ceremonies.[39]

Given the relatively small population of Chinese immigrant women, the numbers of these marriages are impressive. Mission Home workers claimed that by 1888, only fourteen years after the establishment of the institution, fifty-five Home residents had been married; by 1901 they took credit for 160 such marriages.[40] No comparable summary figures are available for the twentieth century, but, extrapolating from the average number of marriages recorded in occasional yearly statistics, I estimate that as many as 266 Chinese women married after residing in the Home between 1874 and 1928.[41] By combining information from Chinese Mission Home publications between 1874 and 1928 with information from the institutional case files between 1907 and 1928 (case files before that date were destroyed in the San Francisco earthquake of 1906), we can locate specific information on 114 marriages.[42] These marriages can be divided into two groups: those of prostitutes marrying suitors chosen well before entering the Mission Home and those arranged directly by Mission Home officials.

For the first two decades of its existence, the Presbyterian Mission Home survived by attracting women of the first group—Chinese prostitutes with suitors who exchanged prostitution for marriage by agreeing to submit to a concentrated Home-administered dose of the Victorian gender system. In the context of immigrant Chinatowns, marriage offered young women social respectability and a chance at financial security without the traditional period of apprenticeship to mothers-in-law, because so many in-laws remained in China.[43] For the typical prostitute, the chance to marry was limited by the virtual slavery of the tong-controlled prostitution system. Tong leaders were reluctant to release prostitutes under any conditions, and when they did let women go, they demanded exorbitant fees (ranging from $300 to $3,000) to offset their initial investment and expected loss of earnings.[44] Women who ran away without paying these fees could expect to be tracked down by tong "highbinders" (enforcers).

Under these circumstances, running away from prostitution was no small feat. To achieve it, young women had to find a way to escape from their owners' control long enough to enter the Presbyterian Mission Home. In fact, rescue homes sometimes lived up to their names when mission workers accompanied by white policemen, hatchets in hand, "rescued" young prostitutes directly from brothels. What prompted most prostitutes to take such a daring step was the hope of marriage. Typically, they had made plans to marry young men who were unable or unwilling to buy out their contracts or purchase their persons.

The early pattern can be seen in a letter addressed to Mission Home workers in 1886 by a young man who asked missionaries to collect his fiancée. He wrote:

> I have the case of a prostitute named Ah _____, to bring forward to your notice . . . I wish to succor her, but fear for my life. I also wish to redeem her, and have not sufficient means for that purpose. I find it hard to rescue her from her state of bondage. I thought of running away with her, but dread her keepers and accomplices' violence to me if intercepted. Even if we are furnished with wings, it is difficult to fly. . . . This girl wishes to enter your school. Here I have few friends of my own surname, so I am powerless to rescue her here. For this reason I have instead written to you for aid. I beseech you, with pitying heart and ability, to save her from her present difficulties and sufferings. This accomplished, there will be happiness all around.[45]

The writer went on to give specifics for the proposed rendezvous with missionaries, telling them, "If you get her I will take her home, and give a reward of $50 to your school. I will not change my words." In this case the young man's hopes came to naught—the missionaries arrived at the agreed site some time after the woman in question did—but the letter outlines a chain of events that was commonplace at the Mission Home.

In the years between 1874 and 1900, a steady stream of prostitutes with suitors approached the Home to obtain protection from the tongs so they could marry. Mission Home workers offered assistance only to women who agreed to reside in the institution for six months to a year.[46] Loi Kum, who entered the Home in July 1879, was one of them. According to Mission Home workers, she "ran away to escape a dissolute life" and appeared at their doorstep "accompanied by a friend, who proposes to make her his Wife."[47] By agreement with Mission Home officials, Loi Kum remained in the Home for several months. When her fiancé returned to arrange for their marriage, the missionaries were reluctant to let her go. They put the young man off several times by requiring him to pay $72 for her board and then obtain a legal marriage license. Finally, however, the wedding took place on July 16, 1880, almost a year after Loi Kum had entered the institution.[48] She and her husband left the Mission Home secure in the knowledge that they would have behind them the force of mission workers' access to police power and judicial authority should they be pursued by tong members.

Because missionaries harbored deep reservations about the young men who brought prostitutes to the Home, they did little to publicize these marriages. Only twenty-seven such cases, a figure I suspect underestimates their frequency, are visible in the sources I collected about Home residents, most mentioned only in passing. When they could, missionaries convinced women to break off their engagements with the men who accompanied them to the Home and choose Mission Home–approved husbands instead. These cases they documented more carefully. Mission officials made so much of the case of Chun Ho, a woman who had, they said, "entered the Home . . . promised . . . in marriage to a Chinese Romanist, but as light came into her mind both the Buddhist and the Romanist religion became distasteful to her, and she voluntarily gave him up" that a group of young women in Ohio offered to contribute to the Home on her behalf.[49] Always ambivalent about their role in facilitating the marriages of prostitutes to non-Protestant men, missionaries wanted to abandon the practice from the first, but not until the turn of the century were they able to do so.[50]

In the meantime, however, San Francisco Presbyterian women had expanded their mission and their rescue work to include neglected or abused children as well as betrothed prostitutes. Some children were brought to the Home by child protection authorities; others were left there by struggling immigrant parents who wanted an inexpensive refuge or an English education for their children. As these young girls grew into adulthood, they, too, were married—again with considerable intervention on the part of Mission Home workers.[51] Eighty-seven of these marriages, which form the second type under consideration, can be followed in resident information sources.

Perhaps the first such marriage was that of Ah Fah, held on Saturday, April 13, 1878. Ah Fah married Ng Noy, a Chinese Christian employed as a servant. The service was conducted in Chinese by a Presbyterian missionary and attended by Mission Home workers as well as friends of the couple. One missionary guest wrote a lengthy account of the event. Displaying typical racial attitudes, she commented approvingly that "this organization of a home on Christian principles" was "the first step upwards from heathenism to civilization." On behalf of Protestant women, she wished the newly married couple well, trusting, she said, that their "future housekeeping" would "indeed be a home-keeping."[52]

To arrange for the marriages of long-term residents like Ah Fah, missionaries screened applicants chosen from the many Chinese immigrant men who approached the Mission Home looking for wives. Matrons quizzed applicants about their previous marital status, religious convictions, and financial prospects in the belief that, as they put it, "he who would win a member of the Mission Home family for his wife must present the very best credentials."[53] Only those Chinese men who fit the white Protestant ideal of the Christian gentleman were allowed to write or call on residents.[54]

Chinese men had several motivations for seeking Mission Home brides. First, they were handicapped in finding wives by the skewed sex ratio of the Chinese immigrant community in San Francisco. Second, they had few other alternatives. Intermarriage was not a possibility for them because Chinese immigrants were prohibited from marrying whites by California miscegenation laws.[55] Bringing a bride from China was at least equally difficult. Few minor merchants had the financial resources to pay for the trip, and those who did found themselves at the mercy of unpredictable immigration officials. For these reasons, there was no shortage of suitors for Mission Home residents. Mission Home employee Tien Fu Wu found that she was approached by potential suitors, even on a trip to Boston. "Everybody is after me for girls," she wrote to Donaldina Cameron back in San Francisco and jokingly added, "I might as well open a Matrimony Bureau here in the east."[56] Mission marriages, then, were sought out by Chinese immigrant men. They also represented a significant advance in social status for Mission Home women, many of whom had originally been destined for lives of prostitution, neglect, abuse, or hard work and poverty.

In fact, marriages arranged by the Mission Home placed immigrant women at a particular level of the emerging social structure of San Francisco's Chinatown. In contrast to the social structure in China, which was dominated by scholars and officials, the social structure in immigrant Chinatowns in America was dominated by merchants. The wealthiest of these merchants tended to disdain immigrant women and had the resources to seek brides in China. A step below the wealthy merchants, however, stood a group of less prosperous merchants who were destined to become significant as growing immigrant communities came to depend on them for goods, services, and community leadership.[57] It was these minor merchants, many of whom had started with very little, who most actively sought—and accomplished— marriage with Presbyterian Mission Home residents. Although historians have largely ignored the immigrant marriages that were formed in this period (commonly referred to as the "bachelor" years of San Francisco's Chinatown), it is possible to argue that, by pairing promising Chinese merchants with young women inculcated with Victorian family ideology, Mission Home–arranged marriages created a core of middle-class Protestant Chinese American families in many cities.[58]

Some Mission Home husbands achieved considerable prominence. One example was Ng Poon Chew, the husband of Mission Home resident Chun Fa. Chun Fa had been brought to the Home at age six when a Chinese informant told the juvenile authorities that she was suffering regular beatings at the hands of the woman who had purchased her. She married Ng, who had studied under a Taoist priest in China, attended a Christian mission school in the United States, and taken a degree in theology from the San Francisco Theological Seminary. After several years of conducting mission work with Chinese immigrants in southern California, Ng returned to San Francisco to edit the *Chung Sai Yat Po,* an influential daily newspaper that catered to Chinatown merchants.[59] The Ngs had five children. Of their daughters, one became a piano teacher, one graduated from the University of California, and a third became the first Chinese American woman to be accepted as a (kindergarten) teacher by the Oakland Board of Education. Their son Edward achieved notice as the first Chinese American man to be commissioned by the U.S. Army in World War I.[60]

It was not only in San Francisco that Mission Home marriages contributed to the development of a Chinese American middle class. Presbyterian Mission Home workers received marriage inquiries from Chinese immigrant men all over the United States and used them to establish Mission Home– influenced satellite communities in other areas. As a result, small communities of Mission Home women formed in Los Angeles, Philadelphia, New Orleans, Portland, Minneapolis, Boston, and Chicago. The Philadelphia community, for example, began when Qui Ngun married Wong John in the late 1890s. In 1901 another Mission Home resident, Choi Qui, traveled to Philadelphia and married Wong John's cousin Wong Moy. At the beginning of their married life, Choi Qui and her husband set up housekeeping with the older couple. In 1915 Mission Home resident Jean Leen married Won Fore in the same city. When Tien Fu Wu, a helper at the Mission Home, brought Jean Leen to Philadelphia for her wedding, she used the occasion to visit all the other former residents of the Home in the area. A few years later, Mission Home officials sent Augusta Chan to live with and assist Qui Ngun. In 1922, Qui Ngun's daughter Eliza sent a wedding invitation to "grandma" Donaldina Cameron.[61]

Thus, for both groups of women—prostitutes with suitors and children raised in the institution—the Mission Home facilitated marriages. Whether residents entered the Home specifically for that reason or came there for other reasons, whether they entered the Home voluntarily or involuntarily, Mission Home–marriages seem to have offered Chinese immigrant women something of value. Despite the missionaries' preoccupation with Protestantism, the number of marriages far exceeded the number of baptisms among Mission Home residents. By 1901, for example, Mission Home officials claimed 160 marriages but only 100 baptisms.[62]

In fact, the prospect of marriages sanctioned by the Mission Home proved so appealing that some already married women came to the Home in search of new husbands. Some, like Wong Ah So, had been the victims of men who had deceived them into technical marriage ceremonies to smuggle them into the country. Others had been married quite legitimately according to Chinese custom but wanted to leave incompatible mates. One such woman wrote to Donaldina Cameron in 1923 to ask, "Let me enter your Home and study English [because] I am going to divorce with my husband for the sake of free from repression. . . . I understand," she explained, "that you as a Superintendent of the Home, always give aid to those who suffer from ill-treatment at home."[63]

Mission workers, who were horrified by the deceptions and conditioned by racial and cultural bias to believe that Chinese marriages were not really marriages at all, did help many women secure annulments or divorces. In at least a handful of these cases, missionaries arranged for new husbands as well.[64] Occasional facilitation of second marriages persisted, despite the fact that it exposed the Mission Home to criticism from observers in the white community. One lawyer who participated in a divorce proceeding initiated by a Mission Home resident could not restrain his sarcasm. When the divorce was declared final, he commented acidly, "The cute little defendant is now at liberty to marry whomsoever the good lord may direct across her path."[65]

The Mission Home offered married women more than the chance to form new marriages—it also offered them a chance to jockey for position with respect to their current husbands. In fact, workers at the Presbyterian Mission Home were repeatedly asked to intervene on behalf of unhappy Chinese immigrant wives. The numbers of these cases were probably considerably larger than the numbers of Mission Home–arranged marriages. In the early years of the Home, matrons were reluctant to acknowledge how many unhappy wives they admitted, but during the twentieth century they faced the issue more squarely. Statistics from the five-year period between 1923 and 1928 show seventy-eight such "domestic cases" admitted (in a period in which fifteen resident marriages were performed).[66] Without more information from the nineteenth-century period, we can only guess at the total number of women who might have entered the Home and had domestic complaints between 1874 and 1928, but eighty-four individual cases can be followed closely from resident information sources.

In domestic cases, several complaints loomed large. The most frequent was wife abuse. When unhappy wives complained of mistreatment at the hands of their husbands, they were granted temporary shelter in the Mission Home while missionaries, shocked at the ritualized complaints they heard, made it their business to shape unhappy marriages into the Victorian companionate mode. Because they believed that "the fault usually lies with the husband," missionaries almost always tried to ensure better treatment for the wife.[67] One woman, Mrs. Tom She Been, entered the Home "badly bruised from a beating" at the hands of her husband. The husband, a well-known Chinese doctor, apologized to the missionaries and asked his wife to return to him, but not until the secretary of the Chinese Legation offered to intercede on her behalf did the woman agree.[68] Missionaries were not, of course, always successful in solving a problem. One young woman who twice sought help from the Mission Home and both times went back to her husband committed suicide in March 1924.[69]

Other Chinese immigrant women approached the Home in order to gain leverage in polygamous marriages. One, "Mrs. Yung," requested help from the Mission Home after her husband took a concubine. Although concubinage was a recognized institution in China, Yung's own mother advised her to resist it. "I know," she wrote to her daughter in the Home, "how the second wife has brought all these accusations against you, causing your husband to maltreat you and act savagely. . . . You must make him send the concubine back to China. . . . It isn't right to acquire a concubine and especially this concubine." Mr. Yung, backed up by his father, apparently refused, but when Mrs. Yung complained to the Mission Home, Protestant women speedily arranged for the deportation of the concubine.[70]

Still other Chinese immigrant women came to the Mission Home to flee from marriages that had been arranged by their parents but were distasteful to them. The unsatisfied ex-resident who committed suicide was one of them. As word got around that Mission Home workers were hostile to arranged marriages, a number of young women found their way to the institution soon after their parents proposed unappealing matches. Bow Yoke, a young woman whose father had accepted $600 for agreeing to make her the second wife of a much older man, refused to go along with the plan. She fled to the police station and then to the Mission Home before the marriage could be carried out.[71]

Still another group of married women sought help from missionaries when the death of their husbands placed them under unprecedented control by relatives. That was the case with one former prostitute who had been known to Mission Home officials for several years. The young woman had refused earlier invitations to come to the Home because soon after becoming a prostitute she was successfully ransomed by a man who paid $4,400 for her; she married her redeemer soon afterward. She later explained to a Mission Home official that "he [her husband] was good to her and therefore she did not have to come to the Mission."[72] She did, however, come to the Mission Home when, after her husband's death, his nephew demanded that she return to him all the jewelry she had received as wedding presents.[73] Other widows, who feared that relatives would send them back to China or sell them or their children, also approached the Home.[74]

The possibility of Mission Home intervention offered Chinese immigrant women in any of these positions bargaining room to improve the terms of their marriages or their relations with relatives. In one typical case, a woman entered the Presbyterian Mission Home in 1925 and did not return to her husband until workers at the Home convinced him to sign an agreement stipulating that he would not use opium, he would treat her with "kindness and consideration" and "provide for them as comfortable a home as his income will permit," he would give her money to care for herself and her children, and if she died he would give the children to the Mission Home or to their grandmother rather than sell them.[75]

Missionaries intervened not only in the marriages of strangers who approached them but also in the marriages of women who had resided in and married from the Mission Home. A look at these interventions shows how Chinese immigrant women, and later their American-born daughters, used the conflict between the traditional Chinese gender system and the Victorian gender system in Mission Home marriages to shape their options in Chinese American communities.

Most public—and some private—accounts of Mission Home marriages stressed how thoroughly Chinese immigrant women adopted the Victorian gender system and its correlate, the ideal of compassionate marriage. A Mission Home woman in Philadelphia, for example, described her marriage to Mission Home superintendent Donaldina Cameron in a letter written during a lengthy illness: "My husband has been nursing me day and night," she reported. "He even gave up his restaurant to another party to look after, so he can nurse me, altho, our restaurant is the largest one in town." She went on to say, "He treats me like a real Christian. I regret very much that Heaven doesn't give me longer time to be with him. Yet, I thank God and you [Cameron] that we have had one another for more than ten years. As husband and wife we are most satisfied."[76]

As this example suggests, some Mission Home marriages did mirror the compassionate ideals of Victorianism, but I think it would be more correct to say that Chinese immigrant women, faced with the conflict between two distinct gender systems, sifted through the possibilities and fashioned their own product, one that reveals some of the weaknesses of the Victorian gender system for women. The argument must remain speculative here, because most of the sources come not from the women who entered the Mission Home, married, and remained in contact with missionaries but from those who refused to enter the Home in the first place or who ran away after a short residence. Still, the Mission Home's case files suggest just how selectively immigrant women responded to missionary overtures.

The files show, for example, the attitudes held by the young prostitutes who refused to enter the Mission Home. Despite their sexual exploitation, they were accustomed to receiving fine clothing and gifts of cash or jewelry from their customers or owners. Unless they had chosen a particular husband or found themselves especially ill-treated by their owners, they were unlikely to trade these material advantages for the general promise of Victorian moral respectability and economic dependence on husbands. On one occasion in 1894 when the Mission Home accepted sixty prostitutes arrested in a government raid, the matron recorded that the women "shrieked and wailed beating the floor with their shoes" and "denounced the Home in no unmeasured terms." The matron removed the angriest prostitutes to another room, but even those remaining rejected her offer of "protection" and residence in the Home "with scorn and derision."[77]

The disdain of these prostitutes was echoed by another group of Mission Home residents—young Chinese American women judged by American courts to be the victims of "immoral" men. Such young women were much more likely than abused children or unhappy wives to criticize the most coercive aspect of the Mission Home—the attempt to mold all women to fit the Victorian belief that women were "naturally" morally pure and pious.[78] In 1924, for example, "Rose Seen," an unhappy fourteen-year-old who longed to be reunited with her lover Bill, a Chinese man who had been charged with contributing to her delinquency, was sent to the Presbyterian Mission Home. In a note addressed "to my dearest beloved husband," Seen pleaded with Bill "to find some easy job and go to work so just to make them think you are not lazy and go to church on Sunday so pretend that you were a Christian cause Miss Cameron does not allow the girls to marry a boy that doesn't go to work."[79] When this plan failed (Mission Home women confiscated the note and reported Bill to his probation officer), Seen tried another tack. Remaining in the Home for more than a year, she and a fellow resident convinced officials of their sincerity to the extent that they were entrusted with the funds of a student group. In December 1925, however, both young women ran away from the Home, taking the money and some jewelry, hoping to reunite with Bill and his friends.[80]

By running away from the Mission Home, Rose Seen escaped the moral supervision of missionaries. "Amy Wong," a married former resident, was not so lucky. When she came to the Mission Home asking for help in a marital dispute, Protestant women decided that she, not her husband, was in the wrong. They promptly suggested that she sign an agreement that echoed those they ordinarily presented to husbands. According to its terms, her husband would take her back if she gave up smoking, drinking, gambling, and attending the Chinese theater and if she agreed "not to be out later than ten o'clock at night without my husband's knowledge and consent, or in his company." In addition, she was to attend church and part-time school regularly and spend the rest of her time working to earn money for further education.[81] The Wong agreement is the only one of its kind among Mission Home sources, but the Victorian pattern of female purity and piety it sought to enforce was a common assumption on the part of Protestant women.

Yet even though women like Rose Seen and Amy Wong eschewed the moral restrictiveness of Victorian culture, the clash between traditional and Victorian ideologies in immigrant Chinatowns rendered certain tenets of the traditional Chinese gender system particularly vulnerable. For Chinese women who had decided to marry, the traditional Chinese family ideals upheld by immigrant communities contrasted with important realities, including the relative absence of in-laws and the difficulty young men had in finding wives. In such a situation, Chinese immigrant women used the Home to help tip the balance between vulnerability and opportunity in immigrant Chinatowns. They sought to facilitate forming marriages and exert some control over relations within marriage itself.

Perhaps we can best understand this process by returning once again to the case of Wong Ah So, whose life so clearly reveals the connection between individual experience and shifts in the gender system of Chinese immigrant communities. After residing in the Mission Home for a year, Wong Ah So married an aspiring merchant who had established a foothold in Boise, Idaho.[82] When she wrote to Donaldina Cameron a few years later, she began by displaying the gratitude expected by Mission Home workers. "Thank you," she wrote, "for rescuing me and saving my soul and wishing peace for me and arranging for my marriage."[83] Wong Ah So had more than thank-yous in mind, though: She had written to ask for help with her marriage. Her husband, she said, was treating her badly. Her complaints were three: Her husband had joined the Hop Sing tong, he refused to educate his daughters (by a previous wife), and he was so unhappy that Wong Ah So did not provide him with children that he had threatened to go to China to find a concubine to have a son for him.[84]

In this letter, it is possible to see not only a conflict between two gender systems but also how Wong Ah So's ideals had changed since she left China. As a former prostitute who had suffered from illness, she may have been unable to have the son whose birth would earn her female authority in traditional culture; in any case, what she wanted now was an education for her stepdaughters. As a result, she had come to question the traditional ideals her husband still held. To retain his power, he threatened to return to China to find a willing concubine, a step that would have reinforced Won Ah So's vulnerability. To offset his power, she invoked the aid of Mission Home women, who, reading the carefully worded charges as an all-too-familiar indictment of "heathen" behavior, promptly sent a local Protestant woman to investigate.

Wong Ah So's case is especially revealing, but it was hardly unique. Because the Presbyterian Mission Home offered immigrant women a pathway to marriage in immigrant Chinatowns, its sources show in concentrated form the clash between traditional Chinese and Victorian gender systems. The clash itself, however, was a societywide process. Many Chinese immigrant women in America, whether in Mission Homes or not, found themselves able to use the gap between gender systems to maneuver for specific protections for individual women. Their dreams were played out over and over again as immigrant Chinatowns transformed themselves into Chinese American communities in the early twentieth century. Yet even as Wong Ah So made her plea to missionary women, the context of the clash between gender systems was changing dramatically.

After the turn of the century, the steps toward individual autonomy that Chinese immigrant women had made in negotiating between gender systems in the United States were overshadowed by the steps women were taking in revolutionary China. By 1937, when social scientists Norman S. Hayner and Charles N. Reynolds conducted a series of interviews with Chinese immigrants, they discovered that the women from China were often "shocked by the attitude of American-born Chinese . . . [and believed] that American Chinese, and women in particular, have stood still or lagged while their sisters in China have been progressing."[85] The emergence of Chinese feminism offered Chinese immigrant women in contact with feminist ideas a critique of traditional male power beyond that offered by Victorian missionary women, thus reducing the appeal of the Mission Home.[86]

At the same time, the strength and vitality of the Mission Home was sapped by the decline of the Victorian gender system within American society, the disintegration of a separate women's reform movement, and a general reevaluation of the thrust of Protestant women's missionary work.[87] Although Donaldina Cameron and many of her San Francisco followers remained devoted to rescue work, the Mission Home became the target of national Presbyterian officials who in 1939 moved mission operations to new quarters with room for no more than six residents. The reshaped mission, under the direction of Lorna Logan, planned to offer "a program of broad community service" instead of rescue work focused on Chinese women and girls.[88]

In such a changed context, the Mission Home had little to offer either Chinese or white women. At its height, however, rescue work had granted white missionary matrons—and a few selected Chinese protégés—an alternative to marriage that reduced their marginality in the Victorian gender system even while it required them to espouse companionate marriage as the proper goal for all women. For Chinese immigrant women, rescue work offered something else. It was a pathway to marriage which, although it required them to espouse the rhetoric of companionate marriage and risk the ethnocentrism of missionaries, gave them some leverage in reducing traditional male power. In this way, the conflict between gender systems seen in the San Francisco Mission Home allowed Chinese immigrant women to shape one set of possibilities for a Chinese American culture.

Notes

This essay is reprinted, with minor editorial changes, from the *Journal of Social History* 23 (June 1989): 123–40.

1. Carol Green Wilson, *Chinatown Quest: The Life Adventures of Donaldina Cameron* (Stanford, 1931), 209.

2. Information about Wong Ah So has been compiled from inmates files 258 and 260, Cameron House, San Francisco (numbers assigned by the author during research); Fisk University Social Science Institute, *Orientals and Their Cultural Adjustment* (Nashville, 1946), 31–35; *Women and Missions* 2 (1925–26): 169–72; and "Slave, Rescued in Fresno, Is Brought Here," *San Francisco Chronicle*, Feb. 10, 1924.

3. Donaldina Cameron biographical file, *San Francisco Chronicle* Newspaper Morgue Collection, California Historical Society, San Francisco.

4. See, for example, Alexander McLeod, *Pigtails and Gold Dust* (Caldwell, Ind., 1947), and, to a somewhat lesser degree, Richard Dillon, *The Hatchetmen* (New York, 1962).

5. See, for example, S. W. Kong, *Chinese in American Life: Some Aspects of Their History, Status, Problems, and Contributions* (Seattle, 1962); Betty Lee Sung, *Mountain of Gold: The Story of the Chinese in America* (New York, 1967); Francis L. K. Hsu, *The Challenge of the American Dream: The Chinese in the United States* (Belmont, Calif., 1971); and H. Brett Melendy, *The Oriental Americans* (New York, 1972).

6. See, for example, Stuart Creighton Miller, *The Unwelcome Immigrant: The American Image of the Chinese, 1785–1882* (Berkeley, 1969); Alexander Saxton, *The Indispensable Enemy: Labor and the Anti-Chinese Movement in California* (Berkeley, 1971); Victor G. Nee and Brett de Bary Nee, *Longtime Californ': A Documentary Study of an American Chinatown* (New York, 1972); Stanford M. Lyman, *Chinese Americans* (New York, 1974); and Ronald T. Takaki, *Iron Cages: Race and Culture in Nineteenth-Century America* (New York, 1979).

7. Only in the 1980s have there been serious scholarly attempts to analyze the significance of prostitution within the Chinese immigrant community or to explore the experiences of prostitutes themselves. See Lucie Cheng Hirata, "Free, Endentured, Enslaved: Chinese Prostitutes in Nineteenth-Century America," *Signs* 5 (1979): 3–29; Lucie Cheng Hirata, "Chinese Immigrant Women in Nineteenth-Century California," in *Women of America: A History*, ed. Carol Ruth Berkin and Mary Beth Norton (Boston, 1979), 223–41; Judy Yung, *Chinese Women of America: A Pictorial History* (Seattle, 1986), 18–23; and Ruthanne Lum McCunn's biographical novel *Thousand Pieces of Gold* (San Francisco, 1981). I would define a gender system as the way in which any given society creates, maintains, and reproduces its ideas about gender for women and men. My definition is adapted from a landmark article by Gayle Rubin: "The Traffic in Women: Notes on the 'Political Economy' of Sex," in *Toward an Anthropology of Women*, ed. Rayna R. Reiter (New York, 1975), 157 210, 159.

8. To date, most historians of women who have focused on missionary sources used them to understand missionary women rather than to understand relations between missionaries and the minority groups they targeted for their work. See, however, Jane Hunter, *The Gospel of Gentility: American Women Missionaries in Turn-of-the-Century China* (New Haven, 1984); Joan Jacobs Brumberg, "Zenanas and Girlless Villages: The Ethnology of American Evangelical Women, 1870–1910," *Journal of American History* 69 (Sept. 1982): 347–71; and Joan Jacobs Brumberg, "The Ethnological Mirror: American Evangelical Women and Their Heathen Sisters, 1870–1910," in *Women and the Structure of Society*, ed. Barbara J. Harris and JoAnn K. McNamara (Durham, 1984), 108–28.

9. For information on the traditional Chinese gender system, see Margery Wolf and Roxane Witke, eds., *Women in Chinese Society* (Stanford, 1975). Scholarship on the Chinese family has been flourishing and is too extensive to be reviewed here. For a sense of

the issues at stake, see Maurice Freedman, "The Family in China, Past, and Present," *Pacific Affairs* 34 (Winter 1961–62): 323–36; Carlotte Ikels, "The Family Past: Contemporary Studies and the Traditional Chinese Family," *Journal of Family History* 6 (Fall 1981): 334–40; and James L. Watson, "Chinese Kinship Reconsidered: Anthropological Perspectives on Historical Research," *China Quarterly* 92 (Dec. 1982): 589–622.

10. This generalization holds true despite the fact that ordinarily only the richest—and luckiest—families were able to reach the cultural ideal of the multigenerational family gathered under one roof. For a twentieth-century example of one of the rare peasant families able to maintain the extended-family ideal, see Margery Wolf, *The House of Lim: A Study of a Chinese Farm Family* (New York, 1968). For an example of a nineteenth-century woman unable—but still determined—to teach the ideal, see Ning Lao Tai T'ai, *A Daughter of Han: The Autobiography of a Chinese Working Woman,* ed. Ida Pruitt (New Haven, 1945).

11. Fisk University Social Science Institute, *Orientals and Their Cultural Adjustment,* 31; *Women and Missions* 2 (1925–26): 169–72.

12. Wong Ah So to Her Mother, n.d., inmate file 260, Cameron House, San Francisco. The letter has been reprinted in Fisk University Social Science Institute, *Orientals and Their Cultural Adjustment,* 34–35, and in *Women and Missions* 2 (1925–26): 169–72.

13. Wong Ah So to Her Mother, n.d.

14. Sue Gronewald, "Beautiful Merchandise: Prostitution in China, 1860–1936," *Women and History* 1 (Spring 1982): 1–114.

15. Olga Lang, *Chinese Family and Society* (New Haven, 1946), ch. 4.

16. Margery Wolf, "Women and Suicide in China," in *Women in Chinese Society,* ed. Margery Wolf and Roxane Witke (Stanford, 1975), 111–42.

17. Wong Ah So to Her Mother, n.d.

18. Lang, *Chinese Family and Society,* ch. 5; Wolf, "Women and Suicide in China."

19. Lang, *Chinese Family and Society,* 53, 108–9; Marjorie Topley, "Marriage Resistance in Rural Kwangtun," in *Women in Chinese Society,* ed. Margery Wolf and Roxane Witke (Stanford, 1975), 67–88.

20. Robert L. Griswold, *Family and Divorce in California, 1840–1890: Victorian Illusions and Everyday Realities* (Albany, 1982), 1–17; Carl Degler, *At Odds: Women and the Family in America from the Revolution to the Present* (New York, 1980), 3–25; Ellen Rothman, *Hands and Hearts: A History of Courtship in America* (New York, 1984), ch. 1.

21. Linda Gordon, for example, points out that what family historians have called the emergence of the companionate family was actually the "reconstruction of patriarchy," and Mary Ryan critiques the development of family history by exploring the gap between family ideology and women's reality. Gordon, "Child Abuse, Gender, and the Myth of Family Independence: A Historical Critique," *Child Welfare* 64 (May–June, 1985): 213–25; Ryan, "The Explosion of Family History," *Reviews in American History* 10 (Dec. 1982): 180–95. Other feminist historians have seen companionate marriage as a development of the twentieth rather than the nineteenth century. See Elaine T. May, *Great Expectations: Marriage and Divorce in Post-Victorian America* (Chicago, 1980); and Christina Simmons, "Companionate Marriage and the Lesbian Threat," *Frontiers* 4 (1979): 54–59.

22. Examinations of the complex relation of women reformers to the Victorian gender system include: Christine Stansell, *City of Women: Sex and Class in New York, 1789–1860* (New York, 1986), 199–216; Linda Gordon, "Family Violence, Feminism, and Social

Control," *Feminist Studies* 12 (Fall 1986): 453–78; Elizabeth Pleck, "Challenges to Traditional Authority in Immigrant Families," in *The American Family in Social-Historical Perspective*, 3d ed., ed. Michael Gordon (New York, 1983), 504–17; Barbara L. Epstein, *The Politics of Domesticity: Women, Evangelism, and Temperance in Nineteenth-Century America* (Middletown, 1981); and Kathryn Kish Sklar, *Catherine Beecher: A Study in American Domesticity* (New Haven, 1973). Examinations that focus directly on Protestant missionary women include: Sarah Deutsch, *No Separate Refuge: Culture, Class, and Gender on an Anglo Hispanic Frontier in the American Southwest, 1880–1940* ((New York, 1987), 63–86; Brumberg, "Zenanas and Girlless Villages"; Hunter, *The Gospel of Gentility;* Rosemary Skinner Keller, "Lay Women in the Protestant Tradition," in *Women in Religion in America,* ed. Rosemary P. Ruether and Rosemary S. Keller (San Francisco, 1983), 1:242–53; and Patricia R. Hill, *The World Their Household: The American Women's Foreign Mission Movement and Cultural Transformation, 1870–1920* (Ann Arbor, 1984).

23. Donaldina Cameron, speech outline, inmate file 260, Cameron House, San Francisco.

24. M.H.F., "A Christian Chinese Wedding," *Occident,* May 1, 1878, 6.

25. Figures taken from "The Ratio of Chinese Women to Men Compared to the Ratio of Women to Men in the Total Population of California, 1850–1970," which is included with Hirata, "Chinese Immigrant Women in Nineteenth-Century California," 241.

26. The dynamics of this network are best described in Hirata, "Free, Endentured, Enslaved," and I have relied on that essay for much of the discussion that follows.

27. Mary Chapman, "Notes on the Chinese in Boston," *Journal of American Folklore* 5 (1992): 321–24; Stanford M. Lyman, "Marriage and the Family among Chinese Immigrants to America, 1850–1960," *Phylon* 29 (Winter 1968): 321–30.

28. See Jaqueline Baker Barnhart, "Working Women: Prostitution in San Francisco from the Gold Rush to 1900," Ph.D. diss., University of California, Santa Cruz, 1976, for the comparison.

29. Hirata, "Chinese Immigrant Women in Nineteenth-Century California," 237.

30. The virtues of true womanhood were first identified in Barbara Welter, "The Cult of True Womanhood, 1820–1860," *American Quarterly* 16 (1966): 151–74.

31. Most earlier accounts of the Presbyterian Mission Home are focused on the life of its most famous matron, Donaldina Cameron. See Wilson, *Chinatown Quest;* Mildred Crowl Martin, *Chinatown's Angry Angel: The Story of Donaldina Cameron* (Palo Alto, 1977); and Laurene Wu McClain, "Donaldina Cameron: A Reappraisal," *Pacific Historian* 27 (Fall 1983): 23–35.

32. *Women's Work* (July 1892): 179; Woman's Occidental Board of Foreign Missions, *Annual Report* (1896), 66.

33. Occidental Branch, Women's Foreign Missionary Society, *Annual Report* (1878), 7.

34. Woman's Occidental Board of Foreign Missions, *Annual Report* (1903), 54–55.

35. Woman's Occidental Board of Foreign Missions, *Annual Report* (1895), 57; Ethel Higgins to Mrs. C. S. Brattan, Feb. 19, 1921, inmate file 109; and Ethel Higgins to C. W. Matthews, Aug. 28, 1922, inmate file 108, both in Cameron House, San Francisco.

36. *Occident,* April 13, 1881, 7.

37. Grace M. King, "Presbyterian Chinese Mission Home," nine months' report for the California State Board of Charities and Corrections, Nov.–Dec. 1919, Cadwallader Papers, San Francisco Theological Seminary.

38. California Branch, Women's Foreign Missionary Society, *Annual Report* (1895), 58–59; Woman's Occidental Board of Foreign Missions, *Occidental Board Bulletin,* Nov. 1, 1901, 15; King, "Presbyterian Chinese Mission Home," 9.

39. For typical examples, see M.H.F., "A Christian Chinese Wedding," 6; Woman's Occidental Board of Foreign Missions, *Occidental Board Bulletin,* Feb. 1, 1902, 34; and *Women and Missions* 5 (1928–29): 184–5.

40. Occidental Board, Women's Foreign Missionary Society, *Annual Report* (1888), 52–61; Woman's Occidental Board of Foreign Missions, *Annual Report* (1901). Mission marriages reflected a larger phenomenon occurring within the Chinese immigrant community in California. Lucie Cheng Hirata's figures indicate that in 1870 there were 3,536 adult Chinese women in California, 2,157 of whom were listed in the census as prostitutes and 753 of whom were listed as "keeping house." She cautions, "Most of this increase [in the number of Chinese housewives] occurred outside of San Francisco County." Hirata, "Chinese Immigrant Women in Nineteenth-Century California," 227–28, 236.

41. Mission Home officials reported a yearly total of marriages in thirty-three of the fifty-four annual reports issued between 1874 and 1928. A total of 163 marriages were reported, for an average of 4.9 per year. If we assume that the same average number of marriages were performed in each of the twenty-one years for which marriages statistics are not available, 102.9 additional marriages would have occurred during these years—thus my estimated total of 266 marriages. That total would be smaller than the summary totals occasionally claimed by Mission Home officials.

42. In addition to the annual reports, which contain a great deal of information about individual Home residents, published Mission Home sources include the Woman's Foreign Missionary Society and Woman's Presbyterian Board of Missions of the Northwest, *Woman's Work for Woman* (1875–78); *Occident* (a San Francisco Presbyterian newspaper, 1876–99); the Woman's Foreign Missionary Societies of the Presbyterian Church, *Woman's Work* (1885–95); the Women's Executive Committee of Home Missions of the Presbyterian Church, *Home Mission Monthly* (1886–1902); the Woman's Occidental Board of Foreign Missions, *Occidental Board Bulletin* (1900–1903); the Woman's Home and Foreign Mission Boards of the Presbyterian Church of California, *Far West* (1907–20); the Board of Missions, Presbyterian Church in the U.S.A., *Women and Missions* (1924–39); the Woman's Occidental Board of Foreign Missions, *"920" Newsletter* (1933–39); and a series of individually titled pamphlets. I have also seen 288 confidential inmates files still in the possession of Cameron House, San Francisco, California. To protect the confidentiality of the women and men mentioned in them, I have referred to the files by the numbers I assigned during research. When my information about a particular resident or her husband comes from case files rather than previously published sources, I have used pseudonyms in the text. All pseudonyms are pointed out in the appropriate footnotes.

43. Hirata, "Chinese Immigrant Women in Nineteenth-Century California," 237; Hirata, "Free, Endentured, Enslaved," 19.

44. Woman's Occidental Board of Foreign Missions, *Annual Report* (1907), 71; *Occident,* Jan. 15, 1879, 6.

45. Occidental Board, Women's Foreign Missionary Society, *Annual Report* (1886), 50–51.

46. California Branch, Women's Foreign Missionary Society, *Annual Report* (1875), 19.

47. *Occident,* Sept. 17, 1879, 6.

48. *Occident*, Aug. 25, 1880, 7.

49. *Occident*, Sept. 6, 1876, 285.

50. The policy is discussed in California Branch, Women's Foreign Missionary Society, *Annual Report* (1875), 19, and "Corrections on Tentative Report of the Presbyterian Chinese Mission Home, San Francisco, California," May 7, 1935, correspondence file, Cameron House, San Francisco.

51. The Presbyterian Mission Home did single out and support a small number of Home resident through higher education programs ranging from kindergarten training to medical school, and these young women were generally encouraged not to marry in order to make the most of their hard-won professional skills.

52. M.H.F., "A Christian Chinese Wedding," 6.

53. Woman's Occidental Board of Foreign Missions, *Annual Report* (1909), 77.

54. On the role of the Christian gentleman, see Rothman, *Hands and Hearts,* ch. 6; Charles E. Rosenberg, "Sexuality, Class and Role in Nineteenth-Century America," *American Quarterly* 25 (May 1973): 131–53; Lewis Perry, "'Progress, Not Pleasure, Is Our Aim': The Sexual Advice of an Antebellum Radical," *Journal of Social History* 12 (Spring 1979): 354–67; and Kathleen D. McCarthy, *Noblesse Oblige: Charity and Cultural Philanthropy in Chicago, 1849–1929* (Chicago, 1982), 53–75.

55. Megumi Dick Osumi, "Asians and California's Anti-Miscegenation Laws," in *Asian and Pacific American Experiences: Women's Perspectives,* ed. Nobuya Tsuchida (Minneapolis, 1982), 1–37.

56. Tien Fu Wu to Donaldina Cameron, June 13, 1915, inmate file 269, Cameron House, San Francisco.

57. June Mei, "Socioeconomic Developments among the Chinese in San Francisco, 1848–1906," in *Labor Immigration under Capitalism: Asian Workers in the U.S. before World War II,* ed. Lucie Cheng and Edna Bonacich (Berkeley, 1984), 370–401; Shepard Schwartz, "Mater Selection among New York City's Chinese Males, 1931–38," *American Journal of Sociology* 56 (May 1951): 562–68.

58. Victor Nee and Brett de Bary Nee, for example, use the term *bachelor society* to describe the years from the beginning of Chinese immigration through the 1920s. Nee and Nee, *Longtime Calforn',* 11.

59. For an analysis of the newspaper *Chung Sai Yat Po*'s coverage of women's issues, see Judy Yung, "The China Connection: The Impact of China's Feminist Movement on the Social Awakening of Chinese America Women, 1900–1911," presented at the Seventh Berkshire Conference on the History of Women, Wellesley College, June 19–21, 1987.

60. *Occident*, May 18, 1892, 11; Woman's Occidental Board of Foreign Missions, *Annual Report* (1892), 52, and (1909), 76; Woman's Occidental Board of Foreign Missions, *Occidental Board Bulletin,* July 1, 1902; Woman's Home and Foreign Mission Boards of the Presbyterian Church of California, *Far West* (Nov. 1918): 3–4; Mrs. E. V. Robbins, *How Do the Chinese Girls Come to the Mission Home?* 4th ed. (N.p., N.d.); Corinne K. Hoexter, *From Canton to California: The Epic of Chinese Immigration* (New York, 1976).

61. *Occident*, Feb. 7, 1900, 18–19; Woman's Occidental Board of Foreign Missions, *Occidental Board Bulletin,* Nov. 1, 1901, 10, Dec. 1, 1901, Jan. 1, 1902, 12, and Feb. 1, 1902, 3–4; inmate files 53 and 98, Cameron House, San Francisco.

62. Woman's Occidental Board of Foreign Missions, *Annual Report* (1901).

63. Letter to Donaldina Cameron, Jan. 3, 1923, inmate file 62, Cameron House, San Francisco.

64. *Occident,* April 4, 1887; Occidental Branch, Women's Foreign Missionary Society, *Annual Report* (1878), 9; *Occident,* Jan. 27, 1886, 11; Woman's Occidental Board of Foreign Missions, *Annual Report* (1915), 87–88; inmate files 12, 119, 189, and 237, Cameron House, San Francisco.

65. V. L. Hatfield to Donaldina Cameron, Oct. 6, 1923, inmate file 189, Cameron House, San Francisco.

66. "Admissions, 1923–1928" and "Dismissals, 1923–28," box 3, folder 6, record group 101, Files of the Department of Educational and Medical Work, 1878–1966, Board of National Missions, Presbyterian Historical Society, Philadelphia, Pennsylvania.

67. Woman's Occidental Board of Foreign Missions, *Annual Report* (1900), 73.

68. *Occident,* Feb. 28, 1900, 11; Woman's Occidental Board of Foreign Missions, *Annual Report* (1900), 73.

69. Biographical sketch and newspaper clippings, *San Francisco Examiner,* March 4, 1924; *San Francisco Chronicle,* March 5, 1924, inmate file 56, Cameron House, San Francisco.

70. Case of "Mrs. Yung," inmate file 167, Cameron House, San Francisco.

71. Woman's Occidental Board of Foreign Missions, *Annual Report* (1907), 68–69.

72. "Statement by Miss Tien Fuh Wu," inmate file 63, Cameron House, San Francisco.

73. "Statement [of resident]," inmate file 63, Cameron House, San Francisco.

74. See, for example, *Occident,* Dec. 23, 1885, 11, Sept. 6, 1876, 285, Jan. 24, 1877, 5, and March 7, 1900, 18; and Woman's Occidental Board of Foreign Missions, *Annual Report* (1910), 64.

75. "Agreement," Aug. 8, 1925, inmate file 30, Cameron House, San Francisco.

76. Ex-resident to Donaldina Cameron, June 1, 1928, inmate file 111, Cameron House, San Francisco.

77. Woman's Occidental Board of Foreign Missions, *Annual Report* (1894), 60–61.

78. See, for example, Woman's Occidental Board of Foreign Missions, *Annual Report* (1899), 74–81.

79. "Rose Seen" to "Bill Wong," n.d., inmate file 176, Cameron House, San Francisco.

80. "Two Slave Girls Flee with $1000," *San Francisco Daily News,* Dec. 22, 1925, and "Slave Girls Turn Thieves," *San Francisco Chronicle,* Dec. 23, 1925, both clippings in inmate file 115, Cameron House, San Francisco.

81. Case of "Amy Wong," "Agreement, September 13, 1927," inmate file 211, Cameron House, San Francisco.

82. Wong Ah So to Donaldina Cameron, Oct. 24, 1928, inmate file 258, Cameron House, San Francisco.

83. Ibid.

84. Ibid.

85. Norman S. Hayner and Charles N. Reynolds, "Chinese Family Life in America," *American Sociology Review* 2 (Oct. 1937): 630–37.

86. One of the major conduits for the dissemination of Chinese feminism was the *Chung Sai Yat Po.* See Yung, "The China Connection," for an analysis.

87. May, *Great Expectations;* Rosalind Rosenberg, *Beyond Separate Spheres: Intellectual Roots of Modern Feminism* (New Haven, 1982); Estelle Freedman, "Separatism as a Strategy: Female Institution Building and American Feminism, 1870–1930," *Feminist Studies* 5 (Fall 1979): 512–29; Paula Baker, "The Domestication of Politics: Women and American Political Society, 1780–1920," *American Historical Review* 89 (June 1984): 620–47; Hill, *The*

World Their Household, ch. 6; Louis A. Boyd and R. Douglas Brackenridge, *Presbyterian Women in America: Two Centuries of a Quest for Status* (Westport, 1983), ch. 4.

88. Presbyterian Church, *Board Reports* (1939), 96–98; (1940), 41. See Lorna Logan, *Ventures in Mission: The Cameron House Story* (Wilson Creek, Wash., 1976), 47–92, for an account of the changes. The new quarters were abandoned in 1949, and all Presbyterian social services for Chinese Americans were once again consolidated in the old building at 920 Sacramento Street, where they remain. The building was later renamed Cameron House.

PART 4

The Twentieth Century

As the nineteenth century gave way to the twentieth century, an egalitarian family appeared to have become the new American norm. The early twentieth century was hailed as the century of the child, and a host of Progressive reforms sought to make America at once more humane and child-friendly. States established juvenile courts in the hope of curbing juvenile crime and at the same time rescuing unfortunate young people. A major national campaign against child labor developed, and everywhere school attendance became compulsory and thus more common. Even the number of students in college expanded. Young women in increasing numbers went on to higher education and began to talk about combining careers with marriage.

Self-appointed experts on the family worried that the families of recent immigrants would not conform to this new pattern. Immigrants themselves, however, found ways to adopt the new family style without abandoning ethnic identity. If there is a dominant theme to family life in the twentieth century it is one of greater individualism. The process whereby families lost their functions, begun before the nineteenth century, continued during the twentieth. Young people of both sexes gained freedoms unheard of earlier. The developments confounded immigrant and native-born families alike and produced many conflicts among the generations.

In the early twentieth century, two great migratory streams came to the United States. The better-known came from Central and Southern Europe; the other, perhaps not as well known, was the migration from Central and South America. People from those regions came for the same reasons Europeans did—to better their lives. In chapter 9, Valerie Mendoza discusses the first Hispanic migrants to the Central Plains, single men seeking their fortunes. There were very few Hispanic women in Kansas, for example, until well into the twentieth century. After 1920 families became more common in the migration. As a result, young women found that unbalanced sex ratios and differing gender norms in the United States gave them more power than in Mexico.

A Norwegian farm family in Minnesota. (Private collection, courtesy of Elizabeth Nybakken, Starkville, Miss.)

The home and family of an oil field roustabout. (LC-USF 34-34057-D, courtesy of the Library of Congress)

In the Concourse. (LC-USF 3T01-15445-M3, courtesy of the Library of Congress)

Old friends in Starkville. (Scrapbook of the Wier Family, Robert and Sayde Wier Papers, courtesy of Special Collections, Mitchell Memorial Library, Mississippi State University)

Conflict characterized many immigrant families, especially those from southern Italy. In his selection (chapter 10), Robert A. Orsi explains how parents sought to counter the course taken by their American-born children who regarded them as hopelessly old-fashioned and backward. Parents saw their children as disobedient, disrespectful, and headed for dire consequences. As the children began to think of themselves as individuals, parents responded with physical and verbal abuse. In the process, they invented a mythical world of southern Italy, where all virtues were observed, parents were always obeyed, and children were always respectful and routinely sacrificed their own interests for the greater good of the family. That mythical world—one of memory and desire—became the litany parents used to try to control rebellious offspring.

Sometimes, conflict, even when anticipated, did not materialize. By the turn of the twentieth century, middle-class young women were enjoying more life choices than had been offered to their mothers. Both educational and vocational opportunities for young women expanded in the late nineteenth century. Given the greater range of choices, Linda W. Rosenzweig investigates how mothers felt about daughters' increased choices and how daughters regarded their more traditional mothers (chapter 11). Social commentators expected conflict to develop between mothers and daughters, and it did exist. The diaries and letters of some young women from the period reveal a more complex pattern, however. Some conventional mothers did encourage their daughters to test their wings and obtain the education that had been unavailable earlier. Then came the depression, and individualization and personal fulfillment became a luxury that many families could not afford. Husbands and fathers lost their jobs and often their self-respect; women accepted menial jobs and used their domestic skills to keep the family fed and clothed; children joined the Civilian Conservation Corps or the part-time labor force to contribute to the family income; and families banded together for survival.

An obligatory individualism descended during World War II when the Armed Forces drafted men, the country pleaded for young mothers to enter the job market, and small children only knew their fathers through photographs and written words. Female-headed households often combined in order to fulfill wage-earning and domestic responsibilities. The necessity for blended and fractionalized nuclear families, however, was not pleasant; many families associated such families with the pain and deprivation of these disruptive years.

During the 1950s, society tried, without success, to repeal the first half of the twentieth century and return to the "good old days" when life was predictable and nuclear families were intact. Prosperity returned, and married couples bought and occupied houses as fast as dwellings could be built. They filled them with large numbers of children, who in turn stretched the limits of the existing school infrastructure. Women returned home to find fulfillment in housework and child-rearing only to discover that their lives lacked the stimulation and excitement of the war years. Although the 1950s seems a tranquil time in American history, discontent seethed beneath the surface calm. During the 1960s, individual freedom expanded at a rate undreamed of a generation before. The discontent of well-educated, middle-class women coalesced into a movement for gender equity in employment (and the politics of housework) and led to the founding of organizations such as the National Organization for Women.

Renewed emphasis on home ownership and domesticity after World War II seemed to recapitulate the separate-spheres ideology of the nineteenth century. Yet the 1950s were different because of the desirability of togetherness. Postwar middle-class husbands were supposed to be heavily involved in family life, and, according to Steven M. Gelber (chapter 12), "do-it-yourself" home repair offered justification for a new male presence in the home and the new role of masculine domesticity.

A great many American families did not participate in the prosperity that characterized American society after World War II. Some would argue that African Americans and Hispanics arrived in inner cities just as the good jobs that offered possibilities for advancement left. In chapter 13, Maxine Baca Zinn examines this argument and others and finds that changes in family structure and dynamics among minority families were largely a response to changing economic circumstances. High rates of out-of-wedlock births and female-headed households thus reflect structural changes—responses to, rather than causes of, poverty.

9

They Came to Kansas Searching for a Better Life

VALERIE M. MENDOZA

In 1910 a person gathering census data for Topeka found Otto and Rosa Gonzalez living in a boxcar on Jefferson Street, along with five male board-ers.[1] Immigrants in similar conditions were becoming familiar sights in the part of town near the railroad shops. The Gonzalezes had emigrated from Mexico the previous year, as had all but one of their boarders. Everyone in this particular household except Rosa worked for the railroad, the Atchison, Topeka, and Santa Fe, which heavily recruited Mexican labor and represent-ed a major force in Kansas industry. Further along the tracks, a Rossville census-taker found six Mexicans rooming together in a boxcar supplied by their employer. It was a common arrangement for Mexican immigrant la-borers to live in boxcars, as was the fact that five of the men had wives who remained in Mexico.

The men, as well as everyone in the Gonzalez household, typified recent Mexican migration to Kansas. At first only males sojourned northward in search of work, as evidenced by the 12:1 ratio of the two groups.[2] They either left wives and children behind, as had the men in the Rossville boxcar, or else did not yet head families. Once they earned enough money or decided to stay permanently in the United States, however, the males sent for their families, which resulted in the transformation of railroad camps into communities—*colonias*—as early as 1920. Women like Rosa Gonzalez represented the rare female who typically took in male boarders in order to earn extra money during the early years of migration and settlement.

Mexican immigrants left behind a life in rural Mexico that offered little hope and where they could not have survived on wage labor alone. Life in the North seemed unimaginable, and very few immigrants had ever heard of Kansas, much less thought they would come to call it home. The same basic immigration experience, however, of moving to a new country, living in a strange setting and being exposed to a new work environment and culture, affected men and women differently. In general, men were frustrated when their expectations of economic enhancement and greater opportunity in the United States were not realized. Although they also met with disillusionment, women enjoyed greater freedom because of a more egalitarian atmosphere. In fact, the areas of demography and employment of immigrants to Kansas, and their contact with Americans, depended upon, and revolved around, gender.

Kansas offers an important area for study because of its similarity to many other northern industrial areas such as Chicago and Detroit in its skewed sex ratio and the work available on the railroads and in meat-packing houses. The fact that Kansas lies beyond the border area is another reason for its importance and differentiates it from the destinations of the traditional migrant stream. Mexican immigrants to Kansas did not have anyone to welcome them or help them adjust to the new environment and guide them through the complex web of northern culture. Precisely because Kansas is not thought of as a destination for Mexican migration, it and other parts of the Midwest have received little study. This essay is an attempt to help rectify that oversight.

Most Mexicans migrated to the United States in search of opportunity. Many wanted the chance to advance their economic situation so their families could lead better lives. The father of Sue Rodriguez, for example, came to the United States in 1900 because of the mistreatment of the poor in Mexico; Leonore Sanchez migrated in 1920 with her husband to work for a better life than they had in Mexico; and Domingo Lopez arrived in Topeka in 1912 with an uncle who had left Mexico because the revolution had presumably precluded any options he might have had there.[3]

Once in Kansas, most Mexicans worked for the Atchison, Topeka, and Santa Fe Railroad, which was largely responsible for attracting the increased Mexican population. One scholar of the Kansas railway industry has estimated that as many as 75 percent of all first-generation Mexican men worked as track laborers.[4] As the railroad became more and more dependent upon immigrant labor, the numbers of Mexicans in the state grew from approximately 71 in 1900 to 8,429 in 1910, and by 1920 that number had escalated to 13,770. The Mexican population increased to such an extent that although Kansas was not among the top ten states in Mexican population in 1900, by 1910 it had the fifth-largest in the nation, behind the border states of Texas, California, Arizona, and New Mexico.[5]

Men usually migrated by themselves the first time they crossed the border. Ignacio Valenzuela of Garden City arrived in the United States in 1916 for six months and returned the following year to work on the railroad.[6] The

1910 census manuscript lists many single men who worked for the railroad and lived in boxcars. Enumeration District 138, for example, contained forty-one Mexican men and no Mexican women. All men worked for the railroad, were in their twenties and thirties, and had immigrated in 1909. Similar patterns existed for both Dover and Soldier Townships.[7] In his study of Mexicans in Kansas, Robert Oppenheimer found that in 1915 one colony in Kansas City contained 181 males and only twenty females, half of whom were under ten years of age.[8] At least until 1915 and probably later, Kansas Mexicans were almost exclusively male. So few Mexican women lived in Kansas that men who wanted brides returned to Mexico to marry.[9]

Because Kansas had such a large Mexican male population, men created their own type of leisure activities. Pool halls and bars represented popular forms of recreation, for example the Hotel Paraiso in Kansas City's West Side barrio, where "scandalous activities" were common, and the pool hall Juan Martinez managed, also in Kansas City.[10] In addition, men formed *mutualistas* as support networks and for companionship. The Union Mexicana Benito Juarez held its first meeting in Kansas City in October 1914, with 150 people in attendance. In Topeka, another mutualista society, the Union Mexicans, met the following month and had 350 initial members. In 1917 another mutualista, the Sociedad Funeraria Miguel Hidalgo, was also founded in Topeka.[11]

Topeka seemed to have a fairly active community. In 1920 a large group of young men formed the El Diamante Club for "education, sports, and entertainment" purposes. The club met in the home of Jose Munoz and had a baseball team known as the "Mexican Nine," a football team, and members who boxed. The group also held dances at the Metropolitan Hall.[12] This club provided its male members with an ample social atmosphere and much camaraderie. It disbanded in 1924, however, perhaps due to the increasing number of families that came into the area, lessening the need for male-only forms of leisure.[13]

The early years of migration proved to be slightly different for females, whose numbers remained limited until the 1920s. Women, initially few in numbers, seldom migrated alone. They usually came with family members or to join them; unlike males, their experiences revolved around husbands or families. The first Mexican family in Chanute, Kansas, including women, arrived in 1905; Adolph Oropeza came to the United States in 1913 at age two, presumably with both his mother and father. The 1910 census listed a few families in Topeka, such as the two a census-taker found on First Avenue. One consisted of a husband, wife, and their twenty-two-year-old son, all of whom had crossed the border in 1909. A couple who had only been married for a year constituted the other family.

Reunion with family members who had already migrated brought other women north. Jose Garcia's wife and two sons followed him once he realized he would be staying in the United States for a long period if not permanently. Sue Rodriguez's father brought his wife north in 1909, nine years after his initial venture across the border.[14] Josefina Aguilem came to Kansas in 1916 with her aunt, uncle, their three children, her sister, and her husband and their child. Josefina's parents, who had been in Kansas since 1908, sent her the money for the trip.[15]

Not until 1920 did women and families arrive in Kansas in significant numbers. Before then, the fact that so few Mexican women lived in Kansas gave them more power than they had in Mexico, especially in relationships, where they represented a precious commodity. So much competition existed for women that in many cases wives deserted husbands.[16] Women had more options regarding mate choice than they did in Mexico, simply because of the uneven sex ratio, and if they felt mistreated by a husband or boyfriend they could leave that relationship in search of someone better.

Work represents another area where male and female immigrants had different experiences. The type of work in the United States contributed to the frustrated hopes of Mexican men. Before immigration, most men experienced great optimism over the opportunities available north of the border. "The worst work in the United States is better than the best here," stated a man who had yet to migrate. "The repatriados say that treatment is good and wages are good. . . . Here," he continued, "we work like burros, from sun to sun."[17] For those who came to Kansas and labored for the railroads, however, a better life did not prove to be the case. Railroads hired Mexicans because they thought of them as exploitable—tractable, obedient, and easily satisfied, cheap labor and nothing more. For these reasons, the railroads viewed Mexicans as the best available labor "from the standpoint of foreign labor" and became dependent upon them. In short, employers viewed Mexicans mainly as cheap laborers and nothing more. They wanted to extract as much work as possible from them. As one observer wrote, "Thus far when the Mexican breaks into industry he works in the dirtiest, hardest positions at the lowest wages."[18]

Men received wages higher than those they earned in Mexico but that were relatively low for the United States. In 1909, 86 percent of Mexicans earned less than $1.25 per ten-hour day on western railroads according to the Dillingham Commission—less than any other nationality. Railroads justified lower wages for Mexicans by citing their lower standard of living, even though the opposite was true and lower wages meant worsened living conditions. In Kansas, the father of Domingo Lopez found work with the Santa Fe in Topeka at $1.10 for a ten-hour day during the decade following 1910.[19]

Not only did Mexicans receive low wages, but they also encountered discrimination by being prevented from job advancement. Not until a 1922 strike by white railroad workers did the immigrants gain the opportunity to move up to being helpers; Marcos Corona and Felipe Rodriguez were even promoted to machinists.[20] The promotions were isolated, however, and conditions did not improve much. Adolph Oropeza, for example, stopped working for the Santa Fe in 1941 because, as he phrased it, "they wanted to keep me as a laborer forever."[21]

Other male immigrants talked specifically about dissatisfactions related to the type of labor they performed. "My life is a real story," stated Elias Garza, "especially here in the United States where they drive me crazy from working so much. They squeeze one here until one is left useless." He had spent some time in Kansas, where he and other immigrants "worked on the tracks, taking up and laying down the rails, removing old ties and putting in new, and doing all kinds of hard work." The father of Domingo Lopez worked for the Santa Fe doing odd jobs and repair work, and Lopez remembered the harsh conditions that his father and other workers faced. "In the summer they worked in the heat without any shade," he recalled, "in the winter from the time you left home until you returned you were cold."[22]

Immigrant after immigrant expressed negative feelings about the exploitative conditions of work in the United States. "It is here where I have worked the hardest and earned the least," one recalled.[23] Mexican Americans recognized that their labor was unappreciated. One immigrant, frustrated, composed the following *corrido* to warn others. He entitled it "Los Enganchados" (The Hooked Ones):

> On the twenty-eighth day of February
> That important day
> When we left El Paso,
> They took us out as contract labor.
>
> Some unloaded rails
> And others unloaded ties,
> And others of my companions
> Threw out thousands of curses.
>
> Said Jesus, "El Coyote,"
> As if he wanted to weep,
> "It would be better to be in Juarez
> Even if we were without work."
>
> These verses were composed
> By a poor Mexican
> To spread the word about
> The American system.[24]

Contract labor may have guaranteed work, but not all Mexicans realized exactly what type of work they had signed up for, as shown by the corrido. Once immigrants experienced harsh working conditions in the United States, they began to think that life in Mexico might be better after all. Railroads treated the laborers with virtual disregard, as expressed by the corrido composer and as seen by the fact that Jose Garcia, for example, did not know he was in Kansas until after he had learned how to swing a pick for the Santa Fe.[25]

The low earnings of Mexican males also forced women to work for wages. This put women into contact with the American values of their co-workers or employers if they worked outside the home and led to feelings of increased autonomy due to a new sense of economic power that further eroded male dominance. Perhaps that is why Mexican men resented women working or wanting to work. The father of Dionicia Vasquez, for example, would not allow females in his family to work despite his inability to do so. After the death of her father in 1936, Trini Torres's brother Adolpho supported the family by obtaining a job with the Santa Fe.

Nonetheless, the pressure of high living costs and low wages forced many Mexican women to work. Most married women worked inside the home, such as Petra Mendoza, who took in laundry, and Mrs. Grace Florez, who advertised in *El Cosmopolita* that she had rooms for rent in her Kansas City boardinghouse. Augmentation of income through boarders occurred often, particularly in a male-dominated community. Rosa Gonulez of Topeka cared for five male boarders, and one family on Monroe Street in Topeka housed seven. In most homes with women, boarders could be found—in part due to the lack of housing and in part as a way for the women to contribute to family income without leaving home. Women also cooked for men other than relatives or those who boarded with them as a way of earning extra money. The mother of Sue Rodriguez, for example, cooked for ten to twenty laborers.[26]

Some women did work outside the home—unmarried daughters, wives with no husbands present, or single women. Jenny Hernandez worked for Seymour Foods in Topeka for fifty-two years, plucking chickens and selecting eggs; Dolores Aguilera was employed by the Santa Fe for twenty-two years. These women not only had to labor for their respective employers, but they also, after long hours of paid employment, faced another set of chores in the home.[27]

Another area of difference between men and women can be found in their different reactions to contact with Americans. Many male immigrants, for example, voiced feelings of despair after living in the United States and being exposed to American prejudice and exploitation. One stated, "Over there in Mexico the majority of us Mexicans act as if we were lions, but as soon as we get to the United States we get humble and let ourselves be insulted in all kinds of ways." He went on to say that "humility is what hurts the Mexicans the most. Almost always when they go to speak to an American they feel themselves to be less worthy and so they speak with fear, and consequently are treated very badly." Some Mexican males experienced a sense of inferiority in relation to Americans that they did not with fellow countrymen. They could not see themselves as equals because it was not their country. Americans clearly expressed their dislike of foreigners. Luis Murillo experienced discrimination while working for the railroad in Kansas during the mid-1920s. "I didn't get along very well," he told an interviewer. "We went to a little town where there were very few Mexicans and they didn't treat us with very much respect."[28] It seemed to Murillo as if everyone in the United States, not just those in the upper classes, discriminated against Mexicans.

Contact with American culture for Mexican women proved to be a bit more rewarding. Although they, too, faced discrimination as Mexicans, they also observed that in the United States their status as women could be improved. One way American ideals came into barrios, and to women, was through Anglo religious and sectarian reform groups. These organizations felt that changes needed to be made within the home so Mexicans would better conform to American norms; in order to accomplish that, they targeted women. By the mid- to late-1920s, many churches and charitable organizations in Kansas became conscious of Mexicans and began to undertake Americanization programs "to indoctrinate Mexicans for United States citizenship." Clergy, labor agents, lawyers, merchants, and employers all vied for control and influence of the migrants, who lacked knowledge of the American system.[29] Kansas City social workers in 1913, for example, wanted Mexicans to "see standards of neatness and cleanliness" because "their ignorance and backwardness had affected their level of living, and values they placed upon hygiene of home and person needed to be raised." Others, such as the Agnes Ward Amberg Club, had "religious and social purposes" in mind with regard to Mexican immigrants.[30]

The state of Kansas contained no less than thirteen Protestant communities engaged in "Spanish-speaking work." The Spanish American Baptist Theological Seminary in Los Angeles, for example, sent Mrs. Clinton Ryan to try to Americanize and convert the immigrants of Wellington.[31] A Mexican Methodist Mission was established in 1921 in north Argentine, a Kansas City neighborhood, to improve conditions in the barrio during the 1921 recession, and it proved to be an important social service agency for three decades. The Methodist Mission provided food, clothing, medical services, and funds and conducted educational, recreational, and religious activities. Most important for women, it operated a day-care center and offered courses in sewing, cooking, and homemaking. Kansas City also had its own communi-

ty center operated by the Disciples of Christ, and the Rev. R. G. Estill presided over the Protestant Mexican Christian Institute in the West Side barrio.
Immigrants might have thought of such services as a godsend that helped
with the transition to life in Kansas, an intrusion, or attempted efforts at
conversion to Protestantism. Or, perhaps, they might have taken the middle
ground. In her examination of an El Paso community, historian Vicki Ruiz
showed that Mexicans who resided near a Methodist settlement house selectively used the facilities available to them and therefore controlled the Americanization efforts of the missionaries.[32]

Such selective use of charity services, and reaction against Protestantiza-
tion, can be seen by an account given by a Mr. Childs of the Mexican Christian Institute in Kansas City. Apparently, many Mexican immigrants took
advantage of the services offered by the Institute and even joined its church,
only to go "over to the Catholic church."[33] Mexican immigrants, therefore,
used Protestant aid and may even have felt compelled to join their churches,
but they did not abandon their Catholic faith. Such selective use of services
shows that women tried to be active agents and did not passively accept social workers' Americanization efforts.

Because these groups often invaded the homes of the Mexicans, immigrant women learned more about American women and culture through
direct contact than they would have otherwise. As Paul Taylor observed, such
contacts "almost invariably compel some cultural adaptations on the part of
the Mexicans." The social agencies unwittingly helped lessen male control
over female family members through interaction between Mexican women
and Americans. While teaching the American way of housekeeping and child
care, female social workers afforded Mexican women the chance to observe
American women in positions of authority and working outside the home.
The female immigrants began to absorb American values and learn to view
American gender roles as more egalitarian and less patriarchal than Mexican. Social workers also went so far as to overtly influence immigrants, particularly females, away from their Mexican culture not just toward an American one.[34] Husbands sometimes knew that visits from social agencies
influenced their wives' thoughts and behavior; as a result, male immigrants
resented the influence of female social workers. Women, however, did not
seem to view them negatively. The observance of American women by Mexican women dealing with social agencies aided in female acculturation and
helped to chip away at male dominance.[35]

Americanisms such as those learned from social agencies spread throughout the Mexican community in a variety of ways. The Spanish-language
newspaper of Kansas City *El Cosmopolita* proved to be one vehicle of prop-

agation or propaganda and control and had a readership as far away as Emporia.[36] One article published in February 1916, "La Reduccion de los Nacimientos," introduced Margaret Sanger and the virtues of birth control.[37] That this article was seen in a Mexican newspaper published by a white male speaks volumes about the dominant attitude toward immigrants. Information also spread through the barrio by way of recreation groups in which people gathered for company and gossip. Female members of the Mexican Baptist church in Topeka, for example, began a sewing circle in 1924, two months after the establishment of the church.[38] Whatever the motivation for the founding of the group, it undoubtedly served as a support network for members and possibly as a vehicle for empowerment and independence, as was the case with Hijas de Juarez, the mutualista society in Kansas City. Females could leave home and domestic duties behind, and they could also share new ideas or Americanisms with others.[39]

The move from a rural society in Mexico to an industrial society in the United States caused many changes within the family due to radical differences in demographic and economic structure and cultural and material values. A complicated dynamic existed between husbands and wives. The reality of family life as known in Mexico became a myth, an ideal that changed after crossing the border. No longer did a father represent the sole and supreme authority of the household. In the workplace, men faced discriminating and often humiliating situations. In addition, male incomes proved inadequate for family support, and women had to find ways to stretch those incomes or add to them. Many Mexican women took in laundry or boarders, which also facilitated their economic independence. Such necessary adaptations for survival chipped away at male honor and reputation while bolstering the image of female strength. American culture found its way into Mexican households through social service agencies that tried to Americanize immigrants through education. Many traditional cultural values were retained, but absolute male dominance became a thing of the past. "Our social structure has changed from the time Mexican families decided to venture into the United States," reflected Carmen Garcia of Topeka. "Our social codes have made many adjustments, and our lifestyles move at a faster pace," continued Garcia, "women can make choices, find goals, meet needs and be independent it desired. We are no longer the second-class citizen."[40]

Notes

This essay is reprinted, with minor editorial changes, from the *Kansas Quarterly* 25, no. 2 (1992): 97–106.

1. Tom Rodriguez, "Bottoms Life," *Fiesta Mexicana* (Topeka, 1988), 49, in the author's possession.

2. U.S. Department of Commerce and Labor, Bureau of the Census, "Thirteenth Census of the United States, 1910 Population Schedule, Shawnee County, Kansas," manuscript (hereafter cited as "1910 Census").

3. Sue Rodriguez, interview by Robert Oppenheimer (1981), Kenneth Spencer Library, University of Kansas; Lenore Sanchez, interview by Robert Oppenheimer (1981), Kansas State Historical Society, Topeka; Domingo Lopez, "La Yarda," *Fiesta Mexicana,* 60.

4. Cynthia Mines, "Riding the Rails to Kansas: The Mexican Immigrants" (1980, manuscript), 1, 28, Kenneth Spencer Library, University of Kansas.

5. Michael Smith, "Beyond the Borderlands: Mexican Labor in the Central Plains, 1900–1930," *Great Plains Quarterly* 1 (Winter 1981): 241; Anita Edgar Jones, *Conditions Surrounding the Mexicans in Chicago* (San Francisco, 1971), 31.

6. Ignacio Valenzuela, interview by Robert Oppenheimer (1981), Kenneth Spencer Library, University of Kansas.

7. 1910 Census.

8. Robert Oppenheimer, "Acculturation or Assimilation? Mexican Immigrants in Kansas, 1900 to World War II," *Western Historical Quarterly* 16 (1985): 436.

9. One Kansan not only returned to Mexico for his first wife but also went back again in 1947 for his second. Hazel Gomez Obituary Collection.

10. Michael Smith, "The Mexican Revolution in Kansas City: Jack Danciger versus the Colonial Elite," *Kansas History: A Journal of the Central Plains* 14, no. 3 (1991): 214; Manuel Gamio Papers, box 1, folder 6, Hubert Howe Bancroft Library, University of California, Berkeley.

11. *El Cosmopolita* [Kansas City], Oct. 1, Nov. 28, 1914; José Garcia, "History of the Mexicans in Topeka, 1906–1966" (1973, manuscript), 21, Topeka Public Library.

12. Garcia, "History of the Mexicans in Topeka," 21.

13. Minnie Miller, *The Mexican Heritage of Lyon County* (1980, pamphlet), 2, Kansas State Historical Society, Topeka; Adolph Oropreza, interview by Laurie Bretz (May 1980), Kansas State Historical Society; 1910 Census.

14. John McCormally, "La Colonia: Story of Emporia's 'Little Mexico,' No. 1: A Question of Democracy," *Emporia Gazette,* Dec. 8, 1947, 3; interview with Sue Rodriquez.

15. Margaret Beeson, Marjorie Adams, and Rosalie King, *Memories for Tomorrow: Mexican-American Reflections of Yesteryear* (Detroit, 1983), 62.

16. Greater female power with regard to relationships due to their limited numbers has been demonstrated for colonial Maryland and represents an analogous situation to the Mexican immigrant communities in Kansas during the first two decades of the twentieth century. See Lois Green Carr and Lorena Walsh, "The Planter's Wife: The Experience of White Women in Seventeenth-Century Maryland," *William and Mary Quarterly* 34 (Oct. 1977): 542–71; for accounts of the desertions of wives, see "Mexican Labor in the United States," Paul S. Taylor Papers, carton 11, Hubert Howe Bancroft Library, University of California, Berkeley.

17. Paul Taylor, *Spanish-Mexican Peasant Community: Arandas in Jalisco Mexico* (Berkeley, 1933), 40.

18. Taylor, *Spanish-Mexican Peasant Community,* 41; Robert N. McLean, *The Northern Mexican* (New York, 1929), 11, 13.

19. Mario Garcia, *Desert Immigrants: The Mexicans of El Paso, 1880–1920* (New Haven, 1981), 90; Lopez, "La Yarda," 60.

20. Oppenheimer, "Acculturation or Assimilation?" 326; Garcia, "History of the Mexicans in Topeka," 10.

21. Interview with Adolph Oropeza.

22. Manuel Gamio, *The Mexican Immigrant* (New York, 1969), 150; Lopez, "La Yarda," 60.

23. Gamio, *The Mexican Immigrant*, 91.

24. Garcia, *Desert Immigrants*, 63–64.

25. McCormally, "'La Colonia.'"

26. 1910 Census; interview with Sue Rodriguez.

27. Garcia, *Desert Immigrants*, 75; Hazel Gomez Obituary Collection.

28. Gamio, *The Mexican Immigrant*, 10, 222.

29. Larry Rutter, "Mexican Americans in Kansas: A Survey and Social Mobility Study, 1900–1970," master's thesis, Kansas State University, 1972, 60; Smith "The Mexican Revolution in Kansas City," 208–9.

30. Michael Smith, "Mexicans in Kansas City: The First Generation," *Perspectives in Mexican American Studies* 2 (1989): 34, 43.

31. McLean, *The Northern Mexican*, 27, 29; Michael Smith, "The Mexican Immigrant Press beyond the Borderlands: The Case of *El Cosmopolita*, 1914–1919," *Great Plains Quarterly* 10 (Spring 1990): 73.

32. Judith Fincher Laird, "Argentine, Kansas: The Evolution of a Mexican American Community, 1905–1940," Ph.D. diss., University of Kansas 1975, 199; Vicki Ruiz, "Dead Ends or Gold Mines? Using Missionary Records in Mexican American Women's History," *Frontiers* 12, no. 1 (1991): 33–56.

33. Paul S. Taylor, interviews on Mexican migration, Kansas City and St. Louis folder, carton 11, Hubert Howe Bancroft Library, University of California, Berkeley.

34. Paul Taylor, *Mexican Labor in the United States,* vol 2: *Chicago and the Calumet Region* (Berkeley, 1932), 255.

35. Taylor, *Chicago and the Calumet Region.*

36. Ibid., 264.

37. "La Reduccion de los Nacimientos," *El Cosmopolita* [Kansas City], Feb. 26, 1916.

38. Garcia, "History of the Mexicans in Topeka," 15.

39. *El Cosmopolita* [Kansas City], Dec. 26, 1914.

40. Carmen Garcia, "La Mujer," *Historia Mexicana* (Topeka, 1984), 51.

10

The Fault of Memory: "Southern Italy" in the Imagination of Immigrants and the Lives of Their Children in Italian Harlem, 1920–45

ROBERT A. ORSI

Conflict between parents and children in immigrant communities over the right way to live is inevitably cast in the idioms of geography. The men and women who had immigrated or migrated to Harlem remembered being children in other places. Their sense of the world—their understanding of what is, what is good, and what is possible—was grounded in memories of these other places, which were always also memories of their mothers and fathers.[1] Immigrants regressed when they remembered the old country, finding their way back to the needs, pleasures, and satisfactions of their early childhoods. But their children had been shaped by other experiences in the new place and remembered different things. Parents and children accounted for themselves—to each other and to themselves—by telling stories about different places. Conflict over the meaning of "America" and "Italy," or "Harlem" and the "South," or "New York" and "Puerto Rico" was the community's most intimate moral discourse. When the generations talked about these two places, they were defining the world, reflecting on the consequences of immigration, measuring the distance that separated parents and children, and marking the boundaries of acceptable and unacceptable behavior.

In geological terms, a fault, according to *Webster's*, is a "fracture of the earth's crust accompanied by a displacement of one side of the fracture in respect to the other and in a direction parallel to the fracture." In the history of immigrant and migrant communities like Harlem, the fracture ran through the crust of memory and was accompanied by a displacement of the generations with respect to each other. A deep fault line has run beneath the tenements, streets, social clubs, and churches of Harlem throughout its history.

Italian Harlem was built on this disjuncture of memory, and the neighborhoods erupted along the fault in the 1920s and 1930s in what was, by all accounts, a severe disturbance. Leonard Covello, who directed the Italian-language program at a Manhattan high school in the 1920s and served as the principal of another high school in East Harlem after 1934, recalled in his autobiography *The Heart Is the Teacher* that he got very little sleep in those years as he struggled, at first alone and then with a large staff, to bring immigrant parents and their New York–born children to some understanding of each other.[2]

Covello's days and nights were spent talking to young men who had run away from home and were sleeping in cars and to parents raging against their children's choices and values. The local police identified generational conflict as the major source of disturbance in Italian homes.[3] Parents and children lived in different linguistic universes, and the way they talked to each other expressed mutual refusal to acknowledge the reality of their respective worlds. In a pattern common to immigrant communities, parents in East Harlem spoke only in Italian to their children, who would respond only in English.[4] One of Covello's graduate students found in a survey he conducted in 1936 that many younger Italian Americans in Harlem either could not or would not identify their parents' *paese*.[5]

The social and economic world of Italian Harlem was changing in these years in ways that would have significant consequences for relations between parents and children. Historians have emphasized the family-centered economy of immigrant communities, noting that parents and children were bound together in the early years of immigration not only by kinship bonds but also by economic necessity. Immigrants and their children needed each other to survive, an arrangement one historian has seen persisting until 1940.[6]

But countervailing social trends became evident in Harlem following World War I as the demographic balance in the community began to tip in favor of the American-born for the first time. Compulsory education laws and restrictions on child labor had an effect on the way people lived in the community despite the well-documented efforts of Italian parents to evade such restrictions. Young Italian Americans began to think of themselves in a new way in these years. They played sports, went to school, listened to the radio, bobbed their hair, and went to movies. Southern Italians did not identify "adolescence" as a distinct period in an individual's development, a person was either a child or an adult.[7] But as Italian American young people took on the lineaments of something like adolescence, their parents found themselves confronting a new kind of being, which made them uneasy, uncomfortable, and angry. "There was no playing" in Italy, an immigrant woman told Covello, but "in America, it's all play and I see young men (*cazzoni*) who should be married and have families of their own playing ball in the streets—

che vergogna! Il giuoco e una ivenzione del diavolo" (the new being is a de-mon).[8] The woman's cry of "shame!" demonstrates the immigrants' disori-entation and confusion at what was happening to their children in the new place and the depth of their anger.[9]

Younger Italian Americans had become more familiar with the ways and language of the city, and their parents feared that this new sophistication would erode the basis of the old family economy grounded in and maintained by mutual dependence during the difficult transition to the industrial work world. The second generation was able to find better-paying work more easily in the years after World War I than their fathers and mothers had in the ini-tial period of Italian immigration.[10] If adolescents were making their own way in the city, would the family economy survive? There was a solid economic fear at the root of the family crisis of the 1920s and 1930s, and particularly bitter fights broke out within families over the control of paychecks as young people demanded some autonomy from the family economy.[11]

As younger people began to think of themselves in new ways, they also began to think of their parents in new ways. Both boys and girls began to re-sist being disciplined in public by their elders. "To be reprimanded by my fa-ther in the street was like having a knife pierced through my heart," one young man told Covello. "I dreaded it frightfully. I even dreaded his presence in the street when I was playing in it." Like other young men and women in Har-lem at the time, the young man looked to his friends for support against his kin, in contrast to the general Southern Italian distrust of friends who were not also family.[12] At the same time, this first generation of Italian adolescents also wished their parents would relent in the harsh discipline and begin to treat them in a new way and with new feelings and attitudes. One young woman told Covello, "Oh, if only our Italian parents were a little more loving and a little less dutiful! I know of many Italian boys and girls who have never known the touch of a loving arm around them or a sweet voice that would give real advice and solace. What the child hears instead is a series of commands and orders as if taken from a long ago written manual of child duties."[13]

Italian parents did not change their ways in the period under consider-ation; rather, Linda Gordon observes, there was an increase in parental vio-lence against children. In the new economy, "based on individual wage la-bor and increasingly requiring formal education . . . traditional patterns of socialization did not necessarily fit children for the world they would face as adults."[14] There were cultural supports as well for the violence of Southern Italian parents who viewed their children with profound ambivalence as both angels and wild animals needing to be tamed. Interview sources from East Harlem report beatings, often severe ones, by parents.

Physical violence was only one way the immigrant generation in Harlem responded to the crisis of the years after World War I. Immigrants also resorted to what must be called a violent discipline of the imagination. In their children's presence they constructed a particular image of "Southern Italy" as well as an inversion of this they called "America." The creation of "Southern Italy" was a public performance built during preparations for and celebrations of weddings and funerals, occasions when the generations found themselves together that marked changes in the social relations and definitions in the community. The clash between the old ways and the new was most clearly evident to the community itself at these times.[15] "Southern Italy" was always cast as a reproach to the younger generation's emerging sense of the world. With this act of the imagination peculiar to immigrant communities, the immigrants sought to discipline their children with the other place.

Most historians have assumed, as Covello also did from within the thick of the crisis, that the immigrants' American-born or -raised children rejected their parents' values and treated contemptuously any mention of the old country. "Everywhere the present mocked the past and turned yesterday's wise man into an old country bumpkin" Moses Rischin writes in *The Promised City* in a sentence that indicates the mood of this interpretation of generational conflict in immigrant communities.[16] Immigrant parents, according to most historians, wanted their children to appreciate, respect, and even share the values and ways of that other place, but the younger generation, under the influence of American ideas and prejudices, turned away. Judith Smith, a historian of Italian Americans in Providence, Rhode Island, has commented that during this transitional period immigrants had begun to find it extremely difficult to share their fundamental values with a younger generation increasingly absorbed into American culture.[17] Likewise, Virginia Yans-McLaughlin, in an important study of Buffalo's Italians, assumed that the most serious threat to the stability of the Italian American family came from the outside, from the individualistic values of American social welfare agencies for example.[18] According to Covello, the culprit was the public school, which taught Italian American children to despise the language and culture of their parents. What resulted was that "the influence of the parental culture [is] unavoidably weakened, its patterns cease to be a strong agency of moral and social control."[19]

Covello and the historians of Italian America who have come after him worked from a particular understanding of the way tradition is transmitted. For them, the older generation "passes on" its values to the younger, which for various reasons may or may not be capable of accepting them. Any resistance in this process comes from the generation on the receiving end. That is both an inadequate model for the historical fate of traditions and an inaccurate representation of what happened in Italian Harlem and other Italian American communities.

Is it possible, for example, that under the pressures of the crisis the immigrants created a particular understanding of "Southern Italy" that could not be passed on and was never intended to be? Could immigrants have shaped an image of "Southern Italy" meant to exclude their children? Could immigrants have used this "Southern Italy" against their children as an instrument of discipline?

The direction of immigrant family history in the United States is well known. It has gone from the tragic historiographies of Oscar Handlin and Marcus Hansen, which emphasized the traumatic consequences of industrialization and immigration for traditional family patterns, to historians of continuity who have stressed the economic importance, cultural authority, and historical stability of the immigrant family. One of the results of that particular historiographical development is that conflicts within the immigrant family in general, and the Italian American family in particular, have been obscured.

John Bodnar, for example, acknowledges familial tension and turmoil in *The Transplanted,* a study of immigration, but only very briefly and almost reluctantly. A "few" children resisted their parents and "individual plans and dreams were often formulated but reluctantly put aside for family needs," but, Bodnar concludes, "the cooperative ideal" so necessary for economic survival "pervaded most immigrant families."[20] As Yans-McLaughlin writes, "The Italian family made a relatively smooth transition from the Old to the New." She is echoed by a student of Italian St. Louis, Gary Mormino: "The Italian family survived the passage of immigration and the rigors of industrialization in remarkably good health." Mormino concludes that St. Louis Italians gave evidence of "dedication to family and commitment to community" and in this way "created and sustained a culture of community stressing integrity, decency, and honor."[21]

Yet the evidence of sharp and persistent conflict between parents and children was clear between the wars—and not only in East Harlem. The examination should shift from the issue of Italian American family persistence in American culture (and the identification of outside threats to this persistence) to the family's inner workings in a proper historical situation and an analysis of the cost of that continuity. I have always seen the much-celebrated success of the Italian American family as a kind of tragedy, of which the years from 1920 to 1945 were the second act. We should listen, as much as we are able, to what immigrants were telling their children about the old world and about the moral topography of that other place.

What kinds of stories did Italian immigrants tell their children about the world before New York and before them? How were the stories told and in what spirit and to what end? How did the younger generation receive them? What did these stories mean in the generational crisis of the 1920s and 1930s?

IMAGINING SOUTHERN ITALY

The family was the source of all bounty in "Southern Italy" as immigrants constructed this place for their children. One woman told Covello, "In our family, every member of the family worked for the family. There were no wages and there was no pay day. . . . The family provided for everything. Once a year, each member of the family had a new suit made from cloth woven at home, also new shoes for Sunday and 'scarponi' for everyday use. We ate as one family. We had no use for money as individuals."[22] Harlem's Italians had emigrated from those regions of the peninsula that were most alienated from the new Italian state. The only memories of "Italy" these men and women had were memories of their families, intimate ties linking them to particular Southern landscapes. As they imagined "Southern Italy" for their children, it became a place of perfectly ordered and secure family relations.[23]

Nothing threatened the intimacy and authority of the family. Marriage, for example, did not mean separation in "Southern Italy," but a deeper closeness to one's family of origin.[24] Families were almost preternaturally close in "Southern Italy." Relatives saw each other whenever they wanted or needed. There seemed to be no distance separating kin, no space between them, and no obstacles to the satisfaction of their needs for each other.[25]

"Southern Italy" was a land of mighty mothers and fathers whom no child would ever dare disobey. Parents reigned unchallenged over their offspring. Children were treated with the usual Southern Italian ambivalence in these stories, but despite their frequent unruliness and potential destructiveness they always finally submitted to parental power. These bad/submissive children never grew up in "Southern Italy." In this construction, children were always children and parents always powerful. One young man told Covello, "In Italy, my father told me, he was slapped in the street by his father despite the fact that he was twenty-five years old."[26]

In "Southern Italy," women knew their place, married the persons they were expected to marry, and never went out at night.[27] This was the land of order and propriety, where the appropriate norms (il buon costume e l'ordine della famiglia) were always obeyed.[28] It was a geographical fantasy of entropy, although as the immigrants spun this tale of "Southern Italy" for their children, they did make it clear that order was achieved against the innate destructiveness of women and children. The latent themes of these stories and the values encoded in them were submission, domination, and the surrender to absolute authority.

Just as the distance that separated family members was obliterated in this imagining of "Southern Italy," so, too, the distinctions between species were blurred. One of Covello's sources lamented that what she missed most about Italy was living with her animals.[29] In another woman's memory, little children and lambs are joined in an image of pastoral harmony.[30] Likewise, the distance between the human and divine was diminished. In "Southern Italy," one man told Covello, everyone always went to church.[31] God, like the family, provided spontaneously and abundantly for everything.[32] "What we have here," an immigrant told Carla Bianco:

> The work we have here, is not like what we had in Italy! In Italy it was far better! If I had a lot of money, I would go to Italy. I would go there, because the air and the people there are not like the air and the people here. The old people here—we are in prison. In Italy, we used to walk four, five miles a day, morning and evening, and we always had to carry heavy things with us. And yet, we used to sing all the time, all the way to work! And loud! They used to hear me from here to down in the valley. It's true! Oh, it was beautiful.[33]

The immigrants' sorrow was real, of course, and they genuinely missed Italy with greater or lesser intensity according to the stages of their lives in the United States. But we have not paid enough attention to the way that nostalgia was transmuted into discipline.

The opposite of "Southern Italy," of course, was "here," "America." The imagining of "Southern Italy" was always structured in contrast to this other, equally imaginary, place where money could be made more easily than in "Southern Italy" the immigrants conceded, but everything else was wrong.[34] "America" was the structural inversion of "Southern Italy." In "America" the dead were not buried properly and went unmourned, women and children ran wild, and men were not really men.[35] In "America" children betrayed their parents, denying the fundamental bonds between them. As one woman told Covello, in "America" "there is no family, or anything."[36] Immigrants in Harlem did not believe that Americans could raise their children properly.[37] "America" was, in the words of one of Garibaldi Lapolla's immigrant characters, an "upside down and crazy" land.[38]

When young Italian Americans expressed their own concerns in Harlem, or discussed plans they had made for themselves apart from the priorities that had been established for them by their families, or sought to arrange some event in their lives in a manner they considered appropriate, their immigrant parents chastised them with a bitter phrase that derived its mean power from this contrast between places. You want to make your life, they would say, "an American comedy"?[39]

But who were these "Americans" who lived in "America"? How could one recognize them other than by their poorly mannered children? A girl who had immigrated with her family from Italy in 1927 told Covello that her Italian neighbors in the Bronx found her family strange. "As we came from a newer Italy and thought and acted differently than the Italians who came to America many years before, my brothers and myself became frequent subjects of discussion. The Italians on Villa Avenue frequently pointed us out, saying: 'Non sembrano Italiani, sembrano Americani.' Whatever that could mean, I felt they disliked us."[40]

Whatever that could mean indeed. The older immigrants identified as "American" any person who did not conform to the norms of "Southern Italy" as they "remembered" them, even if the person came from Southern Italy. They had created a place without history where nothing ever happened, and when someone came from that place bearing the signs of change they concluded that he or she was an "American." A visitor from Sambuca, Sicily, complained to Donna Gabbaccia during a visit to his American relatives in New York in 1980: "Why do these *Americani* [his relatives] always accuse us of having abandoned the old ways? We are Sicilians, but we are proud to have changed. We are *evoluto,* but they. . . . These *Americani!* Why they seem to think that they are the only real Sicilians."[41]

The problem for immigrants in the 1920s and 1930s, of course, was that their children were changing too, which meant that they were becoming "Americani." Covello noted, "When an Italian wants to condemn a young man they say he is an 'American.'" And in her study of Roseto, Pennsylvania, Carla Bianco observes that any departure of younger people from traditional ways appeared to their immigrant parents as a "decline in humanity which they blame on America."[42] The immigrants were saying that there was only one way of being truly human, and that way was identified with a place other than this place.

Young people either submitted to this account of the world, and to the norms encoded in it, or else they were excommunicated by their parents, driven not only from the community but also from the circle of the acceptably human. The tale of parents who refused to recognize the existence of one of their children who had deviated in some way from "Southern Italian" practices was so common as to constitute a particular category of the community's folklore.[43] To refuse to enter the world of "Southern Italy" marked one as a "dog," an "animal," or a "Turk."[44] The younger generation understood that. They knew that the only logic they could use against the image of "Southern Italy" was violent separation.

But could the second generation have entered the world of "Southern Italy"? Was it even intended to be entered? "I was born in a small town called Lucania (Basilicata) in Spinosa," one immigrant began his creation of "Southern Italy." "Some of its traditions are beautiful and it gripes me when I have to listen to unappreciative misunderstanding young people who could never in a million years live up to such fine customs and home life that is carried on in these little towns hidden up in mountains or down in the valleys. We have a wealth of material which more sensible people would give anything to have or be familiar with for the purpose of enlightening other people who would likely feast at coming into such information."[45] This man says explicitly what was implied in every angry imagining of "Southern Italy": Immigrants were telling their children that "never in a million years" could they live life as it was lived in that other place because this place is not that place. The immigrants met each sign of change, hint of autonomy, and new idea or interest of their children with the image of "Southern Italy," making it clear the whole time that they identified the children as "Americans." Covello and most subsequent historians of Italian America have it wrong: The immigrants did not imagine "Southern Italy" for their children but against them.

Piri Thomas calls his mother's public evocations of Puerto Rico "dream talking."[46] The recreation of a place in memory is subject to all the pressures and forces that shape any exercise of memory: the distortions and displacements of desire, repression, fear, and denial. The memories of "Southern Italy" I have described were not frozen at the moment of the immigrant's departure but in the moment they encountered their maturing children. "Southern Italy," in other words, was born of fear, desire, and denial in East Harlem.

The years between the World Wars were a hard time for the immigrants. The experience of the depression was grim in Harlem, threatening the immigrants' always fragile achievements. Italy seemed far away after government restrictions slowed the arrival of newcomers to the community. One of Covello's students, commenting on the mood in Harlem after 1924, claimed that neighborhood cliques based on Southern Italian regional identification were dissolving and fewer people were keeping to the old ways.[47] Whether that was exactly true or not, it is important that this is how the community had begun to think of itself. Italian immigrants came to the United States with the intention of making enough money to return to Italy and live comfortably in the old *paese*. They kept alive their attachment to the old country through remittances sent to relatives, for example, and even through trips back and forth. In the 1920s and 1930s, however, these immigrants suddenly discovered that they were becoming Americans by attrition, and one of the most disturbing ways they discovered this was by looking at their children.

"Southern Italy" was born of that distress. The construction brought the immigrants back to the unchanging world of infantile satisfactions, presided over by all powerful mothers and fathers, in which needs were met by the bounties of nature, family, and God. It is significant in this regard that in the memories of the immigrants "Southern Italy" was always identified with their mothers.[48] It also served them as a satisfying structure of denial. Although immigrants were quite capable of more realistic recollections of their homeland when they were talking among themselves, for their children they suppressed any reference to family turmoil, which was particularly acute in Southern Italy just before and during the period of immigration.[49] Nor did they discuss religious alienation and dissatisfaction, poverty, disease, infant mortality, and suffering. While they were disciplining their children the immigrants were consoling themselves.

"SOUTHERN ITALY" AS EXCLUSIONARY TEXT

The Balinese cockfight, according to Clifford Geertz in his well-known (and often criticized) account, presents to its spectators an image of the world not really as it is but as it ideally is.[50] The cockfight is a text in which the Balinese reads, in the sense of enters into, a characteristic structure of moods, attitudes, and understandings about the world, an encounter Geertz describes as "a kind of sentimental education." "Enacted and reenacted, so far without end, the cockfight enables the Balinese . . . to see a dimension of his own subjectivity. As he watches fight after fight . . . he grows familiar with it and what it has to say to him, much as the attentive listener to string quartets or the absorbed viewer of still life grows slowly more familiar with them in a way which opens his subjectivity to himself." The Balinese "forms and discovers his temperament and his society's temper at the same time" in the cockfight.[51]

The public construction of "Southern Italy" in East Harlem in the 1920s and 1930s was a similar sort of performance. The immigrants were displaying to their children (and themselves) a way of being in the world, a unique "Southern Italian" subjectivity. Their children understood that these stories of place were stories about the world and how to live in it. One of Covello's students angrily complained that he was "tired of hearing about how good the old town was in Italy." His parents had "lived their lives in their own way," he said, and he wanted to live his in his own way.[52] Covello himself was confident that he could read out the codes and norms of the Southern Italian way of life from the way the immigrants presented Italy to their children.[53]

Unlike the Balinese (in Geertz's imagining of them), the second generation did not discover aspects of their subjectivity in these performances but rather encountered a denial of their emergent subjectivities. This suggests that we are dealing with a particular sort of cultural text or performance as well as a particular sort of family dynamic. Geertz's understanding of cultural performances owed a great deal to Paul Ricoeur's theory of the text.[54] Ricoeur believes that the text summons the reader into the world it discloses, or, as he says, "The text seeks to place us in its meaning." In a discussion of the text of ancient "Greece," for example, Ricoeur writes, "We speak about the world of 'Greece,' not to designate any more what were the situations for those who lived them, but to designate the non-situational references which outlive the effacement of the first and which henceforth are offered as possible modes of being, as symbolic dimensions of our being-in-the-world."[55] In the discourse of "Greece," we understand "the outline of a new being in the world." Entry into such worlds of discourse, Ricoeur says, is the action of the world of the text upon the reader. To read, in this understanding, is to be taken up and spun inexorably into the web of the text and into the way of being-in-the-world that it discloses.

"Southern Italy," however, which did disclose a way of being-in-the-world, did so in order to exclude the younger generation. Immigrants in East Harlem constructed "Southern Italy" for their children only to reveal to them how far they had fallen from it and how impossible it would be for them to live up to its standards. Out of their own needs in New York, they created a static paradise into which they demanded their children gaze while making it clear that the children could never enter. The second generation had been born in the wrong place. They were "Americani." This is one way this younger generation discovered who they were in these years, but it could not have been a pleasant discovery.

It was the fault of memory. The younger generation did not remember the other place, the only place where people are truly human. To invert one of Covello's phrases, they were excluded from "Southern Italy" as their birthright by the locus of their memories and by the fact of growing up and developing new ideas in the new place. The immigrants presented their children with an exclusionary text; the latter could not enter "Southern Italy" because it was made to repel them. "Southern Italy" was a "text-against" and meant to disclose and enforce distance.

Southern Italians themselves had been dismissed from the circle of the truly human. The immigrants came from that region of Italy where, as Carlo Levi was told by its inhabitants, Christ had never chosen to come.[56] They had been called, and continued to be called in New York, "Turks" and "Africans." Italian immigrants named as their deepest desire in coming to America the ability to earn enough money to be considered "cristiani."[57] These people were familiar with the discipline of expulsion.

One historian has seen a shift in these years in New York's Italian communities, from externally applied parental discipline (the applications of sanctions within the family economy) to a more inwardly oriented discipline—in particular the manipulation of guilt in the conflict with the younger generation.[58] I would go further. In the generational crisis of the 1920s and 1930s, Southern Italian parents attempted to control their children by denying their humanity and threatening them constantly with exile from the community, tactics with which they had long been familiar themselves. They were applying familiar sanctions against their children but in a radically changed material context that impelled them to a harsher insistence on the absolute authority of "Southern Italy."

The creation of "Southern Italy" was predicated on the denial of the reality of "America." Immigration, in the immigrants' understanding, acquired the status of a fall, and the fault of memory became the second generation's original sin, branding them as "American." History had stopped for "Southern Italy," which became a paradise lost, prehistoric (and antihistoric) and filled with the archaic longings of the immigrants. One can measure the intensity of the need the immigrants had for that imaginary, unchanging world by observing the tragic disappointment and disorientation experienced by those who returned to "Southern Italy" but found instead Southern Italy. Dino Cinel has described their plight: "When Italians returned to Italy, they witnessed additional changes and felt a different and more disturbing kind of alienation. The towns and villages were not the same as those they had left: much had changed in the few years they had gone. Returnees painfully recognized that they no longer had a place that they could call their own. They were aliens both in the United States and Italy."[59] History, change, conflict, dissent within families, and the new concerns of the younger generation all characterized "America." Leaving Italy meant embarking on a process of degeneration. There was no place in this construction of the world, of the two worlds, for new generations trying to make their way in the new place.

CONCLUSIONS

I have described the peculiar role that the imaginative construction of "Southern Italy" played in the intergenerational crisis of the 1920s and 1930s in Italian Harlem. I hope in this way to break with earlier students of the subject and put conflict at the center of the understanding of Italian American family history. The southern Italian "tradition," Yans-McLaughlin observes, "provided the interface between the Old World and the New, lending coherence to the crisis of adjustment."[60] But traditions are not simply handed down in a neutral process of generational transmission. They are first constructed, in particular times and places, out of particular circumstances of crisis and need, in a process with both conscious and unconscious elements. The construction of tradition is contextual, and talk about tradition must be contextual as well.[61] "Traditions" may be shaped by one part of the community against another. It may not be the intention of the older generation to "hand on" a "tradition" but to deploy it against its juniors. It is also clear that "tradition" did not facilitate the process of adjustment to the New World in any simple sense. The imagining of "Southern Italy" was hardly a force for coherence in Italian Harlem.

We must begin to think about Italian American history as endurance through conflict and stability through instability. Dysfunction, pain, and alienation, the result of both internal and external circumstances, were as much, if not more, a part of the history of immigrant families as were mutual support and group cooperation.[62] If that is not understood, then the rest of the immigrant experience, especially religion, will remain opaque.

I have also suggested that what I have called the harsh discipline of the imagination had roots in Southern Italian history. The historians of continuity have emphasized the hardiness of the Southern Italian family in the New World and the persistence of its values and authority. Just how hardy the Southern Italian family was in the first place is debatable, that the particular tragedies of the history of the Mezzogiorno left their mark on these people, and on their relations with their children, is not. The history of the Italian American family is the history of conflict.

That leads to a very different construction of the inner world of immigration, and of immigrant family history, than the one proposed by most recent historians. Consider again John Bodnar's presentation in his authoritative history of immigration.[63] The traditional family, says Bodnar, maintained its strength and usefulness in the new industrial economy because of its "central and enduring attachment to the value of cooperation." Family members worked together, "muting individual inclinations" and stressing "sharing and reciprocity" so "family goals came to supersede individual goals, and parents and children both worked together vigorously to contribute to family welfare."

The picture looks different from East Harlem and from San Francisco as Dino Cinel has presented it and Boston in Linda Gordon's account. Coercion more than cooperation characterized the family in Italian Harlem—perhaps "coercive cooperation" would be the best formulation. Individual inclinations were not muted but suppressed, even if the younger folk participated in their suppression. Family goals did not come to replace individual goals; individuals, especially young women, were subjected to fierce family disciplines that included the discipline of the imagination.[64]

The conflict that characterized what are now the middle years of Italian American history, 1920–45, is not the whole story of Italian American family history. There were forty years before and forty years after in which different problems and structures are evident. Tamara Hareven has written that the family must be studied as a "process over time."[65] The period I have studied represented a particular moment in the history of Italian American families when conflict took a particular form. At earlier and later moments the struggle did not revolve around competing definitions of place, but it did in the 1920s and 1930s and a generation was shaped by the conflict.

It is clear that the moral history of communities like Harlem must be studied in the contrasting accounts of place that are evolved in them. The stakes in the struggle over the meaning of place were high in East Harlem and black Harlem. It was a question of how to live in the world and of what the world was. An old immigrant woman once told Covello that she wanted to die in "Southern Italy." Implicitly at least she understood the true meaning of the place.[66]

Notes

This essay is reprinted, with minor editorial changes, from the *Journal of Family History* 15, no. 2 (1990): 133–47.

1. I have borrowed these categories of what is/what is good/what is possible from Goran Therborn, *The Power of Ideology and the Ideology of Power* (London, 1980), 18. Ideology in this account is not wrong thinking, but comprehensive, historically derived ways of constructing reality within the coordinates of social power.

2. Leonard Covello, *The Heart Is the Teacher* (New York, 1958). Covello and his colleagues make no reference to the split between generations in the charter they drew up for the Italian League for Social Service in 1915 (Covello Papers, Balch Institute for Ethnic Studies, Philadelphia [hereafter cited as Covello Papers]). Other Italian American communi-

ties in the United States were experiencing the same conflict in these years. Dino Cinel notes that hostility between the generations was the topic most often discussed in the files of the Italian Welfare Agency in San Francisco during the 1930s. Parents identified the source of the problem as their offsprings' desire for a wider circle of friends outside of the family; younger people said they were trying to escape the boredom of their parents' world. Cinel concludes, "The children were different from their parents; they had grown up in a different environment." Cinel, *From Italy to San Francisco: The Immigrant Experience* (Stanford, 1982), 125–26. Judith Smith observes widespread occupational and residential mobility in the Italian community in this period along with "the nearly universal acceptance of English as a language." Such changes, she notes, brought on a crisis of identity in the community. Smith, *Family Connections: A History of Italian and Jewish Immigrant Lives in Providence, Rhode Island* (Albany, 1985), 169. Humbert Nelli makes similar observations about the Chicago Italian community; see *Italians in Chicago, 1880–1930: A Study in Ethnic Mobility* (New York, 1970), 204. The Balch Institute has prepared a useful catalog of the documents in the Covello Papers: see Shawn Weldon, "Register of the Leonard Covello Papers, 1907–1974," MSS Group 40, Balch Institute, Philadelphia, 1982.

3. Covello's students conducted a survey of New York police precincts in Italian American neighborhoods in 1932, Covello Papers.

4. Leonard Covello, "Language Usage in Italian Families," *Atlantic* (Nov. 1934): 370.

5. This is in a history of East Harlem, a manuscript prepared for Covello by S. Busacca in 1936, Covello Papers.

6. John Bodnar situates the family economy in the ethnic enclave, "a complex world that was grounded not only in the workplace but also in intricate networks of family, communal, and work associations." The enclave was a "community born of the shared experiences of family and toil" and shaped the "life goals" of immigrants and their children. In this world, "parents assisted children, uncles gained jobs for nephews, and friends forged associations with common boundaries." Bodnar, *Worker's World: Kinship, Community, and Protest in an Industrial Society, 1900–1940* (Baltimore, 1982), 63, 166.

7. Michael James Eula, "Between Contadino and Urban Villager: Italian Americans of New Jersey and New York, 1880–1980, a Comparative Exploration into the Limits of Bourgeois Hegemony," Ph.D. diss., University of California, Irvine, 1987, 116–87.

8. "C.G., First Generation. Came to America at Age of Thirty," interview fragment, Covello Papers.

9. The perception that adolescents are "hostile and uncontrollable" became widespread in the 1920s. See Linda Gordon, *Heroes of Their Own Lives: The Politics and History of Family Violence* (Boston, 1988). Italian Harlem's "discovery" of this, however, was rooted in the peculiarities of immigration in the broader context of a changing American economy, and it differed from the coincident discovery in "Middletown." Although Covello was influenced by the theorists of adolescent crisis in this period, we should keep clear the distinction between the two simultaneous discoveries.

10. Samuel Baily, "The Adjustment of Italian Immigrants in Buenos Aires and New York, 1870–1914," *American Historical Review* 88 (1983): 281–305.

11. Robert Orsi, *The Madonna of 115th Street: Faith and Community in Italian Harlem, 1850–1950* (New Haven, 1985), 111.

12. "Italian Family Discipline, Family Discipline in America, L.H.-31, John Fazio," Covello Papers.

13. "Mores Relevant to Girls, Second Gen. Teacher, Female, L.C.T.-S.B. 1940 II," Covello Papers.

14. Gordon, *Heroes of Their Own Lives*, 188.

15. Orsi, *The Madonna of 115th Street*, 104–49.

16. Moses Rischin, *The Promised City: New York's Jews, 1870–1914* (Cambridge, 1962), 146.

17. Smith, *Family Connections*, 73–75.

18. Virginia Yans-McLaughlin, *Family and Community: Italian Immigrants in Buffalo, 1880–1930* (Ithaca, 1971) 220.

19. Covello made this point repeatly in speeches he gave to audiences outside New York City in these years. I have quoted in the text from page 14 of "Italo American Youth in the War Crisis," which Covello gave at Sarah Lawrence College on March 29, 1943, but see also "Cultural Minorities in the War Effort" (Aug. 1943); "Neighborhood School in the Greatest Metropolis" (Feb. 25, 1939); "The Meaning of the Term 'Juvenile Delinquent'" (Dec. 7, 1939); and "Language Usage," 327–29. All in the Covello Papers. This was the guiding insight of Covello's masterwork, *The Social Background of the Italian American School Child* (Leiden, 1967). In his introduction to that work, Covello's friend and executor Francisco Cordasco bitterly denounced what he called the "public school's assault on cultural identity," which he held responsible for the wellsprings of ambivalence in the second generation (xix). Covello was an eloquent advocate of bilingual education, and the school he built in East Harlem offered a tolerant and supportive educational environment for the children of immigrants and migrants. The curriculum addressed issues of cultural diversity and cultural conflict, and Italian American students were encouraged to explore not only their own cultural traditions but also those of their neighbors. I am not dissenting from Covello's charge against public schools, but I am arguing that there were other, internal, wellsprings of ambivalence. The generations did not need public schools to drive them apart. Covello's understanding was also echoed by other observers of the Italian American community of the time; see, for example, John Howard Mariano, *The Second Generation of Italians in New York City* (Boston, 1921), 29.

20. Bodnar, *Worker's World*, 73–74.

21. Yans-McLaughlin, *Family and Community*, xx, 22-23; Gary Mormino, *Immigrants on the Hill: Italian Americans in St. Louis, 1882-1982* (Urbana, 1986), 110–11; see also Smith, *Family Connections*, 94; and Corinne Azen Krause, "Urbanization without Breakdown: Italian, Jewish, and Slavic Immigrant Women in Pittsburgh, 1900–1945," *Journal of Urban History* 4 (1978): 292-93. In "Does the Family Have a History? A Review of Theory and Practice in Family History," *Social Science History* 6 (1982): 153, Louise Tilly and Miriam Cohen also comment on the revisionist tradition of immigrant historiography.

22. "C.G., First Generation. Came to America at Age of Thirty."

23. See, for example, "Establishment of Life in America. First Generation, Forty-two Years—from Baiano near Naples. . . . American Lawyer"; "Dowries among Italo-Americans, Second Generation Man, Twenty-two Years (T.N.-B.F.-I)"; and Margaret A. Harrington, "Italian Backgrounds," School of Education, New York University, 1939 (an outline description of a family study conducted by Harrington, Covello marked the document, "Keep!"). All in the Covello Papers. See also page 60 of the sketch of East Harlem history and culture prepared for Covello and dated Jan. 24, 1936, Covello Papers.

24. L.C. [Leonard Covello], "La Famiglia in America," Covello Papers.

25. "Family Interaction in U.S. A.J.S"; "Mutual Aid Society as Social Center, Second Gen. Female, College Student, E. Locquaniti"; and "Mutual Aid Societies, Italian Second Generation, Lawyer, Forty-two Years." All in Covello Papers.

26. "Italian Family Discipline, Family Discipline in America, L. H.-31, John Fazio."

27. Untitled interview fragment and "Flora Vastola," fragment. "C.G." also comments on this; see "C.G., First Generation. Came to America at Age of Thirty." All in Covello Papers.

28. "Italians in U.S.," interview fragment, Covello Papers.

29. May Case Marsch, "Italian Sentiments in U.S. Italian Social Heritage," Ph.D. diss., New York University, 1930, 64.

30. "C.G., First Generation. Came to America at Age of Thirty."

31. "Religious Affiliation in the United States. P.C.-B.Y.-III," Covello Papers.

32. "Thrift. C.G.," Covello Papers. "C.G." may be the same person cited earlier, although that is not clear from this fragment.

33. Carla Bianco, *The Two Rosetos* (Bloomington, 1974), 130.

34. "Socio-Economic Adjustment in America, from the Story of an Assimilated Family-Ruth Chase-S.B.-1939," Covello Papers.

35. "Flora Vastola" fragment; "Marriage Concepts of Italian Girls, Italo-American, Forty-two Years Old, Came to US as Boy of Three, Father of Five Girls, One Boy"; and "Mores Relevant to Italian Girls. Second Gen. School Teacher, Female." All in Covello Papers.

36. "C.G., First Generation. Came to America at Age of Thirty."

37. "Rearing of Children Demands a Proper Social Milieu. Second Gen. Thirty-six Years Female. Parents from Near Avellino"; see also "Case Study-R.M.-E.H.Y.S.-1943." Both in Covello Papers.

38. Garibaldi Lapolla, *The Grand Gennaro* (New York, 1931), 37. See a longer discussion of this theme in Lapolla's work in Orsi, *The Madonna of 115th Street*, 157–60. Two novels of Italian immigration popular in San Francisco in these years also emphasized and mourned the fall from Italian ways in the New World. In Paolo Pallavacini's *Tutto il dolore, tutto l'amore* (1937), a character exclaims, "Only in Italy can family life exist in all its beauty." Giovanni Pancrazi had a character say in *L'etrusca all'ovest* (1914), "Family life in the native village is the most cherished dream of those forced to leave their country." Both novels are discussed in Cinel, *From Italy to San Francisco*, 191.

39. "Dowry among Italo-Americans. Male Thirty-six Years—Born in USA of Sicilian Parents," Covello Papers.

40. "Accommodation in America. First Generation Girl, Arrived in 1927 at Age of Eleven," Covello Papers.

41. Donna Gabaccia, *From Sicily to Elizabeth Street: Housing and Social Change among Italian Immigrants, 1880–1930* (Albany, 1984), 116.

42. Leonard Covello, "Cultural Problems among Italians in the United States," given at the Y.M.C.A., Feb. 8, 1940, 9, Covello Papers; Bianco, *The Two Rosetos*, 141.

43. Orsi, *The Madonna of 115th Street*, 107–89.

44. Untitled interview fragment.

45. Thomas DeStefano, "Preservations of Italian Traditions, S.B. 1941" (term paper), Covello Papers.

46. Piri Thomas, *Down These Mean Streets* (New York, 1974), 9.

47. Zappulia history, "Establishment of Life in America. First Generation. Forty-two Years—from Baiano near Naples, American Lawyer," Covello Papers.

48. Orsi, *The Madonna of 115th Street,* 14–25, 163–68.

49. Cinel, *From Italy to San Francisco,* 193; Josef Barton, *Peasants and Strangers* (Cambridge, 1975).

50. A number of useful critical perspectives on this essay of Geertz's can be found in James Clifford and George Marcus, *Writing Culture: The Poetics and Politics of Ethnography* (Berkeley, 1986).

51. Clifford Geertz, *The Interpretation of Cultures* (New York, 1973), 450–51.

52. Untitled fragment beginning with "in my early years, even when I was going to college," Covello Papers. Cinel has commented on the frustration of young Italian Americans in San Francisco in the same period: "The authoritarianism of the immigrant parents simply did not make sense to children born in the United States. It belonged to another world" (*From Italy to San Francisco,* 129).

53. L.C. [Leonard Covello], "Some Basic Mores in Family Life," Covello Papers.

54. Paul Ricoeur, *Hermeneutics and the Human Sciences: Essays on Language, Action, and Interpretation,* ed. and trans. John B. Thompson (Cambridge, 1981).

55. Ricoeur, *Hermeneutics and the Human Sciences,* 202.

56. Carlo Levi, *Christ Stopped in Boli,* trans. Frances Frenaye (New York, 1977).

57. Orsi, *The Madonna of 115th Street,* 18, 85–86, 197.

58. Eula, "Between Contadino and Urban Villager," 143.

59. Cinel, *From Italy to San Francisco,* 71–100, 257.

60. Yans-McLaughlin, *Family and Community,* 260.

61. I want to distinguish this idea of the "construction" of tradition from Hobsbawm and Ranger's idea of the "invention" of tradition. (Eric Hobsbawm and Terence Ranger, eds., *The Invention of Tradition* [Cambridge, 1983].) Construction implies a greater dependence on materials already available, consciously and unconsciously, to the people involved in the act of imagining a tradition or reassembling its pieces into new patterns according to a complex and multileveled logic. Traditions always exist as themes and variations, with the latter determined by and expressing historical circumstance, psychological need, and political pressures. Immigrants did not invent a tradition ex nihilo. Rather, they improvised on the polysemous "tradition" (all that they understood or fantasized about themselves and where they had come from and where they were going) they had inherited in some inchoate fashion from their elders. Traditions are invented, but only in the way that dreams are invented by a dreamer—from the stuff already there.

62. See the useful comments on family dysfunction in history in Rayna Rapp, Ellen Ross, and Renate Bridenthal, "Examining Family History," *Feminist Studies* 7 (1979): 174–200.

63. Bodnar, *Worker's World,* 73–74.

64. Orsi, *The Madonna of 115th Street,* 129–40. Linda Gordon comments in *Heroes of Their Own Lives* (190) that parental violence was often more intense toward girls, and that was certainly the case in East Harlem.

65. Tamara Hareven, "The Family as Process: The Historical Study of the Family Cycle," *Journal of Social History* 7 (1974): 322–29.

66. "Assimilation and Family Establishment, Primary Group Cohesion and Assimilation Process. Story of an Assimilated Family. Francesco Annato. S.B.-N.Y.U.-1938," Covello Papers.

11

"The Anchor of My Life": Middle-Class American Mothers and College-Educated Daughters, 1880–1920

LINDA W. ROSENZWEIG

In 1917 a contributor to the popular women's magazine *Good Housekeeping* made the following assertion:

> In the lifetime of girls even twenty years old, the tradition of what girls should be and do in the world has changed as much as heretofore in a century. It used to be that girls looked forward with confidence to domestic life as their destiny. That is still the destiny of most of them, but it is a destiny that in this generation seems to be modified for all, and avoided by very many. . . . The mothers of these modern girls are very much like hens that have hatched out ducks. Whether they believe in current feminine aspirations or not makes not very much difference.[1]

These observations highlighted a series of dramatic changes that peaked around the turn of the century and significantly altered the expectations and aspirations of American girls and young women. While the earlier nineteenth-century world had offered women few viable alternatives to marriage and a traditional role in the family, the world of the late nineteenth and early twentieth centuries brought new opportunities that disturbed the equilibrium of nineteenth-century domesticity and family life. The middle-class Victorian cultural image of the "angel in the house" remained the ideal, but the distance between that image and the reality of women's lives was growing rapidly.[2]

Broader horizons beckoned the "new woman." New kinds of work—for example, clerical and department store sales positions—offered more independence. Extended educational experiences, including secondary school and college for a growing number of middle-class girls as well, enlarged the boundaries of women's lives, as did the plethora of clubs and women's associations to which they were exposed. Innovations in fashion and social behavior—shorter skirts, different hat styles, and public cigarette smoking—added to the mix.[3] At the same time, socialization toward distinctive emotional styles, especially the control of anger, differentiated girls' experiences from those of their brothers; this contrasted with earlier socialization regarding anger, which had not emphasized gender-based distinctions of this type.[4]

These changes in women's lives reflected the more general cultural and social trends of the period. The years between 1880 and 1920 witnessed the acceleration of urbanization and industrialization, major technological advances, the rise of larger and more formal organizations, and women's struggle to achieve autonomy and self-consciousness. No historical period can be characterized by one set of core values, but the division between tradition and innovation in American culture was particularly pronounced during the early years of mature industrial society as efforts to accommodate to the scope, scale, and speed of change contrasted with an impulse to maintain earlier patterns. The extensive discussion of the "woman question" and the ambivalence on the part of social commentators who both criticized and admired the "new woman" reflected this division.[5]

In this context, the perception of an emerging female generation gap, as articulated in the *Good Housekeeping* commentary, is understandable. Certainly during the period from 1880 to 1920, the world of daughters, particularly in middle-class families, differed from the world their mothers and grandmothers had experienced earlier in the nineteenth century. To the limited extent that historians have considered mother-daughter interactions in the past, they have correspondingly stressed the implications of generational differences in opportunity and behavior for mother-daughter relationships. For example, Carroll Smith-Rosenberg has pointed out that a continuity of expectation and experience had linked earlier female generations and fostered mother-daughter intimacy. She suggests that the disruption of that continuity in the late nineteenth century introduced conflict, estrangement, and alienation into a previously harmonious relationship. In the same vein, Peter G. Filene has underlined the novelty of the choices available to the new female generation and their mothers' anxiety about, if not disapproval of, their increasingly "unladylike" patterns of behavior.[6]

It was this disruption of generational continuity and the apparent attendant tension that concerned the author of the *Good Housekeeping* article and contributors to other contemporary popular periodicals as well. Throughout the late nineteenth and early twentieth centuries, articles, editorials, and advice columns implied that serious problems existed in the area of mother-daughter relationships. Here was a translation into women's family relationships of a concern about adolescence spreading around 1900, but with a potential for socially derived misunderstanding added in. Much magazine discussion centered on a perceived lack of communication, frequently attributing daughters' failures to confide in their mothers to maternal behaviors and attitudes. In 1884, the first year of its existence, the *Ladies Home Journal* took a firm stand on the matter: "It is the companionable mothers who are the only ones to keep their girls' confidences. The severely critical mothers are not of this clan, nor those who are impatient of a child's many failures and shortcomings."[7] Subsequent issues offered advice along similar lines. For example, mothers were told to avoid sending a daughter to boarding school, which would make her "reticent and disinclined to talk of things nearest her heart"; to take an interest in what daughters were doing; to remember what it was like to be eighteen; to keep themselves young; and to avoid "sighing" and melancholy moods.[8]

Daughters were urged to do their part to improve communication: "Never be ashamed to tell her, who should be your best friend and confidant, of all you think and feel. It is very strange that so many young girls will tell every person before 'mother' that which is most important she should know," one writer advised. Another suggested, "Take as much care to cultivate the friendship of your mother as you would that of a stranger . . . it's a thousand times more worth having and she'll always put you first."[9]

Although communication was defined as the major problem, the discipline and training of young women also generated concern. Late-nineteenth-century periodicals characterized American daughters as forward and overindulged and castigated their mothers for the fact that American girls were not as well-behaved as their European counterparts. Disrespectful daughters were viewed as "vulgar." A mother who was "all she ought to be" would see to it that her daughter would respect her.[10]

Popular magazines continued to emphasize mother-daughter conflict after the turn of the century. Additional communication difficulties were cited during the period from 1900 to 1920: the reluctance of mothers to answer their daughters' biological, intellectual, and religious questions; the failure of college-educated daughters and their mothers to respect each others' values and points of view; and the impatience of adult daughters with the whims of aging mothers.[11] While daughters were admonished to do their part to ease the strains in the mother-daughter relationship, they continued to be portrayed as the aggrieved parties. The author of a column for young women began an article entitled "The Mother of My Girl" with a reference to the many letters from readers that caused her to wonder "what the mothers all over the world are doing" regarding their obligations to their daughters. In the same vein, an editorial in *The Independent* in September 1901 observed, "The unnatural burden of filial obligations and scruples imposed by some mothers is the prime factor of the secret antagonism existing between them [mothers and daughters]. . . . As a matter of fact, there is less need of confidences between the two than is generally supposed—and much more need of confidence."[12]

The tendency to depict daughters as the victims of maternal ineptness reflected the more general trend toward the promulgation of "scientific" child-rearing advice designed to foster the development of mothers as experts at their jobs. It also suggested a marketing strategy, an effort to address the perceived concerns of young women and thus to sell more magazines. As the quotation from "The Mother of My Girl" suggests, reader response may have encouraged the continued publication of that point of view.

Advice manuals, like the popular periodicals, identified mother-daughter relationships as a matter for concern and stressed communication as the key problem. The theme of maternal responsibility for the maintenance of peace and harmony pervaded this literature as well. "It is not enough that we encourage our children to talk freely to us. . . . We must prove ourselves worthy and able to give counsel no less than sympathy; must not have 'settled down' below the level of their requirements" the well-known writer Marion Harland reminded readers.[13] In a volume dedicated "to the one who has made my life most complete and ever been my dearest comrade My Daughter," Gabrielle E. Jackson emphasized "the mutual understanding which may and should be as inseparable from a mother's and daughter's intercourse as are life and breathing." Toward the creation of that understanding, she urged mothers to respect daughters, to take their concerns and interests seriously, to involve them in decorating and caring for their rooms, and to talk to them about the books they read. A mother's responsibility was clear: "There should be no one upon earth to whom that daughter should feel so ready to go with every thought, every hope, every plan. If she does not, it is her mother's fault."[14]

Caroline W. Latimer offered a more sophisticated interpretation of the apparent reluctance of daughters to confide in their mothers. She suggested that reticence on the part of a young woman reflected not an intentional desire to shut her mother out but a temporary inability to understand and express coherently the multitude of confusing new ideas, questions, and aspirations passing through her mind during adolescence. She counseled patience and restraint: "If a girl finds that her confidence is not forced and is sensible of that silent comprehension and sympathy which demands no recognition, she will give her confidence again fully and freely as she did before;

but interference with the process of self-evolution just at this period will certainly impair confidence for the future."[15] Here again, mothers were expected to assume full responsibility for fostering open communication with their daughters.

The advice literature also suggested that a mother's job became more difficult if her daughter went away to college. It was vital for her to keep in touch with all aspects of her daughter's college activities, for "college life is, unquestionably, a critical test of the mother's hold upon the daughter and the daughter's love for the mother." Hence mothers should write regularly to their daughters, relating "every little happening of the home life," and visit the college whenever possible to "make them feel that you are in a sense one of them."[16] Additional problems surfaced when daughters finished college. Young women were not likely to return after four years and settle comfortably into home routines; they needed to have constructive activities. Noting that "the breaking up of mental and physical habits that have in four years' time become a kind of second nature" is very painful and difficult, Helen Ekin Starrett advised parents to help their daughters to plan for this transition by encouraging them to find satisfying occupations such as teaching or settlement work, even if that necessitated their leaving home.[17] Margaret Sangster recommended that daughters who did remain at home after college should be treated as adults; a daughter should not be "hampered by an overbearing mother," nor should she be expected to defer to her brothers as was the case in some families.[18]

Advice writers reproved mothers for their daughters' ignorance of, or misinformation about, puberty and the facts of life. Mothers were indicted for their reluctance to discuss these matters and for their inclinations to protect daughters from such knowledge or to invent silly stories rather than provide accurate information, both tendencies that forced young women to learn about these matters from servants and schoolmates. Thus, what should be a daughter's "dower, bearing the seal of the Divine Father" too often became a "foul secret."[19] Again: "The important thing in this matter . . . is that the relation between a girl and her mother shall be of such a nature that she will seek the explanation of things half understood from the legitimate source and thus learn the right way of regarding them."[20]

Advice of this sort suggests that some authors realistically acknowledged the changes in women's lives and their implications as they addressed an audience in need of new guidelines. Other writers, however, projected a distinctly more conservative tone. Articulating a point of view reminiscent of earlier, nineteenth-century ideology, Aline Lydia Hoffman argued that "our lot, our principal office is, then, maternity. . . . motherhood is the paramount duty of woman, *the beginning and the end of her social duty.*" For daughters who did not marry, she envisioned "a future of complete contentment in the motherhood which consists in their self-devotion to humanity and to their suffering and afflicted neighbors." To this end, she maintained that it was a mother's duty to tell her daughter about her responsibilities for the happiness of others.[21] James C. Fernald concurred. Young women from good homes should not compete for jobs with poor girls who really needed the token wages they might be paid he maintained. They should remain at home "and help the dear mother who cared so tenderly for [them] in the weary loving years gone by."[22]

Thus the prescriptive literature presented two clearly different perspectives on the mother-daughter issue. The striking contrast between traditional and modernist views in this literature mirrored the larger cultural tension between tradition and innovation. Whether the tone was conservative or liberal, however, both the substance and the frequency of the discussions of mother-daughter relationships in periodicals and the advice literature emphasized the centrality of the issue and implied that tension and discord between mothers and daughters troubled more than a few middle-class American families during this period of transition in women's lives. The contemporary prescriptive literature clearly supports Smith-Rosenberg's contention that unprecedented conflict intruded upon the mother-daughter relationship during the period from 1880 to 1920.

Although prescriptive literature certainly cannot be assumed to reflect actual family behavior and experiences, it can often mirror real concerns.[23] Given the extent of the changes in women's lives and the frequency with which the theme of intergenerational difficulties appeared in contemporary periodicals, the existence of such a link seems highly plausible in this case. Thus it is reasonable to ask whether the decades of the late nineteenth and early twentieth centuries defined any sort of turning point in female family relationships in fact as well as in perception. Did mother-daughter relationships in middle-class families develop a new element of conflict during these years of cultural and social change? Does this conflict foreshadow the sense of tension and ambivalence in the relationship that would be articulated both formally and informally by even more American women in late-twentieth-century society?[24]

Personal documents that record the actual experiences of middle-class American women provide particularly appropriate sources for the investigation of these issues.[25] This study examines specifically the experiences of the small but significant vanguard of middle-class young women who were able to attend college during this period. They constituted a group whose untraditional behavior clearly and conclusively refuted conventional standards and expectations for daughters. Their activities were particularly likely to generate the sort of mother-daughter tension alluded to in the prescriptive literature.[26]

An examination of the relevant sources corroborates the existence of a range of mother-daughter conflicts, but the documents reveal a far more complex picture of relations in two generations of middle-class mothers and college-educated daughters than that suggested by either Smith-Rosenberg or the periodical and advice literature. Typically, mother-daughter conflict seems to have been balanced, if not outweighed, by powerful support and mutual caring, even in families where daughters' aspirations and experiences differed significantly from those of their mothers. That situation resulted in interactions characterized at least as much by understanding as by alienation. Indeed, mothers appear to have played a vital enabling role in the process of their daughters taking advantage of the new options available to them; in many cases, the "new woman's" best friend was her mother. And daughters seem to have recognized and valued the backing provided by their mothers. Hence, the period from 1880 to 1920 is an important one in the history of mother-daughter relationships not because it heralded the early stages of contemporary matrophobic tendencies but because it sustained positive, supportive interactions, even in the context of significant generational differences in opportunity and experience.

Examples of illustrative relationships span the forty years under consideration. Anne Bent Ware Winsor and her daughter Annie Winsor Allen offer a first-generation case. A collection of nearly thirty years' worth of letters reveals a demanding, critical mother who complained and nagged incessantly and a patient daughter who found their relationship stressful but loved and understood her mother. When Mrs. Winsor scolded her for looking down while speaking, Annie, aged twenty-one, replied, "I am so afraid of the criticysm, [*sic*] correction or dissatisfaction that may be in your face and eyes that I do not dare to look up. I am so afraid you will not like my way of doing things, my opinions and my tastes that I seem indifferent and offish . . . it is because I care so much to please you that I despair and grow discouraged."[27]

Annie not only wanted to please her mother but she was also willing to humor, support, and reassure her: "I cannot imagine myself wishing to prevent my mother from showing her full share of interest in me . . . I want you to understand me and not to worry silently," she told her.[28] Mrs. Winsor took her at her word and continued to express that "full share of interest," feeling free, for example, to ask her daughter, then about thirty-four, "Do you realize that you are habitually stooping a great deal? It's very unbecoming and will soon become so fixed that you can't cure it, unless you set about it at once."[29]

On the surface, this relationship appears to have been a *Ladies Home Journal* classic, but it was more complex. Mrs. Winsor criticized and complained, but she also consistently expressed warm affection for her daughter, encouraged her educational aspirations, and applauded her success as an educator and a contributor (under the pen name Marion Sprague) to the *Ladies Home Journal*. And Annie remained communicative, affectionate, supportive, and tolerant of her mother's needs.[30]

M. Carey Thomas, one of Annie's contemporaries and the future president of Bryn Mawr College, described her relationship with her mother in her journal when she was twenty-two: "I have just had a talk with Mother and I do believe I shall shoot myself. . . . There is no use living and then Mother would see in the morning that she had been cruel. She says I outrage her every feeling, that it is the greatest living grief to her to have me in the house . . . that I make the other children unbelieving, that I barely tolerate Father, and that I am utterly and entirely selfish. . . . O heavens what a religion that makes a mother cast her daughter off!"[31]

This young woman's problems with her mother stemmed from weightier issues than posture and personal appearance. Even as a young girl, she devoted herself to her studies, resisting any notion of traditional female roles and activities. She seriously questioned her family's religious beliefs and eventually rebelled against her strict Quaker upbringing. Conflict with her mother escalated when she lived at home following two years of study at Cornell University. Clearly, as Smith-Rosenberg has also noted, tension was present in this relationship.[32]

Yet it had been Carey's mother who supported and encouraged her educational aspirations in the face of her father's religiously based opposition: "Many and dreadful are the talks we have had upon this subject, but Mother, my own splendid mother, helped me in this as she always has in everything and sympathized with me" she had written four years earlier.[33] And it was her mother who borrowed money to send her abroad for graduate study, whose health she worried over while she was in Europe, and with whom she ecstatically shared the triumph of the successful completion of her dissertation and her comprehensive examinations, asking on November 25, 1882: "Mother, is it not too splendid to be true?"[34] Here, as with Annie Winsor Allen, mother-daughter conflict, in this case over fundamental value issues, was offset by strong maternal support.

Like Carey Thomas in the previous generation, Hilda Worthington Smith, born in 1888, was committed to her studies. She argued frequently with her mother about her clothes, her interpersonal skills, and her sense of responsibility.[35] But her mother, who, like Carey Thomas's mother, had been deprived of higher education herself, understood her daughter's aspirations. She encouraged her college activities, providing both moral support and laundry service for Hilda at Bryn Mawr: "I was sure your speech would be a success. Did you add anything to it! Write me any more said about it! When does the next one come?" she wrote enthusiastically on one occasion.[36]

In this instance, maternal support was somewhat ambivalent, as Mrs. Smith often objected vigorously to any plans proposed by her children that would result in their living away from her. Her ambivalence seems to reflect more the fact that she was widowed at an early age than any fundamental disapproval of her daughter's activities, but in her journal, Hilda complained about her mother's attitude more than once.[37] Yet with her mother's blessing, she became a successful social worker, labor educator, and an administrator at Bryn Mawr, where her mother eventually lived with her. Some twenty pages of her journal record her grief and sense of loss over her mother's illness and death from pneumonia on Christmas morning 1917. "I cannot *bear* to have her gone. I think I was more of a companion to her than the others [her siblings], we had read so much & done so many things together" she wrote.[38]

Among the letters of condolence she received is one of particular interest that was written by M. Carey Thomas (whom she knew from Bryn Mawr) on January 20, 1918: "Ever since I heard of your Mother's death I have been wishing to write to tell you how deeply I sympathized with you, but I have hesitated because I remember as if it were yesterday—and it is thirty years ago—how hard it was for me to get letters about my Mother after she died. There is nothing in the world quite like one's Mother's death and I think one never ceases to miss her however long one survives her."[39]

Neither of these women was a "traditional" daughter. Neither ever married. Both were outstandingly successful, independent, professional people. Annie Winsor Allen followed a more traditional path in that she married and had three children of her own. Although she studied at Radcliffe for several years, she never actually received a degree, but she continued to pursue her career. All three women experienced conflict with their mothers, but all relied on maternal support as they fulfilled their aspirations.

The sources document many other intriguing instances of maternal support for daughters' untraditional activities. For example, Vida Scudder's widowed mother took her sewing and went with her daughter to tutorial sessions at Oxford University because the tutor preferred not to meet alone with female students. She had previously accompanied Vida to Northampton at the beginning of her freshman year at Smith College, where she walked a mile and a half to the dormitory at 6:30 every morning for several weeks to help her daughter, who had never "done" her own hair.[40] Mary Simkhovitch's mother also traveled with her when she went abroad for graduate study. "Girls were not free then to take trips by themselves, and in any case, it was a great adventure for us both" Mary explained in her autobiography.[41]

Few mothers would have had the freedom or the inclination to accompany daughters to European universities, but other examples attest to the fact that unqualified support was certainly not rare in either the first or the second generation under consideration. Louise Marion Bosworth's mother offered enthusiastic encouragement to her daughter at Wellesley. "Oh Louise, I believe you have a future before you . . . I am so glad you could go to college . . . I feel sorry for these girls who have a mother so narrow, that they have to wait until they are married before they can do the things that young people love to do" she wrote in 1902. Her support continued as Louise pursued her career in social work: "I enjoyed reading the clipping you sent. It certainly seems that your work is greatly appreciated. I feel proud that I have a child who can do so much good."[42] The mothers of other Wellesley women between 1880 and 1920 provided comparable support for their daughters' aspirations.[43]

Active maternal advocacy took various forms in different contexts. The mother of Marion Talbot worked to organize the Association of Collegiate Alumnae, predecessor of the American Association of University Women, expressly to build a community for college graduates when more conventional childhood friends ostracized her daughter following her graduation from Boston University in 1880. Later, Mrs. Talbot, herself a former teacher, encouraged Marion to leave Boston to accept a position at the University of Chicago, "though it cost her many a heart pang."[44] Despite the fact that Willa Cather assumed a male identity, cut her hair, and cross-dressed from the age of fourteen to the age of eighteen, her mother encouraged her intellectual and cultural aspirations, provided her with a private attic bedroom of her own, and later, over her husband's objections, supported her wish to go to college.[45] Freda Kirchwey's mother also approved of her daughter's untraditional activities, including participating while she was a student at Barnard on picket lines during a shirtwaist factory workers' strike in 1913.[46]

Finally, Ethel Sturges Dummer, the wife of a prosperous Chicago banker and herself a social welfare advocate, philanthropist, and author, provided unequivocal support for all four of her college-educated daughters in diverse ways. In a letter (which may never have been mailed) to the future mother-in-law of her eldest daughter, for example, she questioned the young man's parents' preference for a postponement of the marriage of their children, arguing that "the content brought by the consummation of love is the right of these young people."[47] When his parents did not change their minds about the wedding date, she and her husband helped the young couple to elope and accompanied them. Equally supportive of another daughter, she assured her, "If any plan comes up that really tempts you, you and your life and work, that which you have to offer to the world, must be considered as of most importance. . . . Your life must not be stunted by us. . . . Our love can make any leaps of time and distance." Not surprisingly, her daughters responded in kind.[48]

Examples of this sort accurately represent a larger body of evidence that impels a distinction between career paths and intergenerational harmony. Although the experiences of daughters who pursued higher education (and also many who did not choose this option) between 1880 and 1920 frequently differed substantially from those of their mothers, that divergence did not generally result in a relationship transformed by fundamental antagonism. One conspicuous exception to that generalization is the unmitigated mother-daughter conflict depicted by Margaret Anderson in her autobiography.[49] Anderson's account of interactions with her mother offers literally the only evidence of a totally negative and hostile mother-daughter relationship gleaned from the examination of forty-eight collections of letters, diaries, and journals, ten autobiographies and biographies, and several compilations of selected letters between mothers and daughters in the northeastern and midwestern United States. Although conflict certainly existed even when young women followed more traditional paths, the sources consistently indicate that middle-class mothers were far more tolerant of daughters' untraditional choices and activities than the periodical and advice literature suggests.[50] Indeed, they appear to have provided essential support in more than a few cases, which may explain why some young women's choices could be particularly untraditional. Thus, while the "new" young women of the late nineteenth and early twentieth centuries to some extent repudiated the world of their mothers as Smith-Rosenberg and others contend, it seems clear that their mothers did not repudiate them or their world.[51]

What explains the presence of strong maternal support for daughters' innovative aspirations and activities during the period from 1880 to 1920? During this transitional time, daughters who pursued higher education certainly moved into a world their mothers had not known or knew only in part. As Peter Filene has observed, many of them "decisively grew into 'new women'" as a result of their college experiences.[52] The "woman question" pervaded the social and cultural climate and placed new and difficult demands on their relationships, but it did not truly divide middle-class mothers from their college-educated daughters. Why did mutuality prevail over estrangement in a situation that appears to have been particularly conducive to conflict and hostility?

First, a reassessment of the earlier nineteenth-century background against which mother-daughter interactions between 1880 and 1920 have been measured suggests that the case for previously untroubled, harmonious relationships has been overstated. Smith-Rosenberg found no evidence of discord in her study of the female world in the first two-thirds of the nineteenth century, but other sources document the presence of mother-daughter tensions during this period.[53] Contemporary observers, who were probably personally uncomfortable with the changes in the world of women, apparently exaggerated the novelty of the tensions between mothers and daughters as well as the extent of the conflict they perceived during the late nineteenth and earlier twentieth centuries.[54] Both the physical and the emotional aspects of puberty in young women had engaged the attention of various medical and educational advisers earlier in the century. The extensive discussion of mother-daughter relationships after 1880, then, continued that trend in the context of the "invention" of adolescence as the concept was elaborated by G. Stanley Hall and others.[55]

Despite this continuity however, evidence of a major intensification of mother-daughter discord after 1880 would not be surprising, particularly where daughters chose to pursue the option of higher education and the accompanying independence. Yet the sources document the absence of systematic conflict. Hence a fuller explanation for this finding must be sought through the further exploration of the complex interaction of social, psychological, and cultural factors with experiences of mothers and daughters between 1880 and 1920—both those experiences intrinsic to the relationship and those unique to the period.[56]

Women's varied personality characteristics and activities shape the mother-daughter relationship during any historical period. Not all mothers nagged and complained as Annie Winsor Allen's mother did, and not all daughters were as patient and tolerant as Annie. Similarly, very few mothers were as sophisticated and open as Ethel Sturges Dummer. Undoubtedly, conflict in the relationship, or its absence, was at least in part a function of the specific traits of individuals.

In the same way, women's particular life experiences help to account for the lack of conflict in specific instances. For example, certain widowed mothers may have felt it essential to remain in their daughters' good graces, because they were otherwise alone in the world. They may have accepted what in some sense was unacceptable to them in the interests of preserving a relationship they needed for their own security. Such women may also have been able to fill the void left in their own lives by the loss of a spouse through their involvement in their daughters' lives. Although that situation would seem more typical in the case of a married daughter with children, it may also describe mothers whose daughters chose less conventional options, for example, the mothers of Vida Scudder and Hilda Worthington Smith. Likewise, mothers whose own educational aspirations had not been fulfilled may have lived out those desires vicariously through the act of assisting their daughters to achieve their goals.[57] Mothers who were satisfied and fulfilled in their own lives, however, comfortable in their marriages and successful in club and charitable work, as Ethel Sturges Dummer was, may have found it perfectly natural and comfortable to support daughters' efforts to move even further from traditional domestic roles.

Research in the new field of the history of the emotions indicates that the collective emotional standards of the period, the "emotionology" as articulated in the prescriptive literature, also played a role in defining mother-daughter relationships.[58] Throughout the nineteenth and early twentieth centuries, for example, the suppression of female anger was specifically encouraged, a pattern that helps explain the general absence of overt expressions of the emotion between mothers and daughters.[59] Failure to express anger, however, certainly does not indicate that women did not feel this emotion throughout the nineteenth century and beyond.[60] Recent research has suggested that for some middle-class young women in the past, unexpressed family conflict, particularly mother-daughter tension, was manifested through serious illnesses, specifically anorexia nervosa and related eating disorders.[61] Although relatively few daughters suffered these illnesses, the possible connection between these disorders and the repression of mother-daughter conflict encourages further consideration of the role of psychological issues in the historical interpretation of the mother-daughter relationship.

Studies of the complex and subtle relationship between emotional standards and actual emotional experience indicate that emotionology may influence the experience, as well as the expression, of emotions. Hence, changes in emotional standards in the past may have resulted in changes in the emotions themselves.[62] It is difficult to document explicitly the influence of collective emotional standards on individual women, but the research suggests that the nature of mother-daughter relationships between 1880 and 1920 reflected in part the emphasis on the importance of intergenerational harmony in the emotionology of the period. If mothers fully internalized the emotional standards prescribed for them, they may not have experienced significant negative emotions about their daughters' activities. Alternatively, they may have altered only their overt expressions of emotions in accordance with societal standards. In either case, maternal support rather than open conflict was the manifest result.

Women's collective experiences, both within and outside their homes, also shaped their family relationships. Although the domestic role still dominated the lives of middle-class women in the late nineteenth and early twentieth centuries, their endeavors were not as narrowly circumscribed as that concept suggests. During most of the nineteenth century, women participated in various religious and social organizations and causes outside the home. Involvement in external activities was not a new idea to mothers between 1880 and 1920, nor was secondary education, which had been available earlier in the century in the form of private female academies and seminaries and even in public high schools. One for girls was founded in Worcester, Massachusetts in 1824. Thus, while their daughters' aspirations extended beyond the boundaries of their own experiences and encompassed both college and career goals, their own socialization had embraced the concept that women's "sphere" reached beyond the home.[63]

Even within the home, evidence suggests that middle-class women experienced a significant increase in power and autonomy during the course of the nineteenth century. That increase, expressed as a kind of "domestic feminism," has been documented with reference to women's exercise of control over sex and reproduction within marriage.[64] The theory of domestic feminism interprets the evolution of female domestic roles and the perceptions that developed from those roles, for example, women's presumed expertise in homemaking and child-rearing, as positive developments. In that context, it is possible that by the late nineteenth century mothers had altered their views of womanhood to such an extent that they felt comfortable supporting daughters' efforts to extend the activism they had developed at home into the public sphere. Thus domestic feminism may have actually encouraged maternal support for daughters' activities, particularly where paternal opposition was involved, as in the case of M. Carey Thomas. If, as Daniel Scott Smith has suggested, the eventual success of women outside the domestic setting can be construed as an extension of their earlier progress within the family, the connection between domestic feminism and mother-daughter relationships may have been a critical component in that success.[65]

Several related factors thus explain why the emergence of a generation gap in opportunity and aspirations did not prove to be the most powerful determinant of mother-daughter relationships in the late nineteenth and early twentieth centuries. Various other influences fostered a pattern of primarily positive, supportive interactions. A final point remains to be explored, however: the yawning discrepancy between the reality of mother-daughter relationships and the tone of the discussion in the contemporary periodicals and advice manuals.

Undoubtedly this discrepancy partly reflected the individual idiosyncrasies of writers and editors; for example, Edward Bok of the *Ladies Home Journal* was not known for his liberal views.[66] More significantly, the double emphasis in the prescriptive literature on the importance of avoiding conflict in the putatively harmonious mother-daughter relationship and the responsibilities of mothers for responding appropriately to daughters' needs mirrored the intensity of the cultural dialectic between tradition and innovation, the "divided mind" of the era.[67] That emphasis also reflected societal anxiety about the changes that challenged the tenets of the nineteenth-century cult of domesticity and threatened to dismantle the barriers between the separate spheres. As Mary Ryan has noted, American women in the past "have been subjected to the most excessive amounts and extreme forms of instructions, all of which have sought to escort them into roles that provide vital services to the social order."[68] In the case of periodicals and the advice manuals, the subtext in the "instructions" was concerned with the preservation of the integrity of the women's sphere. Maintaining harmonious mother-daughter relationships would enable mothers to continue to train daughters to fulfill their domestic roles; mother-daughter conflict would threaten that continuity.

At least two other discernible and important cultural trends emerged in the prescriptive literature: the professionalization of motherhood in the second half of the nineteenth century and the development of formal public concern over adolescence at the beginning of the twentieth.[69] The growing emphasis on the importance of so-called expert advice as essential for proper child-rearing (which was exemplified in the proliferation of advice books) and the attendant tendency to preach to women partially explain the prevalence of literature that blamed mothers for intergenerational difficulties. With the development of the concept of expertise in mothering and the articulation of the social definition of adolescence as a period of storm and stress, tensions that had been viewed formerly as normal parts of family life— moody daughters or impatient mothers, for example—seem to have been upgraded or redefined as serious problems for which properly professional mothers could and should find solutions. The prescriptive literature contributed to the growth of this perception by focusing extensively on mother-daughter issues.

It is difficult to estimate the relative contributions of each of these cultural strands to the creation of the generation gap painted by the prescriptive literature and still more difficult to unravel the intricacies of the connec-tions between that literature and the emotional and behavioral realities of individual women's lives. Yet the latter issue is particularly important to con-sider inasmuch as these women functioned as part of the culture that was reflected in the literature. Hence, although magazines and advice manuals apparently did not express the explicit reality of the experiences of college-educated "new women" and their mothers, this literature was not necessar-ily totally irrelevant to their concerns. No doubt some middle-class mothers and daughters (whether or not they attended college) were troubled by as-pects of their relationships. Probably some found an outlet in the periodical and advice literature for tensions that could not be directly expressed at the conscious level due to the influence of women's socialization patterns and the emotionology of the period. At the other end of the spectrum, readers who did not identify personally with the problems described may have en-joyed reading the advice and congratulating themselves for avoiding such difficulties. As these examples suggest, a complex range of possibilities defines the relation between prescription and behavior in the context of mother-daughter relationships as in women's history more generally.[70]

Despite this complexity and the manifest discrepancy between the por-trayal of mother-daughter interactions in the prescriptive literature and the nature of most actual relationships, it is evident that mutual caring and sup-port rather than conflict dominated the relationships of college-educated daughters and their mothers between 1880 and 1920. Although the sources do reveal some tensions surrounding both trivial and weightier issues, a fun-damental harmony is what stands out.

Research on women's psychological development in late adolescence suggests the possibility of a link between the lack of conflict and the ability of young women in the late nineteenth and early twentieth centuries to un-dertake new and untraditional behaviors. Self-in-relation theory argues that women develop and strengthen a sense of self through their involvement in both external social relationships and in the internal experiences of relation-ships characterized by mutuality and affective connection.[71] This develop-ment is initiated by the early mother-daughter relationship in which children identify with the mother as an active caretaker. In modern Western culture, the full evolution of the image of an interacting self, "a self whose emotion-al core is responded to by the other and who responds back to the emotions of the other," is discouraged in boys but becomes the center of the self-image in girls.[72]

According to this model, mother-daughter attachments foster the devel-opment of positive capabilities, for example, motivations for action, self-esteem, and self-affirmation rather than the restriction of the individual's capacity to function independently as is posited by object-relations theory, which has also been applied to the analysis of mother-daughter relationships.[73] For self-in-relation journal of social history theory, passing conflicts between adolescent daughters and their mothers represent a means of elaborating the continuity of connection to significant others, an important mode of "intense and abiding engagement" not disengagement.[74]

Although research findings that support this theory are based on the experiences of late-twentieth-century women rather than those of mothers and daughters between 1880 and 1920, it is possible to discern elements of congruence between the contemporary self-in-relation model and earlier mother-daughter interactions without claiming any sort of a historical universality for the female experience.[75] Thus self-in-relation research suggests that the mutuality and support that typified late-nineteenth- and early-twentieth-century mother-daughter relationships would generate an important positive effect upon daughters' psychological abilities to function successfully in new roles and settings—on their ability to venture beyond their mothers' worlds. Perhaps that also explains why their mothers were able to cope with their doing so. Yet the apparent congruence between self-in-relation theory and middle-class mother-daughter interactions between 1880 and 1920 raises further questions. Does the theory describe a phenomenon that is characteristic of American women's psychological development over longer spans of time—and if so, why? Or, do the experiences of late-nineteenth- and early-twentieth-century mothers and daughters specifically link them psychologically with their late-twentieth-century counterparts? These issues clearly merit further research.

The middle-class mothers who encouraged and supported their daughters' educational and professional aspirations in the late nineteenth and early twentieth centuries might not have agreed with the thoughts of Lydia Maria Child, who commented in 1863: "I know people are accustomed to congratulate mothers when their daughters are married, but to me it has always seemed the severest trial that a woman can meet, except the death of her loved ones."[76] Probably, however, they would have applauded the view expressed by one outspoken mother in a letter written in 1910: "Daughters are wonderful luxuries; they are well worth a bad husband in my opinion: at least mine are."[77] And no doubt other daughters would have echoed the feelings of a "new woman" who wrote in her journal in 1916: "My mother is desperately ill and the doctors say she can't get well. . . . I have no words to tell her how she is, after all, the anchor of my life."[78]

These sentiments highlight the role of the mother-daughter relationship as a vital and enduring source of support that enabled middle-class American women to face and respond to the challenges they confronted during a period of rapid change in their lives. They suggest the power of continuity rather than disruption and change in women's feelings about the relationship. Such sentiments also indicate that if mother-daughter conflict has actually escalated in the late twentieth century, as some participants occasionally claim, the origins of this increase must be pursued through focused, serious historical investigation of the nature of mother-daughter interactions in the decades following 1920. As the turn-of-the-century data clearly indicate, it is time to reexamine the facile assumption that conflict, antagonism, and guilt necessarily define the modern mother-daughter relationship.

Notes

This essay is reprinted, with minor editorial changes, from the *Journal of Social History* 25 (Fall 1991): 5–25.

1. E. S. Martin, "Mothers and Daughters," *Good Housekeeping* 64 (May 1917): 27.

2. For overviews of the changes in women's lives, see Carl Degler, *At Odds: Women and the Family in America from the Revolution to the Present* (New York, 1980); Margaret G. Wilson, *The American Woman in Transition, 1870–1920* (New York, 1979); Mary P. Ryan, *Womanhood in America* (New York, 1975); and Peter G. Filene, *Him-Her-Self,* 2d ed. (Baltimore, 1986), ch. 1.

3. Filene, *Him-Her-Self,* 18–19.

4. Carol Z. Stearns and Peter N. Stearns, *Anger: The Struggle for Emotional Control in America's History* (Chicago, 1986), especially ch. 4.

5. John Higham, "The Reorientation of American Culture in the 1890s," in John Higham, *Writing American History: Essays in Modern Scholarship* (Bloomington, 1970); Peter Conn, *The Divided Mind: Ideology and Imagination in America, 1898–1917* (Cambridge, 1983), especially ch. 1; Filene, *Him-Her-Self,* 18–19.

6. Carroll Smith-Rosenberg, "The Female World of Love and Ritual," "Hearing Women's Words: A Feminist Reconstruction of History," and "The New Woman as Androgyne: Social Disorder and Gender Crisis, 1870–1936," all in Smith-Rosenberg, *Disorderly Conduct: Visions of Gender in Victorian America* (New York, 1985), 11–52, 53–76, 245–96; Filene, *Him-Her-Self,* 20–25.

7. "Maybell," *Ladies Home Journal* 1 (Oct. 1884).

8. Ruth Ashmore, "My Girls' Mothers," *Ladies Home Journal* 7 (Oct. 1890): 12; Alan Cameron, "A Woman's Most Grievous Mistake," *Ladies Home Journal* 14 (Oct. 1897): 10.

9. Fanny Fern, "Tell Your Mother," *Ladies Home Journal* 5 (June 1888); Ruth Ashmore, "A Girl's Best Friend," *Ladies Home Journal* 8 (May 1881): 12.

10. "How Girls Deceive Their Parents," *Ladies Home Journal* 1 (Nov. 1884); M. E. W. Sherwood, "How Shall Our Girls Behave?" *Ladies Home Journal* 5 (Oct. 1888): 2; "What Is a Lady?" *Ladies Home Journal* 5 (Nov. 1888): 13; 17; Ella Wheeler Wilcox, "An Evil of American Daughters," *Ladies Home Journal* 7 (April 1890): 3; Edward Bok, "The American Skeleton" [editorial], *Ladies Home Journal* 20 (May 1903): 4.

11. William Lee Howard, "Why Didn't My Parents Tell Me?" *Ladies Home Journal* 24 (Aug. 1907): 32; "Where One Girl Began" [editorial], *Ladies Home Journal* 34 (Jan. 1917): 7; "My Mother Didn't Tell Me," *Harper's Bazaar* 46 (Oct. 1912): 484, 523; Alice Bartlett Stimson, "When the College Girl Comes Home," *Harper's Bazaar* 42 (Aug. 1908): 797–99; Charles Edward Jefferson, "A Sermon to Grown-up Daughters," *Woman's Hone Companion* 43 (Feb. 1916): 7; "The Case of the Elderly Mother," *Ladies Home Journal* 36 (March 1919): 112; Harriet Brunkhurst, "The Girl Whose Mother Is 'Old,'" *Ladies Home Journal* 35 (June 1919): 132.

12. Ruth Ashmore, "The Mother of My Girl," *Ladies Home Journal* 11 (Sept. 1894): 16; "Antagonism between Mothers and Daughters," *The Independent,* Sept. 26, 1901, 2311.

13. Marion Harland, *Eve's Daughters; or, Common Sense for Maid, Wife and Mother* (1882, repr. New York, 1978), 311–12.

14. Gabriella Jackson, *Mother and Daughter* (New York, 1905), 3, 63, 81, 85–86, 104, 114, 129.

15. Caroline W. Latimer, *Girl and Woman: A Book for Mothers and Daughters* (New York, 1910), 32–33.

16. Jackson, *Mother and Daughter,* 135–36, 138.

17. Helen Ekin Starrett, *After College, What? For Girls* (New York, 1896), 13, 15–17, 24.

18. Margaret Sangster, *The Little Kingdom of Home* (New York, 1905), 430–31; Margaret Sangster, *Radiant Motherhood: A Book for the Twentieth-century Mother* (Indianapolis, 1905), 195.

19. Latimer, *Girl and Woman,* 138–44; Harland, *Eve's Daughters,* 79, 83.

20. Latimer, *Girl and Woman,* 261–62.

21. Aline Lydia Hoffman, *The Social Duty of Our Daughters: A Mother's Talks with Mothers and Their Grown Daughters* (Philadelphia, 1908), 7, 64–65, 34.

22. James C. Fernald, *The New Womanhood* (Boston, 1891), 235–36.

23. Carroll Smith-Rosenberg has noted the importance of examining the relationship between prescriptive literature and unpublished personal documents specifically for the development of knowledge about women's experiences in the past. Smith-Rosenberg, "The New Woman and the New History," *Feminist Studies* 3 (Fall 1975): 185–98. For a more general example, see the discussion of the relationship between the rise of sibling jealousy in the early twentieth century and the treatment of the topic in the prescriptive literature in Peter N. Stearns, "The Rise of Sibling Jealousy in the Twentieth Century," in *Emotion and Social Change: Toward a New Psychohistory,* ed. Carol Z. Stearns and Peter N. Stearns (New York, 1987), 193–22. On the pitfalls of assuming correspondence between prescriptive literature and family behavior, see Jay Mechling, "Advice to Historians on Advice to Mothers," *Journal of Social History* 9 (Fall 1975): 45–63. Mary Beth Norton has commented on this topic, specifically with regard to the probable discrepancy between the diverse experiences of nineteenth-century women and the social norms formulated mainly by men and articulated in advice manuals. See "The Paradox of 'Women's Sphere,'" in *Women of America: A History,* ed. Carol Ruth Berkin and Mary Beth Norton (Boston, 1979), 140–46; see also Ernest Earnest, *The American Eve in Fact and Fiction* (Urbana, 1974).

24. Judith Arcana, *Our Mothers' Daughters* (Berkeley, 1981); Nancy Friday, *My Mother, Myself* (New York, 1977); Dorothy Dinnerstein, *The Mermaid and the Minotaur: Sexual Arrangements and Human Malaise* (New York, 1976); Signe Hammet, *Daughters and Mothers—Mothers and Daughters: Reflections on the Archetypal Feminine* (Minneapolis,

1976); Lucy Rose Fischer, *Linked Lives: Adult Daughters and Their Mothers* (New York, 1986); and Adrienne Rich, *Of Woman Born: Motherhood as Experience and Institution* (New York, 1976).

25. Many more middle-class women than working-class women in the past have recorded thoughts and feelings in private correspondence, diaries, and journals. Thus, for the historian interested in the analysis of the emotional quality of women's lives, it is feasible to begin with a focus on middle-class women (Smith-Rosenberg, "The New Woman and the New History," 190–92). Even middle-class women's personal documents, however, may not provide totally reliable data regarding family interactions. Mothers and daughters do not necessarily write to one another about hostile feelings. Entries in journals and diaries are often brief and incomplete. Autobiographers typically record their lives as older adults, and their recollections may be faulty or distorted by their biases. For these same reasons, oral histories can also be unreliable.

26. A reappraisal of the literature on Victorian sexuality suggests that a female generation gap in attitudes and beliefs about sex may have separated young women and their mothers during this period. That could also contribute to heightened tensions between college-educated daughters (and other middle-class daughters as well) and their mothers. Stephen Seidman, "The Power of Desire and the Danger of Pleasure: Victorian Sexuality Reconsidered," *Journal of Social History* 24 (Fall 1990): 47–67.

Presumably, young women who went to college were more ambitious and achievement-oriented than their peers. As such, they should be viewed as tokens rather than as representative white middle-class daughters. An investigation of the experiences of "token women," however, can also offer valuable insight into what was possible and likely among a larger generality of women. Nancy Cott has made this point with regard to the study of the development of feminism; see *The Grounding of Modern Feminism* (New Haven, 1987), 7.

27. Anne Bent Ware Winsor to Annie Winsor Allen, Aug. 7, 1886, series 3, box 25, folder 397, Annie Winsor Allen Papers, Schlesinger Library, Radcliffe College.

28. Annie Winsor Allen to Anne Bent Ware Winsor, Nov. 11, 1893, series 3, box 25, folder 400, Allen Papers.

29. Anne Bent Ware Winsor to Annie Winsor Allen, fragment, ca. 1899, series 3, box 24, folder 390, Allen Papers.

30. See extensive mother-daughter correspondence, series 3, boxes 23, 24, 25, and 27, Allen Papers.

31. M. Carey Thomas, journal entry, Jan. 11, 1879, in Thomas, *The Making of a Feminist: Early Journals and Letters of M. Carey Thomas,* ed. Marjorie Dobkin (Kent, 1979), 152.

32. Thomas, *The Making of a Feminist,* 152; Smith-Rosenberg, "The New Woman as Androgyne," 257.

33. M. Carey Thomas, journal entry, July 16, 1875, in Thomas, *The Making of a Feminist,* 100. An earlier journal entry (Feb. 26, 1871) also documents Mrs. Thomas's commitment to education: "An English man Joseph Beck was here to dinner the other day and he don't believe in the Education of Women. Neither does Cousin Frank King and my such a disgusson [*sic*] they had. *Mother of course was for*" (50, emphasis added).

34. Thomas, *The Making of a Feminist,* 263.

35. Hilda Worthington Smith to Mother, Dec. 11, 1903, box 3, vol. 60, and May 16, 1907, box 3, vol. 64, book 6, both in Hilda Worthington Smith Papers, Schlesinger Library, Radcliffe College.

36. Mother to Hilda Worthington Smith, Oct. 3, 1909, box 2, folder 49, Smith Papers.

37. See, for example, journal entry for Jan. 9, 1915, box 4, vol. 78, book 20, Smith Papers: "It seems as if I should never get anywhere, but should stay at home with Mother. *She* hasn't enough to do, & realizes it sadly."

38. Hilda Worthington Smith, journal entry for Dec. 25, 1917, box 4, vol. 81, book 23, Smith Papers.

39. M. Carey Thomas to Hilda Worthington Smith, Jan. 20, 1918, box 10, folder 171, Smith Papers.

40. Vida Scudder, *On Journey* (New York, 1937), 66–67, 88.

41. Mary Simkhovitch, *Neighborhood* (New York, 1938), 47.

42. Mother to Louise Marion Bosworth, Dec. 3, 1902, carton 1, folder 42, and Aug. 8, 1912, carton 1, folder 63, both in Louise Marion Bosworth Papers, Schlesinger Library, Radcliffe College.

43. Patricia A. Palmieri, "Patterns of Achievement of Single Academic Women at Wellesley College, 1880–1920," *Frontiers* 5 (Spring 1980): 63–67.

44. Joyce Antler, "'After College, What?': New Graduates and the Family Claim," *American Quarterly* 32 (Fall 1980): 428; Lynn D. Gordon, "Co-Education on Two Campuses: Berkeley and Chicago, 1890–1912," in *Woman's Being, Woman's Place: Female Identity and Vocation in American History,* ed. Mary Kelley (Boston, 1979), 181; Marian Talbot, *More Than Love* (Chicago, 1936), 3, quoted in Rosalind Rosenberg, *Beyond Separate Spheres: Intellectual Roots of Modern Feminism* (New Haven, 1982), 27.

45. Sharon O'Brien, *Willa Cather: The Emerging Voice* (New York, 1987), 104.

46. Sara Alpern, *Freda Kirchwey, a Woman of the Nation* (Cambridge, 1987), 11.

47. Ethel Sturges Dummer to Mabel Fisher, June 28, 1915, box 45, folder 924, Ethel Sturges Dummer Papers, Schlesinger Library, Radcliffe College. The letter is marked in pencil, "I believe this was never sent."

48. See, for example, letters to Katharine Dummer Fisher, box 45, folder 925; letter to "Happy" (Ethel) Dummer Mintzner, July 8, 1920, box 10, folder 165a; letters from Katherine Dummer Fisher, box 43, folder 895; letters from Frances Dummer Logan, box 12, folder 185; and letters from "Happy" (Ethel) Dummer Mintzner, box 10, folder 162. All in Dummer Papers.

49. Margaret Anderson, *My Thirty Years' War* (1930, repr. New York, 1969). The conflict between Alice James and her mother offers an earlier example of a troubled relationship, in this instance between an intelligent, invalid daughter who did not go to college and a capable, practical Victorian mother. Alice James felt "emotionally undernourished" by her mother and apparently experienced significant relief when her mother died in 1882. Jean Strouse, *Alice James: A Biography* (Boston, 1980), 46, 202–3.

50. For additional representative examples of relationships between college-educated daughters and their mothers, see the following collections: Mary Williams Dewson Papers, Dorothea May Moore Papers, and Morgan-Howes Family Papers, Schlesinger Library, Radcliffe; Ames Family Papers, Sophia Smith Collection, Smith College; and Helen Landon Cass Letters and Helen Lyman Miller Letters, Smith College Archives. Representative examples of relationships between daughters who did not attend college and their mothers may be found in the Hills Family Papers, Amherst College Special Collections; Bradley Family Papers and Emerson-Nichols Papers, Schlesinger Library, Radcliffe; and Richard Lee Strout, ed., *Maud* (New York, 1929). A complete list of sources consulted is available from the author.

51. For a discussion of the positive contribution of families, particularly mothers, to the continuing growth and development of college-educated daughters, see Antler, "'After College, What?'" Barbara Miller Solomon has also documented mothers' support for daughters' educational goals in the late nineteenth century and even earlier. Solomon, *In the Company of Educated Women* (New Haven, 1985), 13, 64–68.

It is possible that college-educated women and their mothers compose a sample self-selected to produce evidence of positive mother-daughter relationships. Maternal support for untraditional female activity, including higher education, may have been a critical precondition for daughters who went to college. It is relevant, therefore, to consider whether a greater disparity between mothers and daughters would be apparent in a larger sample representing the wider middle class. The weight of the evidence in the present study, however, strongly suggests that such a sample would also document maternal support for daughter's activities.

52. Filene, *Him-Her-Self*, 26.

53. See, for example, Margo E. Horn, "Family Ties: The Blackwells: A Study in the Dynamics of Family Life in Nineteenth Century America," Ph.D. diss., Tufts University, 1980, and Mary E. Bulkley, "Grandmother, Mother and Me," mimeographed manuscript, Schlesinger Library, Radcliffe College. Examples of less-than-perfect earlier mother-daughter interactions are also cited in Nancy F. Cott, *The Bonds of Womanhood: "Woman's Sphere" in New England, 1780–1835* (New Haven, 1977), 178; Nancy M. Theriot, *The Biosocial Construction of Femininity: Mothers and Daughters in Nineteenth-Century America* (Westport, 1988), 77; Nini Herman, *Too Long a Child: The Mother-Daughter Dyad* (London, 1989); and Lee Virginia Chambers-Schiller, *Liberty a Better Husband: Single Women in America, the Generations of 1780–1840* (New Haven, 1984).

54. See, for example, discussions of the dangers of too much education for women contained in E. H. Clarke, *Sex in Education; or, A Fair Chance for the Girls* (Boston, 1873).

55. Joseph E. Kett, *Rites of Passage: Adolescence in America, 1790 to the Present* (New York, 1977), 133–43, 215–38.

56. For an analysis of the relationship among cultural, social, and psychological factors and the dynamics of family life, see Stephen Mintz, *A Prison of Expectations: The Family in Victorian Culture* (New York, 1983).

57. Peter Filene suggests that mothers lived vicariously through their daughters' rebellious and emancipated behavior during the late nineteenth century (*Him-Her-Self*, 23); see also Solomon, *In the Company of Educated Women*, 67–68.

58. Peter N. Stearns, with Carol Z. Stearns, "Emotionology: Clarifying the History of Emotions and Emotional Standards," *American Historical Review* 90 (Oct. 1985): 813–36.

59. Stearns and Stearns, *Anger*, ch. 4.

60. Ibid.

61. Joan Jacobs Brumberg, *Fasting Girls: The Emergence of Anorexia Nervosa as a Modern Disease* (Cambridge, 1988), 126–40; Theriot, *The Biosocial Construction of Femininity*, 119–32.

62. For discussions of the relationship between emotional standards and actual emotions, see Shula Sommers, "Understanding Emotions: Some Interdisciplinary Considerations," in *Emotion and Social Change: Toward a New Psychohistory*, ed. Carol Z. Stearns and Peter N. Stearns (New York, 1987), 23–38, and Margaret S. Clark, "Historical Emotionology from a Social Scientist's Perspective," in *Social History and Issues in Human Consciousness: Some Interdisciplinary Connections*, ed. Andrew E. Barnes and Peter N.

Stearns (New York, 1989), 262–69. Other research in emotions history includes Stearns and Stearns, *Anger;* Jan Lewis, "Mother's Love: The Construction of an Emotion in Nineteenth-Century America," and Peter N. Stearns, "Suppressing Unpleasant Emotions: The Development of a Twentieth-Century American Style," both in *Social History and Human Consciousness: Some Interdisciplinary Connections,* ed. Andrew E. Barnes and Peter N. Stearns (New York, 1989), 209–29, 230–61. See also the essays and works cited in the bibliography in *Emotion and Social Change,* ed. Stearns and Stearns.

63. Ethel Sturges Dummer, for example, was involved in a wide variety of activities outside her home. See Degler, *At Odds,* ch. 13, for a discussion of women's world beyond the home. Smith-Rosenberg also comments on the activities of women outside the confines of domesticity. See "The New Woman as Androgyne," 256–57.

64. Daniel Scott Smith, "Family Limitation, Sexual Control, and Domestic Feminism in Victorian America," in *Clio's Consciousness Raised,* ed. Mary S. Hartman and Lois Banner (New York, 1974), 119–36; see also Degler, *At Odds,* ch. 11, 249–78; Cott, *The Bonds of Womanhood;* Norton, "The Paradox of 'Women's Sphere'"; Kathryn Kish Sklar, *Catherine Beecher: A Study in American Domesticity* (New York, 1973); Glenna Matthews, *"Just a Housewife": The Rise and Fall of Domesticity in America* (New York, 1987); Dolores Hayden, *The Grand Revolution: A History of Feminist Designs for American Homes, Neighborhoods, and Cities* (Cambridge, 1981); and Barbara Harris, *Beyond Her Sphere: Women and the Professions in American History* (Westport, 1978). I am grateful to Peter N. Stearns for suggesting a possible connection between domestic feminism and maternal support.

65. Smith, "Family Limitation."

66. Carroll Smith-Rosenberg has commented on the lack of congruence between the perspectives of male authors and the experiences of women: "I ceased to search in men's writings for clues to women's experiences." Smith-Rosenberg, "Hearing Women's Words: A Feminist Reconstruction of History," in *Disorderly Conduct: Visions of Gender in Victorian America* (New York, 1985), 27; see also Norton, "The Paradox of 'Women's Sphere.'"

67. Conn, *The Divided Mind.*

68. Ryan, *Womanhood in America,* 12.

69. For an analysis of the effects on the family of the emphasis on outside expertise, see Christopher Lasch, *Haven in a Heartless World: The Family Besieged* (New York, 1977).

70. Smith-Rosenberg, "The New Woman and the New History."

71. Alexandra Kaplan and Rona Klein, "The Relational Self in Late-Adolescent Women," Work in Progress no. 17, Stone Center for Developmental Services and Studies, Wellesley College, 1985, 1–10.

72. Kaplan and Klein, "The Relational Self," 3. Carol Gilligan's model of female development also stresses the role of affective connectedness in women's concepts of self. Gilligan, *In a Different Voice: Psychological Theory and Women's Development* (Cambridge, 1982).

73. Relevant discussions of object relations theory can be found in Nancy M. Chodorow, *The Reproduction of Mothering: Psychoanalysis and the Sociology of Gender* (Berkeley, 1978), and Jay R. Greenberg and Stephen A. Mitchell, *Object Relations in Psychoanalytic Theory* (Cambridge, 1983). For an example of the application of the theory to the analysis of contemporary mother-daughter relationships, see Friday, *My Mother, Myself.*

74. Kaplan and Klein, "The Relational Self," 5.

75. For an example of a study that supports self-in-relation theory, see Nancy A. Gleason, "Daughters and Mothers: College Women Look at Their Relationships," Work in

Progress no. 17, Stone Center for Developmental Services and Studies, Wellesley College, 1985, 12–22. The issue of the application of historical psychological theories to analyses of the family in the past is considered in Theriot, *The Biosocial Construction of Femininity,* 12. See also Jane Flax, "The Conflict between Nurturance and Autonomy in Mother-Daughter Relationships and within Feminism," *Feminist Studies* 4 (June 1978): 171–89.

76. Lydia Maria Child to "Louise," Nov. 9, 1863, Loring Papers, Schlesinger Library, quoted in Degler, *At Odds,* 106.

77. Hannah Whitall Smith, aunt of M. Carey Thomas, to Mary Berenson, her daughter, Sept. 28, 1910, in *Philadelphia Quaker: The Letters of Hannah Whitall Smith,* ed. Logan Pearsall Smith (New York, 1950), 210.

78. Clara Savage Littledale, Oct. 22, 1916, box 1, vol. 18, Clara Savage Littledale Papers, Schlesinger Library, Radcliffe College.

12

Do-It-Yourself: Constructing, Repairing, and Maintaining Domestic Masculinity

STEVEN M. GELBER

In the 1860s when Harriet Robinson annually set aside a full month for the spring cleaning of her Malden, Massachusetts home, she had the occasional assistance of hired help but none from her husband, William. Over the years, as the Robinsons improved their house by installing weather stripping, re-papering rooms, refinishing furniture, and putting in a new mantle, Harriet's biographer Claudia Bushman notes that neither she nor William "lifted a finger toward household maintenance."[1] Some eighty years later, immediately after World War II, when Eve and Sam Goldenberg moved into a somewhat decrepit apartment in the Bronx, Sam patched the holes in the wall himself, and they both worked to scrub away the residual odor "of people who don't care."[2] After a few years in the Bronx, the Goldenbergs (now the Gordons) moved out to a new subdivision on Long Island, where Sam built a brick patio and the surrounding fence, installed a new front door, and drew up plans to build a dormer window on the front facade. Real estate agents for the development would drive prospective buyers to the Gordons' house so they could admire Sam's handiwork and, in the words of the family chronicler Donald Katz, "see what a homeowner could do with old-fashioned, all American know-how . . . through the agency of his own hands."[3]

There was nothing at all "old-fashioned" about Sam's work around his suburban homestead in Island Park. True old-fashioned husbands in the 1860s, even those in modest middle-class circumstances like William Robinson, usually hired professionals to do the smallest home repair or improvement. Robinson and his socioeconomic peers may have been the titular heads of their households, but they had very little to do there. Their wives raised the children and supervised the servants while they either retired to the library to smoke their cigars or left the house altogether to pass their leisure hours with male friends. One would have to go back to an even earlier time before there were suburbs, when most people lived on farms, in order to find husbands who had the knowledge and inclination to use tools on their own homes. When industrialization separated living and working spaces, it also separated men and women into non-overlapping spheres of competence, and men like Robinson fulfilled their familial obligations by bringing home the money with which their wives ran the household.

The metamorphosis of the restrained and distant Victorian father into the engaged and present suburban dad was one of the more significant changes in the structure of the modern family, and the male use of tools around the house was a critical component of that change. Historians Mark Carnes and Clyde Griffen have asked, "When did Mr. Fixit and the master of the barbecue appear and did these circumscribed modifications in role alter the older division of gender spheres significantly?"[4] This essay answers part of that question: "Mr. Fixit" put in his first formal appearance just after the turn of the century, although there had been calls and precursors as early as the 1870s. Furthermore, his appearance did indeed indicate an important alteration of the male sphere. By taking over chores previously done by professionals, the do-it-yourselfer created a new place for himself inside the house. In theory it overlapped with a widening female household sphere, but in practice it was sufficiently distinct so that by the end of the 1950s the term *do-it-yourself* would become part of the definition of suburban husbanding.

In the process of reacquainting themselves with manual skills, male householders renegotiated the way they functioned with their wives and the way that each related to their residence. The increasingly equalitarian rhetoric of democratic households in the twentieth century acknowledged the right of women to use tools in the same way as men, and calls for female emancipation on the tool front appeared for the first time in the Progressive era. Clearly, there was a steady expansion throughout the twentieth century of the kinds of do-it-yourself tasks women were willing to take on. Nevertheless, in most cases wives limited themselves to helping their handyman husbands and acting as an appreciative audience to their household triumphs.

Men were able to move easily into home-based, do-it-yourself activity because household construction, repair, and maintenance were free from any hint of gender-role compromise. In fact, do-it-yourself can be thought of as a reassertion of traditional direct male control of the physical environment through the use of heavy tools in a way that evoked preindustrial manual competence. If, as numerous historians have asserted, industrialism and the rise of white-collar employment in sexually integrated workplaces made the job a more ambiguous source of masculine identity, then do-it-yourself provided men with an opportunity to recapture the pride that went along with doing a task from start to finish with one's own hands.[5] In periods of economic stress such as the Great Depression, their labor could contribute directly to the family's standard of living and thus be a logical extension of work. Even in good times such as the 1950s, when they might otherwise have been able to hire professional help, what men made or fixed around the house had some theoretical market value that gave do-it-yourself an aura of masculine legitimacy.

There is no doubt that single-homeownership was essential for do-it-yourself activity; apartment dwellers do not normally have the space, the incentive, or even the right to fix up someone else's property. For this reason, the growth of do-it-yourself closely paralleled the growth of suburbs. Not only did the absolute number of owner-occupied homes go from fewer than three million in 1890 to more than thirty million in 1960, but the percentage of dwellings occupied by their owners also increased from 37 percent to more than 60 percent. Thus, by the end of the 1950s there were ten times as many homeowners as there had been in the Gilded Age, and proportionately fewer people lived in rented housing.[6] Nevertheless, there was nothing inevitable about the do-it-yourself movement. The shift from professional to personal home maintenance, the growth of home workshops, the emergence of do-it-yourself as a hobby, and the unequal distribution of authority between men and women were all functions of cultural forces beyond the mere growth in the number of privately owned homes.

The concept of do-it-yourself included a series of distinct elements that permitted it to become virtually a male necessity by the 1950s. First, it drew on a preindustrial yeoman/artisan tradition of mastery over heavy tools. Second, what men did around the house may or may not have been necessary, but it had economic value and thus partook in the masculine legitimacy of skilled labor. Third, although they were worklike, household projects were undertaken more or less voluntarily. Self-directed and even playful, do-it-yourself was leisure—something to be embraced rather than avoided. Finally, do-it-yourself provided justification for men to claim a portion of their homes as workshops for themselves. This new masculine space permitted men to be both a part of the house and apart from it, sharing the home with their families while retaining spatial and functional autonomy. Do-it-yourself was one of a series of roles that suburban men created so they could actively participate in family activities and yet retain a distinct masculine style. Serving as outdoor cook, Little League coach, driver of the car (when the whole family was present), and household handyman were all ways for men to be intimate in family affairs without sacrificing their sense of maleness and to re-create places for themselves in the homes they had left for factory and office.

TOOLS AND GENDER IN VICTORIAN AMERICA

Direct participation in household chores was not anathema to nineteenth-century male homeowners, but neither, it seems, was it something to be actively pursued or highly valued. There were, however, experts who recommended a change in that behavior. Catharine Beecher and her sister Harriet Beecher Stowe assumed that some men would be willing and able "to use plane and saw" to build the elaborate sliding-wall screen they described in their classic advice book *The American Woman's Home* (1869). At the same time, however, they factored in the cost of a carpenter, recognizing that woodworking skills were probably more the exception than the rule among middle-class men.[7] Writing in a somewhat admonitory tone in a related article, Stowe urged the home-owning husband to become a "handy man [who] knows how to use every sort of tool that keeps his house in order." She proceeded to list familiar examples of the kinds of minor household crises that the handyman might address: replacing a broken window pane, soldering a leaking pipe joint, attaching a piece of peeling furniture veneer, tightening a loose hinge screw, and patching a leaky roof.[8] Stowe never implied that home repair might be a satisfying or gender-affirming activity, but both she and her sister did try to break down a widespread reluctance to the occasional use of physical labor in household maintenance.

Although American middle-class men would not embrace the idea of doing manual home work until after 1900, in one sense their wives and daughters had already done so with home decorating and crafts. Throughout the nineteenth century, women who had leisure time filled much of it by making personal items, gifts, and decorative household objects. Women's magazines, and subsequently their rooms, were filled with homemade decorations constructed from shells, dried plants, feathers, human hair, colored paper, paint, wax, needlework, or any other small, colorful items that could be glued to cardboard to make pictures or table-top ornaments.[9] The scope of middle-class female handicraft activities, however, was severely limited by women's reluctance to use what were perceived of as "men's tools." Even the most encouraging advocates of handicrafts for women ultimately conceded woodworking tools to men. Writing in *Godey's Lady's Book* in 1870, "Mertie" urged female readers not to be discouraged from trying to make furniture at home. Mertie acknowledged that most women thought that "even if anything in that line can be made at home, it must owe its production to the hands of one of the gentlemen who may have a taste for, and have learnt, carpentering." But, she said, her plans could "be done by any lady who can manage a hammer and nails, and the little rough work that is needed is within the power of any school-boy or man-servant."[10] Mertie was trying to be encouraging and break down female aversion to men's tools, but what she gave with one hand she immediately retracted with the other. First she urged "do it" but then added that the rough work can be done by schoolboys or manservants. In the final analysis, Mertie's projects for women emphasized the needle arts, and any serious cabinetmaking was left for the "fair amateur carpenter or the village professional," either of whom would have been a man.[11]

The situation was inverted for men; they could use woodworking tools but not needle and thread. In fact, there seems to have been what I will call a "half-pound rule." That is, women did not use any tool weighing more than half a pound, whereas men by and large avoided most tools weighing less, although larger paint brushes sometimes occupied a genderless middle ground. Mertie's reference to "fair amateur carpenters" indicates that as early as 1870 there was a nascent and generally unremarked upon group of urban or suburban male do-it-your-selfers. If there were no expectations that men would work on their own dwellings, as there would be in the next century, or even any assumption that tool work could be a source of pride, in the last decades of the nineteenth century there did at least seem to be a general acceptance of male competence with hammer and saw. Examples are scarce but indicative of the sharp distinctions between what each gender could do. In 1883 one bachelor faced with an unprepossessing rented room refinished the floor, painted the curtain rod and window frame, and purchased old chairs that he painted to match his black, red, and gold color scheme. His greatest achievement, however, was to remove the "common-place marble mantel" and replace it with one that incorporated a set of shelves he constructed out of white pine.[12]

Ultimately, however, very few husbands or wives undertook household repair and maintenance in the nineteenth century. Because they had an on-going tradition of handicrafts, Victorian women, more so than men, had the potential to be the real harbingers of the do-it-yourself movement. They were, however, stymied by their demonstrated reluctance to use heavy tools. On the male side, industrialism had broken the farmer-artisan tradition of manual competence. Men could, if they wished, take up tools around the home, but very few seem to have wanted to and there was no general expectation that they should. Those men who had moved off the farm and out of a home-based workplace had severed their ties to self-sufficiency. They worked away from the house, often in offices, and like their wives were willing to buy what their forebears had made. Among the urban and suburban middle class, both Victorian men and women were disinclined to use heavy tools—women because they considered such tools to be "masculine" and men because they were no longer a part of the way a man earned his living.

Over the course of the twentieth century, increasing numbers of women picked up the tools of household repair. Nevertheless, big tools never lost the aura of masculinity. Strict distinctions about their use broke down at roughly the same rate as strict distinctions in other areas of gender specialization, which is to say that, slowly and unevenly, the rhetoric of equality often outpaced the practice.

NEGOTIATING DOMESTIC SPACE

Before the Civil War, only 12 percent of Americans worked for someone else; by 1910 more than two-thirds of all Americans were employees.[13] On the one hand, work in larger firms was more dependable than self-employment, making postbellum men better able to fulfill what Ileen DeVault has called the "social definition of masculinity"—the imperative to support their families.[14] On the other hand, as the more traditional sense of "manly independence" that came with being one's own boss became increasingly a thing of the past, Victorian men, as Carnes and Griffen point out, were forced to "devise new conceptions of masculinity."[15] Although a job remained a—perhaps *the*—major source of personal identity for men, it appears to have been a less complete, less satisfying basis for feeling manly than self-employment had been.[16] As women began to work in offices, albeit in small numbers and limited roles, the fundamental demography of the workplace shifted and presented white-collar men with additional complications in defining masculinity through their jobs. Angel Kwolek-Folland discovered, for example, that the introduction of women into the life insurance business after the 1890s disturbed the traditional air (and language) of male camaraderie among the old-time clerks who felt they were being "civilized" and losing their manhood as a result."[17]

Historians of the postbellum era have suggested that most male gender anxieties induced by industrialization were resolved away from female-dominated homes. In separate studies, both Mark Carnes and Mary Ann Clawson report that Victorian men spent many evenings at fraternal meetings that, like their jobs, kept them away from the female world of the house. Carnes notes that these ritual-filled meetings may have provided men with the psychological permission to break from the inhibiting bonds that tied them to their mothers.[18] Clawson goes even further, claiming that fraternalism "was an alternative to domesticity, one that worked to preserve rather than deny the primacy of masculine social organization."[19] These conclusions about fraternalism and masculinity have been reinforced by E. Anthony Rotundo's findings that boys and adolescent males formed homosocial groups that allowed them to retreat from the female-dominated household and practice the nonfeminine values of aggression and competition that they would need in the workplace.[20] This picture of the father-as-stranger under his own roof is consistent with the general reluctance of nineteenth-century men to undertake work around the house. Their worlds of both work and leisure lay beyond the white picket fence. The rise of muscular Christianity and organized athletics, the continuation of fraternal orders, and the emergence of the Boy Scouts after 1900 are all indications that male groups remained an important but no longer the sole source of masculine identity into the new century.[21]

Along with this continuation of homosocial bonding, a counter-trend emerged in which men were finding companionship and masculine identity within the home. Beginning very tentatively in the nineteenth century, it took on a recognizably modern form at the beginning of the twentieth as part of the rise of "masculine domesticity." Moving from the position of a somewhat remote paterfamilias, the new suburban husband was, according to Margaret Marsh, willing "to take on increased responsibility for some of the day-to-day tasks of bringing up children" and make "his wife, rather than his male cronies, his regular companion on evenings out."[22] Marsh also notes that part of the new role included increased male attention to home decoration.[23] This increased attention to decoration was more than a part of the broader pattern of masculine domesticity; it was also an expression of a new relationship that developed between men and their houses in the first decades of the twentieth century. This relationship extended the concept of masculine domesticity to the structure itself and served both to broaden the man's sphere within the home and further cement the partnership aspect of suburban married life. Although it is true that men and women worked together more frequently on their houses, it is also important to understand that men staked out areas of activity at home that became their particular domains. By doing so, they created what I prefer to call spheres of "domestic masculinity." Unlike masculine domesticity, which had men doing jobs that had once belonged to women, domestic masculinity was practiced in areas that had been the purview of professional male craftsmen and therefore retained the aura of preindustrial vocational masculinity. The two concepts are complementary, but the introduction of the idea of domestic masculinity recognizes the creation of a male sphere *inside* the house.

When Marsh links the rise of male domesticity to the growth of new suburbs that removed the family from the alternative activities of the city, she recognizes that the physical environment is reciprocally linked to gender roles in the family.[24] As she and others have observed, however, the geographic locus of the family was not the only thing that shifted; the very appearance of the house changed in a way that complemented the new role of the middle-class male homeowner and his relationship with his wife. The fussy, overstuffed, and richly textured designs of high Victorian taste were replaced by two styles of architecture, furniture, and decorative objects that deemphasized the soft, "feminine" complexity of the nineteenth century. As one contemporary noted, both these new looks promoted interiors in which everything was "simple, plain, strong, and vigorous, rich and harmonious in coloring, and absolutely uncrowded."[25]

The first new look, with its emphasis on straight lines, exposed joints, and natural materials, was generically referred to as "arts and crafts," but the architecture of the period was often called "craftsman" or "bungalow," and furniture was labeled "mission." The second new look was the self-consciously preindustrial "colonial" style, also called "early American," which included both "upper-class" styles such as Queen Anne and Chippendale as well as chaste, native forms such as Shaker and vernacular rustic. Although they evoked different historical epochs, many arts and crafts–era decorators were willing to combine mission and colonial styles because they both shared an austerity that produced the desired appearance of simplicity.[26]

It was perhaps only a fortuitous historical accident that these new, masculinized homes were built in the craftsman style, a name derived from *The Craftsman* magazine published by Gustav Stickley, the furniture manufacturer and guru of the American arts and crafts movement. Nevertheless, the image of the craftsman, an artisan in a leather apron and surrounded by the tools of his trade and the products of his own hand, was the perfect one for the new domestic masculinity. "Any fool write a book but it takes a man to dovetail a door," declared Charles F. Lummis, a writer, civic reformer, and romantic primitivist, who, with the help of local Indians, hauled his own fieldstones while building a Pasadena Arroyo home.[27]

The equivalency of man and artisan is central to understanding the meaning of home-based manual skills in the arts and crafts period and the years that follow. Mary Ann Clawson has persuasively argued that in the nineteenth century the masculine artisanal imagery of the Masons was an essential element of the order's success in attracting men who sought affirmation of their besieged maleness.[28] Fraternal orders, however, took men away from their homes and allowed them to become only symbolic artisans. In the twentieth century, basement workshops kept men in their homes and allowed them to become, or at least try to become, actual craftsmen.[29]

Whereas male do-it-yourself activity in the nineteenth century had been limited to minor household repairs, light maintenance, and almost no crafts, building things for pleasure became, as a result of the arts and crafts movement, part of the masculine repertoire in the twentieth century.[30] As a form of work at home that was a relief from work on the job, the arts and crafts movement generated a whole set of psychotherapeutic arguments to augment the heretofore practical ones for do-it-yourself activity.[31] Under this new rubric, work around the house was not work; it was recreation that soothed the troubled minds of men when they returned from the city by providing them with a masculine alternative to effete office work. Typically, a 1910 article entitled "Recreation with Tools" explained that every person needed some interest aside from daily work in order to "maintain that balance and poise—physical and mental—which is so essential to right living."[32] Historian T. J. Jackson Lears seems to regret the palliative aspect of do-it-yourself when he notes that by World War I the arts and crafts ideal had "been reduced to a revivifying hobby for the affluent" in which the "nervous businessman would return refreshed to the office after a weekend of puttering at his basement workbench."[33] It is true that craft work had been "reduced" in the sense that the movement did not revolutionize industrial capitalism as many of its most ardent supporters had hoped, but it would provide generations of men with a sense of satisfaction that may have disappeared from their jobs.

The impact of the arts and crafts movement was amplified by its convergence with the spread of manual training in the public schools. Manual training had been introduced into the United States from Russia in 1876 as a form of vocational education for working-class children, but it combined with drawing instruction around the turn of the century to bring the philosophy and techniques of the arts and crafts movement into middle- as well as working-class school rooms.[34] Shop courses introduced boys to the use of tools at a time when simpler house and furnishing styles made it easier for them and their fathers to make fashionable household items.[35] Ira Griffith, a manual arts teacher and do-it-yourself writer for *Suburban Life*, promoted the "plain, square Mission type of furniture" as both suitable for woodworking beginners and compatible with the aesthetic dictum that form should follow function.[36] Manual arts classes legitimated constructive work for the middle class and re-created a home environment in which fathers could once again pass on specific manly skills to sons, a form of masculine bonding that was virtually universal before the industrial revolution but rare after it.[37] Beginning in the arts and crafts era and continuing through the 1950s, workshop plans frequently contained references to bringing fathers and sons closer.[38]

Although they tended to be smaller than their Victorian predecessors, there was a strong sense that the craftsman-style bungalows so popular at the turn of the century should allow room somewhere for a man's workshop. This "factory in miniature" as one writer called it would serve the practical purpose of storing the tools necessary to do the "numerous small repairs" that would otherwise be left undone because they were "hardly of sufficient importance for the calling in of a carpenter or a plumber."[39] In addition, the shop would be the place where men could pursue messy craft hobbies without bothering their wives.[40] With the disappearance of the library, men still seemed to want a room of their own, and household repair and improvement offered an excellent rationale for setting aside some territory for themselves. The kitchen remained a woman's bailiwick, and the bedroom was shared but, according to decorators writing in 1919, was still considered the "one room in the house above all others where the woman's taste reigns supreme."[41] Because the living room was family space, where could a man turn for a physical place in the home that was his alone?

The problem of gendering limited domestic space faced A. L. Hall when he moved into his moderate-sized house in 1908. Hall reported that he was given a rear room on the second floor as a den. At the same time, however, he encroached on his wife's territory by storing his old tools in the kitchen. When Hall found that he hardly used the den, he gladly followed his wife's suggestion that he convert it to a workshop. Hall was able to turn the room into the location for a new hobby—woodworking. He equipped the workshop with a flywheel-driven circular saw that he used along with a pedal-driven lathe, scroll saw, and grindstone to build furniture of his own design.[42] A surprising number of writers followed Hall's lead and recommended that workshops share space with living quarters.[43] Noise and sawdust, however, made such arrangements impractical, and most of the first generation of male do-it-yourselfers staked a subterranean claim to the space next to the furnace, already considered men's territory because of the labor necessary to shovel coal and ashes. From there, generations of men would produce a steady flow of household objects and regularly emerge with hammer and stillson wrench to keep their homes in tip-top order.[44]

In the Victorian period, most women's painting had been artistic; in the Progressive era, however, women began to undertake more ambitious decorating projects, although they continued to defer to men on those jobs that were arduous or risky. "Women Do Not Paint" proclaimed a paint advertisement in 1911, although, it went on, they should know enough about paint to insist that the professional they hire use the Dutch Boy brand. Because they feared alienating professional customers, manufacturers of building and maintenance materials would not advertise for direct sale to the general public until the do-it-yourself boom of the 1950s, so the advertisement's focus on professional painters is not unusual. Yet the accompanying illustration shows a housewife directing a painter who stands on a ladder outside rather than inside her house.[45]

Two articles published at almost the same time as the Dutch Boy advertisement illustrate how men's and women's do-it-yourself spheres overlapped on the topic of interior painting. The first, directed toward men, urged homeowners not to hand over the redoing of their interiors to professional painters but to do it themselves. In fact, this 1912 article may be the first to self-consciously use the phrase "Do-It-Yourself" (capitals, hyphens, and quotation marks in the original) to refer to owner-completed household projects.[46] The second article, "What a Woman Can Do with a Paint Brush," appeared a month later in the same magazine. The author assured readers that "any woman possessed of average energy and the ability to read and follow directions on a can of paint or varnish can be her own decorator." Nevertheless, by conceding that women could not paint exteriors she explicitly acknowledged that doing so was a masculine activity: "painting a whole house or barn may possibly be tried by the ambitious father, but his wife, who classes ladders and scaffolds among the implements of a dangerous trade, is undoubtedly glad to have professional labor called in."[47]

By 1912, then, suburban homeowners were participating in two related but distinct forms of do-it-yourself. The first, done by husbands and wives together, was an aspect of masculine domesticity. The second, done only by men, was an exercise in domestic masculinity. When men and women undertook, in roughly equal parts, household chores such as interior painting, they were contributing to the de-gendering of the home. When husbands alone took over household jobs previously done by professionals—for example, exterior painting or household building projects—they were doing something different from masculine domesticity because they were carving out a gender-specific role within the house. Such activities were exclusively male, and doing them gave men a sense of special ability that perhaps compensated for some loss of masculine affirmation at work.

THE HOUSE BECOMES A HOBBY

Judging from the dramatic increase in do-it-yourself literature, the role for men in caring for their homes grew so palpably during the interwar years that the house was transformed from a place *in* which to do things to a place *on* which to do things. Continuing the pattern that had begun in the Progressive era and paralleling the general loosening of gender constraints, women also increased their role in home maintenance and repair, thus maintaining a rough proportionality with men. This was no zero-sum situation, however, because both husbands and wives expanded their spheres of household competence. The only losers were professionals, because the need for their services continued to decline steadily. Because do-it-yourself was carving out new territory for householder activity, and because most of that activity was performed by men, home maintenance and repair became a major source of domestic masculinity in the 1920s and 1930s and slowed only temporarily when World War II forced homeowners to exchange hammers and saws for the tools of war.

A change to more traditional architectural and furniture styles after World War I did little to dampen the growing enthusiasm of homeowners for improving their surroundings.[48] Do-it-yourself magazines simply ignored the new styles and continued to publish plans for straight-lined mission-style furniture that made up in simplicity of construction what it lacked in current fashion. Furthermore, the antique craze of the 1920s helped by popularizing easy-to-replicate, rustic colonial styles along with some early-American examples of fine cabinetmaking that were much harder to copy.[49] Although the change in styles may have slightly reduced the number of do-it-yourself furniture projects published in advice magazines, the shortage was compensated for by an increase in general home maintenance and improvement suggestions.

Between 1890 and 1930, the number of privately owned homes more than tripled, and mass distribution of automobiles in the 1920s encouraged the growth of new housing developments beyond the confines of streetcar and rail lines.[50] As had been the case in the nineteenth century, the private housing boom was not restricted to the white-collar middle-class. Richard Harris has shown that by the end of the depression the percentage of skilled workers who owned their own homes was higher than that of professional workers (41.9 percent versus 40.3 percent).[51] Although he has no precise figures, Harris is confident that "the families of male blue-collar workers did more work within and upon the home than did those of other groups."[52]

Blue-collar workers who knew how to use tools (and who risked no loss in status by doing so) had everything to gain by working on their own homes. Trumpeting the benefits of his forty-hour work week in 1926, Henry Ford explained that his men had "been building houses for themselves, and to meet their demand for good and cheap lumber we have established a lumber yard where they can buy wood from our own forests."[53] In lovely symmetry, working men who bought the inexpensive cars produced by Ford's workers spent their free time building shelters for this first generation of cheap automobiles. When social worker Rose Feld investigated the leisure activities of steel workers who had just won an eight-hour workday in 1924, she discovered that a high percentage of them were constructing their own garages—additional testimony to widespread private homeownership among blue-collar workers.[54]

Because do-it-yourself was an artifact of homeownership and because homeownership was widespread among blue-collar workers, do-it-yourself was an activity that transcended class more readily than gender. Although common sense suggests that poorer householders had a greater economic stake in doing their own building, repair, and maintenance than did richer homeowners, men from all classes appear to have had an essentially similar set of attitudes toward do-it-yourself. They recognized it as not-quite-a-chore, that is, something useful undertaken voluntarily. As such, do-it-yourself activities were a jumble of contradictions. They were leisure that was worklike and chores that were leisurely; they produced outcomes with real economic value that might actually cost more in time and money than the product was worth; and they were performed by middle-class men acting like blue-collar workers and blue-collar workers acting like middle-class homeowners. It is precisely this categorical fuzziness that allowed do-it-yourself to become central to domestic masculinity. Its justifications and satisfactions were multiple, permitting men, depending on their circumstances, to rationalize it as money-saving, trouble-saving, useful, psychologically fulfilling, creative, or compensatory. It was, in other words, a hobby.

The large increase in the number of small suburban houses after World War I made for a significant number of homeowners who could treat their homes playfully and provided an audience for increasing numbers of do-it-yourself articles. It was during the 1920s that the wonderful, if slightly eccentric, tradition of homemade labor-savers began.[55] Plans for devices such as bicycle-driven lawnmowers, battery-run hedge trimmers, chicken-operated hen house doors, and remote electric ignition switches for water heaters filled the pages of *Popular Mechanics* and other do-it-yourself magazines.[56] Although such implements may, in fact, have saved some time and effort (if they worked), they contained an element of exuberance that made them as much playful as labor-saving. The house itself was becoming a hobby, both the location and the object of leisure activity.[57] To the extent that it was a hobby, the house was part of a pattern of "serious leisure," which, as sociologist Robert Stebbins has noted, is leisure pursued as though it were work.[58] Serious leisure encompasses a strong source of personal identification, and a hobby that involved the use of traditional male skills contributed to a sense of domestic masculinity. By taking over work from professional craftsmen, the interwar generation of handymen expressed pride in their homes, much as they did in their cars, by tricking them out with gadgets and keeping them polished and purring.

With the new conception of the house as a pastime came the growing belief that do-it-yourself maintenance and repair work could be satisfying in the same way as more obviously creative constructive projects. The hobby label had been applied to furniture-building projects in the arts and crafts era, and during the 1920s its application was broadened to include even routine work on the house itself. "Do It Yourself" urged the title of the first chapter in a 1924 home-repair book, because the best form of rest was taking up a "work hobby" that would provide a sense of accomplishment and ward off nervous collapse.[59]

Saving money and avoiding inconvenience would remain the primary reasons for do-it-yourself household repair, but writers increasingly recognized the psychological satisfaction that could make household care as much a satisfying hobby as a chore.[60] The shifting balance between necessity and pleasure meant that for the first time how-to writers could begin to acknowledge what most homeowners had discovered for themselves: Do-it-yourself did not necessarily save either money or aggravation but could be pleasurable nevertheless. In a general how-to article on setting up a home workshop, James Tate advised "Mr. Amateur Mechanic" to be sure he had the tools necessary to fix a loose coffee pot handle, put up a few shelves, make the screen door fit, and repair the cord on the toaster. Tate was not advocating do-it-yourself repairs because they would save the homeowner money. On the contrary, he said he was addressing "the man who gets more fun out of twenty dollars' worth of time spent in tinkering with tools than in paying out five to have the job done."[61] In other words, Tate turned some of the traditional rationales for home repair upside down. It was neither the cost saving nor the convenience of bypassing professionals that mattered. It was the satisfaction of doing it yourself—even if you lost money in the process.

Following up on the inroads they had made during the 1910s, wives moved on to new challenges in do-it-yourself repair and maintenance in the 1920s, when for the first time detailed articles on such things as electrical appliance repair began appearing for women.[62] Although there is little hard data on female participation in do-it-yourself, home-care literature indicates that the trend toward including wives in a house maintenance team continued and even expanded during the Great Depression. With limited money to hire professionals or buy new household items when old ones wore out, the economic incentive to do it yourself became preeminent.[63] Indeed, the mid-1930s appear to have been something of a watershed for female incorporation in do-it-yourself. Women enjoyed the fact that they, too, could do it themselves and did not have to depend on men. In 1936, when she instructed women how to hammer in a nail and how *not* to hammer in a screw, Martha Wirt

Davis did not cite financial savings as the reason women should gain competence with tools. What she did stress was the convenience and pride of being independent of men. She discovered that "there is quite a bit of satisfaction in being able to fix one's own cords, open stubborn windows, unstop stopped-up sinks, put new washers in leaky faucets or replace burned-out fuses without calling for male assistance."[64] Similarly, in 1938, when J. C. Woodin published what appears to be the first American textbook on home mechanics for girls, he explained that he hoped to "allow housewives to deal with minor, everyday problems without having to call professional repairmen or wait for their husbands to come home."[65] That women had to be encouraged to learn do-it-yourself tasks as elementary as hammering a nail or changing a fuse is testimony to how andric household repair and maintenance remained and to a new rhetorical willingness to advocate female use of nontraditional tools.

Like hobbies in general, home workshops enjoyed a great boom during the depression. In a society where jobs were at a premium and the work ethic was under siege from unemployment, leisure activities that replicated work activity and reinforced work values gave employed people a way to confirm the importance of productive labor as the core activity in modern society.[66] Advocates of do-it-yourself in the 1930s praised it both for its practicality in allowing homeowners to save money by doing their own work and for the sense of satisfaction it provided.[67] Workshop hobbyists consumed the fruits of their own production and could argue that they were saving money in the bargain. "I am sitting on a home-made chair," wrote one author, and "the greatest reward coming out of this piece of work was the fun of making it with my own hands." He went on point out, however, that there was also a "dollar-and-cents moral to be drawn" because it cost him less than a commercially produced chair.[68]

Underlying the claims of pride and practicality during the depression was a poignant sense of self-reliance. Men who could take care of their homes and build their furniture had special resources with which to face the vicissitudes of life. There was a new stress on the corruptibility of the physical environment and the key role of the homeowner in staving off breakdown and decay. Advisors stressed that houses, like cars, needed to be maintained. The work could be done professionally if necessary but would be much more satisfying if done by the owner himself.[69] The quirky household hints and oddball projects that had established the home as a hobby in the 1920s kept appearing in pulp how-to magazines like *Modern Mechanix*. Where else could one learn how to use dynamite to dig a hole in which to plant a tree or how to make a door-closer from an automobile water-pump?[70] The 1930s, however, subordinated these aspects of do-it-yourself to a sense of the household workshop as a redoubt where a beleaguered homeowner could exercise those masculine skills that enabled him to keep a very dangerous world at bay.[71] "If you can cook a meal, sew on a button and use a saw and hammer, you can face almost any situation" observed one atypically androgynous do-it-yourselfer. "If you can't do these things, you may be a railroad president but you are not a completely self-reliant human being."[72]

Even while declaring the superiority of skill over wealth, do-it-yourselfers in the 1930s seemed to crave the affirmation that their mundane hobby was shared by those who were not economically constrained to work around the house. In good times craftsmanship was a sign of manly self reliance, but in bad times it could be a sign of economic impotence. Thus, the knowledge that rich people were also do-it-yourselfers contributed to the sense, however illusory, that do-it-yourself was still more leisure than chore. In other words, gender transcended class. Home craftsmen could (and presumably rich ones did) look upon their efforts as an expression of masculinity rather than frugality or even necessity. The *New York Times* made a point of describing doctors, lawyers, and bankers who rolled up their sleeves in workshops that sometimes took up large portions of their homes.[73] Similarly, the Leisure League of America, a depression-era organization that promoted the productive use of spare time, explained that "tucked away in a closet of one of the swankiest of New York's apartment hotels there happens to be a woodworker's bench, a power lathe and an amazing assortment of hand tools ready, at a moment's notice, to make the sawdust fly!"[74]

Just as less affluent do-it-yourselfers might feel less self-conscious by knowing that the wealthy shared their hobby, home workshops allowed wealthier professionals and executives to establish their connection to the tradition of manly labor, which was experiencing a visual revival at the hands of New Deal artists. From the walls of public buildings throughout the country, as Barbara Melosh points out, a disproportionately large number of broad-shouldered, barrel-chested workers peered down in mute disapproval of those who did not work with their hands or did not work at all.[75] In a depression-era home workshop, however, the symbolic could still become real, and every office worker could imagine himself the heroic figure on the post office wall. Indeed, the little data available for the 1930s confirms the classless nature of do-it-yourself. Approximately half of all home workshops were owned by middle-class college graduates and half by skilled blue-collar workers.[76]

The most dedicated and wealthy do-it-yourself hobbyists, like the one in the swanky New York apartment, equipped their shops with electrically driven tools. Some craft workers had motorized their foot-powered jigsaws and lathes early in the century, as soon as small electric motors and electrically wired homes appeared. But it was not until the end of the 1920s that craft writers could begin to assume that any significant number of their readers would have power tools at home.[77] The Delta Corporation produced the first home power tool, a scroll saw, in 1923, and the new industry experienced a boomlet during the cash-starved years of the Great Depression.[78] It was a boomlet not a boom because of the price of the electrical tools. Walker-Turner, the leading manufacturer of home power tools in the 1930s, offered a motor-driven jigsaw, drill press, or lathe for about $20, and they were carried, at least for a while, by large department stores such as Macy's.[79] Other companies sold similar machines for $30 to $40 apiece, which included the cost of the motor used to run them. Because such a price amounted to 2 to 3 percent of an average worker's gross income, the market was limited to the wealthy or the highly motivated hobbyist.[80] A survey of home workshops in Lima, Ohio, in 1935 found that significantly fewer than half had any power equipment at all—and much of that was homemade.[81] A poll the same year of more serious craftsmen who had joined the National Homeworkshop Guild determined that almost two-thirds of them had some sort of electrically driven tool, most commonly a lathe and a circular saw.[82]

Expensive equipment distinguished wealthy from middle-class amateurs, but that difference was secondary to the sense of common masculine experience they shared. When one magazine printed an illustration of what it called a "typical" power-driven basement workshop in 1937, it belonged to a hardly typical Milwaukee industrialist, Louis Allis. Yet the image is typical in a number of ways. Like the average Joe, Allis's workshop retreat was in his basement. It was, furthermore, a man's space, or at least a male's space, because Allis was pictured smoking a cigarette as he worked at his drill press while his son cut a pattern on an electric scroll saw. A second illustration depicts a similarly equipped basement shop and a large dog lying at the feet of his master. The article implies that Allis, although the millionaire manufacturer of electric motors, was also a craftsman participating in the democratic fraternity of home-based artisans along with "bank and industrial executives, opera and movie stars, salesmen, professional men, mechanics and laborers," all of whom were numbered "among the ranks of the home shop operators."[83]

Whether for reasons of pride, practicality, or self-reliance, home workshops proliferated during the 1930s. A variety of specialized magazines that catered to home handymen promoted the workshop movement, headed by the perennial leaders in the field: *Popular Mechanics* and *Popular Science*

Monthly. Popular Mechanics pioneered the category before World War I and remained one of the most successful magazines for do-it-yourselfers well into the 1950s.[84] Arch-rival *Popular Science* was able to carve out a particular place for itself in the 1930s by promoting the National Homeworkshop Guild, a network of three hundred local clubs—in forty-four states—that supported home handicrafts.[85] The Guild represented a midpoint between the Victorian period, when a relatively few men participated in do-it-yourself as a convenient but unnecessary activity, and the 1950s, when it would become a virtual obligation for the suburban homeowner. As a formal institutionalization of workshop hobbies, the Guild was evidence that work around the house was neither unexpected nor commonplace. That which is never done cannot be institutionalized, and that which is ubiquitous does not have to be. In other words, by the Great Depression significant numbers of householders were engaged in do-it-yourself projects, but they still felt a sufficient sense of distinctiveness to join an organization of like-minded men.[86]

Members of the National Homeworkshop Guild did not distinguish between small projects and large, between work in the house or on it, or between the creative and the routine. By the 1930s, do-it-yourself had become a category embracing all household jobs requiring the use of tools, a fact recognized by the author of an early home-care manual who said that his book "should prove particularly valuable to the man who has his own workshop and makes a hobby of woodworking and home maintenance."[87] Not only did the author categorically link woodworking and home maintenance to the workshop, but he also labeled them parts of the same hobby. Thus when more than six hundred members of the Guild were asked why they had a home workshop, the largest number (592) said it was for recreation, and a substantial majority (465) also said they kept a shop for home repairs.[88] The survey did not ask, and there is no way to know, whether respondents perceived recreational activities and repair activities as separate, but given the way household repair, maintenance, and improvement suggestions appeared alongside constructive projects in the literature, there is no reason to assume that householders made much of a distinction. Working in your own house thus contained the basic components of both work and leisure; it was a source of wealth and a source of pleasure.

By putting home repair on a par with creative crafts, the movement spawned a new subset of do-it-yourself literature: home maintenance manuals. The pioneer book in the field, C. T. Schaefer's *The Handy Man's Handbook,* published in 1931 by Harper and Brothers, proclaimed itself "the first attempt to present all of the fundamental [repair and maintenance] information in a single volume, carefully arranged for instant reference."[89] Previous books had been hybrids of creative furniture projects and household maintenance hints, but Schaefer's book focused almost exclusively on home care.[90] In a holdover from the earlier style, it began with an extraneous description of cabinetry wood joints, but instead of printing the usual plans for woodworking projects, the rest of the book dealt strictly with repairs to woodwork; to hinges and locks; to ceilings, walls, and floors; to plumbing and wiring; and to some electric appliances.

The new category of dwelling-maintenance books took for granted a husband's role as handyman. What had been, before the depression, convenient but voluntary householder incursions into the realm of professional craftsmen were becoming expected if not yet required exercises in manual competence. What was once a hobby that had consisted of small creative projects was now also a hobby of maintenance and repair. *Homo faber* had returned to the cave. It was now in his basement and contained a workbench that allowed middle-class homeowners to reintegrate the meaning of work. Although he might be limited to more routine or intellectual production on the job, at home, like his forefathers, he could produce items with his hands and at a *work*bench in a *work*shop. These terms were not anachronisms. They survived because they continued to express the sense that using tools to make and repair things was man's work as well as his leisure. A definitional loop was beginning: To be a man, one used the tools; using the tools made one a man.

ROSIE AND JOE IN WAR AND PEACE

During the brief period of prosperity between the outbreak of fighting in Europe and American entry into World War II, the pragmatic reasons for do-it-yourself shifted from lack of money to a shortage of qualified professional workers. American production for the European war absorbed skilled workers, which may be why attitudes changed toward women doing heavier work at home. As they had since the 1910s, most male do-it-yourselfers took it for granted that their wives would set the agenda, but that they would do the work.[91] Thus, the illustrator of a 1942 article in *Parents' Magazine* showed a wife directing her husband's use of heavy tools in four pictures but doing light work herself in only one.[92] Yet three other articles from the same two-year period had women participating with their husbands in fairly heavy household projects such as putting in a parking area and refinishing a basement.[93] There was some ambivalence at the idea of women doing men's work. For example, when Rachel McKinley Bushong wrote an inspirational (as opposed to an instructional) article for *American Home* that described how she painted walls and made furniture, the cartoon illustrations showed a woman hammering and sawing with much less competence than the determined, self-taught, do-it-yourselfer of the text.[94]

Official American entry into World War II at the end of 1941 erased that ambivalence. Women took over men's jobs in factories and at home. Sabina Ormsby Dean remembered being embarrassed as a girl by her mother, who made her own window screens and installed her own plumbing. But when the war came and women everywhere were forced to learn skills Dean had grown up with, she could boast in the title of a 1943 article, "It Didn't Take a War to Make a Carpenter Out of Mother."[95]

A variety of organizations established adult education classes for women during the war so they could nurse ailing homes and appliances along for the duration. The Young Women's Christian Association (YWCA), the U.S. Extension Service, and especially the American Women's Voluntary Services (AWVS, a private wartime support organization) held classes to teach women to change fuses, splice wires, trouble-shoot appliances, paint, plumb, and do simple wood repairs.[96] Wartime magazine articles on household repair routinely showed women using the heavy tools that had once been almost exclusively men's. "Every woman her own handyman!" one proclaimed.[97] Seldom did one find a traditional reference to the woman as instigator but not participant in household improvement—and even then she might be vulnerable to her husband's uniquely wartime response: "How can you say such things when you are a riveter?"[98]

From the perspective of household do-it-yourself, Rosie the Riveter and her GI Joe husband returned home after the war transformed by their experiences. Historians of the family often characterize gender roles in the 1950s as "neo-Victorian"—and for good reason.[99] The crises of the 1930s and 1940s made the prospect of a husband at work and a wife at home with their children extremely attractive. The Victorian "cult of domesticity" returned with a vengeance in the late 1940s. Three million women left the labor force during the year after the war ended, and they gave birth at a rate 20 percent greater than during the war years.[100] Although by 1953 the number of women in the labor force had regained its wartime peak, even women's return to work was domestically oriented. Most who found jobs did so not to pursue careers but to support a material lifestyle, a major portion of which was a private home.[101]

The home of the 1950s, however, was not the home of the 1850s. Middleclass men and women did more with their own hands, and did more together, than their Victorian great-grandparents did. Rather than neo-Victorian, a more apt characterization of a family of the 1950s would be neo-preindustrial. Like farm and artisan couples, husbands and wives had distinct jobs around the house, but ones done within sight of and in cooperation with each other.[102] Men were expected to be there for their wives, for their children, and for themselves. Being a father was no longer limited to bringing home the paycheck; men were also supposed to be warm and nurturing parents. At the same time, popular images of emasculated suburban men seemed to warn of dangers in the role of suburban dad.[103] Increased calls for paternal presence clashed with continuing assumptions of traditional gender models, catching men in a no-win position. Do-it-yourself provided at least a partial solution because household maintenance and repair permitted suburban fathers to stay at home without feeling emasculated or being subsumed into an undifferentiated entity along with his wife.[104]

The workshop in particular remained the man's realm. A 1954 advertisement for Corby's Whiskey shows five men standing in a garage workshop of what is clearly a very new house. The foreground is dominated by a large wood-lathe, with just enough wood shavings scattered about to make it clear that this is a working shop. Hand tools and parts of power tools are hung neatly on the far wall. The casually dressed men have obviously stepped out of the house and away from their wives to admire a half-finished colonial-style Windsor rocking chair while helping themselves to whiskey from a homemade serving cart.[105] Their collective retreat to the garage workshop to smoke, drink, and admire the artisanal prowess of the householder all bespeak male camaraderie built on a shared appreciation of the masculine role of suburban handyman.

These were just the men *Business Week* referred to in its June 2, 1952, issue when it christened the new movement. Proclaiming the 1950s the "age of do-it-yourself," the magazine located the home improvement movement in the rapidly expanding postwar suburbs. Although the phrase *do-it-yourself* had been used from time to time at least as far back as 1912, this appears to be the earliest prominent use of the term in the 1950s and the one that gave it widespread currency.[106] Within the year the phrase had become commonplace, spread in part by a series of do-it-yourself expositions, themselves additional evidence of the hands-on ownership trend.

In March 1953, New Yorkers turned out at a rate of more than six thousand per day to visit the first of its kind do-it-yourself trade exposition in Manhattan. Although most of the crowd was male, the show, like the do-it-yourself movement, gave women a visible if ambiguous role.[107] Marianne Shay, pictured in a New York newspaper as Miss Do-It-Yourself, had recently moved with her husband from Iowa and was looking for work. Back in Davenport she had laid tile and linoleum and also done a lot of painting.[108] The show's organizers found Shay photogenic and sufficiently knowledgeable about tools to hire her as a demonstrator for everything from wallpaper to welding.[109] Wielding heavy tools and dressed in jeans and plaid shirt, Shay was far removed from Victorian predecessors who would have lifted hardly anything heavier than an artist's paint brush. Nevertheless, it is clear that many of the tools with which she posed for photos were not ones she used in her own home. Rather like a foreigner who has mastered most but not all of the nuances of native culture, Shay was admired for her perseverance in the face of great odds. In the end, she was still a curiosity rather than a natural member of the clan.[110]

Home workshops originated in basements and also colonized garages as they were added to houses in the 1920s and 1930s. Do-it-yourself was not, however, dependent on a dedicated space. It is true that no man could set up a fully equipped shop unless he could set aside space somewhere, but a desire to work around the house overcame even the most formidable obstacle thrown up by postwar builders. Almost two million new single-family homes were started in 1950, up from a wartime low of 139,000, the largest number of housing starts in American history.[111] A surprisingly large number of these new houses, built by the most prominent developers of the time, had neither basements nor garages. In the thousands of northern California houses constructed by Joseph Eichler, for example, there was literally no place to put a workshop unless the homeowner were to follow the suggestion of the Armstrong linoleum company and create a combination kitchen-workshop, which was just what most suburban husbands and wives were trying to avoid.[112] Eichler's modern-style homes, like all houses built in California after 1945, completely abandoned what had been only rudimentary basements even before the war. Their shallow roofs offered no attic for expansion or work space, and most models substituted an unenclosed carport for a garage.[113] Frank Lloyd Wright–inspired houses, however, did have the advantage of providing a perfect backdrop for what was usually referred to as "modern furniture." The style relied heavily on plywood and used simple carcase construction for everything from cabinets to couches. Any man who could cut a straight line with a panel saw could, with some help from his wife, furnish the entire house, from basement (if he had one) workshop to children's attic (if he had one) bedrooms.[114]

On the East Coast, the massive developments put up by William J. Levitt, including more than seventeen thousand houses in Long Island's Levittown alone, were only slightly more conducive to do-it-yourself.[115] Like Eichler's, Levitt's houses lacked both basements and garages, but they did provide an unfinished attic where a handy homeowner could add extra bedrooms.[116] In her definitive social-architectural history of Levittown, Barbara

Kelly notes that remodeling the attic was taken for granted by both the builder and residents.[117] At least one contemporary commentator attributed the do-it-yourself movement to a combination of this attic expansion room and the fact that "some of the less expensive new houses are so uniform in appearance that their owners go in for craftsmanship in order to give them a bit of individuality."[118] *Better Homes and Gardens,* one of a series of shelter magazines that experienced rapid growth in the 1950s in response to the housing boom, found that more than half of its readers had attics, and almost half of the attics were unfinished.[119] Furthermore, the perennially popular rustic colonial furniture style, easily made at home, was compatible with the Cape Cod style that Levitt adopted for his developments.[120]

Even if there were some homes that did not make it particularly easy for the GI generation to work around the house, the facts that there were so many new homes and that the families who occupied them had growing children and felt financially pressed were enough to elevate do-it-yourself to a national fad. Do-it-yourselfers in the 1950s seem to have been, for the most part, middle-aged, middle-income, white-collar workers, a pattern that remained unchanged for the subsequent thirty years.[121] Although recent studies indicate that wealthier people perceive do-it-yourself activity as a hobby and poorer people as a necessity, the popular literature of the 1950s indicates that if the movement were a necessity, then it was a pleasurable one.[122] Although strapped for cash, men were proud of their new houses and comfortable with tools as a result of wartime activities. With help from their wives, they undertook home repair and maintenance with what appears to have been a maximum of enthusiasm and a minimum of complaint.[123]

DAD THE HANDYMAN

By the mid–1950s, only reading and watching television were more popular forms of recreation than do-it-yourself among married men.[124] There were eleven million home workshops in the United States, and do-it-yourselfers were, by some estimates, spending $4 to 6 billion a year on newly developed materials and tools. Among the most popular innovations in materials were pretrimmed wallpaper, washable, water-based latex paint applied with a roller, and floor-covering tiles that did not require full-size layout and cutting. Painting and wallpapering became the most common do-it-yourself projects, more than twice as popular as either electrical work or wood work, which followed in rank order.[125]

The most significant new tool was the hand-held quarter-inch drill. The Black and Decker Manufacturing Company had patented the first portable hand-held drill in 1914.[126] The half-inch drill was large, expensive, and beyond the reach of most homeowners, who before World War II had jury-rigged portable drills by mounting drill bits on small jigsaw motors. The result was both awkward and weak.[127] In 1946 Black and Decker decided to try again. This time it produced a smaller, cheaper, quarter-inch drill designed for homeowners.[128] It was the right tool at the right time and became the symbol of the do-it-yourself movement. Suburbanites bought an estimated fifteen million drills from Black and Decker and a variety of other manufacturers in the next eight years.[129] Originally priced at $16.95, the portable electric drill brought power equipment down to a price that fit a young family's budget and to a size that fit in a toolbox as well as a workshop. Whereas drills (in fact, drill presses) had lagged far behind lathes, saws, and grinders in popularity during the 1930s, a survey in 1958 found that almost three-quarters of the nation's handymen owned an electric hand drill, twice as many as the next most popular power tool, a table saw.[130]

The postwar proliferation of power tools sharply increased the capacity of amateur craftsmen to undertake larger, more complex projects. They could cut and drill quickly and accurately with much less training than that required for the effective use of hand tools. The widespread use of the new tools also confirmed a trend that had been apparent since the late 1920s: Home craftsmanship in the United States was as much product- as process-oriented. William Morris, the English founder of the arts and crafts movement, had envisioned a world in which "all work which would be irksome to do by hand is done by immensely improved machinery; and in all work which it is a pleasure to do by hand, machinery is done without."[131]

At the grass-roots, home workshop level, that world had come to pass in the 1950s, a fact Americans grasped more quickly than Morris's own countrymen. When a group of English experts toured American industrial education programs in 1950 they were disturbed by the large number of power tools they found in school shops. "What do your pupils do later if they wish to take up woodwork as a hobby, since they have been accustomed in school to do everything with power tools?" they asked. The answer was obvious: "[T]hey would, in taking up any hobby, first acquire the necessary machine tools."[132] For the English, hobbies were, almost by definition, activities that involved traditional methods of hand construction. For the Americans, hobbies were useful ways to occupy free time, and the instruments of that usefulness did not define the legitimacy of the enterprise.

For heavy tools, the new rule seemed to be "men must, women may," but women were still ceded aesthetic preeminence with paint brush and needle.[133] For example, an exhaustively complete sixteen-hundred-page home repair handbook written by veteran do-it-yourself author Emanuele Stieri in 1950 pictured women on only two pages, those dealing with upholstery.[134] Victorian assumptions about inherent female superiority in aesthetic expression, especially with needle and brush, survived into the 1950s, but advice-givers continued to promote new possibilities for more substantial participation in household repair and improvement. Despite ongoing male domination of do-it-yourself, writers occasionally urged women to undertake heavy work on their own.[135] A certain amount of this was journalistic hyperbole, but it was also an indication that as men took on new household responsibilities women were not going to surrender the right to participate. If power tools gave men additional opportunities, then do-it-yourself advocates could claim that using power tools to saw wood and drill holes was "simpler than threading, adjusting and running a sewing machine."[136] As they had periodically in the past, women pointed with pride to being able to do a "man's job." That claim gained support from schools around the country, which began to open shop classes to girls as well as boys.[137]

From a gender perspective, the changes in do-it-yourself during the 1950s continued to enlarge the spheres of both men and women, but it was men who cemented their position as home handyman; at best, women expanded their role as assistant handyman. They were now free to help with home improvements if they wanted, but men were expected to. Most frequently, women were depicted as helpers or partners for their husbands. In fact, almost half the men in one survey said they sometimes had help from their wives in performing do-it-yourself jobs. Most of the time, however, more than two-thirds of the men did these chores alone.[138] In an adult version of the tomboy pattern, a wife who did a man's work around the house was admired for competence, but a husband who did not was less than a man. By the 1950s, being handy had, like sobriety and fidelity, become an expected quality in a good husband. A sociological survey of male Little Rock–area homeowners near the end of the decade found that a significant number of them attributed their household activities to the "insistence of the wife," leading the interviewer to conclude that women were "the boss in the homes of Pulaski County, Arkansas."[139] That do-it-yourself environment gave rise to the ironic "honeydew" syndrome (honey do this, honey do that). Humorous complaints about "henpecked husbands" were a traditional form of male self-pity, but they had previously hinged on wives telling their spouses what they should not do (drink, gamble, and ramble) rather on what they should do (fix the faucet, put up a shelf, and paint the kitchen).[140]

The "henpecked do-it-yourselfer" was not only being told to do something he was expected to but also to do something his wife did not expect to do herself, even if she could. In other words, the image of the henpecked handyman was an image of continuing male dominance over the world of heavy tools. "He loves to putter around the house / To the great enjoyment of his spouse" ran the opening lines of an advertising ditty in 1945. It ended by noting the admiration of the community: "Neighbors marvel; you'll hear them utter: / 'Wise little handyman, Peter Putter.'"[141] Such references imply that the male role of handyman was passing from voluntary to mandatory and confirm the social value placed on work around the house. The kinds of household repair, maintenance, and construction projects done by men did not change significantly during the 1950s, but the very doing of those projects became a requirement of masculinity.[142] Do-it-yourself was becoming for adult males what sports were for youths, a badge of manhood. Just as boys took pride in their athletic ability, grown men boasted about their craft skills: "A man makes a chair, a desk, a house, puts a washer in a leaky faucet, builds a kayak, paints a crib, he spends the rest of his life and yours telling you about it."[143]

Writing in 1958, Albert Roland, the only academic analyst of do-it-yourself in the 1950s, said that household projects were perceived as a "real" (that is, manual) activity that confirmed masculine competence and reflected an observation of Henry David Thoreau: "Drive a nail home and clinch it so faithfully that you can wake up in the night and think of your work with satisfaction." Working on their own homes, as Thoreau did on his cabin, gave do-it-yourselfers "the satisfying feeling of individual identity and measurable accomplishment" they failed to get from their everyday jobs. Roland concluded that "millions have taken to heart Thoreau's example, withdrawing to their basement and garage workshops to find there a temporary Walden."[144]

The literature's casual interchange of the leisure term *hobbyist,* the practical label *handyman,* and the mutually inclusive *do-it-yourselfer* reflects this sense of emotionally satisfying work.[145] Do-it-yourself was a morally superior kind of leisure because it was worklike. It is "no longer fashionable for a man to spend his leisure time just doing nothing" observed a workshop article in the *New York Times* in 1957.[146] Likewise, *Harper's* was prompted to reassure readers that they were not losing the work ethic and that "the grim forebodings about American 'non-participation,' the fear that we were turning into a nation of passive consumers of amusements, were largely unjustified" because they were taking to their workshops during their leisure.[147] The sense of masculine accomplishment evoked in Roland's Walden metaphor was at least as important as financial incentives for the explosive growth of do-it-yourself in the postwar suburbs. Surveys at the time indicated that do-it-yourselfers often cited financial reasons for their hobby, but the dollar amounts saved were actually quite modest.[148]

As they had as early as the 1920s, home handymen in the 1950s admitted that far from saving money, doing it yourself could actually be an economic liability. A mordant commentator on the new do-it-yourself craze suggested that men who decided to build their own furniture usually ended up by spending more just on the wood than a store-bought suite would have cost and that they alienated wives and children in the process.[149] Furthermore, frequent articles and even a syndicated cartoon series of do-it-yourself disasters made it clear that home-built was not necessarily better-built. In sharp contrast to earlier periods, almost no one complained about poor professional work during the 1950s. It was, after all, unlikely that a professional would forget to install a staircase in a house he was building, wall his wife into the attic bedroom he was constructing, or build a boat on the third floor of a New York City building so that it had to be lowered to the sidewalk by piano movers.[150] "Make a professional feel better by viewing an amateur's botch," said one not-too-handy man, "and you've scattered a little sunshine."[151] To the extent that do-it-yourself had become part of the standard male repertoire, cost savings were secondary, and even men who could afford to buy their work clothes at Abercrombie and Fitch took power tools to their country property to work on second homes.[152]

Something more important was going on than saving money. The constant, often indulgently humorous, references to handyman disasters make it clear that for do-it-yourselfers there was pleasure in pain. The quintessentially male pastime of reveling in self-inflicted discomfort had moved indoors. One no longer had to play football, climb mountains, or sail outside the harbor to experience the perverse joy of suffering. Now even an unathletic man could waste money, bruise his fingers, and make six return trips to the hardware store, thus participating in the community of manly perseverance. The ham-handed homeowner might make a mess, but at least it was his own mess and he could take pride in confronting, if not always overcoming, obstacles.[153]

CONCLUSION

Just before World War II, a newspaper columnist and do-it-yourself author named Julian Starr praised leisure woodworking by describing the psychological benefits of creativity. The cure for the boredom caused by repetitive jobs, he said, was to find recreation "as far removed from daily occupation as a man can achieve." Starr claimed that sports could not fill that role because their competitiveness made them too worklike, but he went on to promote shop work as a change of pace for white-collar workers precisely because it had the qualities of traditional artisan labor. For example, Starr celebrated the fact that "skill takes the place of thought, because twelve inches today is twelve inches tomorrow. A good joint, once learned is a good joint forever," and he noted that "fixed values of this sort are a tremendous consolation in a world where the most fundamental concepts are subject to change without notice."[154] In other words, Starr's justification for do-it-yourself as leisure was an appeal to its intrinsically worklike qualities. Do-it-yourself might not be work yet it had to be done, if not by the homeowner then by a paid professional. It might not be work, yet it was the exercise of creativity and productivity. It might not be work, yet it required planning, organization, knowledge, and skill, the same values necessary for success on the job. It might not be work as it was—it was work as it might be.

Starr's contradictory assessment of the meaning of do-it-yourself derived from the culturally marginal location of the activity—it was leisure yet it was work. By embracing two oppositional categories, do-it-yourself was able to become an instrument of domestic masculinity. As leisure, it could be done voluntarily, distinct from the arena of alienation that was the modern workplace. As manual work, it could confirm the homeowner's ties to his yeoman or artisan forefathers, thus creating and responding to a new cultural stereotype of masculinity. Over more than a century, homeowner maintenance and amateur home production grew from somewhat suspect activities into a hobby that was a core component of suburban masculinity. The rise of do-it-yourself did not take place at the expense of women. They, too, expanded their role in the care and improvement of their suburban homes, albeit in a secondary capacity. Women, however, already had a place in the home (not in the workplace), which is why male do-it-yourself fits Margaret Marsh's definition of masculine domesticity. Do-it-yourself was an element in the more general pattern of increasing male involvement in the household. Unlike other aspects of masculine domesticity, however, do-it-yourself was always dominated by men and was therefore part of a process in which men reclaimed a legacy that had been lost when they swapped household for factory production.

Household maintenance, which started off as a money-saving convenience in the Victorian era, combined with amateur woodworking after the turn of the century to become a predominantly male domain defined by the use of heavy tools. There was a general acknowledgment of the activity as a hobby in the 1930s, when its practicality complemented both the need to save money and the stress on traditional work values in an economically unstable world. The movement culminated after World War II with the great suburban expansion and baby boom. Building on wartime experience, women joined men in improving their new tract homes, but female participation was optional. It seems likely that they did not challenge their husbands' dominance of do-it-yourself because it kept men usefully occupied and close to home. By ceding them space for a workshop and proprietary interest in the house, women helped perpetuate a male domestic sphere.

In 1959 *Popular Mechanics* reported that when a tourist asked actor Dick Powell's six-year-old daughter if a movie star lived in the house where she was playing, she answered, no. She admitted, when pressed, that it was where Dick Powell lived but assured the curious tourist that he was not a movie star. When asked what he did, she replied, "He fixes things." Headed by a picture of cowboy star Roy Rogers and his two young sons in his workshop, the article went on to list the do-it-yourself exploits of a dozen male actors, several of whom were described as building things with and for their children.[155] The article observed that these residents of a town known for "wild parties and wild spending" were now "climbing out of their glamorous occupational trappings into levis and becoming Mr. Fixits."[156] By the end of the 1950s, it would seem that actors, the most highly visible examples of idealized American manhood, could be held up as models of frugality, practicality, family orientation, and manual work through their participation in the do-it-yourself movement that had attracted men back into the home by turning their houses into hobbies.

Notes

This essay is reprinted, with minor editorial changes, from *American Quarterly* 49 (March 1997): 66–112.

1. Claudia L. Bushman, *A Good Poor Man's Wife* (Hanover, 1981), 116–17; see also Faye E. Dudden, *Serving Women: Household Service in Nineteenth-Century America* (Middletown, 1983), 158; and Margaret Marsh, "Suburban Men and Masculine Domesticity, 1870–1915," *American Quarterly* 40 (June 1988): 172.

2. Donald Katz, *Home Fires: An Intimate Portrait of One Middle-Class Family in Postwar America* (New York, 1992), 29.

3. Katz, *Home Fires*, 71.

4. Mark Carnes and Clyde Griffen, "Constructions of Masculinity in Friendship and Marriage," in *Meanings for Manhood: Constructions of Masculinity in Victorian America*, ed. Mark Carnes and Clyde Griffen (Chicago, 1990), 83. None of the historical data used in this essay acknowledges race and is presumed to refer to whites. Whether African Americans or any other ethnic group behaved differently is a question that remains to be explored.

5. For discussions of masculinity and the workplace, see Peter G. Filene, *Him-Her-Self:*

Sex Roles in Modern America (New York, 1974), 73; Peter N. Stearns, *Be a Man! Males in Modern Society* (New York, 1979), 47–48, 109, 131; Michael S. Kimmel, "The Contemporary 'Crisis' of Masculinity in Historical Perspective," in *The Making of Masculinities: The New Men's Studies,* ed. Harry Brod (Boston, 1987), 138–39; Ava Baron, "Acquiring Manly Competence: The Demise of Apprenticeship and the Remasculinization of Printers' Work," in *Meanings for Manhood: Constructions of Masculinity in Victorian America,* ed. Mark Carnes and Clyde Griffen (Chicago, 1990), 152–63; Ava Baron, ed., *Work Engendered: Toward a New History of American Labor* (Ithaca, 1991); Joe L. Dubbert, *A Man's Place: Masculinity in Transition* (Englewood Cliffs, 1979), 15–28; and Anthony E. Rotundo, *American Manhood: Transformations in Masculinity from the Revolution to the Modern Era* (New York, 1993), 167–68.

6. U.S. Bureau of the Census, *Historical Statistics of the United States, Colonial Times to 1970,* part 2 (Washington, D.C., 1975), 646.

7. Catharine E. Beecher and Harriet Beecher Stowe, *The American Woman's Home* (New York, 1869), 32, 87, 91.

8. [Harriet Beecher Stowe], "The Handy Man," *Arthur's Home Magazine* 34 (Oct. 1869): 230.

9. The best survey of female crafts in England and America is Jan Toller, *The Regency and Victorian Crafts: or, The Genteel Female—Her Arts and Pursuits* (London, 1969).

10. "Home Made Furniture," *Godey's Lady's Book* 81 (Sept. 1870): 273; see also Mrs. John A. Logan, *The Home Manual: Everybody's Guide in Social, Domestic and Business Life* (Chicago, 1889), 270.

11. "Home Made Furniture," 273. For other examples of women doing light woodwork, see "Hints on Home Adornment," *Godey's Lady's Book* 99 (Oct. 1879): 374–75; and Janet E. Ruutz-Rees, *Home Occupations* (New York, 1883), 79–80.

12. *Treasures of Use and Beauty: An Epitome of the Choicest Gems of Wisdom, History, Reference and Recreation* (Detroit, 1883), 363–64.

13. Kimmel, "The Contemporary 'Crisis' of Masculinity," 138.

14. Ileen A. DeVault, "'Give the Boys a Trade': Gender and Job Choice in the 1890s," in *Work Engendered: Toward a New History of American Labor,* ed. Ava Baron (Ithaca, 1991), 211; see also Baron, "Acquiring Manly Competence," 153.

15. Mark Carnes and Clyde Griffen, "Introduction," in *Meanings for Manhood: Constructions of Masculinity in Victorian America,* ed. Mark Carnes and Clyde Griffen (Chicago, 1990), 6.

16. Stearns, *Be a Man!* 47–48; Dubbert, *A Man's Place,* 15, 18, 22, 28; Mary H. Blewett, "Manhood and the Market: The Politics of Gender and Class among the Textile Workers of Fall River," in *Work Engendered: Toward a New History of American Labor,* ed. Ava Baron (Ithaca, 1991), 94–95; Rotundo, *American Manhood,* 167–68.

17. Angel Kwolek-Folland, "Gender, Self, and Work in the Life Insurance Industry, 1880–1930," in *Work Engendered: Toward a New History of American Labor,* ed. Ava Baron (Ithaca, 1991), 176–77.

18. Mark C. Carnes, "Middle-Class Men and the Solace of Fraternal Ritual," in *Meanings for Manhood: Constructions of Masculinity in Victorian America,* ed. Mark Carnes and Clyde Griffen (Chicago, 1990), 38–39, 46–48.

19. Mary Ann Clawson, *Constructing Brotherhood: Class, Gender, and Fraternalism* (Princeton, 1989), 174.

20. Rotundo, *American Manhood,* 31–74; see also Dubbert, *A Man's Place,* 99, 143.

21. Jeffrey P. Hantover, "The Boy Scouts and the Validation of Masculinity," in *The American Man,* ed. Elizabeth H. Pleck and Joseph H. Pleck (Englewood Cliffs, 1980), 285–301.

22. Marsh, "Suburban Men and Masculine Domesticity," 166.

23. Ibid., 181.

24. Ibid.

25. M. Cutler, "The Arts and Crafts Movement," *Harper's Bazaar* 40 (Feb. 1906): 162–66.

26. Cheryl Robertson, "House and Home in the Arts and Crafts Era," in *"The Art That Is Life": The Arts and Crafts Movement in America, 1875–1920,* ed. Wendy Kaplan (New York, 1987), 350.

27. Eileen Boris, "'Dreams of Brotherhood and Beauty': The Social Ideas of the Arts and Crafts Movement," in *"The Art That Is Life": The Arts and Crafts Movement in America, 1875–1920,* ed. Wendy Kaplan (New York, 1987), 211. It is unclear exactly how or why one would dovetail a door, but the point is made nevertheless.

28. Clawson, *Constructing Brotherhood,* 153–54, 164.

29. See, for example, Robertson, "House and Home in the Arts and Crafts Era," 341n27; and Wendy Kaplan, "Spreading the Crafts: The Role of Schools," in *"The Art That Is Life": The Arts and Crafts Movement in America, 1875–1920,* ed. Wendy Kaplan (New York, 1987), 299.

30. For some isolated examples of male hobby craftsmanship in the nineteenth century, see "Napkins and Handicrafts," *Godey's Magazine and Lady's Book* 42 (Feb. 1851): 127; and "Hobbies," *Arthur's Home Magazine* 8 (Sept. 1856): 167–68.

31. T. J. Jackson Lears, *No Place of Grace: Antimodernism and the Transformation of American Culture* (New York, 1981), 47–58; Ruth Ellen Levine, "The Influence of the Arts and Crafts Movement on the Professional Status of Occupational Therapy," *American Journal of Occupational Therapy* 41 (April 1987): 240.

32. Ira S. Griffith, "Recreation with Tools," *Suburban Life* 10 (June 1910): 22; see also John R. Stilgoe, *Borderland: Origins of the American Suburb, 1820–1939* (Cambridge, 1988), 262.

33. Lears, *No Place of Grace,* 65.

34. Eileen Boris, *Art and Labor: Ruskin, Morris, and the Craftsman Ideal in America* (Philadelphia, 1986), 82–98; Paul Hopkins Rule, "Industrial Arts in Education for Leisure," master's thesis, University of Washington, 1940, 20–23; M. F. Johnston, "Arts and Crafts in Civic Improvements," *Chautauquan* 43 (June 1906): 382; Edgar Morton, "Home Work Shop," *American Homes and Gardens* 9 (Oct. 1912): sup. 18; Lewis Flint Anderson, *History of Manual and Industrial School Education* (New York, 1926), 188–90, 198.

35. Ira S. Griffith, "Three Things to Make in Your Own Workshop," *Suburban Life* 13 (Nov. 1911): 269.

36. Ira S. Griffith, "Cabinet Making as a Handicraft," *Suburban Life* 7 (Sept. 1910): 346; see also D. H. Culyer, "Making a Magazine Stand," *The Circle* 2 (July 1907): 48; Griffith, "Three Things to Make," 269; and A. Neely Hall, *Handicraft for Handy Boys* (Boston, 1911), 111.

37. Robert L. Griswold, *Fatherhood in America: A History* (New York, 1993), 13–17, 26.

38. See, for example, Arthur Wakeling, ed., *Things to Make in Your Home Workshop* (New York, 1930), v; and Emanuele Stieri, *Home Craftsmanship* (New York, 1935), 277.

39. Morton, "Home Work Shop."

40. Ibid.

41. Robertson, "House and Home in the Arts and Crafts Movement," 342.

42. A. L. Hall, "My Workshop at Home," *Suburban Life* 7 (Nov. 1908): 256.

43. Griffith, "Cabinet Making," 345.

44. Paul Ellsworth, "A Portable Workshop," *Suburban Life* 16 (March 1913): 133; see also Floyd H. Allport, "This Coming Era of Leisure," in *These United States*, ed. Louis Jones, William Huse, Jr., and Harvey Eagleson (New York, 1933), 201–2; Hall, "My Workshop at Home," 3; Marvin A. Powell, "A Survey of the National Home Workshop Guild," master's thesis, Colorado State College of Education, Greeley, 1935, 43; and Dean F. Kittle, "Activities and Equipment Found in the Home Workshops of Sixty Boys in Lima, Ohio," master's thesis, Iowa State College, 1936, 15.

45. Advertisement, *Suburban Life* 12 (April 1911): 259; Roger W. Babson, "Do It Yourself—A New Industry," *Commercial and Financial Chronicle*, March 5, 1953, 177:1012; *New York Times*, June 10, 1956, 8:1.

46. Garrett Winslow, "Practical Decoration for the Home Interior," *Suburban Life* 15 (Oct. 1912): 187.

47. Agnes Athol, "What a Woman Can Do with a Paint Brush," *Suburban Life* 15 (Nov. 1912): 268.

48. For an example of the more traditional style of the period, see the plans in Frederick Grinde, "Homemade Furniture That You Can Make," *Illustrated World* 35 (July 1921): 823–25.

49. R. O. Buck, "Colonial Bric-a-brac for the Amateur," *Make It Yourself* (Chicago, 1935), 88–92; *Modern Priscilla Home Furnishing Book* (Boston, 1925), 313; L. M. Roehl, *Household Carpentry* (New York, 1927).

50. U.S. Bureau of the Census, *Historical Statistics*, 646; Kenneth T. Jackson, *Crabgrass Frontier: The Suburbanization of the United States* (New York, 1985), 116–37, 157–71.

51. Richard Harris, "Working-Class Home Ownership in the American Metropolis," *Journal of Urban History* 17 (Nov. 1990): 58.

52. Harris, "Working-Class Home Ownership," 54.

53. Samuel Crowther, "Henry Ford: Why I Favor Five Days' Work with Six Days' Pay," *The World's Work* 52 (Oct. 1926): 615.

54. Rose C. Feld, "Now That They Have It," *Century Magazine* 108 (Oct. 1924): 753, 756.

55. Mary Sies notes that architect-designed (rather than homemade) household gadgets got their start a generation earlier. Mary Corbin Sies, "American Country House Architecture in Context: The Suburban Ideal of Living in the East and Midwest," Ph.D. diss., University of Michigan, 1987, 110.

56. Buck, "Colonial Bric-a-brac for the Amateur."

57. Note, for example, the title of Walter J. Coppock, *Make Your Home Your Hobby* (Yellow Springs, 1945).

58. Robert A. Stebbins, *Amateurs, Professionals, and Serious Leisure* (Montreal, 1992).

59. Henry H. Saylor, *Tinkering with Tools* (New York, 1924), 3–11.

60. Arthur Wakeling, ed., *Fix It Yourself* (New York, 1929), 5; Arthur Wakeling, ed., *Home Workshop Manual* (New York, 1930), 1–2.

61. James Tate, "Tools for the Home Mechanic," *Make It Yourself* (Chicago, 1927), 2.

62. Stilgoe, *Borderland*, 266–67. See also, for example, James Tate, "Soldering for the Home Mechanic," *Make It Yourself*, 158; and Wakeling, ed., *Fix It Yourself*, 149.

63. Marge E. Staunton, "Marge Does it Herself!" *American Home* 18 (Aug. 1937): 42.

64. Martha Wirt Davis, "Some Tips for Mrs. Fixit," *American Home* 15 (April 1936): 44.

65. J. C. Woodin, *Home Mechanics for Girls* (Wichita, 1938), iii. For girls using wood-working machinery in a school in the 1930s, see W. Brewer, "Boys Not Allowed," *Texas Outlook* 33 (Dec. 1949): 16–18.

66. Steven M. Gelber, "A Job You Can't Lose: Work and Hobbies in the Great Depression," *Journal of Social History* 24 (Summer 1991): 741–66.

67. Arthur W. Wilson, "Home Hobbyists Offer a Market," *Printers' Ink,* May 4, 1933, 69; H. J. Hobbs, "Fifty-one Hours a Week," *Better Homes and Gardens* 12 (Jan. 1934): 24.

68. Harry J. Hobbs, *Working with Tools* (New York, 1935), 63; see also Clemens T. Schaefer, "Home Mechanics," in *Hobbies for Everybody,* ed. Ruth Lampland (New York, 1934), 216; and Wakeling, ed., *Things to Make,* v.

69. Godfrey Ernst, "Things That Make You Say Damn!" *House and Garden* 70 (July 1936): 38–39; Julius Gregory, "Keep Your Home from Slipping Back," *House and Garden* 64 (Oct. 1933): 56.

70. *Handy Man's Home Manual* (Greenwich, 1936).

71. This attitude even extended to manual training in the schools, which increasingly taught home repair skills. William H. Johnson, "New Day for the Arts and Crafts in Chicago," *American School Board Journal* 94 (June 1937): 21; Earl L. Bedell and Ernest G. Gardner, *Household Mechanics: Industrial Arts for the General Shop* (Scranton, 1937).

72. Hobbs, *Working with Tools,* 12.

73. *New York Times,* Jan. 10, 1937, 112.

74. Ibid., 9.

75. Barbara Melosh, "Manly Work: Public Art and Masculinity in Depression America," in *Gender and American History since 1890,* ed. Barbara Melosh (London, 1993), 182–206; see also Steven M. Gelber, "Working to Prosperity: California's New Deal Murals," *California History* 61 (Summer 1979): 98–127.

76. Powell, "A Survey of the National Home Workshop Guild," 5, 20–21, 26, 28–29, 37; U.S. Bureau of the Census, *Historical Statistics,* 380.

77. Wakeling, ed., *Fix It Yourself,* 233; For illustrations of these tools, see Wakeling, ed., *Home Workshop Manual,* 51–65.

78. "History of the Delta Specialty Company, Rockwell Manufacturing Company, Rockwell International, Delta Machinery Corp." [timeline], Delta International Machinery Corp., n.d. [ca. 1993]; Allen Murphy, "Sales Boom in Hobby Goods," *American Business* 6 (May 1936): 51.

79. Murphy, "Sales Boom," 51, 55; Robert K. Leavitt, "Mr. Macy, Meet the Guppy . . . and Mr. Advertiser, Meet the Hobby," *Advertising and Selling,* June 22, 1933, 17.

80. "Millions in Power Tools for Craftsmen Hobbies," *Steel,* May 17, 1937, 28–29.

81. Kittle, "Activities and Equipment," 26.

82. Powell, "A Survey of the National Home Workshop Guild," 53; see also Kittle, "Activities and Equipment, 26; and C. L. Page, "Survey of the Home Workshops in Ottumwa, Iowa," master's thesis, Colorado State College of Education, Greeley, 1941, 32.

83. "Millions in Power Tools," 28–29.

84. Joseph J. Corn, "Educating the Enthusiast: Print and the Popularization of Technical Knowledge," in *Possible Dreams: Enthusiasm for Technology in America,* ed. John L. Wright (Dearborn, 1992); Joseph J. Corn, *"Popular Mechanics,* Mechanical Literacy and American Culture, 1900–1950," in *Reading in America,* ed. Kathryn Glover (Westport, in press); Kittle, "Activities and Equipment," 24; Powell, "A Survey of the National Home Workshop Guild," 77; Elmer W. Cressman, *Out of School Activities of High School Pupils*

in Relation to Intelligence and Socio-Economic Status (State College, 1937), 50; Page, "Survey of the Home Workshops," 41.

85. Wakeling, ed., *Things to Make*, v; Powell, "A Survey of the National Home Workshop Guild."

86. Powell does not indicate how many women might have been among the three thousand members, but only two of the 633 responses were from women. Ibid., 15.

87. C. T. Schaefer, *Handy Man's Handbook* (New York, 1931), xi.

88. Powell, "A Survey of the National Home Workshop Guild," 65.

89. Schaefer, *Handy Man's Handbook*, xi.

90. For examples of hybrid books, see A. C. Horth, *101 Things for the Handyman to Do* (Philadelphia, 1938) and *Handy Man's Home Manual*. The first imitator was published five years later: Hawthorne Daniel, *The Householder's Complete Handbook* (Boston, 1936).

91. Dick Ramsell, "Diary of a Desperate Daddy," *Better Homes and Gardens* 20 (May 1942): 22–23.

92. Harold J. Hawkins, "Fixing Things around the House," *Parents' Magazine* 17 (Aug. 1942): 48–49.

93. Esther Boulton Black, "Confessions of a Hostess," *American Home* 28 (June 1942): 77; "Family's Day for Repairs," *Parents' Magazine* 16 (Feb. 1941): 55; see also William Klenke, *Furniture a Girl Can Make* (Kansas City, 1940); and *Giant Home Workshop Manual* (New York, 1941), 67.

94. Rachel McKinley Bushong, "Get Going! Not Brains, Not Talent, Not Skill—but Just Plain Work . . . Try It," *American Home* 25 (March 1941): 30–31; see also Klenke, *Furniture a Girl Can Make*, 2; and Ruth Wyeth Spears, *Let's Make a Gift* (New York, 1941).

95. Sabina Ormsby Dean, "It Didn't Take a War to Make a Carpenter Out of Mother," *House Beautiful* 85 (Oct. 1943): 118–19; see also *New York Times*, Dec. 27, 1942, 112; and F. C. Minaker, "Promotion to Hold Customer Interest," *American* 12 (March 1942): 40.

96. For background on the AWVS, see Janet Flanner, "Ladies in Uniform," *The New Yorker*, July 4, 1942, 21–29.

97. Mary Mardison, "Fixing It Yourself," *New York Times Magazine*, March 7, 1943, 24; see also "How to Fix It: Home Owners All over U.S. Learn to Make Own Repairs," *Life*, July 26, 1943, 87–95; Mrs. Robert C. Baker, "Everywoman's Primer of Home Repairs," *House and Garden* 83 (March 1943): 35–42; and Arthur Bohnen, "Be Your Own Handyman: Maintenance—Not Repair," *American Home* 29 (Jan. 1943): 36–38.

98. S. S. Pheiffer, "Never Tell Your Wife," *House Beautiful* 86 (Nov. 1944): 160.

99. See, for example, Stephanie Coontz, *The Way We Never Were: American Families and the Nostalgia Trap* (New York, 1992), 27; and Arlene Skolnick, *Embattled Paradise: The American Family in an Age of Uncertainty* (New York, 1991), 52.

100. U.S. Bureau of the Census, *Historical Statistics*, 49.

101. Filene, *Him-Her-Self*, 169; Skolnick, *Embattled Paradise*, 53; U.S. Bureau of the Census, *Historical Statistics*, 131.

102. H. L. May and D. Petgen, *Leisure and Its Uses* (New York, 1928); Clifford Edward Clark, Jr., *The American Family Home, 1800–1960* (Chapel Hill, 1986); Jackson, *Crabgrass Frontier*, 231–45; Gwendolyn Wright, *Building the American Dream: A Social History of Housing in America* (New York, 1981), 248–55; Albert Roland, "Do-It-Yourself: A Walden for the Millions?" *American Quarterly* 10 (Spring 1958): 161.

103. Griswold, *Fatherhood in America*, 207; Skolnick, *Embattled Paradise*, 71; Filene, *Him-Her-Self*, 173.

104. For an extended discussion of gender and lawn care, see Virginia Scott Jenkins, *The Lawn: A History of an American Obsession* (Washington, 1994), 117–32.

105. Reproduced in Donna R. Braden, *Leisure and Entertainment in America* (Dearborn, 1988), 107.

106. "New Do-It-Yourself Market," *Business Week,* June 14, 1952, 70.

107. "New Do-It-Yourself Market"; "Do-It-Yourself-Idea on Parade," *Business Week,* March 21, 1953, 33; "Sap Is Running in Do-It-Yourself," *Business Week,* March 27, 1954, 122.

108. Lenore Hailpam, "She Did It Herself," *Independent Woman* 32 (June 1953): 203.

109. Hailpam, "She Did It Herself."

110. See, for example, David Dempsey, "Home Sweet (Homemade) Home," *New York Times Magazine,* March 31, 1957, 26.

111. U.S. Bureau of the Census, *Historical Statistics,* 639.

112. Reproduced in Karal Ann Marling, *As Seen on TV: The Visual Culture of Everyday Life in the 1950s* (Cambridge, 1994), 57.

113. *San Jose Mercury-News,* Jan. 5, 1994, extra, 3, 4, Jan. 12, 1994, extra, 3, 5, and Jan. 19, 1994, extra, 3, 5.

114. "Is There a Handy Man in the House?" *American Home* 38 (Nov. 1947): 38–39; J. Holmes, "Hammer-and-Saw Unit Furniture," *Popular Science* 147 (July 1945): 154–55; Ruth Stumpf, "You Can Be Your Own Cabinet Maker," *Better Homes and Gardens* 30 (Oct. 1952): 186; Betty Pepis, "Ideas for an Amateur Craftsman," *New York Times Magazine,* Sept. 2, 1951, 24–25; Betty Pepis, "Home Handymen Tooling Up," *New York Times Magazine,* June 28, 1953, 28–29; J. H. Bowman, "A Shadow Box for a Kitchen Wall," *Workbench* 13 (March–April 1957): 15; Elizabeth Matthews and Guy Henle, "Young Designer Furniture You Can Build Yourself," *Woman's Home Companion* 81 (Oct. 1954): 60–63.

115. For a complete analysis of the social and architectural history of Levittown, see Barbara M. Kelly, *Expanding the American Dream: Building and Rebuilding Levittown* (Albany, 1993).

116. Wright, *Building the American Dream,* 248–54; Clark, *The American Family Home,* 221–25; "Houseful of Ideas with One Aim, Sell the Fixup Market," *Business Week,* Feb. 14, 1953, 66–68.

117. Kelly, *Expanding the American Dream,* 71–73.

118. Phil Creden, "America Rediscovers Its Hands," *American Magazine* 156 (Dec. 1953): 20, 113; see also Hubbard Cobb, *The Home Owner's Complete Guide to Remodeling* (Boston, 1953), 3.

119. "New Do-It-Yourself Market," 70. Attic conversion was also the subject of several early do-it-yourself television shows. J. Paul Taylor, "Four Do-It-Yourself Trends That Mean Extra Profits to Advertisers," *Printers' Ink,* Oct. 2, 1953, 29.

120. Jerome Parker, "I'm Proud of My All-Thumbs Craftwork," *Popular Science* 152 (March 1948): 194–97.

121. Hukill, "The Do-It-Yourself Movement in Pulaski County, Arkansas," 17–21; Ronald E. Bagley, "A Study to Determine the Contributions of Industrial Arts to the Leisure Time Activities of the Graduates of Northeast Missouri State Teachers College," Ed.D. diss., Colorado State College, 1965; U.S. Bureau of the Census, *Homeowners and Home Improvements 1987* (Washington, 1992), 3–4, 9.

122. Anne Swartzlander, "Consumer Characteristics Related to the Frequency of Do-It-Yourself Maintenance and Repair," Ph.D. diss., Ohio State University, 1984, 19–20; Michael Young and Peter Willmott, *The Symmetrical Family* (New York, 1973), 212; David

A. Cunningham, H. J. Montoye, H. L. Metzner, and J. B. Kell, "Active Leisure Activities as Related to Occupation," *Journal of Leisure Research* 2 (1970): 109.

123. "The Shoulder Trade," *Time,* Aug. 2, 1954, 63; "New Do-It-Yourself Market," 61. Despite frequent references to it, wartime experience may not have been as critical for men as for women. Hukill, "The Do-It-Yourself Movement in Pulaski County, Arkansas," 88.

124. William Astor and Charlotte Astor, "Private Associations and Commercial Activities," *Annals of the American Academy of Political and Social Science* 313 (Sept. 1957): 96.

125. Hukill, "The Do-It-Yourself Movement in Pulaski County, Arkansas," 39; Creden, "America Rediscovers Its Hands," 111; Nathan Keine, "Is Your Product Ripe for the Four Billion Dollar Do-It-Yourself Market?" *Printers' Ink,* Nov. 12, 1953, 46; "Do-It-Yourself Gives America a New Look," *Senior Scholastic,* April 7, 1954, 14.

126. Keine, "Is Your Product Ripe?" 46; "Do-It-Yourself Gives America as New Look," 14; *New York Times,* Jan. 3, 1955, 91; see also "Shoulder Trade," 66; U.S. Bureau of the Census, *Expenditures on Residential Owner-Occupied Properties January to May 1954,* Housing and Construction Reports, series HIOI, no. 1: *Alterations and Repairs* (Washington, 1954), 3, 5; "Off the Editor's Chest," *Consumer's Research Bulletin* 34 (Nov. 1954): 2; *New York Times,* Sept. 19, 1954, 3:7.

127. Wakeling, ed., *Home Workshop Manual,* 65.

128. *Highlights of Progress* (Towson, 1992).

129. Leonard A. Stevens, "America's Most Popular Gadget," *Collier's,* July 9, 1954, 80–81.

130. Hukill, "The Do-It-Yourself Movement in Pulaski County, Arkansas," 30; see also Stevens, "America's Most Popular Gadget," 83; *How to Use Power Tools* (Greenwich, 1953), 116; Kittle, "Activities and Equipment," 28; and Powell, "A Survey of the National Home Workshop Guild," 53.

131. Quoted in Robert W. Winter, "The Arroya Culture," in *California Design,* ed. Timothy J. Anderson, Eudorah M. Moore, and Robert W. Winter (Santa Barbara, 1980), 20.

132. "Armory Show 1953," *Harper's Magazine* 206 (May 1953): 93.

133. See, for example, Reed Millard, "Hobbies That Hold Your Family Together," *Coronet* 31 (Jan. 1952): 136–38.

134. Emanuele Stieri, *Complete Home Repair Book* (New York, 1950), 354–55; see also Keine, "Is Your Product Ripe?" 48; Babson, "Do It Yourself," 1012; and Darrell Huff, "We've Found a Substitute for Income," *Harper's Magazine* 207 (Oct. 1953): 28, 29.

135. "Do-It-Yourself Gives America a New Look," 15–16; Walt Durbhan, "Our House Is Different—Yours Can Be Too," *American Magazine* 157 (Jan. 1954): 73.

136. *How To Use Power Tools,* 9. For examples of woodworking by women, see H. Gunderson, "Hobby Crafts for Adults," *Industrial Arts and Vocational Education* 39 (Nov. 1950): 341–42; Dorothy Lambert Trumm, "Pleasure from Your Leisure, and Why Not?" *American Home* 54 (July 1955): 31–33; Rose McAfee, "A Lady and a Jig Saw," *Profitable Hobbies* 11 (Feb. 1955): 2–5; and Elizabeth Krusell Hall, "My Wood Working Hobby Paid Off," *American Home* 57 (March 1957): 109–10.

137. Mary N. Borton, "Hobbies Can Build Character," *Parents Magazine* 26 (May 1954): 44–46; William G. Poole, "Coeducation Wood Shop," *Industrial Arts and Vocational Education* 47 (Sept. 1958): 205–6.

138. Hukill, "The Do-It-Yourself Movement in Pulaski County, Arkansas," 65.

139. Ibid., 85–86; see also Sprague Holden, "Education of a House Husband," *House Beautiful* 89 (Sept. 1947): 128.

140. Edward C. Fisher, "You're Going to Make a Chair," *Profitable Hobbies* 7 (Jan. 1951): 44–47.

141. "The ABC of Home Repair" [advertisement], *American Home* 31 (Sept. 1945): 43.

142. For examples, see John Webster, "Handsome Furniture You Can Build," *Better Homes and Gardens* 29 (March 1951): 258–59; *Build It* (Greenwich, 1954), 2, 66, 104–5; *Woman's Home Companion Household Book*, ed. Henry Humphrey (New York, 1950), 501; Herbert J. Gans, *The Levittowners: Ways of Use and Politics in a New York Suburban Community* (New York, 1967), 270; *New York Times*, Oct. 24, 1955, 24, and Feb. 9, 1958, 3:1; "Sap Is Running in Do-It-Yourself," *Business Week*, March 27, 1954, 122; "What's New in Do-it-Yourself," *Changing Times* 10 (Feb. 1956): 37; and Babson, "Do It Yourself," 1012.

143. Eugene Rachlis, "How Not to Do-It-Yourself," *New York Times Magazine*, Aug. 15, 1954, 6:34; see also the *New York Times*, Sept. 19, 1954, 6:4.

144. Roland, "Do-It-Yourself," 154.

145. "New Do-It-Yourself Market," 61, 70; "Shoulder Trade," 62; see also Harry Zarchy, *Here's Your Hobby* (New York, 1950); and "Personal Business," *Business Week*, April 2, 1955, 131.

146. Dempsey, "Home Sweet (Homemade) Home," 71.

147. "Armory Show 1953," 95.

148. Hukill, "The Do-It-Yourself Movement in Pulaski County, Arkansas," 54.

149. Rachlis, "How Not to Do-It-Yourself," 34.

150. "Shoulder Trade," 64, 66; Dempsey, "Home Sweet (Homemade) Home," 26; Huff, "We've Found a Substitute for Income," 27, 29 [illustrations by Julius Kroll]; *New York Times*, Sept. 10, 1955, 32.

151. Holden, "Education of a House Husband," 129; see also V. C. Barnett, "Hints for the Gentleman Mechanic; or, How to Use a Tinker's Dam," *Better Homes and Gardens* 25 (May 1947): 190–93; "Off the Editor's Chest," 29; and Margaret E. Mulac, *Hobbies: The Creative Use of Leisure* (New York, 1959).

152. Dempsey, "Home Sweet (Homemade) Home," 71.

153. See, for example, Huff, "We've Found a Substitute for Income," 28; Francis Coughlin, "Is There a Handyman Handy?" *Science Digest* 43 (March 1958): 72.

154. Julian Starr, Jr., *Fifty Things to Make for the Home* (New York, 1941), 3–5.

155. Bill Tusher, "Do It Yourself . . . Hollywood Does," *Popular Mechanics* 112 (Aug. 1959): 125–29. For earlier and somewhat more modest versions of the craftsman, see "Our Hobby Parade: Sixty-eight Unusual American Collections," *House and Garden* 82 (July 1942): 43; and Kay Campbell, "And What's Your Hobby?" *American Home* 37 (April 1947): 32–36. Some of these stories may have been the result of a deliberate campaign by the Screen Actors' Guild to promote family values. Coontz, *The Way We Never Were*, 27–28.

156. Tusher, "Do It Yourself . . . Hollywood Does," 126.

13

Family, Race, and Poverty in the 1980s

MAXINE BACA ZINN

The 1960s civil rights movement overturned segregation laws, opened voting booths, created new job opportunities, and brought hope to black Americans. As long as it could be said that conditions were improving, black family structure and lifestyle remained private matters. The promises of the 1960s faded, however, as the income gap between whites and blacks widened. Since the middle 1970s, the black underclass has expanded rather than contracted, and along with this expansion emerged a public debate about the black family. Two distinct models of the underclass now prevail—one that is cultural and one that is structural. Both focus on issues of family structure and poverty.

THE CULTURAL DEFICIENCY MODEL

The 1980s ushered in a revival of old ideas about poverty, race, and family. Many theories and opinions about the urban underclass rest on the culture-of-poverty debate of the 1960s. In brief, proponents of the culture-of-poverty thesis contend that the poor have a different way of life than the rest of society and that these cultural differences explain continued poverty. Within the current national discussion are three distinct approaches that form the latest wave of deficiency theories.

The first approach—culture as villain—places the cause of the swelling underclass in a value system characterized by low aspirations, excessive masculinity, and the acceptance of female-headed families as a way of life.

The second approach—family as villain—assigns the cause of the growing underclass to the structure of the family. Although unemployment is often addressed, this argument always returns to the causal connections between poverty and the disintegration of traditional family structure.

The third approach—welfare as villain—treats welfare and antipoverty programs as the cause of illegitimate births, female-headed families, and low motivation to work. In short, welfare transfer payments to the poor create disincentives to work and incentives to have children out of wedlock—a self-defeating trap of poverty.

CULTURE AS VILLAIN

Public discussions of urban poverty have made the "disintegrating" black family the force most responsible for the growth of the underclass, which is by definition poor and both overwhelmingly black and disproportionately composed of female-headed households. The members are perceived as different from striving, upwardly mobile whites. The rising number of people in the underclass has provided a catalyst for reporters' and scholars' attention to this disadvantaged category. The typical interpretation given by these social commentators is that the underclass is permanent, being locked in by its own unique but maladaptive culture. This thinking, although flawed, provides the popular rationale for treating the poor as the problem.

The logic of the culture-of-poverty argument is that poor people have distinctive values, aspirations, and psychological characteristics that inhibit their achievement and produce behavioral deficiencies likely to keep them poor not only within generations but also across generations through socialization of the young.[1] In this argument, poverty is more a function of thought processes than of physical environment.[2] As a result of this logic, current discussions of ghetto poverty, family structure, welfare, unemployment, and out-of-wedlock births connect these conditions in ways similar to the 1965 Moynihan Report.[3] Because Moynihan maintained that the pathological problem within black ghettos was the deterioration of the Negro family, his report became the generative example of blaming the victim.[4] Furthermore, Moynihan dismissed racism as a salient force in the perpetuation of poverty by arguing that the tangle of pathology was "capable of perpetuating itself without assistance from the white world."[5]

The reaction of scholars to Moynihan's cultural-deficiency model was swift and extensive although not as well publicized as the model itself. Research in the 1960s and 1970s by Andrew Billingsley, Robert Hill, Herbert Gutman, Joyce Ladner, Elliott Liebow, and Carol Stack, to name a few, documented the many strengths of black families, strengths that allowed them to survive slavery, the enclosures of the South, and the depression of the North.[6] Such work revealed that many patterns of family life were not created by a deficient culture but were instead a "rational adaptational response to conditions of deprivation."[7]

A rapidly growing literature in the 1980s documents the disproportionate representation of black, female-headed families in poverty. Yet recent studies on black, female-headed families are largely unconcerned with questions about adaptation. Rather, they study the strong association between female-headed families and poverty, the effects of family disorganization on children, the demographic and socioeconomic factors that are correlated with single-parent status, and the connection between the economic status of men and the rise in black, female-headed families.[8] Although most of these studies do not advance a social-pathology explanation, they do signal a regressive shift in analytic focus. Many well-meaning academics who intend to call attention to the dangerously high level of poverty in black, female-headed households have begun to emphasize family structure and the black ghetto way of life as contributors to the perpetuation of the underclass.

The popular press, however, openly and enthusiastically embraced the Moynihan thesis both in its original version and in Moynihan's restatement of the thesis in his book *Family and Nation.*[9] Here, Moynihan repeats his assertion that poverty and family structure are associated, but he contends that the association holds for blacks and whites alike. This modification does not critique his earlier assumptions; indeed, it validates them. A profoundly disturbing example of that is revealed in the widely publicized television documentary *CBS Reports: The Vanishing Family.*[10] According to this refurbished version of the old Moynihan Report, a breakdown in family values has allowed black men to renounce their traditional breadwinner role, leaving black women to bear the economic responsibility for children.[11] The argument that the black community is devastating itself fits neatly with the resurgent conservatism that is manifested among black and white intellectuals and policymakers.

Another contemporary example of the use of the culture of poverty is Nicholas Lemann's two-part 1986 *Atlantic Monthly* article about the black underclass in Chicago.[12] According to Lemann, family structure is the most visible manifestation of black America's bifurcation into a middle class that has escaped the ghetto and an underclass that is irrevocably trapped in the ghetto. He explains the rapid growth of the underclass in the 1970s by pointing to two mass migrations of black Americans. The first was from the rural South to the urban North and numbered in the millions during the 1940s, 1950s, and 1960s; the second was a migration out of the ghettos by members of the black working and middle classes who had been freed from housing discrimination by the civil rights movement. As a result of the exodus, the indexes of disorganization in the urban ghettos of the North (crime, illegitimate births) have risen and the underclass has flourished.[13] High illegitimacy rates, family disintegration, and loose attitudes toward marriage are said to be a heritage of the rural South. In Lemann's words, they represent the power of culture to produce poverty:

> The argument is anthropological, not economic; it emphasizes the power over people's behavior that culture, as opposed to economic incentives, can have. Ascribing a society's condition in part to the culture that prevails there seems benign when the society under discussion is England or California. But as a way of thinking about black ghettos it has become unpopular. Twenty years ago ghettos were often said to have a self-generating, destructive culture of poverty (the term has an impeccable source, the anthropologist Oscar Lewis). But then the left equated cultural discussions of the ghetto with accusing poor blacks of being in a bad situation that was of their own making. . . . The left succeeded in limiting the terms of the debate to purely economic ones, and today the right also discusses the ghetto in terms of economic "incentives to fail," provided by the welfare system. . . . In the ghettos, though, it appears that the distinctive culture is now the greatest barrier to progress by the black underclass, rather than either unemployment or welfare.[14]

Lemann's essay, his "misreading of left economic analysis, and cultural anthropology itself," might be dismissed if it were atypical in the debate about the culture of poverty and the underclass.[15] Unfortunately, it shares with other studies the problems of working "with neither the benefit of a well-articulated theory about the impact of personality and motivation on behavior nor adequate data from a representative sample of the low-income population."[16]

The idea that poverty is caused by psychological factors and passed from one generation to the next has been called into question by the University of Michigan's Panel Study of Income Dynamics (PSID), a large-scale data collection project conceived, in part, to test many of the assumptions about the psychological and demographic aspects of poverty. This study has gathered annual information from a representative sample of the U.S. population. Two striking discoveries contradict the stereotypes stemming from the culture-of-poverty argument. The first is the high turnover of individual families in poverty, and the second is the finding that motivation cannot be linked to poverty. Each year the number of people below the poverty line remains about the same, but the poor in one year are not necessarily the poor in the following year. "Blacks from welfare-dependent families were no more likely to become welfare dependent than similar Blacks from families who had never received welfare. Further, measures of parental sense of efficacy, future orientation, and achievement motivation had no effects on welfare dependency for either group."[17] This research has found no evidence that highly motivated people are more successful at escaping from poverty than those with lower scores on tests.[18] Thus, cultural deficiency is an inappropriate model for explaining the underclass.

THE FAMILY AS VILLAIN

A central notion within culture-of-poverty arguments is that family disintegration is the source and sustaining feature of poverty. Today, nearly six out
of ten black children are born out of wedlock compared to roughly three out
of ten in 1970. In the twenty-five- to thirty-four-year age bracket, the probability of separation and divorce for black women is twice that of white wom-
en. The result is a high probability that an individual black woman and her
children will live alone. The so-called deviant, mother-only family, common
among blacks, is a product of the "feminization of poverty," a shorthand
reference to women living alone and being disproportionately represented
among the poor. The attention given to increased marital breakups, to births
to unmarried women, and to the household patterns that accompany these
changes would suggest that the bulk of contemporary poverty is a family-
structure phenomenon. Common knowledge—whether true or not—has it
that family-structure changes cause most poverty and that changes in family structure have led to poverty rates much higher than they would have been
had family composition remained stable.[19]

Despite the growing concentration of poverty among black, female-headed households since the late 1960s, there is reason to question conventional
thinking. Research by Mary Jo Bane finds that changes in family structure
have less causal influence on poverty than is commonly thought.[20] Assumptions about the correlation and association between poverty and family
breakdown avoid harder questions about the character and direction of causal relations between the two phenomena.[21] Bane's longitudinal research on
household composition and poverty suggests that much poverty, especially
among blacks, is the result of already poor, two-parent households that break
up, producing poor, female-headed households. This differs from the event
transition to poverty that is more common for whites: "Three-quarters of
whites who were poor in the first year after moving into a female-headed or
single person household became poor simultaneously with the transition; in
contrast, of the blacks who were poor after the transition, about two-thirds
had also been poor before. Reshuffled poverty as opposed to event-caused
poverty for blacks challenges the assumption that changes in family structure have created ghetto poverty. This underscores the importance of considering the ways in which race produces different paths to poverty."[22]

A two-parent family is no guarantee against poverty for racial minorities. Analyzing data from the PSID, Martha Hill concluded that the long-term
income of black children in two-parent families throughout the decade was
even lower than the long-term income of non-black children who spent most

of the decade in mother-only families: "Thus, increasing the proportion of Black children growing up in two-parent families would not by itself eliminate very much of the racial gap in the economic well-being of children; changes in the economic circumstances of the parents are needed most to bring the economic status of Black children up to the higher status of non-Black children."[23]

Further studies are required if we are to understand the ways in which poverty, family structure, and race are related.

WELFARE AS VILLAIN

An important variant of the family-structure and deficient-culture explanations, one especially popular among political conservatives, is the argument that welfare causes poverty. This explanation proposes that welfare undermines incentives to work and causes families to break up by allowing black women to have babies and encouraging black men to escape family responsibilities. That position has been widely publicized by Charles Murray's influential *Losing Ground*.[24] According to Murray, liberal welfare policies squelch work incentives and thus are the major cause of the breakup of black families. In effect, increased Aid to Families with Dependent Children (AFDC) benefits make it desirable to forgo marriage and live on the dole.

Research has refuted that explanation for the changes in the structure of families in the underclass. Numerous studies have shown that variations in welfare across time and in different states have not produced systematic variation in family structure.[25] Research conducted at the University of Wisconsin's Institute for Research on Poverty found that poverty increased after the late 1960s due to a weakening economy through the 1970s. No support was found for Murray's assertion that spending growth did more harm than good for blacks because it increased the percentage of families headed by women. Trends in welfare spending increased between 1960 and 1972 and declined between 1970 and 1984, yet there were no reversals in family-composition trends during this period. The percentage of these households headed by women increased steadily, from 10.7 percent to 20.8 percent between 1968 and 1983.[26]

Further evidence against the "welfare-dependency" motivation for the dramatic rise in the proportion of black families headed by females is provided by William Darity and Samuel Meyers. Using statistical causality tests, they found no short-term effects of variations in welfare payments on female headship in black families.[27]

Other research draws similar conclusions about the impact of welfare policies on family structure. Using a variety of tests, David Ellwood and Lawrence Summers dispute the adverse effects of AFDC.[28] They highlight two facts that raise questions about the role of welfare policies in producing female-headed households. First, the real value of welfare payments has declined since the early 1970s, whereas family dissolution has continued to rise. Family-structure changes do not mirror benefit-level changes. Second, variations in benefit levels across states do not lead to corresponding variations in divorce rates or numbers of children in single-parent families. Their comparison of groups collecting AFDC with groups that were not found that the effects of welfare benefits on family structures were small.[29] In sum, the systematic research on welfare and family structure indicates that AFDC has far less effect on changes in family structure than has been assumed.

OPPORTUNITY STRUCTURES IN DECLINE

A very different view of the underclass has emerged alongside the popularized cultural-deficiency model. This view is rooted in a substantial body of theory and research. Focusing on the opportunity structure of society, these concrete studies reveal that culture is not responsible for the underclass.

Within the structural framework there are three distinct strands. The first deals with transformations of the economy and the labor force that affect Americans in general and blacks and Hispanics in particular. The second is the transformation of marriage and family life among minorities. The third is the changing class composition of inner cities and their increasing isolation of residents from mainstream social institutions.

All three are informed by new research that examines the macrostructural forces that shape family trends and demographic patterns that expand the analysis to include Hispanics.

Employment

Massive economic changes since the end of World War II are causing the social marginalization of black people throughout the United States. The shift from an economy based on the manufacture of goods to one based on information and services has redistributed work in global, national, and local economies. Although these major economic shifts affect all workers, they have more serious consequences for blacks than whites, a condition that scholars call "structural racism."[30] Major economic trends and patterns, even those that appear race-neutral, have significant racial implications. Blacks and other minorities are profoundly affected, first, by the decline of the industrial manufacturing sector and the growth of service sectors of the economy and, second, by shifts in the geographical location of jobs from central cities to the suburbs and from the traditional manufacturing cities (the Rustbelt) to the Sunbelt and to other countries.

In their classic work *The Deindustrialization of America,* Barry Bluestone and Bennett Harrison revealed that "minorities tend to be concentrated in industries that have borne the brunt of recent closing. This is particularly true in the automobile, steel, and rubber industries."[31] In a follow-up study, Bluestone, Harrison, and Lucy Gorham have shown that people of color, particularly black men, are more likely than whites to lose their jobs due to the restructuring of the U.S. economy and that young black men are especially hard-hit.[32] Further evidence of the consequences of economic transformation for minority males is provided by Richard Hill and Cynthia Negrey.[33] They studied deindustrialization in the Great Lakes region and found that the race-gender group that was hardest hit by the industrial slump was black male production workers. Fully 50 percent of that group in five Great Lakes cities studied lost their jobs in durable-goods manufacturing between 1979 and 1984. They found that black male production workers also suffered the greatest rate of job loss in the region and in the nation as a whole.

The decline of manufacturing jobs has altered the cities' roles as opportunity ladders for the disadvantaged. Since the start of World War II, well-paying blue-collar jobs in manufacturing have been a main avenue of job security and mobility for blacks and Hispanics. Movement into higher-level blue-collar jobs was one of the most important components of black occupational advancement in the 1970s. The current restructuring of industries creates the threat of downward mobility for middle-class minorities.[34]

Rather than offering opportunities to minorities, cities have become centers of poverty. Large concentrations of blacks and Hispanics are trapped in cities in which the urban employment base is shifting. Inner cities are shifting from being centers of production and distribution of physical goods toward being centers of administration, information, exchange, trade, finance, and government service. Conversely, these changes in local employment structures have been accompanied by a shift in the demographic composition of large central cities away from European white to predominantly black and Hispanic, with rising unemployment. The transfer of jobs away from central cities to the suburbs has created a residential job opportunity mismatch that literally leaves minorities behind in the inner city. Without adequate training or credentials, they are relegated to low-paying, nonadvancing exploitative service work or they are unemployed. Thus, blacks have become, for the most part, superfluous people in cities that once provided them with opportunities.

The composition and size of cities' overall employment bases have also changed. Since the late 1960s, most older, larger cities have experienced substantial job growth in occupations associated with knowledge-intensive service industries. Job growth in these high-skill, predominantly white-collar industries, however, has not compensated for employment declines in manufacturing, wholesale trade, and other predominantly blue-collar industries that once constituted the economic backbone of black urban employment.[35]

While cities once sustained large numbers of less-skilled persons, today's service industries typically have high educational requisites for entry knowledge, and information jobs in the central cities are virtually closed to minorities given the required technological education and skill level. Commuting between central cities and outlying areas is increasingly common. White-collar workers commute daily from their suburban residences to central business districts while streams of inner-city residents commute to blue-collar jobs in outlying nodes.[36]

An additional structural impediment that inner-city minorities face is their increased distance from current sources of blue-collar and other entry-level jobs. Because industries that provide these jobs have moved to the suburbs and nonmetropolitan peripheries, racial discrimination and inadequate incomes of inner-city minorities have the additional impact of preventing many from moving out of the inner city in order to maintain access to traditional sources of employment. The dispersed nature of job growth makes public transportation from inner-city neighborhoods impractical, requiring virtually all city residents who work in peripheral areas to commute by personally owned automobiles. The severity of this mismatch is documented by John Kasarda: "More than one-half of the minority households in Philadelphia and Boston are without a means of personal transportation. New York City's proportions are even higher, with only three of ten black or Hispanic households having a vehicle available."[37]

This economic restructuring is characterized by an overall pattern of uneven development. Manufacturing industries have declined in the North and Midwest while new growth industries, such as computers and communications equipment, are locating in the southern and southwestern part of the United States. This regional shift has produced some gains for blacks in the South, where black poverty rates have declined. Given the large minority populations in the Sunbelt, it is conceivable that industrial restructuring could offset the economic threats to racial equality. Sunbelt expansion, however, has been based largely on low-wage, labor-intensive enterprises that use large numbers of underpaid minority workers, and a decline in the northern industrial sector continues to leave large numbers of blacks and Hispanics without work.

Marriage

The connection between declining black employment opportunities (especially male joblessness) and the explosive growth of black families headed by single women is the basis of William J. Wilson's analysis of the underclass. Several studies conducted by Wilson and his colleagues at the University of Chicago have established this link.[38] Wilson and Kathryn Neckerman have documented the relationship between increased male joblessness and female-headed households. By devising an indicator called "the index of marriageable males," they reveal a long-term decline in the proportion of black men, particularly voting black men, who are in a position to support a family. Their indicators include mortality and incarceration rates as well as labor-force participation rates, and they reveal that the proportion of black men in unstable economic situations is much higher than indicated in unemployment figures.[39]

Wilson's analysis treats marriage as an opportunity structure that no longer exists for large numbers of black people. Consider, for example, why the majority of pregnant black teenagers do not marry. In 1960, 42 percent of black teenagers who had babies were unmarried; by 1970 the rate jumped to 63 percent, and by 1983 it was 89 percent.[40] According to Wilson, the increase is tied directly to the changing labor-market status of voting black males. He cites the well-established relationship between joblessness and marital instability in support of his argument that "pregnant teenagers are more likely to marry if their boyfriends are working."[41] Out-of-wedlock births are sometimes encouraged by families and absorbed into the kinship system because marrying the suspected father would mean adding someone who was unemployed to the family's financial burden.[42] Adaptation to structural conditions leaves black women disproportionately separated, divorced, and solely responsible for their children. The mother-only family structure is thus the consequence, not the cause, of poverty.

Community

These changes in employment and marriage patterns have been accompanied by changes in the social fabric of cities. "The Kerner Report Twenty Years Later," a conference of the 1988 Commission on the Cities, highlighted the growing isolation of blacks and Hispanics.[43] Inner-city poverty was worse and more persistent than in the late 1960s, and ghettos and barrios have become isolated and deteriorating societies with their own economies and with increasingly isolated social institutions, including schools, families, businesses, churches, and hospitals. According to Wilson, this profound social transformation is reflected not only in the high rates of joblessness, crime, and poverty but also in a changing socioeconomic class structure. As black middle-class professionals left the central city, so too did working-class blacks. Wilson uses the term *concentration effects* to capture the experiences of low-income families who now make up the majority of those who live in inner cities. The most disadvantaged are disproportionately concentrated in the sections of the inner city plagued by joblessness, lawlessness, and a general milieu of desperation. Without working-class or middle-class role models, these families have little in common with mainstream society.[44]

The departure of the black working and middle classes means more than a loss of role models, however. As David Ellwood has observed, the flight of black professionals has meant the loss of connections and networks. If successfully employed persons do not live nearby, then the informal methods of finding a job, by which one worker tells someone else of an opening and recommends her or him to the employer, are lost.[45] Concentration and isolation describe the processes that systematically entrench a lack of opportunities in inner cities. Individuals and families are thus left to acquire life's necessities although they are far removed from the channels of social opportunity.

THE CHANGING DEMOGRAPHY OF RACE AND POVERTY

Hispanic poverty, virtually ignored for nearly a quarter of a century is now capturing the attention of media and scholars alike. Demographic and economic patterns have made "the flow of Hispanics to urban America among the most significant changes occurring in the 1980s."[46]

As the Hispanic presence in the United States has increased, Hispanic poverty rates have risen alarmingly. Between 1979 and 1985, the percentage of Latinos who were poor grew from 21.8 percent to 29 percent. Nationwide, the poverty rate for all Hispanics was 27.3 percent in 1986. By comparison, the white poverty rate in 1986 was 11 percent; the black poverty rate was 31.1 percent.[47] Not only have Hispanic poverty rates risen alarmingly but also, like black poverty, Hispanic poverty has become increasingly concentrated in inner cities. Hispanics fall well behind the general population on all measures of social and economic well-being: jobs, income, educational attainment, housing, and health care. Poverty among Hispanics has become so persistent that if current patterns continue, Hispanics will emerge in the 1990s as the nation's poorest racial-ethnic group.[48] Hispanic poverty has thus become a trend to watch in national discussions of urban poverty and the underclass.

Although Hispanics are emerging as the poorest minority group, poverty rates and other socioeconomic indicators vary widely among Hispanic groups. Among Puerto Ricans, 39.9 percent of the population lived below the poverty level in 1986. For Mexicans, 28.4 percent were living in poverty in 1986. For Cubans and Central and South Americans, the poverty rate was much lower: 18.7 percent.[49] Such diversity has led scholars to question the usefulness of this racial-ethnic category that includes all people of Latin American descent.[50] Nevertheless, the labels "Hispanic" or "Latino" are useful in general terms in describing the changing racial composition of poverty populations. In spite of the great diversity among Hispanic nationalities, they face common obstacles to becoming incorporated into the economic mainstream of society.

Researchers are debating whether trends of rising Hispanic poverty are irreversible and if those trends point to a permanent inner-class among Hispanics. Do macrostructural shifts in the economy and the labor force have the same effects on blacks and Latinos? According to Joan W. Moore, national economic changes do affect Latinos, but they affect subgroups of Latinos in different ways:

> The movement of jobs and investments out of Rustbelt cities has left many Puerto Ricans living in a bleak ghetto economy. This same movement has had a different effect on Mexican Americans living in the Southwest. As in the North, many factories with job ladders have disappeared. Most of the newer Sunbelt industries offer either high-paying jobs for which few Hispanics are trained or low-paying ones that provide few opportunities for advancement. Those industries that depend on immigrant labor (such as clothing manufacturing in Los Angeles) often seriously exploit their workers, so the benefits to Hispanics in the Southwest of this influx of industries and investments are mixed. Another subgroup, Cubans in Miami, work and live in an enclave economy that appears to be unaffected by this shift in the national economy.[51]

Because shifts in the subregional economies seem more important to Hispanics than changes in the national economy, Moore is cautious about applying William Wilson's analysis of how the underclass is created.

Opportunity structures have not declined in a uniform manner for Latinos. Yet Hispanic poverty, welfare dependence, and unemployment rates are greatest in regions that have been transformed by macrostructural economic changes. In some cities, Puerto Rican poverty and unemployment rates are steadily converging with, and in some cases exceeding, the rates for blacks. In 1986, 40 percent of the Puerto Ricans in the United States lived below the poverty level, and 70 percent of Puerto Rican children lived in poverty.[52]

Family structure is also affected by economic dislocation. Among Latinos, the incidence of female-headed households is highest for Puerto Ricans—43.3 percent—compared to 19.2 percent for Mexicans, 17.7 for Cubans, and 25.5 percent for Central and South Americans.[53] The association between national economic shifts and high rates of social dislocation among Hispanics provides further evidence for the structural argument that economic conditions rather than culture create distinctive forms of racial poverty.

FAMILY, POVERTY, AND GENDER

The structural model I have described advances our understanding of poverty and minority families beyond the limitations of the cultural model. It directs attention away from psychological and cultural issues and toward social structures that allocate economic and social rewards. It has generated a substantial body of research and findings that challenge culture-of-poverty arguments.

On matters of gender, however, the structural model would benefit from discussion, criticism, and rethinking. This is not to deny the structural model's value in linking poverty to external economic conditions but rather to question the model's assumptions about gender and family structure and point to the need for gender as a specific analytic category.

Although several key aspects of the structural model distinguish it from the cultural model, both models are remarkably close in their thinking about gender. Patricia Hill Collins exposes the gender ideologies that underlie cultural explanations of racial inferiority. Those same ideologies about women and men, about their place in the family and their relationship to the public institutions of the larger society, reappear, albeit in modified ways, in the structural model.

Collins shows how assumptions about racial deficiency rest on cultural notions about unfit men and women. In contrast, the structural approach focuses on the social circumstances produced by economic change. It therefore avoids drawing caricatures of men who spurn work and unmarried women who persist in having children. Yet both models find differences between mainstream gender roles and those of the underclass. Indeed, some of the most striking and important findings of the structural approach focus on that difference. Clearly, the reasons for the difference lie in the differing economic and social opportunities of the two groups, yet the structural model assumes that the traditional family is a key solution for eliminating racial poverty. Although the reasons given for the erosion of the traditional family are very different, both models rest on normative definitions of women's and men's roles. Two examples reveal how the structural perspective is locked into traditional concepts of the family and women's and men's places within it.

Wilson identifies male joblessness and the resulting shortage of marriageable males as the conditions responsible for the proliferation of female-headed households. His vision of a solution is a restoration of marital opportunities and the restoration of family structures in which men provide for their families by working in the labor force and women have children who can then be assured of the economic opportunities afforded by two-parent families. He offers no alternative concept of the family, no discussion of lesbian families or other arrangements that differ from the standard male-female married pair. Instead of exploring how women's opportunities and earning capacities outside of marriage are affected by macrostructural economic transformations, instead of calling "for pay equity, universal day care and other initiatives to buttress women's capacities for living independently in the world . . . Wilson goes in exactly the opposite direction."[54]

Ellwood's comprehensive analysis of American family poverty and welfare, *Poor Support: Poverty in the American Family,* contains a discussion that says a great deal about how women, men, and family roles are viewed by authoritative scholars working within the structural tradition. Looking at the work of adults in two-parent families, Ellwood finds that all families must fulfill two roles—a nurturing/child-rearing role and a provider role—and that in two-parent families these responsibilities are divided along traditional gender lines. Therefore, Ellwood raises a question: "Do we want single mothers to behave like husbands or like wives? Those who argue that single mothers ought to support their families through their own efforts are implicitly asking that they behave like husbands."[55] Although Ellwood's discussion is meant to illustrate that single mothers experience difficulty in having to fulfill the dual roles of provider and nurturer, it confuses the matter by reverting to a gendered division of labor in which women nurture and men provide. By presenting family responsibilities as those of "husbands" and "wives," even well-meaning illustrations reproduce the ideology they seek to challenge.

Structural approaches have failed to articulate gender as an analytic category even though the conditions uncovered in contemporary research on the urban underclass are closely intertwined with gender. In fact, the problems of male joblessness and female-headed households form themselves around gender. Although these conditions are the result of economic transformations, they change gender relations as they change the marital, family, and labor arrangements of women and men. Furthermore, the economic disenfranchisement of large numbers of black men, what Clyde Franklin calls "the institutional decimation of Black men," is a gender phenomenon of enormous magnitude.[56] It affects the meanings and definitions of masculinity for black men, and it reinforces the public patriarchy that controls black women through their increased dependence on welfare. Such gender issues are vital. They reveal that where people of color "end up" in the social order has as much to do with the economic restructuring of gender as with the economic restructuring of class and race.

The new structural analyses of the underclass reveal that the conditions in which black and Hispanic women and men live are extremely vulnerable to economic change. In this way, such analyses move beyond feminization-of-poverty explanations that ignore class and race differences among women and ignore poverty among minority men.[57] Yet many structural analyses fail to consider the interplay of gender-based assumptions with structural racism. Just as the feminization-of-poverty approach has tended to neglect the way in which race produces different routes to poverty, structural discussions of the underclass pay far too little attention to how gender produces different routes to poverty for black and Hispanic women and men. Many social forces are at work in the erosion of family life among black and Hispanic people. Careful attention to the interlocking systems of class, race, and gender is imperative if we are to understand and solve the problems resulting from economic transformation.

Notes

This essay is reprinted, with minor editorial changes, from *Signs: Journal of Women in Culture and Society* 14, no. 4 (1989): 856–74.

1. Mary Corcoran, Greg J. Duncan, Gerald Gurin, and Patricia Gurin, "Myth and Reality: The Causes and Persistence of Poverty," *Journal of Policy Analysis and Management* 4, no. 4 (1985): 516–36.

2. Mary Corcoran, Greg J. Duncan, and Martha S. Hill, "The Economic Fortunes of Women and Children: Lessons from the Panel Study of Income Dynamics," *Signs: Journal of Women in Culture and Society* 10 (Winter 1984): 232–48.

3. Daniel P. Moynihan, "The Negro Family: The Case for National Action," in *The Moynihan Report and the Politics of Controversy,* ed. Lee Rainwater and William L. Yancy (Cambridge, 1967), 39–132.

4. Margaret Cerullo and Marla Erlien, "Beyond the 'Normal Family': A Cultural Critique of Women's Poverty," in *For Crying Out Loud,* ed. Rochelle Lefkowitz and Ann Withorn (New York, 1986), 246–60.

5. Moynihan, "The Negro Family," 47.

6. Leith Mullings, "Anthropological Perspectives on the Afro-American Family," *American Journal of Social Psychiatry* 6 (Winter 1986): 11–16. See the following revisionist works on the black family: Andrew Billingsley, *Black Families in White America* (Englewood Cliffs, 1968); Robert Hill, *The Strengths of Black Families* (New York, 1972); Herbert Gutman, *The*

Black Family in Slavery and Freedom (New York, 1976); Joyce Ladner, *Tomorrow's Tomorrow: The Black Woman* (New York, 1971); Elliott Liebow, *Talley's Corners: A Study of Negro Street Corner Men* (Boston, 1967); and Carol Stack, *All Our Kin* (New York, 1974).

7. William J. Wilson and Robert Aponte, "Urban Poverty," *Annual Review of Sociology* 11 (1985): 231–58, esp. 241.

8. For a review of recent studies see Wilson and Aponte, "Urban Poverty."

9. Daniel Patrick Moynihan, *Family and Nation* (San Diego, 1986).

10. *CBS Reports: The Vanishing Family, Crisis in Black America*, narrated by Bill Moyers, Columbia Broadcasting System, Jan. 1986.

11. "Hard Times for Black America," *Dollars and Sense*, no. 115 (April 1986): 5–7.

12. Nicholas Lemann, "The Origins of the Underclass, Part 1," *Atlantic Monthly* (June 1986): 31–55; Nicholas Lemann, "The Origins of the Underclass, Part 2," *Atlantic Monthly* (July 1986): 54–68.

13. Lemann, "The Origins of the Underclass, Part 1," 35.

14. Ibid.

15. Jim Sleeper, "Overcoming 'Underclass': More Jobs Are Still the Key," *In These Times*, June 11–24, 1986, 16.

16. Corcoran, Duncan, Gurin, and Gurin, "Myth and Reality," 517.

17. Martha S. Hill and Michael Ponza, "Poverty and Welfare Dependence across Generations," *Economic Outlook U.S.A.* (Summer 1983): 61–64, esp. 64.

18. Anne Rueter, "Myths of Poverty," *Research News* (July–Sept. 1984): 18–19.

19. Mary Jo Bane, "Household Composition and Poverty," in *Fighting Poverty*, ed. Sheldon H. Danziger and Daniel Weinberg (Cambridge, 1986), 209–31.

20. Bane, "Household Composition and Poverty."

21. Betsy Dworkin, "40 Percent of the Poor Are Children," *New York Times Book Review*, March 2, 1986, 9.

22. Bane, "Household Composition and Poverty," 277.

23. Martha Hill, "Trends in the Economic Situation of U.S. Families and Children, 1970–1980," in *American Families and the Economy*, ed. Richard R. Nelson and Felicity Skidmore (Washington, 1983), 9–53, esp. 38.

24. Charles Murray, *Losing Ground* (New York, 1984).

25. David T. Ellwood, *Poor Support* (New York, 1988).

26. Sheldon Danziger and Peter Gottschalk, "The Poverty of Losing Ground," *Challenge* 28 (May–June 1985): 32–38.

27. William A. Darity and Samuel L. Meyers, "Does Welfare Dependency Cause Female Hardship? The Case of the Black Family," *Journal of Marriage and the Family* 46 (Nov. 1984): 765–79.

28. David T. Ellwood and Lawrence H. Summers, "Poverty in America: Is Welfare the Answer or the Problem?" in *Fighting Poverty*, ed. Sheldon H. Danziger and Daniel Weinberg (Cambridge, 1986), 78–105.

29. Ellwood and Summers, "Poverty in America," 96.

30. "The Costs of Being Black," *Research News* 38 (Nov.–Dec. 1987): 8–10.

31. Barry Bluestone and Bennett Harrison, *The Deindustrialization of America* (New York, 1982), 54.

32. Barry Bluestone, Bennett Harrison, and Luc Gorham, "Storm Clouds on the Horizon: Labor Market Crisis and Industrial Policy," 68, as cited in "Hard Times for Black America."

33. Richard Child Hill and Cynthia Negrey, "Deindustrialization and Racial Minorities in the Great Lakes Region, U.S.A.," in *The Reshaping of America: Social Consequences of the Changing Economy*, ed. D. Stanley Eitzen and Maxine Baca Zinn (Englewood Cliffs, 1989), 168–77.

34. Elliot Currie and Jerome H. Skolnick, *America's Problems: Social Issues and Public Policy* (Boston, 1984), 82.

35. John D. Kasarda, "Caught in a Web of Change," *Society* 21 (Nov.-Dec. 1983): 41–47.

36. Kasarda, "Caught in a Web of Change," 45–47.

37. John D. Kasarda, "Urban Change and Minority Opportunities," in *The New Urban Reality*, ed. Paul Peterson (Washington, 1985), 33–68, esp. 55.

38. William J. Wilson with Kathryn Neckerman, "Poverty and Family Structure: The Widening Gap between Evidence and Public Policy Issues," in *The Truly Disadvantaged*, ed. William J. Wilson (Chicago, 1987), 63–92.

39. Wilson with Neckerman, "Poverty and Family Structure."

40. Jerelyn Eddings, "Children Having Children," *Baltimore Sun*, March 2, 1986, 71.

41. As quoted in Eddings, "Children Having Children," 71.

42. Noel A. Cazenave, "Alternate Intimacy, Marriage, and Family Lifestyles among Low-Income Black Americans," *Alternative Lifestyles* 3 (Nov. 1980): 425–44.

43. "The Kerner Report Updated," Racine, Wis., March 1, 1988.

44. Wilson, *The Truly Disadvantaged*, 62.

45. Ellwood, *Poor Support*, 204.

46. Paul E. Peterson, "Introduction: Technology, Race, and Urban Policy," in *The New Urban Reality*, ed. Paul E. Peterson (Washington, 1985), 1–35, esp. 22.

47. Jennifer Juarez Robles, "Hispanics Emerging as Nation's Poorest Minority Group," *Chicago Reporter* 17 (June 1988): 1–3.

48. Robles, "Hispanics Emerging as Nation's Poorest Minority Group," 2–3.

49. Ibid., 3.

50. Alejandro Portes and Cynthia Truelove, "Making Sense of Diversity: Recent Research on Hispanic Minorities in the United States," *Annual Review of Sociology* 13 (1987): 359–85.

51. Joan W. Moore, "An Assessment of Hispanic Poverty: Does a Hispanic Underclass Exist?" *Tomás Rivera Center Report* 2 (Fall 1988): 8–9.

52. Robles, "Hispanics Emerging as Nation's Poorest Minority Group," 3.

53. U.S. Bureau of the Census, *Current Population Reports* series P-20, nos. 416, 422 (Washington, 1987).

54. Adolph Reed, Jr., "The Liberal Technocrat," *The Nation*, Feb. 6, 1988, 167–70.

55. Ellwood, *Poor Support*, 133.

56. Clyde W. Franklin II, "Surviving the Institutional Decimation of Black Males: Causes, Consequences and Intervention," in *The Making of Masculinities*, ed. Harry Brod (Winchester, 1987), 155–69, esp. 155.

57. See Maxine Baca Zinn, "Minority Families in Crisis: The Public Discussion," working paper no. 6, Center for Research on Women, Memphis State University, 1987, for an extended critique of the culture-of-poverty model.

Epilogue

We are struck by the contradictory trends that continue in American life. Increasingly, individualism has become the norm in society. Courts have come to interpret the laws in line with individual freedom and equal rights. Some even wonder if families and the idea of family will continue. A reaction to individualism and an "anything goes" approach to family life has emerged. Rooted in conservative religious circles with a focus on traditional, even patriarchal, "family values," the movement has attracted the support of many Americans who fear that individualism has gone too far. During the late 1990s, welfare reform laws were passed that were designed to force families off welfare rolls and into the world of work. Although scholars have repeatedly demonstrated that welfare programs did not cause family pathologies (chapter 13), the new approach was hailed as promoting "family values" even as it forced single mothers into the work force.

Those who oppose the rising tide of individualism can take heart in more recent developments. By the end of the century, the divorce rate had leveled off because more Americans were cohabiting than marrying, or they were marrying later than their parents did. Many same-sex couples seek the trappings of marriage and wish not only to exchange wedding vows but also to be recognized as a family. Traditional church-style weddings are once again the norm for those who choose to marry, but individualism seems not to have been diminished by these counter-trends. Older Americans, if given a choice, prefer to live independently as long as they possibly can. Young people move across the country in order to seek their fortunes and establish their own relationships, which may or may not lead to matrimony. Who can say where these trends will lead. Statements about the study of contemporary and future families is beyond the scope of this volume, but we remain convinced that a complete understanding of contemporary family diversity will depend on sound knowledge of the rich and varied history of past American families.

Contributors

SUSAN BRANSON is an assistant professor at the University of Texas at Dallas. Her study on *Women and Political Culture in Early National Philadelphia* is in press.

KARIN CALVERT is the director of the National Faculty's Delta Teacher's Academy in Louisiana and author of *Children in the House: The Material Culture of Early Childhood* (1992).

STEVEN M. GELBER is a professor of history at Santa Clara University and author of *Hobbies: Leisure and the Culture of Work in America* (1999).

ROBERT L. GRISWOLD is a professor of history at the University of Oklahoma and the author of *Fatherhood in America: A History* (1993).

JOSEPH M. HAWES is a professor of history at the University of Memphis and the author of *Children between the Wars* (1993).

JAN LEWIS is a professor of history at Rutgers University Newark–New Jersey Institute of Technology and the author of *Pursuit of Happiness: Family and Values in Jefferson's Virginia* (1983).

KENNETH A. LOCKRIDGE is a professor of history at the University of Montana and author of *The Sources of Patriarchal Rage: The Commonplace Books of William Byrd and Thomas Jefferson and the Gendering of Power in the Eighteenth Century* (1992).

VALERIE M. MENDOZA is an assistant professor of history at the University of Kansas. She is completing a study on gender and community among Mexican Americans in Kansas City between 1900 and 1940.

STEVEN MINTZ is a professor of history at the University of Houston and coauthor of *Domestic Revolutions: A Social History of American Family Life* (1988).

ELIZABETH I. NYBAKKEN is an associate professor of history at Mississippi State University. Her study *Francis Alison: American Philosophe, 1705–1779* is in press.

ROBERT A. ORSI is a professor of religious studies at the University of Indiana and editor of *Gods of the City: Religion and the American Urban Landscape* (1999).

PEGGY PASCOE is an associate professor of history at the University of Oregon and author of *Relations of Rescue: The Search for Female Moral Authority in the American West* (1990).

LINDA W. ROSENZWEIG is a professor of history at Chatham College and author of *Another Self: Middle-Class American Women and Their Friends in the Twentieth Century* (1999).

MARYLYNN SALMON is an adjunct professor of history at Smith College and author of *The Limits of Independence: American Women, 1760–1800* (New York, 1994).

NANCY SHOEMAKER is an assistant professor of history at the University of Connecticut and author of *American Indian Population in the Twentieth Century* (1999).

MAXINE BACA ZINN is a professor of sociology at Michigan State University. She is the coeditor, with Pierette Hondoyneyo-Sotelo and Michael A. Messner, of *Gender through the Prism of Difference* (2000).

Index

Typeset in 10.5/13 Adobe Minion
with Helvetica Neue Extended display
Designed by Paula Newcomb
Composed by Jim Proefrock
at the University of Illinois Press
Manufactured by Cushing-Malloy, Inc.

University of Illinois Press
1325 South Oak Street
Champaign, IL 61820-6903
www.press.uillinois.edu